Japan's Musical Tradition

Japan's Musical Tradition
Hogaku from Prehistory to the Present

Miyuki Yoshikami

McFarland & Company, Inc., Publishers
Jefferson, North Carolina

LIBRARY OF CONGRESS CATALOGUING-IN-PUBLICATION DATA

Names: Yoshikami, Miyuki, 1938– author.
Title: Japan's musical tradition : hogaku from prehistory to the present / Miyuki Yoshikami.
Description: Jefferson, North Carolina : McFarland & Company, Inc., Publishers, 2020. | Includes bibliographical references and index.
Identifiers: LCCN 2019055237 | ISBN 9781476675596 (paperback : acid free paper) ∞ ISBN 9781476635118 (ebook)
Subjects: LCSH: Music—Japan—History and criticism.
Classification: LCC ML340 .Y7 2020 | DDC 780.952—dc23
LC record available at https://lccn.loc.gov/2019055237

BRITISH LIBRARY CATALOGUING DATA ARE AVAILABLE

ISBN (print) 978-1-4766-7559-6
ISBN (ebook) 978-1-4766-3511-8

© 2020 Miyuki Yoshikami. All rights reserved

No part of this book may be reproduced or transmitted in any form or by any means, electronic or mechanical, including photocopying or recording, or by any information storage and retrieval system, without permission in writing from the publisher.

Front cover: Hand-tinted 19th century photograph by Kimbei Kusakabe of Japanese women posing with traditional musical instruments (Arthur M. Sackler Gallery Archives, Smithsonian Institution)

Printed in the United States of America

McFarland & Company, Inc., Publishers
 Box 611, Jefferson, North Carolina 28640
 www.mcfarlandpub.com

To Dojun and Tami who can now stop saying,
"What? Still working on your book?"

Table of Contents

Acknowledgments — ix
Preface — 1
Introduction — 5

1. Aesthetic Heritage — 11
2. Ancient Music and Its Properties — 23
3. Simple Instruments — 44
4. Two Modes and Tuning of the Instruments — 68
5. Singing the *Uta* (Song/Poetry) — 82
6. The Format of Continuity in Hogaku Compositions — 110
7. Decorating the Melodic Line — 145
8. Why We Are Able to Hear Ancient Music Today: The Iemoto System — 159
9. The West, Hogaku Today and the Future — 176

Epilogue — 188
Glossary — 191
Chapter Notes — 207
Bibliography — 227
Index — 231

Acknowledgments

In 1980, I was in Tokyo when one of my sisters asked me to translate koto lyrics, which I took as a straightforward request. The lyrics of each hogaku composition revealed how all Japanese art is interwoven with legends, stories, events, literature, history, and religious beliefs—each an element of Japan's culture—and so the task turned out to be a lifetime project. I turned for assistance to experts in Japanese classical literature, first to Mrs. Yanagita, a retired teacher of Japanese classical literature in Kamakura who later moved to Finland and then to Dr. Sayo Yotsukura of Virginia, Fusako Teramoto of Japan, and Kazuko (Kay) Wain of Rockville, Maryland. Sadly these four eminent and knowledgeable friends passed on before getting to see their names in this book. Today, I consult with Dr. Yoshio Akiyama and Yodo Kurahashi-sensei.

Noh, kyogen, and kabuki artists who helped me by bringing their perspectives through lessons and performances throughout my study of hogaku include kyogen's Nomura Mansaku, percussion's Katada Kissaku, noh teachers of Kita-ryu, Kita Nagayo and Uchida Anshin, and gagaku's Togi Suenobu. In addition I thank nohgaku's Richard Emmert and Jonas Salz, and the late Dr. Howard Hamilton. Kabuki's Larry Kominz and Keiko Yoshikawa of Tokyo were invaluable resources. I am grateful to Yasuko Nainan of Chevy Chase, Maryland, who introduced me to Osaka's Hanayagi Shifu, a *buyo* (dance) artist, and her husband, the late Tokiwazu Sanso. Shifu in turn introduced me to bunraku puppeteer Yoshida Kazuo, who became a Living National Treasure in 2017. In addition, I am indebted to Onoe Kikuyuki and her husband, Ralph Orlandella, of Chantilly, Virginia. From Kikuyuki, her Bokusetsu (retired iemoto), and the Iemoto, Onoe Kikunojo III, I learned much about kabuki dance and music.

My academic influences have been my friends at the University of Maryland. Art historian Dr. Gail Weigl and I discussed and gave lectures together on Japanese aesthetics from our respective disciplines which laid the foundation for the interweaving of the arts with music offered in this book. I received countless years of support from Drs. Marlene Mayo, Eleanor Kerkham, Lindsay Yotsukura, Robert Ramsey, and Michele Mason of the University of Maryland, College Park, and the members of the University of Maryland, College Park's Center for East Asian Studies (CEAS). And at the University of Maryland at Shady Grove, I am grateful to librarian Irene Munster of the Priddy Library who found a crucial quote for me. At Gettysburg College, my supporters have been Noriko Garofalo, who opened doors for me there, and Dr. Marta Robertson, with whom I discussed Japanese music while she learned to play the koto.

In my research on indigenous culture, I received enthusiastic confirmation of my hogaku approach from Mr. and Mrs. Hiromasa Shinkura of Hokkaido Newspaper and Television and Chief Priest Michio Kasuga of Niigata's Koenji temple, who connected me with Dr. Yastami Nishida, director of education and science of the Niigata Prefectural Museum of History. Dr. Nishida graciously granted permission to use several of my photographs of the museum's Jomon and Kaen pottery exhibits. The Rev. Toshihisa Enoki of Los Angeles introduced me to Shinto priest the Rev. Izumi Hasegawa and Dr. Hatsune Natsuyama, whose specialty is Jomon megalith and woshite. My late in-laws, the Reverend Masamichi and Mieko Yoshikami, and the late Rev. Dr. Mokusan Miyuki answered many questions about Buddhist music, as did the Rev. Mas Kodani of Senshin Buddhist Temple through Satoshi Miyata, a friend from my college days.

Columbia University Press kindly granted permission to reproduce the score to *Togan* from Stephen Addiss's "Singing the Wakan Roei Shu," Chapter 4 in *Japanese and Chinese Poems to Sing: The Wakan Roei Shu*, translated by J. Thomas Rimer and Jonathan Chaves. Thank you, Yi Deng.

American shakuhachi students of Kyoto's Yodo Kurahashi will agree that he is the most interesting resource and storyteller. I am indebted to him and to the generous Tokyo koto disciples of the late Tomiyama Seikin I, Tominari Seijo and Tomio Seiritsu. Also I thank koto artist Kazue Sawai and her disciple Masayo Ishigure who prevailed upon the kotoya, Tanikawa Kazuhiro of Tokyo. He generously introduced my student, Mia, and her mother, Toshiko Saidel, and me to koto makers and players on a koto journey funded by Andrew Saidel.

In the Washington, D.C., and Maryland area, I thank the Embassy of Japan through the Japan Information Culture Center, namely Ministers Hiroshi Furusawa, Izumi Seki, Masato Otaka, and Tamaki Tsukada. I owe much gratitude to my lifelong friends Timothy and Susan Healy of the International Conservatory of Music and composer and friends Lori Laitman, Winifred Hyson, and Gary Davison. I also thank my constant fans who unfailingly attend my concerts and lectures, David and Mariko Baasch, Christine Johnson, Johnny Park, Gail Yano, Ed Celarier, Sanae Reeves, and Trin Xue.

Close to me personally are my sisters Youko Kagawa, Sanaye Kagawa, and Ritsuko Nakata, with whom I practiced and performed the koto. I also thank my deceased parents, Hatsuki and Otoku Kagawa, for not letting me quit and for making me practice. I thank my children, Dojun Yoshikami and Tami Gaertner, my grandsons, Ryan, Collin, and Akira Brown, and my husband and critic, Shuko. Thank you all for your patience.

Innumerable thanks to Meagan Healy of Meagan Healy Studios who created most of the fine drawings in this book as well as doing the graphic design of many of the scores and diagrams. And a special shout-out to Cathy Healy, who introduced me to Susan Simmons. Susan gave me encouragement and the will to shape this work to its final stages.

Last in this list but not last in my fountain of gratitude are Gary Mitchem and Lisa Camp, my editors at McFarland. They had faith in me, quickly returned serious and gentle responses to my many questions, and walked me and my book through the mysteries of the publishing process. Thank you.

Preface

I confess. I was a weekend Japanese. Born in Los Angeles to parents from Japan, my exposure to *hogaku* (pre-Western Japanese music) felt as natural as speaking English at school and Japanese at home. During the week I learned to play the viola for the junior high orchestra, joined high school and college glee clubs, and took college music appreciation and music education courses. Weekends, however, were devoted to Japanese language school, Buddhist Sunday School, and performing in kimono on the *koto*, a thirteen-string instrument, for the Japanese American community.

My koto lessons were with Nakashima Chihoko, the first bona fide Ikuta-ryu koto teacher in Los Angeles. Later I studied with Kimio Eto from Japan and consulted with Kagawa Seishi, my sister, who studied with Tomiyama Seikin of Tokyo. Nakashima-sensei taught in the traditional rote method, so I learned many koto classics by imitating her passage by passage and memorizing each piece. Eto Kimio expanded my repertoire to the Westernized koto music of Miyagi Michio. My exposure to koto music was through private lessons, but I also had the opportunity to learn *noh, kyogen, tsuzumi,* and *gagaku* at UCLA's Classical Performing Arts Friendship Mission of Japan in the summer of 1981. I consider myself bi-musical and love and appreciate the music of both cultures.

When asked to teach college classes on hogaku, the available materials were a mixture of information and misinformation with incongruent Western explanations. Many textbooks begin hogaku with music from China, thereby giving the impression that Japan was a musical vacuum before the Chinese arrived in Japan. And some writers contend today that nothing new happened in Japanese music until Western music was introduced, again implying that the Japanese sat in a musical lull for centuries. Hiroyuki Iwaki, the conductor of the Nippon Hoso Kyokai (NHK) orchestra, put the lie to these perceptions when he said, "[Japanese composers] go well beyond the limits of Japan ... [and their music is] strongly founded on Japanese philosophy [and as a result] ... could not have been composed by non–Japanese."[1]

What is the "Japanese philosophy" or the musical capital from which contemporary composers emanate their Japanese-ness? Unlike pitch-based Western music, Japanese music grew from a word-based tradition steeped in history, culture, and literature. Japanese music was conceived outside of Western parameters and as such Japanese and Western music exist poles apart. Thus, any explanation of Japanese music from the Western template is like explaining the game of go from the perspective of chess or explaining baseball using football rules. We cannot overlay Western rules of aesthetics, mode, tuning, etc., on Japanese music. Nevertheless Western audiences want to know: "What key is it in?" "What is the phrasing of your music?" "Doesn't your music fit into a bar?" "Is it rhapsodic?" "How do you notate bended notes?" "How can you learn a piece without written scores?" These questions are not answerable in Western musical terms. When others apologize to Western audiences for the strangeness of hogaku, I transform into Mr. Hyde and growl as I decry the many missed opportunities for a real cultural exchange of musical ideas.

Denise Patry Leidy,[2] curator of the Department of Asian Art of the Metropolitan Museum of Art, lamented that the Metropolitan's Asian visual art collection is misconstrued because books on the subject are written from a Western perspective. She is my kindred spirit! Books and studies on Japanese music require a reexamination to reflect a Japanese paradigm of its history, literature, and culture.

I begin the story of Japanese music in the Jomon Era (circa 13,000–250 BCE) to explore how primal beliefs affected the aesthetics of early music, such as Shinto *norito* (invocation, sacred spell, or incantation) and ancient songs. My foundational assumption is that a culture's aesthetics permeate all of its arts—like mitochondria permeate all living things. And as mitochondria have been transmitted from one generation to the next, the elements of music have been transmitted from their Shinto inception through all of hogaku, even into the imported music from the Asian continent. By the time Western music was introduced, Japan had developed its sophisticated classical performance arts from Shinto priests to the purveyors of *gagaku, biwa, noh, shamisen, koto, shakuhachi,* and others. All seem different and daunting, but they are all similar for they share the same musical commonalities and a cultural finesse that rivals their visual counterparts.

Although it is exciting to see young hogaku instrumentalists playing with acoustically amplified sounds and gyrating in the bright lights to popular Western music, the real nexus of Japanese musical exchange is hogaku, Japan's pre–Western music. This original musical form was spawned as people listened to and mimicked nature's multifarious voices. Hogaku's longevity is not coincidental; hogaku was a part of everyday life that was institutionalized over the millennium in the iemoto system and as such, the music was preserved. The music is a mirror and a record of the Japanese people's emotional concerns at different times in history. Understanding this music requires one to step outside of one's comfort zone, but discovering what hogaku has to offer is an enlightening ramble.

Introduction

When I was comparing Western and Japanese music with a koto student from Japan, her face grew increasingly puzzled. She suddenly asked me, "Are you talking about cowboy music?"[1] To her, Western music was cowboy music; the music of Bach and Beethoven was classical music. I was perplexed and wondered when she absorbed our Western definition for cowboy music when there is the word *yogaku* meaning Western music in her own language! Then I realized she was a product of Japan's music education. Beginning in 1872, Japan successfully trained all Japanese ears to hear Western music, leaving *hogaku* (pre-Western Japanese music) in its wake. For the purpose of this book, Western music will mean compositions of European or Western origin, including classical, popular, and even cowboy music of the American West.

Speaking about definitions, we in the West have one word to mean "music." In Japan, there are many terms. New ones were invented and old ones changed with time and function. The word yogaku came into use with the introduction of Western music during the Meiji Era (1868–1912). Additionally, the word *ongaku* (sound pleasure) became necessary to mean "music" in the general sense of music as in the West. Hogaku (Japanese music) came to distinguish Japanese from Western music. Also, depending on the scholar, hogaku may include all pre-Western music from prehistoric to Edo Era music. Other scholars apply hogaku only to Edo Era (1868–1912) music of *biwa, shamisen, koto,* and *shakuhachi*.[2] For the purpose of this book, hogaku will be inclusive, meaning anything pre-Western from the Jomon Era (13,000–250 BCE) to today.

The Timeline on the following page shows many different words for music, including *kagura, asobi, gagaku,* and *geido*. In many cultures music grew out of religious rites, and Japan is no exception. *Kagura* (music of, for, or from the *kami* [gods or spirits]) is the earliest music with Shinto *norito*

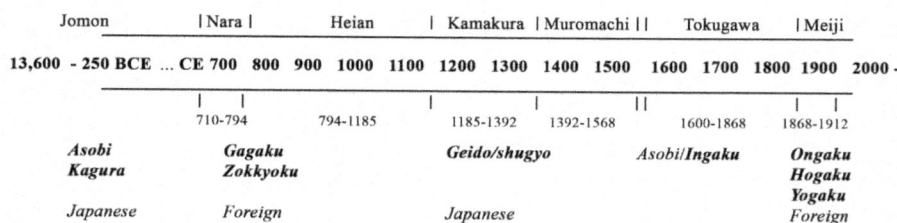

Timeline of the names for music

(invocation, sacred spell, or incantation) pronounced by a priest. Kagura is divided into the two categories of *sato-kagura* (hometown regional shrine) for the general public and *mi-kagura* (honorable kagura) for the emperor's entertainment. Some mi-kagura is part of public domain for songs like *Asakura* were once ancient songs played for entertainment.

Music outside of kagura is *asobi* (play) and as the word implies, it is secular music for fun and diversion played by musicians called *asobi-o*. Among asobi, often mentioned is Azuma asobi, or songs from the northeastern Kanto and Tohoku regions. At the finale of the *noh* play *Hagoromo*[3] (Feather Mantel) the angel dances to the words, "*Azuma asobi no kazu kazu ni—.*" Translated, it says asobi from Azuma are countless. The song proceeds to tell about the angel who showered the land with good fortune.

The merriment implied in asobi became transplanted in the eighth century by China's *gagaku*[4] (elegant music). Anything outside of gagaku was labeled *zokkyoku* (miscellaneous) insinuating that asobi and any other music outside of gagaku was frivolous and belonged to a lower, less serious order of music. With the passage of time, gagaku has become a category that now includes any ancient music, religious or secular, and asobi that was once zokkyoku is now part of gagaku music (see the end of the discussion on gagaku in Chapter 3).

When gagaku music diminished after the Gempei War (1160–1185), two prominent musical genres came from the temples and shrines, biwa music and *sarugaku* (monkey mimes). Sarugaku later became noh. Biwa musicians sang about the Heike clan's demise and the heroic deeds of the samurai who then ruled Japan. Noh was favored by the military class and the actors and musicians followed *geido*, the "Way of the Art" as in *bushido*, or the "Way of Warrior" like Zen's "Way to Enlightenment." Henceforth, geido and *shugyo* (austere training of a single-minded, self-sacrificing pursuit towards the Way) became the maxim for anyone in pursuit of the arts including biwa, shamisen, koto, and shakuhachi.

Introduced in the mid–1500s, the three-stringed shamisen became the commoner's instrument. Its music was asobi (play), stylish, smart, chic, *tsu* (savvy), and also *iki* (sexy). The aristocracy called the commoner's asobi *ingaku* (vulgar music). Nevertheless, ingaku musicians pursued the art with the fervor of geido and shugyo practiced by samurai and noh actors. Combined with the organizational structure of the *iemoto* system (a quintessentially Japanese apprentice system; iemoto is explored in Chapter 8), the philosophy behind the pursuit of an art allowed commoners to gain status, pierce class barriers, and lead Edo Era music to sophisticated heights.

Returning to the word "hogaku," calling it "traditional music" is misleading. The word "traditional" implies that hogaku is folk music. It is true that Japan's *minyo* (folk music) and hogaku are both passed by rote. But according to the dictionary, classical music is formal and artistic music "more sophisticated and enduring ... as distinguished from popular and folk music."[5] Also, folk music comes from an unknown source, but hogaku's composers are known professional musicians who transmitted their music by rote to students within strict guidelines practiced in the iemoto system.[6] Evidence of precise transmission can be seen in the visual arts of *buyo* (dance),[7] noh, *kyogen*, *bunraku* puppet, woodblock printing, ceramics, and other arts where the skill is passed fastidiously and exactly. Hogaku in this book focuses on what is considered Japan's classical genre. The concepts presented here also apply to minyo and all other genres not covered here because all Japanese pre-Western music shares the same philosophical basis for aesthetics and its art.

Format of the Book

Many books on hogaku specialize in one genre or historically devote one genre per chapter. In this book, each chapter explores one musical concept shared by all the genres. The goal is to show that hogaku's logic springs from its own land, people, religion, culture, language, and history. I avoid comparing the hogaku with Western music for "never the twain shall meet" and any comparison only enhances the oddity of each.[8]

Fortunately for us, Japanese culture grew in isolation and has a long continuous history. The Jomon people left evidence of their aesthetic sensibilities with their Jomon pottery and Shinto *norito* (invocation, sacred spell, or incantation) purported to be unsullied by foreign influence.

To set the scene, Chapter 1 begins with the aesthetics goal of the Jomon people that was transmitted to the modern Japanese. Jomon aesthetics were based on good etiquette, or building good relationships between humans and kami, and humans and the environment. Scholars list many words describing Japanese aesthetics but I find that each word fits one or more of the categories listed in the Four Principles of the Way of Tea (tea ceremony). The ultimate goal is to have beauty felt. It must touch the heart to the point of tears. Recurring themes in *uta* (songs/poems) associated with seasonal plant and fauna evoke *awa-re* (pathos), and they show why songs have touched people for generations.

Chapter 2 examines the pre-historic Jomon aesthetics that grew from the Jomon people's mythology and relationship with the environment. From the artistry of the Jomon pottery, I look for musical parallels in Shinto's norito, mi-kagura's *Asakura,* and *miko* dance music. Common musical elements gleaned from the three examples—such as the simplicity of the instruments, modes used, singing, format, and decoration—are discussed separately as topics in Chapters 3 through 7.

Chapter 3 examines instruments of indigenous people and those that came from the Asian continent. The foreign instruments adopted by the Japanese were remodeled within the premise of keeping the instrument simple and were made from materials found in the environment.

In Chapter 4, I show that Japanese music is set in two modes—the IN (shade) and YO (sunshine)—with no set pitch except in ensemble works. Even with the initial flurry of new scales from China, the Japanese preferred the Chinese music that sounded closest to their accustomed indigenous scale. The tuning of each instrument accommodates the voice, but the koto best illustrates how the so-called different tunings across the instrument may look and feel like a new scale, but in actuality remain in either the IN or YO mode.

Singing dominates hogaku, and there is hardly a composition without the uta. Noh, bunraku, and kabuki without the uta have no storyline. The adage is that the uta is the heart of Japanese music. The singing style from norito and Buddhist chants is like recitation of poetry and this style recurs in every genre, even with different instrumental accompaniment. Chapter 5 shows how the spoken word becomes a sophisticated melodic coordination of voice and instrument.

Every hogaku piece has structure even when it unrolls in ever-flowing different melodies. Chapter 6 shows that amorphous sounding melodies have definite sections that organize the music into predictable sequences. Detailing the format ensconced in every genre is beyond the scope of this book, therefore, I chose to examine the format of the noh play with its music accompaniment and the influence of lyrical music *utai-mono* (lyrical music), such as ji-uta shamisen and koto music, and its off-shoot of *katari-mono* (narrative music) of sighted musicians that shows how each genre morphed out of previous genres to share similar formats.

Chapter 7 considers how hogaku decorates a melody without Western-type harmony. Gagaku and noh use contrasting instruments to decorate a composition, whereas other genres use the timbre of the instruments to embellish the vocal and melodic lines; the koto techniques discussed here serve as good examples. In other compositions, the main melody may have two or more instruments with different melodic lines to heterophonically weave each around the other.

The iemoto system, discussed in Chapter 8, is the reason for the continuation of music from pre-historic times to today. The iemoto concept encapsulates the teacher–pupil behavior fundamental to understanding Japanese individual and group behavior and the society. It explains why we can rely on live performers to perpetuate the art with fidelity.

Chapter 9 examines Western music and hogaku in modern Japan, and the epilogue discusses the status of hogaku today. In modern Japan, the properties of hogaku permeate the works by contemporary Japanese composers trained in Western music. But in conferences that feature today's Japanese composers, expectations and confusion occur when Japanese and Western musicians face each other to discuss: What is "Japanese" music?

Hogaku genres are interrelated. Depending on the purpose of the music, audience addressed, instruments used, style of vocalization, and lyric content, all genres share the same musical premises of aesthetics, simple instruments, scale, timbre use, and singing, and were shaped by Japan's history, literature, and society.

1
Aesthetic Heritage

Aesthetics is defined tautologically as what brings pleasure through beauty; beauty is defined as what brings pleasure. Japanese aesthetics reside in Shinto's precepts of purity, simplicity, and *makoto* (sincerity). These qualities shape how the Japanese make things aesthetically pleasing and beautiful.

I find Japanese aesthetics closely linked with etiquette in the desire to present something beautiful and pleasant to a guest, friend, or someone special. The Jomon people shared everything, according to philosopher Takeshi Umehara, and were *reigi tadashii* (good mannered). The Japanese were courteous to Jesuit Alessandro Valignano, SJ, who wrote in the late 1500s that "even common folk and peasants are well brought up and so remarkably polite that they give the impression that they were trained at court."[1] Westerners encountering the Japanese subsequently noted the same civility and continue to comment on it even to this day. Courtesy is extended to other people by presenting what the Japanese consider the best, beautiful, artistic, and compatible. In this way, good relationships are built and lasting friendships, trust, and respect cemented.

In the sixteenth century, Sen Rikyu (1522–1591)[2] codified Japanese etiquette into the Four Principles—*wa* (harmony), *kei* (respect), *sei* (purity), and *jaku* (tranquility)[3]—of the Way of Tea (tea ceremony). The Way of Tea requires unique accouterments of utensils, cuisine, dress, and a special environment. As such the Way of Tea serves as a powerful summary of Japan's fine arts.[4] Moreover, the Four Principles encapsulate the ideal and essence of Japanese aesthetics. At its core, for instance, reside Shinto purity and simplicity in partnership with nature as espoused in Buddhism, Confucianism, and Taoism. The essence of wa or harmony with nature is captured in the aesthetic descriptions of *sabi* and *wabi* (rustic, patina, refined), suggestibility, perishability, *shibui* (astringent), noh's *yugen* (mysterious, suggestive, hidden beauty), and even the profundity of performance, as in Zeami's *hana* (flower). The aesthetics idea of refinement and elegance, as in *sui/iki* (meaning both fashionable and sexy), that became prominent during the Edo Era is also a component of the Four Principles of the Way of Tea. Basically, extraneous motions in the tea-making are stripped away, leaving the essential of what is pure, elegant, and harmonious with the environment. When each principle of the Way of Tea is applied to music, one finds that hogaku's goal is to touch people with stirring words and quieting melodies.[5]

Wa (harmony) in the Pythagorean sense of chordal harmony does not exist in hogaku. Wa is harmony between people where all ranks and cares of the world are shed. Everyone is in synchrony with the occasion of sharing tea, listening to music, or enjoying poetry, flowers, or partying. Compatibility is key. In music, harmony is the concept of being in tune with the listener's expectation. The audience is in a sedentary state and music begins with *jo* (slow), and then gently moves to *ha* or the main part of the piece, and then ends quickly with *kyu*, so *jo-ha-kyu*. The melodies unroll like an expertly chauffeured car in which the driver accelerates slowly at the beginning, passes

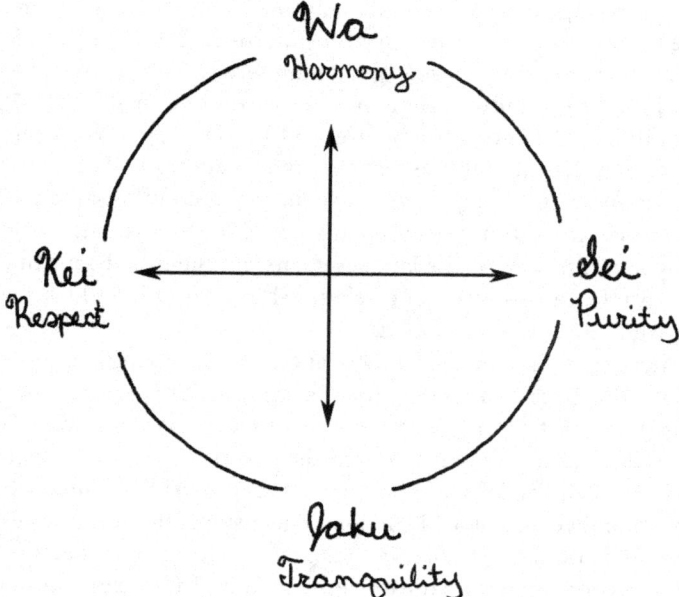

Figure 1.1. Diagram of *Wa, Kei, Sei* and *Jaku*. The Four Principles of the Tea Ceremony in a circle and cross in the center depicts that when one principle is practiced, the other principles fall into place. The principles summarize the aesthetics found in Japanese art, which strives for unassuming elegance, natural beauty, quietness, and sentiments that touch the heart (drawing by Meagan Healy).

and turns gently through many scenes, and finally ends at a different aesthetic place. Sudden braking or swerving would be jarring and unwelcomed, like an earthquake.[6]

The quiet demeanor of the music suggests that it should be heard in an intimate setting or from afar, letting the sounds steal up to affect a listener's feelings and mood. Applause are intrusive and break the spell of silence that allows people to reflect upon what just transpired.[7] To ensure that a performance is harmonious with the occasion, blind musicians signed oaths to play only before deserving audiences and at appropriate venues.

Kei (respect) in hogaku means to be respectful to the audience. Music is a journey that should move people to a higher aesthetic plane. Japanese children learn not to cause *meiwaku* (problem, inconvenience) to others, and music likewise should not be intrusive. The low bow at the beginning and end of a lesson or performance may appear to be automatic, a habitual act, but the gesture honors, respects, and shows gratitude towards the legacy of the art—to teachers, predecessors, and anyone connected with the performance—and to the audience. It is believed that a respectful relationship between teacher and student carries over to the performer and instrument, and to the performer and audience.

Hogaku musicians during a performance are unexpressive, motionless, and stoic, which can be puzzling to American audiences. Gesticulating or emoting is considered rude for it calls attention to the performer and detracts from the music that came from the *kamis* via the composer.[8] Full attention of the audience to the musician-as-medium is expected. At the end, the listener is left to imbibe the beauty that transpired.

Sei (purity, simplicity) is the fundamental precept of Shinto displayed through *makoto* (sincerity). Beauty and elegance of music come from a heart that is pure. Actors and musicians, like hosts at tea, train and practice until the music is second nature and effortless. Performers are known to visit shrines or temples to ensure a good performance.[9] A Tsukushi koto player went through bodily and spiritual lustration. He followed a strict diet and burned incense to cleanse the air before sitting before the koto. One goal in performance is to reach hana (flower) or performance described in Zeami's *Noh Treatise* that transcends words and moves audiences to tears.[10] Tears are water that purifies the heart, and any performance with such power is rare and to be cherished.

The Japanese believe a true human being has passion, and tears from men and women show feeling. The slightest provocation—impending parting, nostalgia, regret, sad events, and even admiration and happiness—evokes tears. Literature is filled with teary moments from the earliest *Kojiki*. Edward S. Morse (1838–1925) noticed that audiences upon hearing biwa players "are often affected to tears by the exceedingly sweet and caressing notes the instrument emits in the hands of a master."[11] To find hogaku's mysterious appeal, he sought *utai* lessons with a master.[12]

The writer Lafcadio Hearn (1850–1904) listening to a blind shamisen street musician saw that "those who listened began to weep silently. I did not distinguish the words; but I felt the sorrow and the sweetness and the patience of the life of Japan pass with her voice into my heart—plaintively seeking for something never there."[13] And although Hearn found nothing extraordinary in the lyrics, the unassuming sincerity of the musician moved everyone.

Contrary to common belief, *awa-re* (pathos) is a pleasant feeling for it stirs yearning, blitheness, romance, reconciliation, and peace. Vicariously *felt* and *perceived* emotions from poignant songs are removed from real discomfort and are therapeutic.[14] Beauty that touches the heart and evokes tears has *yugen* (hidden beauty) which is hard to define or touch, but is desired.

Jaku (tranquility) occurs when any one of the Four Principles is practiced and the other three principles fall into place in a cyclical manner. For example, purity leads to quiet, harmonious, and respectful music, and respect leads to pure, harmonious, and tranquil music, and so on. Tranquility is equilibrium without earthquakes, famine, pestilence, or personal problems to disturb life. Having jaku is happiness. And in the Jomon scheme of the world, having tranquility and harmony with other people, the environment, and the kami is desirable.

Sad Songs to Evoke Tears

Most hogaku music leaves people contemplative, wistful, nostalgic, or in tears. During the Edo Era, tear-producing music was carried to an extreme to provoke what I call "cheap tears." The sorrowful songs reflected the lives of the commoner class, rich merchants, and farmers who were bound by strict governmental codes of social immobility. Their surrogate was the *yujyo* (prostitutes) and geishas whose pitiful situation was recognizable.[15] One piece, *Yuki* (Snow), is held up as the epitome of this genre. The song begins, "Will I be purified if I brush the snow off my sleeve?" Once lovers like Mandarin ducks, he is now absent. She hears footsteps, but they are not his, and she cries inconsolably (tears turn to icicles) as she waits, she contemplates suicide, but finally resigns herself to her situation. When I played a recording of *Yuki* at one of my lectures, a lady walked out wiping her eyes.[16] Thinking that her contact lens must be bothering her, I later learned about her impending divorce that made her identify with the song. Rejection is real and universal.

Sad, contemplative songs need not always be about rejection of the yujyo or of the commoner's demise. One folk song, *Nagoya Obi*, sounds very sad but the lyric is joyous to evoke tears of happiness because she is walking away with her lover. The last verse of koto's *Chidori no Kyoku* asks, "How many sleepless nights are there for the Barrier Keeper at Suma?"[17] The intention of this poignant verse is to empathize with the Imperial Barrier Keeper who wishes to be in Kyoto enjoying the activities at court. One is reminded of a scene from the *Tale of Genji* where the exiled Prince Genji at Suma sang, "Waves break on the shore, and their voices rise to join my sighs of yearning / Can the wind be blowing from all those who long for me?"[18] Waking his companions, they cried to the quiet beauty of his song and the longing to be in Kyoto from where Genji was banished.

Tomiyama Seikin I's (1913–2008) arrangement of six waka poems for *Miyako Wasure*[19] purposely evokes melancholy at the end. The first and last

1.	Hana mo yuki mo haraeba	Flower petals, snowflakes, if brushed away,
2.	kiyoki tamoto ka na?	will my sleeves [heart] be cleansed?
3.	Hon ni mukashi no mukashi no koto yo	I remember not long ago that the person
4.	waga matsu hito mo ware wo machiken.	I waited for now, once yearned for me. [We were]
5.	Oshi no otori ni mono omoi ba no	like mandarin ducks—such fond memories.
6.	kōru fursuma ni nakune mo sazona.	In this freezing room, I disparately wish for him.
7.	Sanaki da ni kokoro mo	Ah, to know the ways of the world—
8.	toki yo wa no kane	far away temple bells
9.	(ai-no-te)	(interlude of depicting a winter scene)
10.	Kiku mo samishiki hitori ne no	The bells saddens me while I sleep alone.
11.	makura ni hibiku arare no oto mo	My pillow vibrates! Is it hail, or
12.	moshi yato isso seki kanete	my love's footsteps? I cannot stop
13.	otsuru namida no	my overflowing tears that turn
14.	tsurara yori tsuraki inochi wa	into icicles. This intolerable life I would
15.	oshikara nedo mo koishiki hito wa	cast it away if it weren't for my love
16.	tsumi fukaku omowane	who'd feel remorse. Instead, I'll
17.	koto no kanashisa ni suteta uki	leave this Floating World [take tonsure].
18.	suteta ukiyono yamakazura	Dawn, at last, breaking through mountain clouds!

Figure 1.2. Lyrics to *Yuki* (Snow). The piece was composed by Minezaki Kōtō (1780s) with lyrics by Ryusekian Hazumi. Hailed as the epitome of elegance on a disconsolate theme, the agony of this woman of the Pleasure Quarters mirrors the dilemma of the commoner class suffering under the Tokugawa government's sumptuary laws. Any mention of snow or a snow scene triggers the famous *ai-no-te* melody after the words "temple bells."

1. ARIHENA BA
   MATA MO KAERAN
   TSUNOKUNI NO
   SUMIYOSHI GAWA NO
   MATSU NO KOKAGE NI
2. FURU SATO NO
   HANA NI KOKORO WO
   NOKOSHI TSUTSU
   TATSUYA KASUMI NO
   UBARA SUMIYOSHI
3. YAMAZATO WA
   SAKURA FUBUKI NI
   AKE KURETE
   HANA NAKI NIWA MO
   HANAZO CHIRISHIKU
4. HANA NO NA WA
   MIYAKO WASURE TO
   KIKU KARA NI
   MINI YOSOETE ZO
   WABISHI KARIKERU

Some day, when possible,
I'd like to return
to Tsunokuni's
Sumiyoshi River
to a pine tree's little shadow.
Upon my homeland
flower, my heart
was left when I
departed hazy, misty
Ubara Sumiyoshi.
My mountain homeland has
swirling cherry blossoms
throughout the day.
Even flowerless gardens are
strewn with blossoms everywhere.
The flower's name is
Miyako Wasure.
Whenever I hear [its name]
my soul is engulfed
with wistful longing.

(TEGOTO: Instrumental interlude in 2 sections: Part 1 depicts a reunion, and Part 2 is festival music of typical shamisen passages and drums.)

5. KURENAI NO
   AME TO SHIDARESHI
   SONO HARU NO
   ITO ZAKURA KAYA?
   YUME NO ATO KAYA?
6. ASA NE GAMI
   MAKITE MEDENISHI
   IKUTOSE NO
   TANARE NO KAO MO
   YASE NI KERASHI NA
7. (1) ARIHENA BA
   MATA MO KAERAN
   TSUNOKUNI NO
   SUMIYOSHI GAWA NO
   MATSU NO KOKAGE NI

[Are they] crimson
rain falling softly
or that spring's
weeping cherry blossoms?
Or a dreamy afterglow?
Morning's tousled hair—
my love by my side.
The countless times
my hands felt my face—
thinner— it seems!
Some day, if I can,
I'd like to return
to Tsunokuni's
Sumiyoshi River
to a pine tree's little shadow.

Figure 1.3. Lyrics of *Miyako Wasure* (translation). *Miyako* means capital, and *wasure* means forget not. Tomiyama Seikin premiered this piece at the Mombusho Geijitsu Sanko Ensokai concert in 1960. The title is from the fourth poem about a purplish wild daisy-like flower that literally translates as "forget not the capital." Tanizaki Junichiro, who supplied the lyrics, lived in Tsunokuni. He points to his home under a pine tree's shadow. *Matsu* means pine so the lyrics also refer to his wife, Matsuko. After he left for Tokyo, he reminisced about his hometown. Tomiyama was attracted by the archaic words in the poems, such as *ubara Sumiyoshi* or *arihenaba* (if I survive life's course) and arranged six wake poems to evoke nostalgia and wistfulness.

verses are the same: "Someday, when possible, I'd like to return to Tsunokuni's Sumiyoshi River to a little pine tree's little shadow." The poems in between reminisce and include an instrumental interlude with frolicsome festival music. In the penultimate stanza, the poet notices that "my face has grown thinner!" The first poem introduced a narrative of hope, but its repetition at the end resonates with uncertainty and the final sad question: "Will I *ever* be able to visit my hometown? Or, will I die before I do?"

Seasonal Themes That Evoke Feeling

Recurring themes in Japanese poetry and music touch emotions communally in the same way that Jomon pottery used symbols that people shared and recognized. For music, lyrics are associated with the seasons that coincide with the Chinese lunar calendar[20] to our confusion today. According to the lunar calendar, the first month begins with New Year's Day, Mutsuki (our third month) or spring. The tenth month, Kannazuki, is not a god-less month but the time when all of the local, regional, and national gods are conferring at Izumo Taisha of the god, Okuninushi. The other months' names correspond with their activities.

The Jomon people's sensitivity to the seasons is ingrained in the modern Japanese so much so that certain cognoscenti today have further segmented the seasons into twenty-four gradations with seventy-two more increments approximately five days apart.[21] Each appearance or disappearance of an herb or bird, or any other sign of change is a poetic and lyrical inspiration. Many Imperial collections of poems by courtiers and commoners traditionally categorize their anthologies by the seasons.[22]

Names of plants and fauna evoke emotional associations and appear in many songs like emotional shorthand. Even when a vowel is elongated, the context sufficiently triggers feelings like a red rose symbolizing true love in the West. Poetic references are common and recur in the majority of songs. For example, the *sho* (pine), *chiku* (bamboo), and *bai* (plum) or the *shochikubai* are three symbols used at the New Year just as an evergreen tree or wreath is brought out at Christmas. Each one has emotional significance. *Sho/matsu*[23] (pine tree) stands for steadfastness and endurance and conjures up the pines of Takasago and Sumiyoshi that represent connubial bliss, longevity, and good fortune, as in the noh play *Takasago*.[24] The Tokiwa pine of Karasaki represents a beautiful woman with a virtuous heart immortalized in the koto piece *Godan Ginuta* (see Figure 1.6: Lyrics of *Godan Ginuta*). *Chiku/ta-ke* (bamboo) stands for flexibility and resilience for it bends under the weight of snow. The *bai/ume* (plum) is the delicious fragrance of the first flower blossoming at the first sign of spring, bringing hope and happiness.

Mutsuki	Month of mutual goodwill	1st month, our 3rd
Kisaragi	Clothes changing time	2nd month, our 4th
Yayoi	Month of new life	3rd month, our 5th
Uzuki	"U" no hana (white field flower)	4th month, our 6th
Satsuki	Rice planting month	5th month, our 7th
Minazuki	Month of water	6th month, our 8th
Fumizuki	Month of books	7th month, our 9th
Hazuki	Month of changing & falling leaves	8th month, our 10th
Nagazuki/Kikuzuki	Long nights/Chrysanthemum	9th month, our 11th
Kannazuki	Gods away month (at Ise Shrine)	10th month, our 12th
Shimozuki	Month of frost	11th month, our 1st
Shiwasu	Teacher/priest running month	12th month, our 2nd

Figure 1.4. The Lunar Calendar. Any seasonal reference in Japanese literature is based on the Chinese calendar until 1873 when the Gregorian calendar became the standard to be in sync with the Western world. The Jomon people had an astute sense of the seasons and knew when to fish and hunt and when to gather nuts, seaweed, and vegetables.

Also associated with spring is *ume* (plum) and the *uguisu* (bush warbler) with its endearing cries of *"ho—hokekyo!"* that herald the approach of warmer weather. With spring, the *sakura* (cherry blossom) and hana (flower) remind listeners of the impermanence of things and thus, the sakura is an insignia of the *samurai* and the Japanese army. Its fragility is reconciled in the ninth century by poet Ariwara no Narihira who wrote, "How carefree our hearts would be if there were no sakura to worry about."[25] In Washington, D.C., when the cherry blossoms will appear and how long they will remain on the trees is a constant source of conversation and speculation. The cherry blossoms cause much anxiety among residents, businesses, and tourists.

LONGEVITY/ ETERNITY	AUSPICIOUS	PROSPERITY/ HAPPINESS	NOSTALGIA/ PATHOS	TIME PASSAGE
Pine tree	pine	Seven Gods	chidori (plover)	temple bell
Bamboo	bamboo.	sake	miyako wasure	layered snow
Crane	crane	sea food (tai)	moon	lapping waves
Turtle	sake	snow on bamboo	autumn leaves	swift rapids
Tsuzumi	lion dance.	pounding waves	deer cry	wind
Mandarin ducks.	bird cries	sakura		insect cries
Ebi (shrimp)				

Figure 1.5. Common Symbolic Words. The list is limited to a few reliable words that trigger shared emotions. Generally people react to words depending on their experience and knowledge of literature, art, music, etc., and it is natural for each generation to add their list of trigger words.

Songs naming rivers such as Sakuragawa in Ibaraki-ken and Sumidagawa in Tokyo conjure two famous noh plays concerning mothers in search of their sons. The Japanese people know that the Kamo River in Kyoto was the meeting place of the bully-priest Benkei and agile and clever child, Ushiwakamaru (koto's *Chigo Zakura*). Two concrete statues on Gojo Bashi (Fifth Bridge) commemorate their encounter. In poetry, the mention of the river Asukagawa conjures the passage of time like its swift rapids.

Hana wa Yoshino	The best flowers are of Yoshino
Momiji wa Takawo	The best maple leaves are of Takawo
Matsu wa Karasaki	The best pines are from Karasaki
Kasumi wa Toyama	the best mists are in Toyama
Itsu mo Tokiwa no	But always Tokiwa's
Furi wa sanza	figure is like Sanza (River)
Shihorashi ya	Exquisite!
(Tegoto in five sections, or go-dan)	
Matsu wa Tokiwa yo	Tokiwa is the pine
Matsu wa Tokiwa yo	Tokiwa is the pine
Itsumo kawara nu	Always never changing
Sai no hagoto ni	with time.

Figure 1.6. Lyrics of *Godan Ginuta*. (Kinuta in Five Sections). Minezaki Kengyo (d. 1853) composed this composition for two kotos as part of the pure koto music movement that excluded the shamisen. The complex instrumental interlude challenges kotoists, and musicians who specialize in contemporary instrumental works often perform this piece. The lyrics list places noted for flowers, mists, and pine trees, but a frequenter to the tea houses during Edo times would recognize that they are also names of famous courtesans. Tokiwa, who is compared to the Sanza River, means she is the most beautiful of all.

Summer is less inspiring for poetry except for the *hototogisu* (lesser cuckoo) that heralds the beginning of summer.[26] The hot weather brings the *tombo* (dragonfly) believed to bring the spirit of the deceased at Obon (Memorial Day) time. The *hachisu* (lotus) blossom symbolizes Buddha's teachings, a refreshing sight of purity rising from murky water. The *semi* (cicada) is loud, but it won't be around for long because the sky is exchanging summer winds for cooler ones of autumn.

Autumn stirs the *awa-re* feeling of pathos. One leaf falling from a *kiri* (Paulownia) tree means fall is here. Singing insects like the *matsumushi* (pine/waiting bug), *suzumushi* (bell bug), and *kirigirisu* (cricket) increase the feeling of impending winter. A deer is depicted with its outstretched head pointing to the moon. Desolation and isolation are poetic themes. "When I look at the moon, I am enveloped in incredible sadness / I know it is not for me that autumn exists."[27] The full moon is significant in the story of *Kagoyahime, the Bamboo Princess*. How sad when she must return to her castle on the moon on the fifteenth day of the tenth month of the lunar calendar. Another poem says, "It is only at autumn that I am melancholy while at my mountain home. I awaken to the cry of deer."[28] The cries of the small *chidori* (sea plover) also stir a feeling of abandonment when one hears its plaintive "*chi-chi!*"[29]

Besides pathos evoked at autumn, gold and red foliage stirs warmth. In the kabuki nagauta music's *Kokaji*, the *Inari* (fox deity) assists an iron forger to craft a special sword. We can hear hammering against steel with the word *utsu* (strike/hit), and striking/hitting flax to the beats of *kinuta* (softening cloth with bat), and the word *utsu*, in Utsunoyama (Strike/Hit Mountain). Similarly we feel the heat from the hot anvil at the mention of red as *momiji* (red maple leaves).

Winter is cold, but even then, "White snow falling here and there / Flowers seem to be blossoming on boulders."[30] The tale of unrequited love told in *Yuki* (see Figure 1.2: Lyrics to *Yuki*) is again heard in *Kurokami* (see Figure 7.4: *Kurokami* Lyrics) where the accumulated snow signifies the passage of time. A rooftop that once held a statue of Mandarin ducks now covered with frost is a sad vision of marriage torn apart.[31] Not every song is cold and dank in winter. In the koto piece *Ginsekai* (Silvery World),[32] two people enjoy tea on a snowy day. A muted sound of a bell, the hiss of a steaming kettle, and amiable conversation projects a warm cozy scene.

In times past before modern medicine, longevity was a common wish. To live as long as aged people with backs curved like the *ebi* (shrimp) was one. Other symbols yearning for longevity are pine tree, turtles, many sake flasks, unrelenting waves on a shore, and the *tsuru* (crane). Five symbols in the koto piece *Shin Sugomori* (New Nesting) are stacked to pile good fortune upon fortune. They are the (1) cranes (2) building a nest in an (3) old pine tree on (4) Imperial ground, whose (5) cries are wishing for the Meiji Emperor's long reign. The voice of the crane is the voice of authority. The lyrics of *Tancho no Tsuru* (Red Headed Crane) also stack good luck upon good luck like sake flasks. The dancing cranes ensure peace and prosperity to the island surrounded by the four seas where waves ceaselessly cast good fortune on its shores.

When the audience hears the word *tai* (sea bream), they think *medetai*, meaning felicitations or congratulations. The fish is associated with the god, Ebisu, who holds a fishing pole with a tai at the end.[33] The reddish fish is on the menu of auspicious events such as weddings and New Year's Day.

Although the basis of Japanese aesthetics is Jomon and Shinto sensibilities (explored more in Chapter 2), with time foreign and indigenous elements melded to become culturally ingrained as Japanese. Lyrics reflect the fads, wishes, and emotional state of past Japanese people just as the lyrics of any culture reveal the changing values and trends of its society.[34]

Kazu kazu no	Many, many stacks of
Saka zuki wo	sake carafe to
Chiyo yorozuyo to	toast eternity, piled
Kasane, kasane te	one on top of the other—
Megurasu	pass the drinks!
Choshi mo tori dori	Keep tempo with the
Ito take no	string and wind instruments—
Koe mo nigi wo	let our voices blend with the
Sasatsu no matsu no kaze	sound of the wind through the pine trees.
Tancho Tsuru wa	The red headed crane
Na teijyo ni	in the garden
Mai wo kanade	dances as an
Yo wai o sasazu	longevity offering
Kimi ga miyo	to the Emperor.
(tegoto)	(instrumental interlude)
Tsuki ji tsukiseji	Blowing back and forth
Yomutomo tsuki se nu	the ceaseless wind over
Masago no kazu	countless sand grains of the
Hito tsu futasu	one, two,
Mitsu no hama	three beaches and
Yottsu no umi	four seas with the
Nami wo shizuka ni te	Waves quietly lapping to
Yutaka ni osamaru	beckon peace for
Miyo zo medeta ki	an eternal Reign.

Figure 1.7: Lyrics for *Tancho no Tsuru*. This piece named for the red-headed crane is by Fukafusa Kengyo (mid–1700s). Considered early naga-uta music, Fukafusa Kengyo celebrated the peace and prosperity in Japan by listing the symbols that bring good fortune.

Summary

Following the Jomon people's aesthetic sensitivity to nature and beliefs in the life cycle of things, Japanese preferred music through the Shinto precepts of simplicity, purity, and harmony with nature. Thus Shinto tinged with Buddhism, Confucianism, and Taoism shaped what is considered beautiful, and the concept of the beautiful can be generalized in the premises of *wa* (harmony), *kei* (respect), *sei* (purity), and *jaku* (tranquility). These are the Four Principles of the Way of Tea.[35] Etiquette, with its precept of forming good relationships, brought forth beauty in objects, music, and poetry.

In Japan's uta-driven music, beautiful feeling is triggered by references to seasonal flora and fauna, literature, and events in stories and history, which are communally shared to evoke *awa-re* (pathos)—melancholia, wistfulness, nostalgia, or tears. Helen Keller (1880–1968) said, "The best and most beautiful things in the world cannot be seen or even touched. They must be felt within the heart."[36] Thus, hogaku's elegant calming melodies are intended to touch the heart.

2

Ancient Music and Its Properties

On my first visit to Japan in 1975, I expected to see a Buddhist country from what I knew of the Japanese Americans in Los Angeles. But it soon became evident to me that the feeling of the *kan nagara-no-michi* (the Way of the Kami or Shinto) permeated Japan deeply and indelibly. When I visited my aunt on the same trip, her 3-year-old granddaughter reinforced my hunch. She insisted on showing me the *omiya* (shrine). Not knowing what to expect, I followed her across the streetcar tracks and past a shrine built by my aunt, who claimed it helped her business. As we wound up the hill, we came to a small clearing with countless well-tended omiya nestled on the mountainside. I realized then that the Japanese do not exaggerate when they say they have over 800,000 Shinto shrines; the spot where the granddaughter escorted me was a microcosm of similar shrines all over Japan hidden from the eyes of tourists. In fact Shinto shrines appear everywhere, even in the middle of town on street corners, between high-rise buildings, inside shops, homes, and gardens, or anywhere else a kami may reside.

In the remote mountains, people tend to their private shrines but generally, it is the larger and famous local, regional, and national shrines—such as Ise, Izumo, and Kasuga—that gain our attention. Tended by professional priests and *mikos* (shrine maidens), the priests perform daily rituals and preside over the *matsuri* (ritual/festival). These community activities have ancient roots, going back as far as the Mid-Jomon Era (6,000 BCE). The Jomon Era is renowned for its pottery, but it is also the period when Shinto evolved and shaped Japanese culture, including its music (see Table 1).

Because Shinto underlies the beliefs and customs of the Japanese, it is prudent to examine Japan's mythological beginnings to understand what inspired the Jomon people in their music-making. The orally transmitted

Years	Name	Pottery type
13,600-9,200 (10,000-7,500)	Incipient	Low temperature firing, thick porous, small, built upside down in small sheets, rim added, round or flat base. Secondary items, small circular clay discs, engraved stones.
9,200-5,300 (7,500-4,500)	Initial	Coil technique from base up, thicker larger, unglazed, tempered with fiber, dark brown, red with black patch. Rolled cord and shell imprint markings. Secondary items: triangular or violin shaped figurines.
5,300-3,500 (4,500-3,000)	Early	Larger thicker vessels, 700 C firing, not fired to core, cracked from bottom up. Fiber for uneven surface. Thick cord decorations, herring bone marks, stub drags, flat base jar with wide mouth. Secondary items: engraved pebbles, figurines, earrings, shell bangles, phallic stone bars.
3,500-2,500 (3,000-2,000)	Middle	Pit fireplace for indoor cooking. Grit added, 2 layers, coil, thick wall, dramatic decoration, lavish application of relief, rims are large, and associated with ritual, cords, grooved wood grain patterns, cooking pots, storage jars flat base, shallow eating bowls, large handles for suspending vessel, burial jars, pots with pedestals. Pots with holes for drums, Secondary items: Wavy rim elaborate pots. incense burners, large phallic stones, triangular pottery plaques, stone and pottery flutes, stone bar shaped swords & daggers; special clay and well fired figurines with limbs and head but no face.
2,500-1,200 (2,000-1,000)	Late	Carefully made by specialized potters, less elaborate, heavy but thinner, uniformly refined, smooth surfaced, brown, blue, black. Zoned cord decoration, large spiral, curves, vertical oblique panels. Larger undecorated surfaces. Shell markings, figurines, human faces. Pouring spout for alcohol, ritual. Rim projections, fine cords, knobs, raised foot, some pots had lids, ceramic incense burners & lamps.
1,200-900 (1,000-300)	Final	Still no kiln or potter's wheel. Hand-coil or molded method used. Firing brown and black pots. Flowing water pattern from China esp. in Kyushu. Complex, refined, excised decoration, cloud, spiral, S-shape. Underside is decorated. Black or red-brown lacquer surface for ceremonial use. Production of figurines to ward away Yayoi people that fizzles away.

Table 1: Jomon Era Names and Pottery Types

Shinto mythology or the Way of the Kami, became written as the *Kojiki* and the *Nihon Shoki*.[1]

The head of the Shinto pantheon is Amaterasu, the Sun Goddess.[2] Tall stone markers in Jomon villages point towards the sun to indicate the summer or winter solstices, or the beginning of the seasons.[3] Amaterasu is the progeny of two creator gods, Izanagi and Izanami, who descended from a heavenly mist to form the Japanese islands and many other gods. Among them, the Fire God (fever) caused Izanami's death. Izanagi journeyed to the underworld to retrieve her, but to his dismay he found her decaying. Izanagi fled and Izanami gave chase hurling insults and evil spirits at him, but Izanagi was able to block her from entering this world. Izanagi then immediately purified himself, some say in the sea, others say in Hyuga River in Kyushu. This act commenced the symbolic water purification rites of Shinto. Unfortunately the scattering debris from Izanagi's washing caused problems to humanity. Fortunately, Amaterasu appeared from Izanagi's left eye and Tsukiyomi, the Moon God, from his right eye. Susanowo, the Storm God, came from Izanagi's nose. We hear little about Tsukiyomi, but the ribald antics of Susanowo forced Amaterasu to conceal herself in a cave that plunged the world into darkness. The god Futotama organized and directed the goddess Uzume to perform a dance to entice Amaterasu out of the cave. Uzume tied her sleeves, wore a *hachimaki* (head band) around her head, and danced and stamped on a *uke* (round drum) with *sasa* (sacred) leaves in her hand and sang,

Hito futa miyo	Assembled gods, look at the cave door.
Itsu muyu nana	Her Majesty appears.
Ya koko-no tari	We are satisfied!
Momo chi yorodzu.[4]	Behold my bosom and thighs!

Uzume then exposed herself to the uproarious laughter of onlookers. A rooster crowed and Amaterasu peeked out of the cave but caught her reflection in a mirror whereupon the other gods seized her before she could retreat into the cave.

Uzume's performance is purported to be the first ritualistic dance of *chinkon-sai* (spirit pacification). Japanese dancers of every style attribute Uzume's dance as their origin and enter the stage from the *anoyo* (other world) to the *konoyo* (this world)[5] sometimes from a bridge to the stage, holding a branch, bells, wand, or fan in the trance-like countenance of a medium. They stamp the ground or stage as Uzume did on the uke, to awaken souls or seeds, an integral part of *buyo* (dance), kyogen, noh, and kabuki.

From Kyushu, the site of early Japanese civilization, Amaterasu's grandson, Ninigi-no Mikoto, led an expedition northward and established the Yamato state in the Nara-Ise area. His great-grandson Jimmu-tenno headed the Yamato clan, a name synonymous with Japan, its people, and language (Yamato *kotoba*). Thirty-two emperors succeeded Jimmu-tenno, all from the Imperial line of Amaterasu. Hence, the concept of family lineage gained social cachet—a worthy goal to be emulated, as in the long line of priests of Shinto shrines and Buddhist temples, musicians, dancers, artists, tradesmen or craftsmen, industrialists, and even politicians (see Chapter 8 on the iemoto system).

The Way of the Kami and belief in Amaterasu and Jomon society's view of the world not only affected Japan's respect for lineage but also the daily customs and routines of the modern Japanese, according to philosopher Takeshi Umehara.[6] On an island that is 70 percent mountain and forest, Japan sits precariously on the Tuscarora Deep, an ocean abyss five miles deep along the volatile Pacific Rim making people vulnerable to sudden calamities, disasters, and pestilence or misfortunes showing the kami's displeasure. The heavily forested island produced a culture of the *mori no bunka* (forest culture). Everything—living and non-living—had *tamashi* (soul, sentience), even the land, mountains, rocks, and trees. Sacred places are cordoned off with *shimenawa* (sacred rope) such as two rocks in the sea called Meoto Iwa representing the two creator gods.[7] The shimenawa is found around any natural phenomenon that exudes numinous qualities. Roads in Japan wind and twist around sacred trees, rocks, and places deemed sacred in every community, even in Tokyo. The cities of Nara and Kyoto are exceptions. Modeled after the Chinese city of Chang An roads are not windy but blocked and gridded and so cause culture shock to people like Professor Umehara, who had lived in the Tohoku (northern) area of Japan with its twisting streets and roads.

The Incipient Jomon people lived in caves but later dwelled in several primary and secondary villages depending on food sources. Having to live in harmony with the invisible spirits of the environment while getting along with their neighbors, the Jomon people were a classless, egalitarian, semi-nomadic, and semi-sedentary society.[8] They were hunters and gatherers who followed the food supply, cultivated foodstuff, and studied the cycle of grains, nuts, and fruits, and the migration of birds, animals, and fish. The modern Japanese are also cognizant of the seasons and celebrate each season with appropriate cuisine, clothing, art, poetic themes, and even girls' names like Hanako (flower child), Momoyo (peach), Yukiko (snow child), Chikiku (thousand chrysanthemums), and Matsuko (pine child).

The Jomon people knew the techniques of smoking, salting, and drying food to preserve vegetables, fish, and shellfish with methods continued to this day.[9] Archeologists found nuts ground into flour to make soup dumplings or to bake into cookies[10] and also found wine made from elderberries and wild grapes.[11] Fortunately, the poor dishwashing habits of the Jomon people allowed archeologists to analyze their culinary creations; one of them was *nabe-mono* (boiled food),[12] a Japanese favorite made of seafood, broth, and vegetables. Perhaps the women in cooking the meal noticed how mud transformed into waterproof and heatproof items of utility. Credit goes to the Jomon women as artists and creators of the acclaimed Jomon pottery.[13]

When the Jomon people moved from caves to villages and arranged their dwellings in concentric circles, the center accommodated graves and an open area for communal and religious observances. Surrounding the center were pits for dwellings covered over with thatched roofs. Beyond the pit dwellings, structures with raised floors held dry storage, and at the perimeter of the community, there were storage pits for chestnuts and similar nuts according to Tatsuo Kobayashi.[14] At the Sannai Maruyama site in Aoyama, graves lined both sides of a pathway[15] making the living ever cognizant of the dead.

Figure 2.1: Diorama of Jomon Women and Children Working on Pottery. Using the pinch pot method, hands shape the clay to the desired size. Making clay pottery was women's work and here a woman adds an elaborate design to the rim. Children learned the skill early by creating smaller pots. The room displays a number of Jomon pottery pieces and shows creative hands fashioning pottery of different shapes, sizes, and styles (author's photograph taken at Niigata Historical Museum, May 2015, courtesy Yastami Nishida, Niigata Prefectural Museum of History).

In some villages, two different groups lived side by side and distinguished themselves by orienting the direction of their pit dwellings and arranging their round or rectangular hearthstone either east–west or north–south. The two groups identified themselves physically with different tooth ablation, hairstyles, tattoos, painted faces, and different styles of pottery. They swapped goods, cooperated, mixed genes, and apportioned responsibilities at births, weddings, and funerals, depending on the occasion.

Tatsuo Kobayashi likens the dual living condition to the black and white pieces of a Go game, or red and white as in the Japanese flag, necessary for cooperative living.[16] Residing side by side, the two different groups fostered the concept of duality—*uchi/soto* (inside/outside), *anoyo/konoyo* (that world/this world), and *honne/tatemae* (real/façade feelings)—concepts that survive today. In an egalitarian society, Jomon people shared goods equally and practiced *reigi tadashii* (good manners) to get along. Significantly each dwelling had a small *kamidana*[17] (shrine/altar) to honor the *seken* (other world) of spirits and descendants.[18] Many modern households also have either or both a Shinto *kamidana* and a *Butsudan* (Buddhist altar).[19]

Adversities were the signs of the kami's displeasure to the Jomon people's neglect of rites and the environment. This belief permeates the modern Japanese who is reluctant to publicize any personal or family malady.[20] Even the Edo Era (1600–1868) people were careful to behave properly on *konoyo* (this world) as it may affect the spirits of the invisible *anoyo* (other world). People's spirits mill around the area after death and return quickly if they were good while alive. Jomon parents, in an unusual ritual, buried children in earthenware and placed the vessel in front of the house for people to stomp on to expedite their rebirth.[21]

The predictability and unpredictability of Nature is reflected in art and poetic expression. Modern ceramicists deliberately add imperfections to their pieces. Artists' open spaces in drawings represent continuity. Writers prefer uneven numbers in poetic lines just as salespeople sell goods in uneven numbers from candies, tea cups, to bowls. The odd numbers provide a sense of continuity as opposed to the symmetry of even numbers.[22]

It is evident that the Way of the Kami formed the theological basis of the Jomon people from Incipient Jomon times. Shinto rituals, according to Kobayashi, were clearly established by the Mid-Jomon Era with the appearance of familiar religious regalia[23] such as incense burners, lamps, burial urns, pottery plaques, phallic stones, figurines with round mouths shaped like an "O" either in song or in calling the kami, and elaborately rimmed pottery. Other secondary regalia included ornaments, masks, and musical instruments, like the *ishibue* (stone flute), clay rattle, and bells, and small wooden stringed instruments. Engraved stones, small circular clay discs, jade beads, and figurines with no faces also appeared.[24]

Beginning in the Late Jomon Era (2500–1200 BCE), small palm-size *o-mamori* (charms) were used to ward off evil. Neither gods nor toys, the number of figurines increased during the Final Jomon period, probably to get rid of Yayoi[25] immigrants from northern China. The immigrants were a menace to the Jomon way of life, a life that was balanced with the seasonal goods from the land, forest, and sea. The Jomon's efforts were ineffectual, and their production of figurines diminished with the advent of the Yayoi Period (250 BCE–250 CE). The immigrants settled in the mid-portion of Honshu, splitting the indigenous people to become Ainu descendants in Hokkaido and Okinawans to the south.[26] The Yayoi people introduced metallurgy, rice cultivation, and the concept of social ranking and private ownership. Buried remains with armlets, big ear ornaments, engraved deer antlers, and slaves showed ranking. For the equality-minded Jomon people, hierarchy such as the ancestor worship brought by the newcomers was a contentious issue, according to

Makoto Takemitsu. However the Yayoi people joined the Jomon people in their belief in the *ujo* (sentience) of all creatures and assimilated the culture of the Jomon people.[27]

Following the Yayoi Period, which lasted 500 years, the Kofun or Tumulus Era (250–538) began. It is distinguished by the appearance of keyhole shaped burial mounds that eulogized the Imperial family, a practice adopted from the Asian continent. The Tumulus mounds remain unopened today in respect for the dead, but some have revealed *haniwa* (terracotta cylindrical clay) figures, animals, houses, transport wagons, and utensils. Musical instruments discovered included the *uke* (drum), a figure holding a *wa-gon* (indigenous koto), and two delightful haniwa figures with "O" shaped mouths and arms as if singing and dancing in reflection of their religious and secular activity.

The Kofun or Tumulus Era (250–538), Asuka Era (552–645), and Early Nara and Nara Eras (646–710, 710–794), collectively called the Yamato Era (300–710), had many immigrants from the Asian continent. Some *toraijin* (Chinese and Korean immigrants) with special knowledge of writing, Buddhism, Confucianism, or music became aristocrats.[28] Gagaku music, which was religious music in China, was relegated as Imperial court ceremonial music because the Japanese already had their Shinto music that had the power to communicate with the gods. The *Kojiki* describes several of such direct communications. For example, Princess Onagahimi, at the death of her parents, played the *wa-gon* (indigenous koto) to summon the gods to hear how she could placate the kamis to quell the reason for her parents' death. She was told to be vigilant and to observe Shinto rites regularly. Is this caution the reason why priests today diligently continue rituals to appease the kamis at Shinto shrines?

In another story, the fifth century Emperor Chudai summoned the kamis with the wa-gon to hear their accolades about his recent Eastern conquest. The possessed Empress Jingu spoke on the kami's behalf and told him to conquer lands to the west, or Korea. Seeing only an ocean in that direction, the Emperor accused the kami of being mistaken. Soon thereafter, the strums of the wa-gon ceased. Chudai, in defying the kamis' message, was struck dead.[29] Did he not know that the kami's message should not be refuted?

Aesthetics of Jomon Pottery and Shinto Music

Undoubtedly, beliefs in the power of music shaped the aesthetics, melodic contour, and sound. Like DNA, the scale and tones found their way into new genres of Japanese music. Fortuitously for us, a stone flute appeared in a 4,000-year-old archeological site to clue us into the sounds heard by

Jomon people. When it was blown, it was a noh flute come alive! The sound came from Japan's ageless past just like the Western 35,000-year-old bone flute whose range of notes was similar to Western modern flutes.[30] Although the Jomon flute is "younger" than the bone flute, its sounds may be as old as the world's oldest Jomon pottery that goes back, according to some scholars, 16,000 years.

If we assume that the aesthetics of a culture permeate all its artistic endeavors, Jomon pottery and music must share common properties. The first similarity is that Jomon pottery is constructed from simple handmade clay pinch pots that are unglazed and earthy looking; musical instruments have no mechanical parts and are made of materials found in the environment and look like their sources are from nature.

Secondly, both the pottery and music are constructed and decorated simply, using limited techniques. The exquisite *kaen* (fire) pottery from

Figure 2.2: *Kaen* pottery, attributed to the Mid-Jomon Era around the Niigata area. Note the earthy quality honoring its raw material, clay. The cylindrical base fans out to a rim with elaborate designs. The large display room shows a variety of pots of different sizes with different functions and decorations (author's photograph taken at Niigata Historical Museum, May 2015, courtesy Yastami Nishida, Niigata Prefectural Museum of History).

Niigata is divided into top or rim, middle area, and long body portion. The rim consists of "C" clay coils shaped into combs of a rooster, leaping flames, a crown, goggles, bags, or serrations. The middle region and long body is imprinted with a rope coiled on a doweling (hence the name *jo* (rope) *mon* (imprint). Over it, a cleared space holds symbolic designs of recognizable figures, plants, or fauna. The longitudinal decorations are again a series of "C" shaped coils in "S," spirals, inverted "U," or elongated "J" designs. Strict rules apply to each design having meanings significant to the community. Some pottery served as objects to dance around.[31]

Thirdly, asymmetry is the rule on Jomon pottery. The Katsusaka pottery of Figure 2.3 shows the middle region of pottery with a J-like motif that morphed from a "J" to J, J, J."[32] As in the Figure 2.2, the motifs or designs change around the body of the pottery. Similarly, hogaku's musical motifs repeat and vary with subtle timbre changes through compositions.[33]

Fourthly, the early Jomon pottery had pressed fibers as decoration to resemble woven baskets but later became more elaborate, like the kaen pottery. The fragile, fanciful kaen pottery with impractical designs served as cooking pots.[34] Similarly, hogaku's musical melodies evolved from a few abstract motifs with some recognizable imitations of nature's musicians like swishing water and bird or insect cries. The simple melodic line on

Figure 2.3: Mid-Portion of Katsusaka Pottery and Its Changing Design. In this illustration the designs change slightly across the pottery, thereby sharing an intriguing characteristic with the melodic variations in music. The organic designs are of human dimension that change with time (drawing by Meagan Healy based on Kobayashi's *Jomon Reflections,* p. 47).

several instruments became several melodic lines intertwining around each other in a complex sounding composition (see Chapter 7 on decoration).

Lastly, Jomon pottery is held up as having well-defined Japanese sensibilities that are rooted in its ancient population. Neil MacGregor said of a 7,000-year-old Jomon pot that "the Jomon's meticulous attention to detail and patterning, the search for ever-greater aesthetic refinement and the long continuity of Jomon traditions seem already very Japanese."[35] According to artist Okamoto Taro (1911–1996), Jomon pottery reflects the ultimate artistry of the Japanese; anything thereafter is mere imitation.[36]

Music, which is harder to grasp, hold, and examine than its visual counterpart, is ephemeral, now here and now gone. It requires memory to appreciate its sophistication and elegance that is singularly Japanese.[37] Jomon Era music cannot be scrutinized like Jomon pottery and so there is no testimony to it being the ultimate in artistry. Still Eta Harich-Schneider said, "The ritual sound as a means to effectuate magic has survived in Japan not only in the rural districts but also in the large cities."[42] It *is* music heard throughout Japan even today.

Jomon Era Music

The prime music we can trace back to the Jomon Era is the solemn *norito* (invocation, sacred spell, or incantation) performed only by a qualified Shinto priest. Devoid of Asian continental influences,[38] they represent a "precious resource for reconstructing the religious tradition of the primitive Japanese."[39] They came from the time of Amaterasu and the prehistoric Urabe[40] (priest's) family who controlled the Department of the Affairs of the Kami. Which norito chant to perform depends on the function it must facilitate.[41]

Is Jomon Era music as profound as its pottery? Joseph Kitagawa said that Shinto music is "shrouded in the misty past" and "most likely embraced a wide variety of prayers, charms, and spells that had been developed in different places by the local *ujis* (clans)."[43] Played today are *kume-uta* (military songs) and Yamato-*uta* music from Jimmu-tenno's reign (660–585 BCE). The two types of music date back to the Late Jomon Era[44] and have no known Asian continental influence.[45]

However, some Japanese musicologists[46,47] question the validity of Shinto ritual and ancient music and dismiss them as products of "primitive people" belonging to isolated hunters and gatherers, barbaric nomads, or simple savages with no written language. Of the ritual practiced today by Shinto priests at various shrines, Eishi Kikkawa said that they are "imitations of primitive music and ... a befitting accompaniment to the devotional ceremonies dedicated to ancestral deities."[48] Kikkawa essentially dismisses Shinto music as patronizing obsolete practices.[49] Accordingly, Japanese and Western musicologists[50] begin the study of hogaku with the introduction of Korean and Chinese music,[51] thereby implying that before them, Japan existed in a musical vacuum. Failure to acknowledge Shinto ritual music misses the ancient Japanese practice of what became known as the iemoto system where music, art, and other skills are transmitted precisely from one generation to the next. The evidence left of the Jomon people's social practices and their pottery suggests that they were very civilized people transmitting their arts from one generation to the next over thousands of years, and not as primitive as some scholars suggest. The music, as simple as it may sound, contains subtleties that are reflected on their visual counterparts.

Shinto music of norito, *mi-kagura,* and *sato-kagura* ranges from sacred to ceremonial. Ceremonial music can be sublime or raucous using voice, percussion, strings, and flute to enliven countless matsuri festivities at almost any place in Japan.[52] The musicality found in sacred *norito* (invocation, sacred spell, or incantation), a mi-kagura song *Asakura,* and sato-kagura ceremonial music are examined here for common musical elements that also appear in all hogaku.

Norito. Norito sounds like monotonic recitation of mumble jumble, but I find it musical and fortunately, some scholars agree with me. John Nelson said that the "voices are practiced and beautiful in their intonation of a poem said to be nearly 1,100 years old."[53] It "begins in a murmur that steadily rises in pitch and volume ... ending with a vowel that slides down an octave in pitch and lasts a full five seconds."[54]

Some prayers have continuous small spiraling melodic pronouncements of words in a short–long rhythm.[55] The word, or elongated syllable at the end of the prayer, moves upward in pitch. Donald Philippi speaks of "evidence that there was a special musical technique to reciting these rituals, and that there were books on musical notation for this purpose."[56] The delivery requires power, elegance of expression, and preciseness to effectuate magic.

Norito uses flowery language with "repetition, parallelism, long enumerations of names of deities and offerings, metaphors, the use of mythological accounts to explain the origin of certain forms of worship, and the all-pervading sonority."[57] The norito contains no doctrine but is "performed text" showing people how to observe rituals and prayers.[58]

Norito consists of two types: the *senge-tai* (word from the deity) and *sojo tai* (addressing a deity). The senge-tai from the kami starts with, "Hear me, thus I speak," and ends with "Thus I declare." Of the two, the *senge-tai* may be the older, evolving when the Jomon society was forming. Today it is logical that there are more *sojo tai* or requests to the kami. The format of the two tais is similar except for the ending of "senge-tai" ("Thus, I speak") or "sojo tai" ("I humbly speak"),[59] and both are official and public pronouncements from the kami.

Type	Beginning	Qualification	Request	End
Senge-tai	Kami addresses the emperor through the priest, giving the Kami's name and august status.	Petitioner or priest of the Nakatomi or Imibe family or who is one of Amaterasu's descendants	*Semmyo*: "Hear me, thus I speak."	"Thus I speak."
Sojo tai	Priest addresses a deity by name and with exaltations listing things, fruits, and the beauty of the environment.		*Mowasu:* "I humbly petition." A humble address to the kami insures the blessing and pacification of the spirit. A plea is made to hold safe and protect the Imperial family, and a list of offerings is promised for good fortune, harvest, etc.	"I humbly speak."

Table 2: Format for Norito Recitation of Senge-tai and Sojo tai. Senge-tai is a command from the kami, and sojo tai is a request to the kami. The format of the incantations begins with a flourish of praises to the kami. The requester states his qualifications by identifying himself. A list either in praise and gratitude follows which mentions the land and the products provided by the kami. The list gives insight into the desires and goods enjoyed by the community. Near the end of the norito, a command or request is made, and the incantation finishes humbly and quietly. This norito structure is the general form of hogaku's uta-centric music.

As an example, the Hirano Matsuri norito begins by exultations of the kami followed by the name of the qualified petitioner (usually a descendent of the Nakatomi [Urabe] family) to speak on the emperor's behalf. A list of offerings of everyday products provides a glimpse of goods of the day, such as swords, silk, horses, garments, wine, sweet and bitter herbs, fish, and seaweed.[60] Towards the end,[61] the petitioner requests blessings upon the emperor and the court as they work for the people's behalf. The prayer ends with the priest humbling himself.[62] After listening to many noritos, their stylized and formulaic words become familiar and recognizable.

> By command of the Emperor,
> I humbly speak in the solemn presence
> > Of the Great Sovereign Deity
> > > Who has been brought hither from Imaki and worshipped:
>
> In accordance with your desires, oh Great Sovereign Deity
> In this place,
> > The shrine posts have been broadly set up in the bed-rock below,
> > The cross-beams of the roof soaring towards the
> > > High Heavenly Plain,
> >
> > And [a shrine] established as a heavenly shelter, as a sun-shelter,
>
> And **I (office, rank, surname, and name) of the Office of Rites,**
> > **Have been designated as *kamu-nishi*,**
>
> Do **present the divine treasures:**
> > Bows, swords, mirrors, bells,
> > Silken awnings, and horses have been lined up in rows;
> > Garments of colored cloth, radiant cloth,
> > Plain cloth, and coarse cloth have been provided;
>
> **The first fruits of the tribute presented by the lands of the**
> > four quarters have been lined up:
> > The wine, raising high the soaring necks
> > > Of the countless wine vessels filled to the brim;
> >
> > The fruits of the mountain fields—
> > > The sweet herbs and the bitter herbs—
> >
> > As well as the fruits of the blue ocean—
> > > The wide-finned and the narrow-finned fishes,
> > > The sea-weeds of the deep and the sea-weeds of the shore—
>
> All these various offerings do I place, raising them high
> > Like a long mountain range, and present.
>
> Receive, then, tranquilly, I pray, these noble offerings;
> **Bless the reign of the Emperor as eternal and unmoving.**
> > Prosper it was an abundant reign,
>
> And grant that he may abide for a myriad ages,
> [Thus praying] I fulfill you praises. Thus I humbly speak.
>
> Also I humbly speak:
> **Guard, I pray, the princes of the blood, the princes,**
> > The courtiers, and the many officials have assembled
> > Who serve [the Emperor];
> > Guard them in the guarding by night and the guarding by day,
>
> **And grant that they may serve in the Emperor's court**
> > Ever higher, ever wider, always prospering
> > Like luxuriant, flourishing trees.
>
> [Thus praying] I fulfill your praises. Thus I humbly speak.

Figure 2.4: Norito for the Hirano Festival. In this sojo tai found in Donald L. Philippi's *Norito* (pp. 32–33), the priest addresses the Iwaki deity on the fourth and eleventh months of the year to ensure the Imperial family's safety and health. The norito opens with extravagant praise, the identification of the priest, and a list of goods and food stuff from the land and sea as offerings. Near the end a request is made to bless the Imperial court and then finishes with the priest humbly praising the kami. (Bold added by author to emphasize the form.)

From the text of the Hirano norito we find these musical elements:

- Norito is solemn, quiet, and fills the heart.[63]
- The voice is the simplest ubiquitous instrument.
- The voice moves within a few notes of the IN scale.
- Special words are enunciated to effectuate magic in a grounded but natural voice.
- The norito unrolls within a prescribed structure: (1) Naming the kami (2) Making the request, and (3) Humbling oneself.
- Interest or decoration of the norito comes from the timbre of the priest's sincere voice and intonation.

In norito incantations, the *kotodama* (words) have the power to move the kami. It is the earliest form of mantra-like secret prayer; likewise, the ancient *waka* (poems of 5, 7, 5, 7, 7 syllables per line) continue to invoke wishes and blessings to this day at the annual Imperial New Year's waka contests. Thus, kotodama is a sophisticated recitation like singing. Every instrument—biwa, shamisen, koto, and even the various kinds of flutes—accompany the voice. Theater music noh, bunraku, kabuki, and *buyo* (dance) are set in motion by the songs, and the correct words with the right intonation and conviction effectuate magic and move listeners.

Mi-kagura's *Asakura*. Kagura is performed at matsuri and comes in two forms: *Mi* (honorific)-kagura is Imperial and *sato* (hometown)-kagura is kagura for the public and outside of the Imperial purview. Norito, special incantation by priests is also under the category of kagura.

Mi-kagura is performed for the sole attendance of the emperor who is the high priest of Shinto. On behalf of the Japanese people he honors the kami to ensure peace and good fortune for Japan.[64] Mi-kagura is performed at the equinoxes and February 11 for Kigensetsu, April 3 for the commemoration of Jimmu-tenno's ascent, October 17 for Chinkonsai, November 23 for Shinjosai, December 15 for Gorei-no-mikagura, December 25 for the Taisho Tennosai, and at other times.

A mi-kagura ceremony held on December 15[65] provides a glimpse of a program for the emperor. Shortened to six hours, this private concert in the past took all night. The emperor arrives at dusk. The officiating priest, a descendent of the god Futotama (who organized the performance to lure Amaterasu out of the cave) lights a fire in front of Amaterasu's shrine with a sacred mirror. In a defined area he dances slowly toward the fire to purify the area and induce divine possession. After the norito, musicians entertain with twelve songs accompanied by the *kagura-bue* (kagura flute), wa-gon (indigenous koto with six strings and six wooden bridges), *shakubyoshi* (sticks), and the imported *hichiriki* (reed flute). A lead singer followed by other singers in

2. Ancient Music and Its Properties

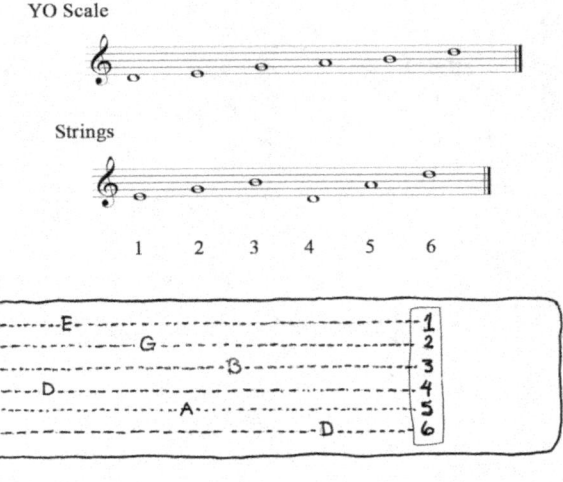

Figure 2.5: Wa-gon Tuning and Bridge Placement. The unusual bridge placement, compared to most instruments, allows the melody to be played on adjacent strings without searching for the notes that are usually arranged by pitch from low to high. In addition to the wa-gon melody, a mesh of up or down strums, the voice, and shakubyoshi add interest to the music. Note that the YO scale on the strings does not ascend up the wa-gon (drawing by Meagan Healy).

unison, sing *Azuma asobi*, *saibara* (folk songs),[66] and *tanka* or waka poems. When the head priest calls "Oooh"[67] at heart of the mi-kagura ritual, he opens an expansive sanctum for the kamis take their temporal abode in the *sakaki* branch that is in his hand.[68] A *saibara* and *Senzai no Ho* (Thousand Years of Eternal Existence) songs entertain the emperor and the kamis. The emperor leaves with the sakaki branch infused with life's energy. The kamis then retreat.

In another ceremony held on November 21, as the penultimate number at dawn, a priest sings an ancient song called *Asakura* accompanied by a *wa-gon*. From Harich-Schneider's partial recording,[69] one can hear musical properties found in all Japanese music in terms of singing, instrumentation, and tempo. The wa-gon[70] accompanying the singing is made of lightweight Paulownia wood with moveable bridges suspending the six strings. The *shakubyoshi* (two long flat sticks) slaps together to punctuate the vocal line which sings in the IN mode. The wa-gon is tuned to the YO mode but unlike most instruments, the bridges are not placed in the ascending pitch but rather arranged to facilitate playing the notes on adjacent strings (see Chapter 4 for discussion of YO mode).

Figure 2.6 shows *Asakura* with four instrumental patterns that repeat.

Figure 2.6: Score of *Asakura* with Melody Patterns. While playing the wa-gon, a priest sings in a chant-like fashion and holds a vowel over the two wa-gon melody of A, B, A, A, B, A, A, B, A, A, B, etc. The arrows indicate the strums of *zan* (up) and *ji* (down) across the strings and an asterisk shows the sharp snaps of the *shakubyoshi* (wooden sticks).

The right hand holds a small wooden stick to strum the meshed tones of *zan* (up) and *ji* (down) indicated by arrows on the score. The soft plucks of the melodic patterns of *ori* (A) and *tsume* (B) are played with bare fingers beginning on string 5. Plucking the adjacent strings starting on 4, 3, 2, 1, 2, 3, 4, 5, 6 make the melodic sequences of ori and tsume as in the score. The sharp slaps of the shakubyoshi sticks (indicated by x's) tell when to start singing and when to change pitch. Although rules exist for the shakubyoshi, its timing is organic.[71] The piece begins slowly and stealthily gathers speed as in the *jo-ha-kyu* or *jo* (slow), *ha* (fast), *kyu* (faster) phenomenon or tempo that mimics life as it begins, matures, and ends.

In *Asakura* the focus of the music is the voice that does not soar like Gregorian chants but is heavy and grounded. Nevertheless, volume, breath control, and conviction must hold the open vowels melismatically. In the meantime the wa-gon's soft plucks, mesh of sound, and occasional slap of the shakubyoshi coordinate to make music.

Asakura concerns a castle of Emperor Yuryaku (456–479), possibly a lament of a deposed successor, evoking melancholia. The same person plays and sings[72] the song.

> Asakura, oh! The place built of undamaged trees,
> If I were there! If I were there And gave my name,
> They would wonder: Whose child is he?[73]

Imported instruments accompanied mi-kagura singing that developed later in the seventh or eighth centuries. For example, the imported hichiriki and *komabue* (Korean flute)[74] accompanied Azuma asobi with wa-gon and shakubyoshi. Even with the addition of foreign instruments, the elements of singing in the indigenous scale to produce *awa-re* (pathos) persisted.

Ceremonial Music of Sato-kagura: Sato-kagura is any ceremonial music or energetic music at matsuri outside Imperial observance performed by the community at matsuri time. Matsuri celebration occurs at a shrine's anniversary or a special occasion like changing the mats of the inner sanctum or sprinkling water for purification. The Internet lists countless festivals in Japan for different reasons and different times of the year. Before the celebration, the area is ceremonially prepared for the religious portion by the miko[75] who dances to sanctify a space for the kami's attendance—a task usually ignored by the general public. (Tourists mistakenly regard the act of sanctifying as performance and believe the dance and music is for them as the audience and not for a more profound purpose.) After the miko sanctifies the stage, priests through norito chants ask for blessings or make a request. Following the solemn ceremony, the entertainment and festivities begin.

Large shrines rally the neighborhoods to raise funds for games, food, and floats, enlist and engage carriers of the *mikoshi* (portable shrine),[76] and organize a parade of dancers and performers. The Hirano Shrine matsuri in Kyoto has continued since 794. People wear *yukata* (cotton kimono) or *happi* (short-kimono jackets) and freely shout, sing, and dance uninhibitedly to drums, cymbals, and flutes.[77]

Another famous festival is the Onbashira Matsuri in Nagano, where every six years hardy participants risk their lives to ride downhill on huge logs destined for the Suwa Grand Shrine. Different regions have their variation of the *hadaka* (naked) matsuri that challenges young men to run in loincloths on a cold day and be drenched with water. The purpose of the matsuri is for the people to commune with the local, regional, or national kami while participating and enjoying uninhibited fun.[78]

Entertainment, also part of the matsuri festivities, is varied. It includes reenactments of mythological or religious stories of Amaterasu's reappearance from the cave and Susanowo's slaying of the eight-headed serpent. Imported forms of entertainment[79] later featured the Dojoji legend from the Lotus Sutra. The instruments from China, such as the hichiriki, *sho*, flute, and the thirteen-stringed koto, accompanied the kagura.[80] Today kagura entertainment in cities such as Kyoto, Osaka, and Tokyo is diverse. At the Yasaka Jinja in Kyoto, *kyogen* (comic) performances from the noh theater please the crowds. Farmers of the Yamaoka region perform *Kurokawa noh* for the Kasuga Shrine. And depending on local talent, the performances may include a town band, flamenco dancers, and jazz bands. Essentially, the matsuri keep people in touch with their kami and heritage while presenting new talent.[81]

In another setting of a more traditional sense, sato-kagura music[82] is played at shrines to accompany private ceremonies, such as an infant's 100 days or the presentation of offerings at Izumo Shrine. Heard often at shrines and in movies is the following that uses three instruments—a flute, drum, and *suzu* (bells on a stick) held by a miko. The flute plays four notes of the IN scale over a consistent long, short–long, short–long, short–long, long drum pattern. Soft bells held by a dancing miko follow the drum patterns and then she later shakes them freely as if spreading magic. The structure of the music repeats three or more times until the ceremony is completed. Aesthetically, the overall music just described and found in Figure 2.7 is gentle, mesmerizing, serious, and calming.

The kagura of norito, mi-kagura with song, and instrumental music of sato-kagura performed by priests are three examples that contain musical

Opposite: **Figure 2.7: Sato Kagura Ceremonial and Miko Dance Music. Heard at shrines and in videos about shrine ceremonies, the flute's few notes over the steady drum beat is calming and mesmerizing. Small bells on a stick are shaken by a miko (shrine maiden) to the drum beat or at will when showering blessings over those present at the appointed ceremony.**

2. Ancient Music and Its Properties

elements common in all hogaku. Overall, their aesthetics include the sounds of unassuming simplicity of the instruments, scale, and songs and an organic format and tempo with melodies decorated by timbre.

Summary

In ascertaining hogaku's musical elements from ritual music, the prehistoric Jomon pottery is an aesthetics mirror because it "sings" like its auditory counterpart. For example, in the construction of pottery, the hand-pinched clay is earthy looking and unglazed. Similarly, musical instruments cannot hide their source materials from nature. From the simplicity of the construction of instruments, countless timbre are teased out to decorate melodies in one of two modes, the IN and YO.

Symbolic decorations on Jomon pottery are made from rolled rope to imprint textures or appliqués of C-shaped clay rods shaped to tell familiar narratives to the community. Musical narrative comes from the *kotodama* (words) recited by priests to charm, pacify, and cajole the kami to bring good fortune. The uta is the tool to convey feelings, images, and mood, and it is magical like the kotodama.

Designs on the Jomon pottery move asymmetrically across the body of the vessel. Hogaku melody also moves with different melodies taking listeners to another place in time. As in nature's musicians, timbre from the voice or instrument make tantalizing sounds to color the melody line.

The ultimate purpose of both visual pottery and ephemeral music is to touch and quiet the heart. The purveyor–priests who perform Shinto rites have generationally passed the musical elements to new priests in the same manner that the Japanese people continue the Way of the Kami in their daily lives from the naming of their children to cuisine, paintings, literature, architecture, consumer goods, pottery, music, or practically everything.

Musically Shinto and ancient music share the following:

- Aesthetics: Uplifting elegance, quieting, pathos
- Simple instruments of flute, drums, and bells made from nature's gifts with no mechanical parts
- Scale: IN/YO modes
- Structure: *Jo-ha-kyu* with words and patterns affecting rhythm and melodic flow
- Singing: The uta (song/poetry) dominates every genre and moves emotion and the melody

- Decoration: Contrast and timbre of instrument and voice to evoke atmosphere

Except for aesthetics, which was covered in the first chapter, these musical elements are the topics for discussion in the following chapters beginning with simple instruments.

3
Simple Instruments

When I talk about simple instruments, I mean using a tube with holes punched in it for a flute, blowing over reeds or a soda pop bottle, pounding on wood or stones for percussion, or plucking strings stretched across a stick or bone. Tomiyama Seikin contrasted a palanquin with an automobile in that a palanquin can traverse any terrain—steep, rough, windy, and paved or unpaved roads—whereas an automobile needs paved roads.[1] A simple instrument is like a palanquin. Seikin is a master at cajoling and wheedling subtle flavors from the vibrating strings of simple instruments such as a shamisen or koto, a practice that may have passed from the Jomon people when trying to produce interesting sounds from simple instruments.

Jomon Instruments

According to Jomon beliefs, musical instruments made of natural materials like bivalve shells and small stones for castanets or clappers were the kami's gifts to people. In the Jomon sites of Aomori, Hokkaido, and Shiga Prefectures, archeologists found flutes made of deer antlers and remnants of stringed instruments made of wooden spatula-shaped frames of Paulownia, mulberry, bamboo, and hardwood. Also found were rattles made of clay with some shaped like tortoises with small hard balls inside for noise-making.

The clay pots, however, with their different sizes and regularly spaced holes proved puzzling. Were they for wine storage or for drums?[2] Percussionist Tsuchitori Toshiyuki noticed similar pots in Africa and decided to cover the Jomon pots with deerskin and have a concert. He imagined the Jomon people's rhythm taken from the heartbeat, walking, jogging, tool-making, grain pounding, and other common daily pursuits.[3] Certainly they must have accompanied their activities with singing, a favorite Japanese pastime.

3. Simple Instruments

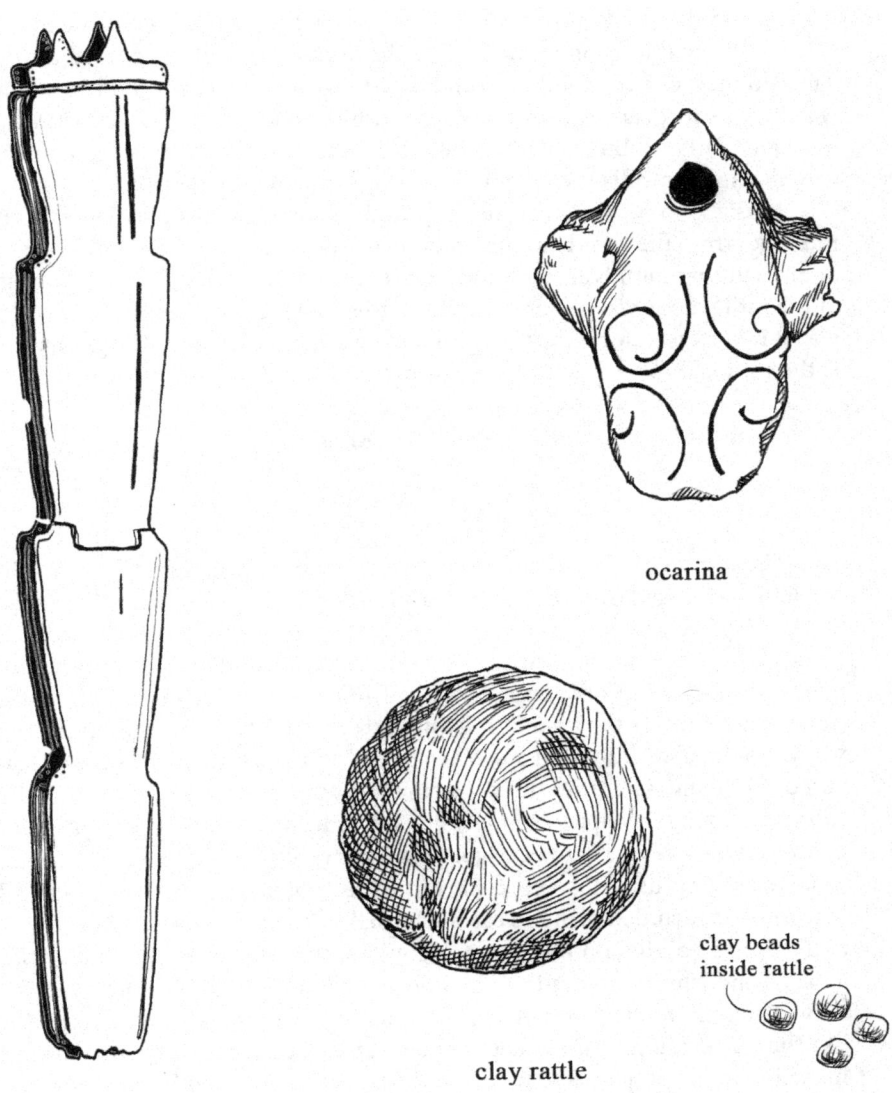

Figure 3.1: Jomon Instruments. Found in Jomon sites, wooden objects may have had strings strung across the length to pluck for making music. Other instruments played to invoke the deities were the ocarina, clay rattle, and *ama no iwabue* (stone flute). It is known that shells and objects to beat, shake, blow, or pluck were used as musical instruments (drawing by Meagan Healy).

As for the preferred sound of the Jomon people, one instrument, the *ishibue* (stone flute) sometimes called the *ama-no-iwafue*,[4] provided a clue. The ishibue came from a three-thousand-year-old Jomon site, and its sound was like a soft ocarina with four unfixed high-pitched notes similar to the nohkan.[5] This ishibue called deities from anoyo to konoyo, similar to the way the nohkan calls the actors to the stage of make-believe.[6]

Music is to be pleasing, calming, and cleansing and the melodies were messages from the gods beautiful enough to evoke tears. Nature is an example of unassuming sounds as in the Shinto premise of purity. The vibrating strings of the indigenous wa-gon are likened to the swaying motions (*saya, saya*) of plants in water. Water is purifying, and the wa-gon's vibrating strings *in water* is the ultimate description of pure or natural sound.[7]

> When its strings were plucked—
> It was like the brine-soaked plants
> Growing in the underwater rocks
> In the YURA Channel
> Which sway slowly—Saya—.[8]

The Jomon Era lasted over 10,000 years before immigrants from northern China changed the scene to begin what is called the Yayoi Era (250 BCE–250 CE). The newcomers brought rice cultivation, iron and bronze, the potter's wheel, and the concept of monarchy and social class. The Yayoi Era ended when people from Korea launched the Tumulus Era (250–550). The era is noted for tombs or burial mounds that interred aristocrats until cremation was introduced with Buddhism. When some Tumulus Era mounds were excavated, archeologists unearthed fascinating terracotta *haniwa* (terracotta tubes)[9] figures of people, animals, houses, transport wagons, and utensils. They found a *uke*, the drum the goddess Uzume danced upon, and a *meigen*, a bowed-string used for exorcism until the Heian times.[10] Other musical instruments included bamboo castanets, bells on a stick, a *kagura bue* (flute), and a figure holding on his lap a wa-gon that was 30 centimeters long with a flared end, similar to a miniature koto relic found in Okinoshima and the Ainu *tonkori*.[11] Some types of instruments have disappeared while some—like the wa-gon, tonkori, and kagura bue—give evidence that Japanese simple instruments accompanied dancing and singing, as depicted by two figurines with mouths shaped in an "O" as if singing and with their arms raised high in dance.

First Records of Imported Instruments

Although the Yayoi and Tumulus eras are evidence of the early exchanges between Japan and the continent, documentation of imported musical instruments is recorded with the death of Emperor Ingyo (374–454). The Korean king of Silla sent eight tribute ships with eighty musicians and dancers. Upon arriving at Naniwa (Osaka), the performers changed into white mourning clothes, and wept, wailed, sang, and danced until they reached the site of the Emperor's temporary internment.[12] After his burial in Kawachi, the mourners sailed home but left behind many stringed instruments, such as the biwa, *shiragi* (Korean koto), *dai-kin* (big koto), *chu-kin* (middle-sized koto), and *sho-kin* (small koto). Although it seemed musicians came and went, later in the year 467 a koto player arrived from the Kure Kingdom of Korea. Known as Irare no Kure Koto Hiki (Koto Hiki means koto player), he was a southern Chinese by birth and brought the koto and the art of *gigaku* (miscellany performing arts). (The words **gi**gaku and **ga**gaku may look confusing in English but they are easily distinguishable in Japanese kanji. Gigaku is of Chinese and Korean origin and points to various skills of performance that include dancing and singing. Gagaku is the musical ensemble from either China or Korea.) According to the *Nihon Shoki*, Korean gagaku music with no stringed instruments was introduced to the Japanese court in year 684,[13] suggesting that Korean gagaku preceded the Chinese gagaku ensemble with stringed instruments. As mentioned previously, gagaku was originally religious music in China but religious music already existed in Japan with Shinto. Therefore, gagaku music served as the ceremonial music for the pomp and circumstance of the Japanese Imperial court.

Japanese interest in foreign music was keen but as I will explore later, Japanese aesthetics crept over imported music in the way they selected instruments for the gagaku ensemble, chose compositions in a familiar mode, and sang Japanese songs using foreign instrumental accompaniment.

Buddhist Instruments

Buddhist chants and their percussion instruments came from Asia officially in the year 538 during Emperor Kimmei's (507–571) reign. Kimmei was presented a statue of Buddha, pictures, scrolls, and other Buddhist paraphernalia. The introduction of a new religion was a contentious issue between two Shintoist families (Mononobe and Nakatomi) and the Emperor, who, backed by the Soga clan, was ready to adopt Buddhism. In a fight for control, the Soga clan defeated the two families, thereby enabling Prince Shotoku Taishi (574–622) to become regent for Empress Suiko (592–628). As regent, Shotoku adopted Buddhism as the state religion[14] and built the temple Shitennoji in Osaka in the year 593. He encouraged gigaku and used the performance art with songs, dances, and plays to spread Buddhism to the masses. Gigaku lasted until the thirteenth century, but *shomyo* (radiant songs or chants), which contain the Buddha's teachings, had an everlasting effect. Different shapes and sizes of percussion instruments kept chanters together.

Most sects use the large *daikin* (bowl-like bell) shaped like a giant Buddha's begging bowl. It sits on a circular stand under a cushion and is struck to set the tempo, change sections, and indicate when to end. An elaborate lacquered stick covered with leather strikes the side of the bowl to produce a pleasant mellow, hollow, resonating tone that gradually fades to remind one of life's ephemeralness.

When chanting privately, the *sawari* (metal inverted bell) is handy. Struck with a smaller brocaded stick, the tone is higher in pitch than the daikin. For outdoor ceremonies, an *inkin* (draw-bell) or a miniature daikin is struck with a metal rod and functions like the daikin to set the tempo of the chants. Sometimes two hardwood *settaku* (wooden clappers) beat the tempo constantly during chanting, particularly chants of foreign origin that are monotonic and of an even rhythm.

Seldom used but for very formal rituals is the *kyotaiko* (large drum on a stand). The kyotaiko has a "majestic sound, which calls all sentient beings to the truth of the Dharma." The small *nyohachi* (cymbals) "represent thunder, lightning, and the power of the Buddha's teachings."[15] Another instrument is the *dora* (gong) used only for formal rituals of certain sects. Notice that the chants were mainly accompanied by percussion instruments.

Gagaku Instruments

Favored by the Imperial court for ceremonial use, gagaku instruments were introduced around the same time as the Buddhist shomyo. It is unfathomable how the instruments ever reached Japan considering the rickety ancient boats traveling over treacherous seas. For example, in the ninth century four ships set sail for China with an *urabe* (diviner) as navigator! Two Buddhist scholars, Kukai (Kobo Daishi of the Shingon sect) and Saicho (Dengyo Daishi of the Tendai sect) sailed to study Buddhism on a journey that should have taken ten days. The first boat with Saicho arrived near the target, but Kukai's ship tossed and drifted on the high seas and reached southern China fifty-four days later. The third ship wrecked in the South Seas, and the forth was lost forever.[16]

The gagaku ensemble came with thirty-four different instruments. Inundated with foreign music, the government established a Gagaku-ryo (Foreign Music Department) to study Chinese, Korean, and Manchurian music the first year of the Nara Era (701–794).[17] Empress Komyo, wife of Emperor Shomu (724–749), enjoyed Chinese music so much that she played the koto. At the premature death of her husband, Emperor Shomu, Komyo fortuitously stored his belongings in Shosoin, the storehouse of Todaiji. Here, musical instruments, costumes, masks, and many precious artifacts from as far as the Roman Empire were preserved for over a thousand years. The lists of instruments in bold in Figure 3.2 indicate their use today.

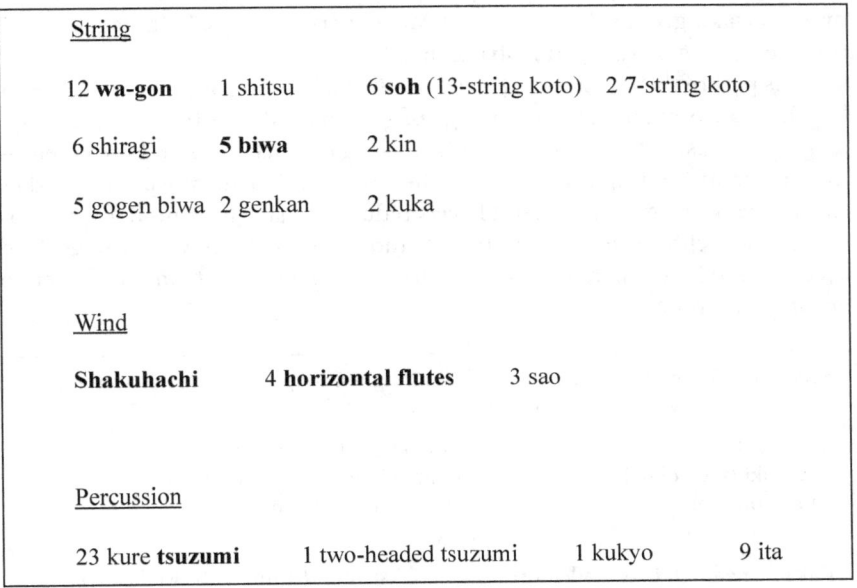

String			
12 **wa-gon**	1 shitsu	6 **soh** (13-string koto)	2 7-string koto
6 shiragi	**5 biwa**	2 kin	
5 gogen biwa	2 genkan	2 kuka	

Wind		
Shakuhachi	4 **horizontal flutes**	3 sao

Percussion			
23 kure **tsuzumi**	1 two-headed tsuzumi	1 kukyo	9 ita

Figure 3.2: List of Instruments Stored in Shosoin. Except for the wa-gon which is indigenous, the ensemble consisted of many stringed instruments of different size, volume, and number of strings. Those with little appeal were stored at Shosoin. Initially the shakuhachi was part of the gagaku ensemble but was later replaced by the hichiriki.

By the ninth century, the unstable political situation of the T'ang Dynasty of China (618–906) affected emissary visits between the two countries. Without outside intrusion, indigenous Japanese aesthetic rose in paintings, literature, and music. The realistic Chinese steep mountain landscape paintings became familiar flat rolling round hills with bird's eye views of house interiors to peek into the activities of courtiers. In literature, pathos as expressed in the *Manyoshu*[18] re-emerged and the Japanese vernacular replaced the scholarly Chinese language in diaries and poetry. Women excelled as writers as seen by the appearance of the *Pillow Book of Sei Shonagon* and Murasaki Shikibu's *Tale of Genji*. In music, the Saga Emperor (reigned 809–823) initiated changes in the gagaku ensemble. He reduced its size to eight instruments, keeping the higher pitched instruments and eliminating lower pitched *hichiriki* and the "U" (bass *sho*).[19]

Foreign music waned even further during Emperor Murakami's reign between 946 and 967. The Japanese music department was separated from the Chinese music department. Gagaku music was further divided into *kangen* (instrumental ensemble) and *bugaku* (dance music) and also into two categories, *saho* (left) or Togaku groups of Chinese origins, and *uho* (right) or Komagaku groups of Korean and Manchurian origins.[20] Komagaku does not use the *sho* or stringed instruments.[21]

As part of the Japanese's beloved pastime of singing, gagaku instruments began to accompany Japanese songs of *saibara* and *roei* (see Chapter 5 on singing). Thus, between 986 and 1011, the gagaku ensemble and the ceremonial music of the Imperial court reached the familiar form we know today. In summary, the gagaku ensemble was reduced in size for simplicity, instruments were chosen for contrasting sound, compositions were categorized according to instrumental or dance music, and gagaku instruments began to accompany songs.

Saho: Left Group, Chinese	Uho: Right Group, Korean, Manchurian, etc.
Wind:	
Ryuteki (flute)	Koma bue (Korean flute)
Hichiriki (reed oboe)	Kagura bue (Kagura flute)
Sho (mouth organ)	Hichiriki (reed oboe)
Percussion:	
Kakko (medium, two headed drum)	So no Tsuzumi (drum with two heads)
Taiko (large bass drum)	Taiko (large bass drum)
Shoko (small metallic gong)	Shoko (small metallic gong)
String:	
Biwa (4-stringed lute)	
Koto (13-stringed)	No stringed instruments

Figure 3.3: **List of Instruments of the Left and Right Groups. The Japanese organized gagaku instruments according to their national origin to study and preserve the values of indigenous and imported music. Imported music was classified into the left and right groupings; left for Chinese and right for Korea, Manchuria, etc. The right group has no stringed instruments.**

When facing the gagaku ensemble on stage, the audience is impressed with the beautiful arrangement of the ensemble, especially with the front row that is dominated by three contrasting percussion instruments. From the right comes the distinctive tapping sound of the *kakko* (two-headed drum) that sits on a stand. Two sticks hit the two drumheads alternately in a roll of beats that begins slowly and then speeds up. On the extreme left of the stage is the *shoko* (brass pan) that is struck with the brass balls on two sticks that strike the pan together or one at a time, leading with the left hand. The tendency for a right-handed person is to hit the shoko with the right hand first, but one is cautioned to play the left hand first and then the right.[22] Although mere mortals cannot tell the difference which hand strikes the shoko first, the saying is that the "kami will know" so it is in one's interest to "get it right." The largest drum with ornate designs sits prominently in the center of the stage. Two ball-covered drumsticks hit the drum resulting in a soft, low commanding "boom." The three drums with different and contrasting timbre—sharp, clanky, and low boom—suit Japanese ears which like the contrasting sounds.

It is easy to identify the wind instruments in the back row because of their distinctive sounds. On the right, facing the stage is the *sho* (mouth organ) consisting of seventeen thin bamboo pipes of different lengths for different pitches. A metal reed is attached to each pipe and when a pipe is closed, sound is produced. Open pipes are mute, thus there is a cluster of harmonious sound with fingers closing certain pipes while the player inhales and exhales through the sho. The sho must be kept dry so the players are often seen rotating the instrument around a charcoal brazier or an electric hotplate.

In the middle of the wind instruments is the loud 7-inch *hichiriki* (double reed flute) which, along with the flute, plays the melody. Made of bamboo and wrapped with cherry or birch bark, its characteristic nasal and strident oboe-like sound is ideal for any outdoor setting.[23] On the left is the 16-inch *ryuteki* (dragon flute) which is also made of bamboo. It has a mellow, pleasant sound associated with most flutes of the world. Having seven holes, the left-hand phalanges (not the tips) cover three holes while the right phalanges cover four holes.[24]

Also at the gagaku center stage are two stringed instruments in between the percussion and wind instruments. On the right is the gagaku biwa or *gakubiwa* with four frets played with a smaller *shakushi* (rice scooper type) plectrum. It is held sideways and plays distinct patterns of a few notes.[25] The other stringed instrument is the *gaku-soh*, the thirteen-stringed koto often called the Chinese koto in the *Tale of Genji*. The gaku-soh uses the thick 25-gauge strings[26] and low bridges. The deerskin plectrum band covers the distal phalange of the thumb, index, and middle fingers. A small thin bamboo plectrum protrudes out of the band. Both the koto and biwa play like percussion instruments with loud plunk sounds. The melodic tones associated with the two instruments appeared later with their respective songs. I discuss their construction later in this chapter.

Today, gagaku musicians have a repertoire of 200 pieces. However, gagaku that once pointed to elegant music from the Asian continent now in the twenty-first century has an expanded definition and is separated into four categories:

1. Instrumental ensemble called kangen
2. Dance music called bugaku
3. Songs. Ancient songs that include saibara and wakan-roei. Saibara is accompanied by ryuteki, hichiriki, sho, biwa, and shakubyoshi. Wakan-roei is accompanied by ryuteki, hichiki, and sho.
4. Ritual music for Shinto ceremonies. It includes music from Shinto ceremonies that include:

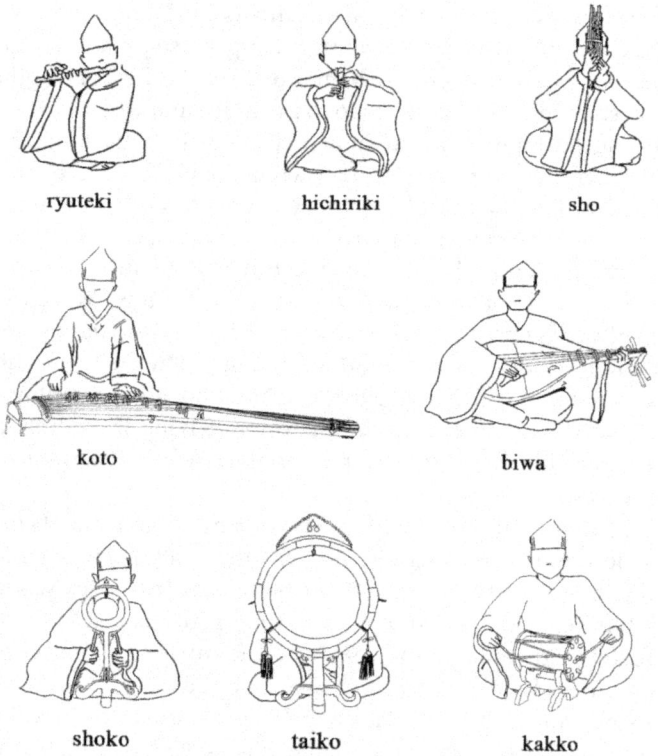

Figure 3.4: The Gagaku Ensemble Today. The ensemble consists of contrasting percussion, string, and wind instruments. The percussion instruments are in the front row with the largest o-daiko in the very front. The stringed instruments are in the middle row, and the wind instruments are at the back. The arrangement seems incongruous since the musicians who play the wind instruments carry the melody but are hidden in the back row. Ensemble-wise, the sound is balanced because the strident and loud hichiriki and the soaring flute carry above the other instruments. When the wind and percussion switch places, the music seems to lack the backbone provided by the drums (drawing by Meagan Healy).

- Kagura of mi-kagura and sato-kagura music
- Yamato-mai
- Kume-mai
- Azuma-asobi

In other words, gagaku once meant elegant music, but today it includes *any ancient* music from Heian times. Under the fourth category, kagura and other ancient songs are categorized under gagaku by virtue of being ancient.

The categorization of ritual music under the heading gagaku became an issue between a Japanese scientist and me. She said kagura is gagaku, and I said it is not. Yes, kagura does belong to the broadened *category* of gagaku but kagura is indigenous religious Shinto music and is different. Gagaku is imported music from China and Korea. Kagura was placed recently under gagaku for convenience because gagaku musicians today play the same instruments as those used in Shinto music, particularly in accompanying Azuma Asobi, kume- and Yamato-mai and kagura music. Our disagreement illustrates the shifting categorization of hogaku music when the finer aspects of music are forgotten with time.

Biwa

Biwa players. As shown in the Timeline, biwa *hoshi* (blind priest) originated with India's Prince Asoka's blind son who chanted the sutra to the

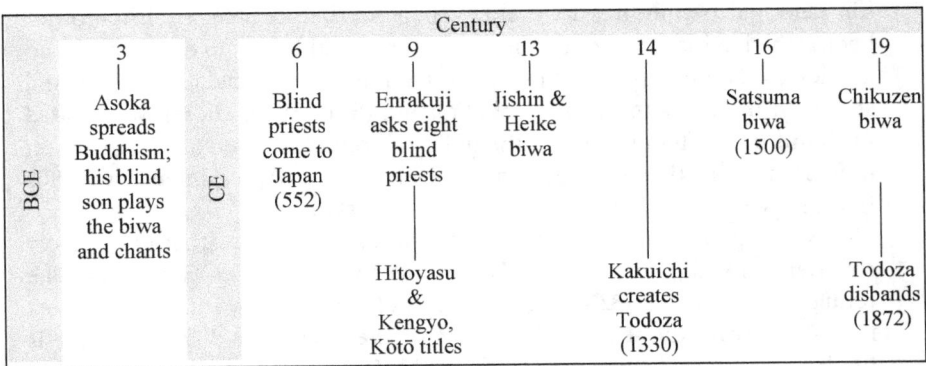

Figure 3.5: Timeline of Biwa Music. The biwa, said to be of Persian origin, spread to India. There, around 3 BCE, Prince Asoka's blind son played the biwa to accompany his sutra chanting and began the association of biwa with blind musicians. These blind musicians were part of the entourage that spread Buddhism. In Japan, blind priest musicians through Prince Hitoyasu Shinnyo earned the titles of Kengyo and Kōtō. Their status as musicians was secured when a professional guild was formed in 1330 by Kakuichi. This guild lasted until 1872.

strums of the biwa. The biwa hoshi were part of Asoka's spread of Buddhism through Asia because, according to tradition, their blindness enabled them to hear the Buddha's message better. Because of their purported special powers, they received welfare and were frequently called upon to dedicate new temples. They were among some of the twenty thousand Buddhist monks from China, India, Manchuria, and Vietnam asked to dedicate the Great Eye Opening Ceremony of Todaiji's giant Buddha in year 752.[27] For Tendai sect's Enryakuji on Mount Hiei completed in 806, the head priest Saicho commissioned eight blind Tendai monks to dedicate this important temple.

Famous biwa hoshi included Man'ichi, who passed on his skill to two equally prominent successors, Mansei-in and Myotoku-in. But the most famous is the legendary blind musician, Semimaru[28] (late 800s) who helped the Tendai priests from Kyushu gain official titles and priest's names. One group of *moso* (blind) biwa players from Kyushu performs even to this day.

At court in year 839, the famous biwa musician Fujiwara Sadatoshi led an exchange to the T'ang court before all exchanges ceased in 894. Sadatoshi learned from Renshobu, a Chinese teacher, the most secret pieces called *Ryusen* (Running Spring) and *Takobuku* (Hitting Wood).[29] These pieces passed only to serious and promising students but were lost with the Heian court's demise.

An important biwa player is Prince Hitoyasu Shinno (844–886), the fourth son of Emperor Nimmyo (810–850), who became blind at age 28. Empathizing with the plight of blind priest–musicians, the Prince gave all his personal belongings to them. When he died at age 42, his mother bequeathed in his memory the titles of Kengyo and Kōtō[30] to deserving blind musicians. These Imperial titles gave blind musicians official recognition and status. In the 1330s the Tōdō Shoku Yashiki (Tōdōza for short) was created for blind men. Membership in the guild offered blind men an organization to market their skills. Hitoyasu Shinno became its patron saint and was thus immortalized (see Chapter 8 on the iemoto system).

Many people even today lament the loss of the aesthetically savvy courtiers with the defeat of the Heike clan that ended the Heian Era. The Kamakura Era (1185–1333) began the age of the shogun. Innovators of art then came from the temple's *hoshi* and shrine attendants.[31] One example is the Heike biwa that came directly from the Tendai temple. Their narrations of *The Tale of the Heike* (or *Heike Tales*) catapulted the popularity of itinerant priest–musicians who earned extra income beyond sutra chanting. Spectacular offshoots of the Heike biwa music came later with Satsuma biwa and Chikuzen biwa.

The biwa construction. Originally from Persia, the biwa came with four strings with four frets or bridges, but the Japanese play the four-string or five-string biwa depending on the school. Biwa of all the schools are made with two pieces of either mulberry or Paulownia wood. The front flat piece has two moon-shaped holes and the back is rounded for a hollow sounding board. Its pear-like body tapers to a long neck that is bent to hold pegs for tightening silk strings.

The strings come in different gauges. The first and thickest string makes the open string drone sound. The fourth string is the thinnest and best for melodic passages.

Four tall bridges suspend the strings. Different pitches and its ½ and ¼ tones come from pressing the strings between the bridges.

The *bachi* (plectrum) is either a small *shakushi* or large and pointed fan-shape bachi. The Satsuma biwa bachi is the largest and picks out melodic passages with the points and makes a different timbre from the scrapes, whacks, flutter, and swishes, and many other sounds with its long sides.

Japanese musicians honor and pray to the goddess Benzaiten or Benten-sama, who holds a biwa and reigns over music, letters, and the arts. The Indians call her Sarawasti, but she came from Persia via the Silk Road to India, China, and then to Japan. One biwa stored at Shosoin of the Todaiji Temple in Nara journeyed across a desert. A date tree and camel, two items alien to Japan, are depicted on its biwa guard.

Musical Instruments of Noh

From the temples and shrines came sarugaku that was polished to noh in the 1400s. The *noh bayashi*[32] (noh ensemble) consists of a *ko-tsuzumi* (shoulder drum), *o-tsuzumi* (larger drum), *taiko* (drum hit with two sticks)[33] and *nohkan* (flute).[34] The musicians sit along the rear of the stage. Also, the noh stage itself is a big percussion instrument for actors to dance and stomp for dramatic emphasis. There are three clay pots under the bridgeway, four to six pots under the main stage, and two to three pots under the rear stage.[35] Stomping was Uzume's dance to entice Amaterasu out of the cave, and it is the Sambaso god's dance to awaken seeds in the soil. Jomon people practiced stomping to hasten a dead infant's spirit to return to the land. Stomps are part of Japanese dance and drama.

O-tsuzumi (big drum) *and* ko-tsuzumi (little shoulder drum). Unlike a Western drummer who has a variety of drums before him, two people holding one drum each must coordinate beat, create timbre, and act as one drummer. The o-tsuzumi delivers the dominant beat and the ko-tsuzumi reacts with the back note. This seemingly impossible task is a learned stimulus–response reaction that comes naturally after practice.

The larger of the two drums, the o-tsuzumi or *okawa* (big skin) is made

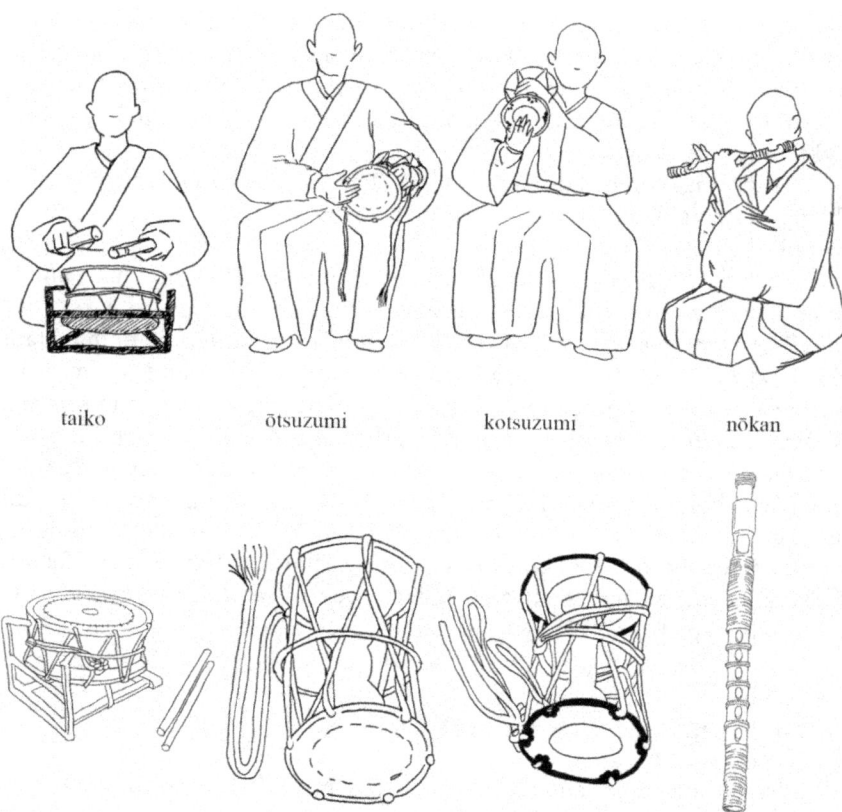

Figure 3.6: The *Noh Bayashi* (Ensemble). The flute and two drums begin the program with the actors and singers narrating the story. The taiko enters at the end of some plays for festive or celebratory dances (drawing by Meagan Healy).

of two horsehide drumheads and is held on the left lap. The drumheads are tied by flaxen rope on both sides of an hourglass-shaped body. The drumhead is hit with the right hand's middle and fourth fingers that are covered with papier mâché socks. A sharp whip-like whack results, especially on a heated drumhead with taut skin. The solmization of the o-tsuzumi sounds are *don*, *tsu*, and *chon*, depending on the patterns required because the play is coordinated with the ko-tsuzumi (see Chapter 7 on decoration).

Two ko-tsuzumi drumheads also consist of horsehide on a metal rim. On an hourglass-shaped, cherry-wood lacquered body, flaxen cords hold the two drumheads at either end. Unlike most drums, the ko-tsuzumi rests on the right shoulder while the left hand holds the flaxen cords. The third and fourth fingers of the right hand hit or tap the center or edge of the drum for four subtle but distinct sounds called *chi, ta, pu, pon*. The ko-tsuzumi's unusual and delightful feature is its ability to produce pitch change. As the right hand hits the drumhead, the left hand simultaneously squeezes and relaxes the cords connected to the drumhead to produce pitch. The control and coordination show mastery and skill on the ko-tsuzumi.[36]

Taiko. Of the three noh drums, the taiko is found everywhere in the streets as well as at shrines and temples. The drummer sits on the floor before a taiko placed on a small stand. The two drumheads are tied with flaxen ropes to the body and struck towards the end of the play in at least half of the two hundred noh plays. With dramatic fanfare the drummer aims the sticks at a small round paper at the center of a drum. Depending on the strength and tempo that is applied, the sound moves the audience to a festive celebration of dancing gods, heroes, or supernatural characters or to an exciting conclusion of dancing demons and other apt endings.

With no conductor, the o-tsuzumi, ko-tsuzumi, and the taiko coordinate rhythmic patterns with the *kakegoe* (shouts) used for aural timing (see Chapter 7 on decoration).

Nokhan. In addition to the drums, there is the nohkan, a flute that soars above the voice and drums. It is made of smoke-cured female bamboo consisting of eight to twelve insertions of bamboo tubes affecting the distances between the nodes and producing a slight conical shape. The outer portion of the nohkan is cherry or oak bark tied with vine. The inside is painted with red lacquer. There are seven finger holes and, unlike the Chinese ryuteki or gagaku flute, each nohkan is slightly different in length so that calibrating the notes with other nohkan or other instruments is nearly impossible. It is played alone. The scale of one nohkan is B, C#, D#, F, G, A#, C#, D#.

The noh flute creates atmosphere and evokes primordial emotions.[37] The amount of air forced through the flute determines its sound, which can be mellow, sweet, ghostly, or screechy. A wax plug inserted around the mouthpiece stops the air for the characteristic ear-piercing screech.

The Sankyoku Instruments: The Sangen/Shamisen, Koto and Shakuhachi

Imported Buddhist chants, gagaku, and noh music are associated with the upper class. Tsukushi koto music belonged to priests and noblemen, and biwa music was played by biwa hoshi as they roamed the public streets. During the 1500s, percussion accompanied most songs of the Japanese commoners until the introduction of the shamisen.

Sangen/Shamisen. When the small three-stringed *sansen* came from China via the Ryukyu Islands to Sakai in Osaka between 1558 and 1570, it became the rage. The word *sansen* was difficult for the Japanese to say until the first syllable "sa" became "sha," and the "mi" was thrown in to become shamisen.[38] The blind ji-uta musicians prefer to use the term *sangen* (three strings) but the terms are interchangeable.

As mentioned earlier, everyone, even the *oni* (demon), picked up this versatile and portable instrument. Basically, there are four groups of shamisen players—blind, sighted, men, and women—each with sub-groups with distinctive styles.[39] The sangen and koto later combined with the *kokyu* (bowed shamisen) and shakuhachi to create music quintessentially of the Edo Era.

	Blind	Sighted
Men	Members of the Todo Shoku Yashiki	Narrative popular music like Shinnai bushi
	Ji-uta lyrical music of kumi-uta, naga-uta, ha-uta, tegoto-mono	Theater music of Bunraku (gidayu) & Kabuki such as Nagauta, Tokiwazu, Tomimoto, and Kiyomoto
	Combined with Ikuta koto	
Women	Goze: Women from Echigo House for Blind Women	Geisha musicians played ko-uta shamisen music, and nagauta and ji-uta music
	Traveled in groups of five to entertain	
	Sang folk songs of the Echigo area with shamisen	

Table 3: Blind, Sighted, Men, and Women Shamisen Styles. The grid shows that shamisen music was segregated by sex and whether the musician was blind or sighted. Of the different styles, members of the Tōdō Shoku Yashiki were the authorized professional musicians and took the lead in creating art music that others emulated.

The first shamisen players were blind biwa musicians of the Tōdōza who were entranced with the new instrument but did not know how to play it until Naka Shoji or Ishimura Kengyo[40] remodeled the snakeskin drum and, using the biwa tuning and techniques, made the shamisen accessible to everyone. Today, the shamisen comes in three sizes—small, medium, and large—all similarly constructed. The blind musicians played the medium size.

The main part is a drum made of cat skin or cat and dog skin on the front and back of a sandalwood drum frame. Projecting out of the drum is a *sao* (pole). The other parts of the shamisen are the *neo* (braided twine) and a *koma* (horse). A *bachi* (fan like plectrum) is used to pluck the strings.

Shamisen size	Bachi (plectrum)	Musical style
Small	Small wooden	Folk songs, Ko-uta, Narrative music of Nagauta, Tokiwazu, Tomimoto, Kiyomoto Shinnai
Medium	Pointed—medium to thin	Lyrical ji-uta music of blind musicians of the Kansai (Osaka, Kyoto) region
Large	Thick bachi	Folk Tsugaru shamisen music Bunraku's gidayu

Table 4: Types of Shamisen. Principally similar in construction, the shapes and sizes of the drums and plectra affect volume. Different sizes of shamisen were developed to accommodate the musical taste of composers and their audiences.

Humidity and temperature affect the drum skin's sound and tension. A little half moon-shaped guard protects the playing area on the drum.

The sao of hard mahogany comes as one piece or in three segments to be assembled as one pole. There are no fret marks on the sao and, like a violin player, pitch stops are learned. Depending on the school, the sao section that inserts into the drum is either sloped or made into a straight edge to allow the fingers to stop the strings for higher notes. The older Yanagawa-ryu sangen sao slopes into the entry point of the drum. During the 1800s, Kyushu-area musicians like Mitsu Seichi, Sakamoto Jinoichi, and Hase Kengyo straightened the sloping end to an angle for a straight edge to make high pitches (see Figure 3.8: Yanagawa and Tsuyama Sao).

The neo made of brocaded cloth hooks onto the extended end of the sao protruding out of the drum so as to hold three strings of different thickness. The strings extend up the sao onto two small komas and then are wound around pegs made of ivory, water buffalo horn, or plastic. The pitch depends on the tension of the wound strings.

Two komas are crucial to sound production on the drum. The *kami koma* (top horse/bridge) elevates the top two thinner strings nearest the pegs of the sao. The thickest or lowest string hits the sao directly and that affects the other strings to produce *sawari* (sympathetic vibration). The second koma made of water buffalo horn comes in different heights and sits on the drum to elevate all of the strings. In Kyushu, improvement on the koma came by inserting lead shot, thus improving the balance of the drum skin and the sympathetic vibration of the first string.[41]

The sangen bachi looks like the biwa bachi from whence it came. Shaped like a fan or gingko leaf, it is made of ivory, water buffalo horn, tortoise shell, or plastic. Depending upon the various schools and styles of shamisen, the size and shape differ. The ji-uta bachi is generally larger than other genres

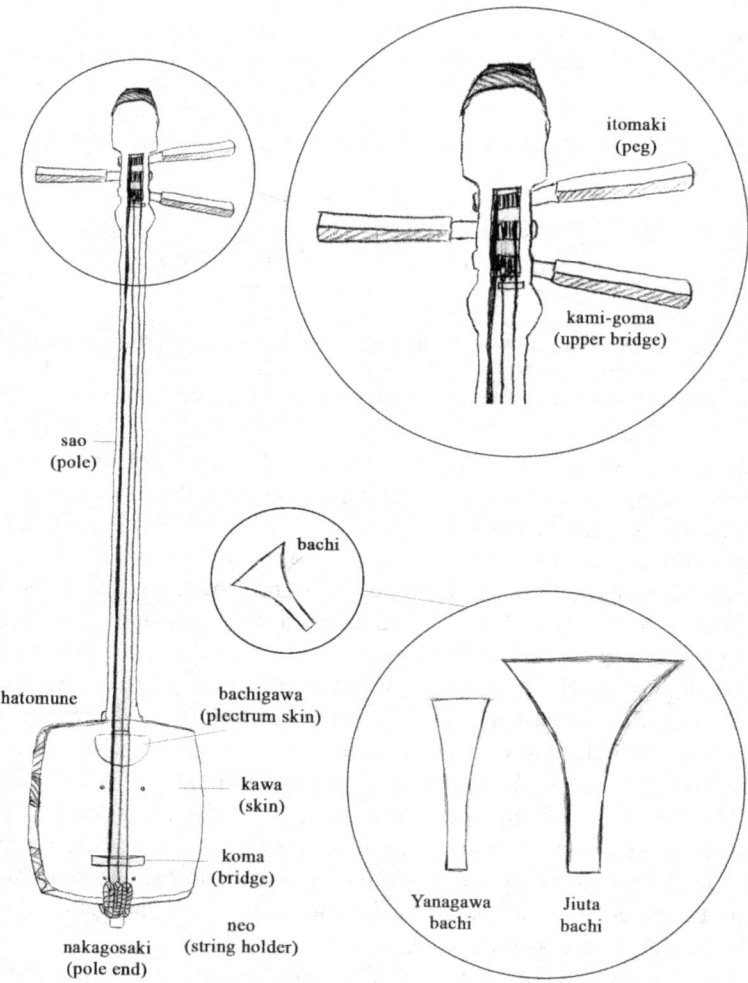

Figure 3.7: Parts of the Shamisen. Basically a drum with a pole for strings on which the strings are stopped at different spots for pitch. Three strings of different sizes are tied to a braided *neo* (string holder) and wound on three pegs. Two *koma* (bridges) include one on the drum to elevate the strings. The *kami-goma* (upper bridge) elevates only the two higher strings and allows the first string to make *sawari* (sympathetic vibrations). Originally a snake-skinned instrument plucked with a small plectrum, biwa musicians handy with the large biwa plectrum no doubt destroyed the snake skin *sansen* and had the drum skin replaced with more ubiquitous skins of feral cats. Today, synthetic skins are available. The plectrum simultaneously plays and hits the drum on the plectrum skin or guard. The result is a characteristically Japanese sound of the Edo Era and of bunraku, kabuki, buyo (dance), tea houses, and music of the merchant class (drawing by Meagan Healy).

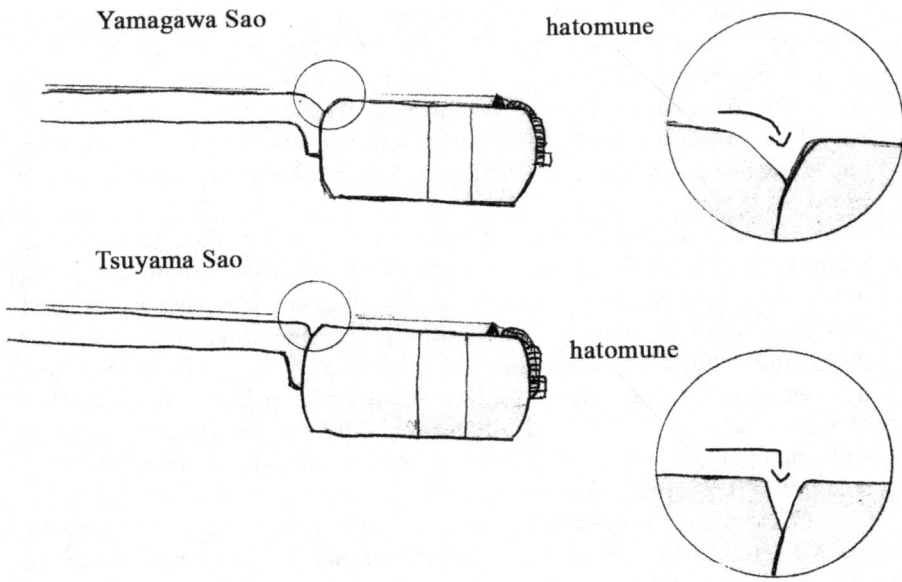

Figure 3.8: Yanagawa and Tsuyama Sao. Yanagawa and Tsuyama are ji-uta shamisen of the blind art musicians. The difference is the *hato-mune* innovation area. Tsuyama Kengyo straightened the end of the *sao* (pole) or the *hato-mune* (pigeon breast) before it enters the drum. This straightened area provided a flat area for fingers to play more high notes closer to the drum. Most ji-uta musicians use the Tsuyama shamisen but the Yanagawa-ryu musicians keep true to their tradition and stick with the rounded pigeon breast, as do most other schools (drawing by Meagan Healy).

of shamisen bachi inspired by Tsuyama Kengyo of Osaka who designed a larger sangen drum and a bachi of about 4.3 inches at the widest point. It is also thicker and heavier with a square handle that tapers to a thin edge to give balance and control to the sound. Kyoto's Yanagawa-ryu sangen is smaller with a bachi of 1.3 inches at the widest point.

The blind men of the *ji–uta* Yanagawa and Tsuyama schools played the medium drum with a medium pole. Ji-uta musicians at times rearranged regional folk songs and made them accessible to a wider audience. In the West, similar transpositions are found with the Shaker hymn "Simple Gifts" in Aaron Copeland's *Appalachian Spring* and the Beatles' songs played by the Boston Pops Orchestra. The London Philharmonic Orchestra plays video game songs, a niche genre of today's youth.[42] Also, the University of Maryland's Gamer Symphony Orchestra[43] makes game themes accessible to the symphony going public, thereby inadvertently storing and raising incidental music to a symphonic level.

The largest shamisen accompanies *gidayu* (vocal narration) singers of the puppet theater. The shamisen player sits to the left of the singer and plays loud, plunkish sounds like a pitched drum, effective for puppet drama on stage. The Tsugaru shamisen players also use the large shamisen, producing what I call "bluegrass music of the shamisen" because of their tremendously appealing fast passages. This folk Tsugaru genre has made shamisen popular in the West.[44]

The traveling *goze* (blind women musicians) of the Niigata area spread the folk songs of northern Japan and preferred the smallest shamisen, being light for traveling. Sighted women or *geisha* (professional women performers) also used the small shamisen, as did the sighted men of narrative music for dance and kabuki. To a shamisen player, shamisen varies to accommodate different styles of songs. Mumonsai/Miyako-Itchu XII of Tokyo, like a number of musicians today, studied both Tokiwazu and Itchu-bushi styles of shamisen and when performing the songs of either school, he switches shamisen to be true to the respective styles.

The shamisen is basically a drum with strings that are struck by a fan-like plectrum. Some schools have replaced animal skins with new materials, such as plastic drumheads. And to appeal to contemporary audiences, rock bands like the Aun-J strum the shamisen to suit the music. Even Maurice Ravel's *Bolero* and Debussy's *Pavane pour une infante défunte* are played on the Tsugaru shamisen, thereby crossing cultural borders.

Kokyu (bowed shamisen). The *kokyu* looks like a shamisen, but it is held parallel to the body and bowed with horsetail hair stretched tautly across a long sandalwood bow.[45] The long sao (pole) protrudes out the bottom part of the drum enabling the player to hold the kokyu upright between the knees to easily rotate the drum while playing.[46] The kokyu's drum is cat skin and the bowed strings produce the sounds of a thin violin or a mosquito. Its origin is said to be the pear-shaped *rebec* that came with the Portuguese, but when Japan expelled all Christians in 1638, the Japanese invented the kokyu to replace the rebec. Yatsuhashi Kengyo of the koto fame is said to have improved the playing techniques of the instrument.

The kokyu's thin quiet sounds almost disappeared from 1673 to 1735, and it is on the verge of disappearing again today. There were two schools, one in the Kansai (Kyoto/Osaka area) developed by Shinagawa Kengyo and the other developed by Masajima Kengyo. The Masajima-ryu survives. Around 1736 to 1750, Fujiue Kengyo in Edo created the Fujiue-ryu. He added a fourth string to add volume and better tone and tuned it to the same pitch as the third string. Fujiue teamed with the newly created Yamada-ryu koto (1800s) to play together.

Honte (main pieces) are pieces for the kokyu alone and written before 1751. Others are *gaikyoku* (outside pieces) that include ensemble pieces with koto. *Yachiyo Jishi* (Eternal Lion) is one of two famous gaikyokus. The genealogy of *Yachiyo Jishi* begins as kagura flute music. Masajima Kengyo transposed it to the kokyu. Fujinaga Kengyo then transposed it to the shamisen and then the koto. The famous koto piece *Chidori no Kyoku* by Yoshizawa Kengyo II[47] was first composed on a kokyu and then transposed to the koto. Today, the shakuhachi replaces the kokyu in most sankyoku ensembles for it offers a stronger contrast to the kokyu. The kokyu, however, has a quieting, ancient-sounding effect preferred for certain pieces at concerts.

Shakuhachi (vertical bamboo flute). The shakuhachi gets its name from its length, the standard being 1.8 feet or equivalent to "one *shaku*,[48] eight (*hachi*)" as in its name shakuhachi. The shakuhachi comes in lengths of 1.3, 1.6, 1.8, 1.9, 2.0, 2.1, 2.3, and 2.9. The shorter the instrument, the higher the pitch range. For example, the "*ro*" note is D for the 1.8, and C sharp for the 1.9, and so on. The longer 2.1 and 2.3 are often preferred for honkyoku and contemporary works but recently some sankyoku players prefer the 1.9 flute or the lower pitch range to suit the voice. The inside is coated with lacquer and only five holes, four in front and one in back, produce the chromatic scale and two and a half octaves.

Legend says a demon gave Minamoto Hiramasa a shakuhachi during the Heian Era (794–1185). A stalk of female bamboo, roots and all, is required for a shakuhachi, as seen in the woodblock by Torii Kiyomatsu (1690–1720) of the kabuki actor Ichikawa Danjuro as Takenuki Goro (*ta-ke* meaning bamboo, *nuki* meaning pulling out, and *goro* meaning heroic figure in an impossible feat). The shakuhashi musician, Yodo Kurahashi, said that the shakuhachi was part of the original gagaku ensemble. In the ninth century, the oboe-nasal sounding hichiriki replaced it. Set aside, the shakuhachi died out, or so it was believed.[49] Clues to the shakuhashi's fate appeared in a scroll painting of a biwa hoshi. Among his neatly laid out possessions was a shakuhachi, which was unusual: Why would an itinerant blind biwa player carry a shakuhachi? This mystery was solved when the blind Tsugaru shamisen player, Takahashi Chikuzan, explained how he had to work every day for his meals. On rainy days, water would ruin the shamisen, or for the hoshi, his biwa, so he played the shakuhachi in place of the shamisen.[50] It seems that itinerant musicians kept the shakuhachi alive out of economic necessity.

Around the fifteenth century there were several styles of shakuhachi players among Buddhist monks. Some belonged to Zen temples and the others belonged to the *komuso* (mendicant Zen priests) of the Fuke sect organized by the Tokugawa government to check the activities of *ronin* (masterless samurai). The attraction of the Fuke sect was that the ronin monks could achieve enlightenment without memorizing chants or sitting through long meditation. Their only requirement was to play the shakuhachi. Covering their identity in deep straw hats that came to their shoulders, they traveled freely and learned about the lords in distant provinces and were soon enlisted as spies for the Edo government. With the shogun's protection, they acted with impunity and were despised. The Meiji Restoration put an end to their spying and the Fuke sect.

Another group of shakuhachi players were *fukiawase* (priest-teachers). The priest-teachers could not teach non-priest students but Kurosawa Kinko (1710–1771), a retired samurai, learned and founded the Kinko-ryu. He rearranged some of the Fuke shakuhachi music to *honkyoku* (main pieces) music exclusively for the shakuhachi. Later towards the Meiji Era, *gaikyoku* (compositions outside the main pieces) with sangen and koto increased their repertoire.

Also during the Meiji Era, Nakao Tozan (1876–1956) learned Kinko-ryu shakuhachi music and started another school with a louder instrument that employed more decorative techniques that showed off a player's ability. The Tozan-ryu, together with koto's Miyagi Michio, led the Shin Nihon Ongaku (New Japanese Music) with music of Western format and influence. In addition, Nakao Tozan published shakuhachi music, making it simpler for students to acquire a teaching degree. His school spread widely and quickly, which accounts for the first shakuhachi players in America to be of the Tozan-ryu.

Like all Japanese instruments, the shakuhachi is also simple, a mere long hollow tube with five holes[51] that can produce several octaves and many sounds and timbre. Its expressiveness, association with Zen Buddhism, and pleasant sound are very appealing worldwide. Today schools dot the United States and the world and include many non-Japanese players of the shakuhachi.[52]

Koto. On the island of Okinoshima there is a 27-centimeter (about 11 inches) copper koto relic with five copper bridges and a flared tail. Similar to the Haniwa figure that held a flared-tail koto on his lap, this koto was most likely an ornamental offering to the kami at matsuri, similar to offerings made at Ise and other shrines. The wa-gon is an indigenous koto with six strings played at Shinto ceremonies. Most people are acquainted with the thirteen-stringed *soh no* koto made of Paulownia wood. It was created during China's Shin Dynasty (220–206 BCE). Legend says it came from the clouds like the auspicious Chinese dragon. The parts of the koto have the prefix *ryu* (dragon), such as *ryu-to* (dragonhead) and *ryu-o* (dragon tail).

The two kanjis[53] for koto are 琴 and 箏. Each kanji is pronounced "koto" by itself. When the 琴 kanji is used in a compound with another kanji, it becomes "kin" or "gon" like 和琴 for wa-gon. The 琴 kanji is a general term to mean any stringed instrument. The second kanji 箏 or *soh*, is specifically for the thirteen-stringed koto and is pronounced soh when combined with another kanji like 箏 曲 or *soh-kyoku* (koto compositions).

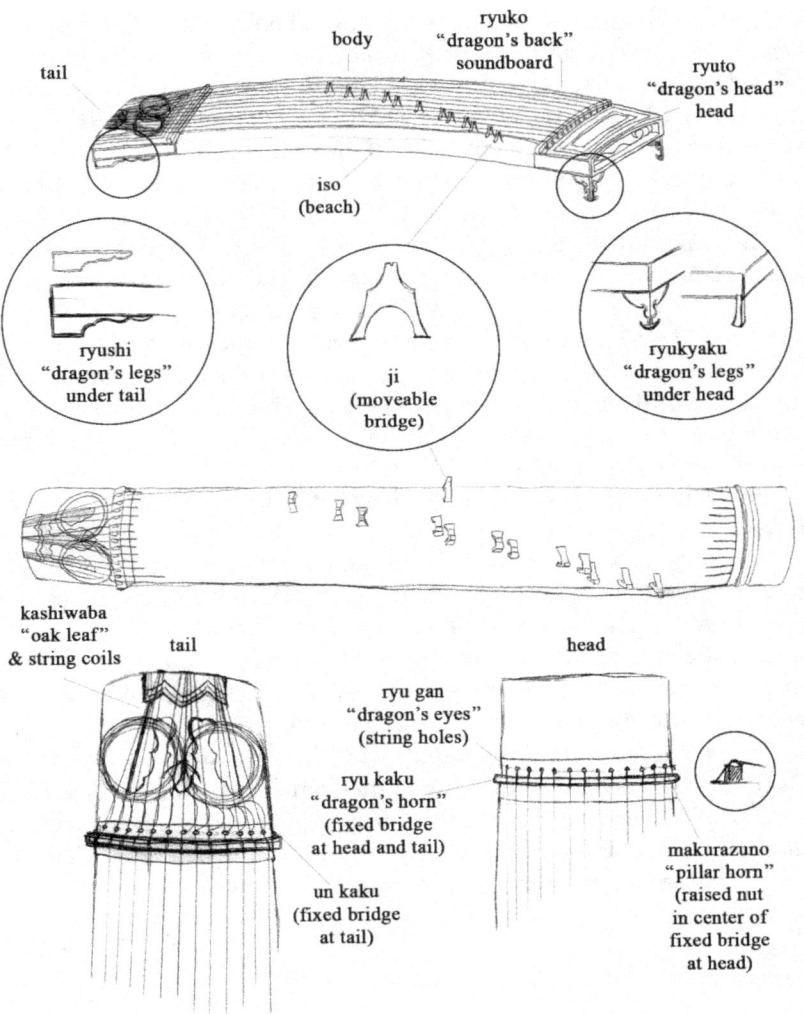

Figure 3.9: Parts of the Koto. The lengthy koto is likened to the auspicious *ryu* (dragon) and so the prefix *ryu* precedes the names of the koto parts. This diagram shows only the pertinent parts. Picturing the relationship of the parts to their metaphoric meaning takes imagination. The *ryu-to* (head) section includes the *ryugaku* (forehead), *ryuken* (eyelids), *ryukyo* (cheek), *ryushin* (lips), *ryuku* (mouth), and *ryuzetsu* (tongue). Some other parts are the *ryufuki* (belly), *ryuhai* (back), and *ryushi, ryushu, ryukyaku,* and *ryusoku* (four names of the legs). The koto has a *ryude* (hands), *ryubi* (tail), and *makurazuno* (raised center portion) of the *unkaku* (fixed bridge) at the head of the koto. The average koto player is not cognizant of the intricate details of the koto, but the craftsmen who make kotos are very aware of them (drawing by Meagan Healy).

The actual origin of the thirteen-stringed koto is blurred, but recurring dates and themes suggest that it was a combination of a plucked thirteen-stringed bamboo instrument remodeled onto a Paulownia wood *shitsu* body. The people of the Shin (Qin) Dynasty (221–206 BCE) enjoyed the instrument and by the year 150 BCE, it became part of the Chinese court ensemble. When mutual exchanges began in 665 during the T'ang Dynasty (618–907), the koto came to Japan as a solo instrument and as part of the gagaku ensemble.

As I mentioned earlier, the Nara Era Empress Komyo liked Chinese music and played the thirteen-stringed koto. But her koto came in six pieces: top, bottom, two sides, and two ends. During the Heian Era, a sturdier instrument from Paulownia wood was constructed with the tops and sides as one piece. Attached to the underside, a bottom board completed the long, hollow sound box. For the finish, burning and polishing brought out the natural luster and tree rings of the wood. Two holes on the underside allowed for resonance and for inserting the thirteen strings.

Pure Paulownia wood makes the best kotos. Cheaper ones of pinewood covered with Paulownia veneer have dubious soul. Expensive silk strings fray easily and weaken from constant playing and last for one concert.[54] Polyester strings are more durable and last many years without retightening.[55] Even the stylized bridges once made of wood with ivory tips or all ivory are now plastic white bridges that look like ivory. Plastic plectrum may soon replace ivory ones because of the ivory restrictions. Silk strings, ivory bridges, and plectrum are available if one is willing to pay the price.

The koto is basically a long sound box with strings suspended by bridges. This timbre box has extraordinary qualities and is favored for its sound and versatility. By moving the bridges the strings can be set to any pitch. Played with three plectrums on the right hand, and sometimes plucked with the left, the koto can sound like almost any stringed instrument in the world.[56]

Summary

The materials for musical instruments are identifiable in the environment. They were left by the kami for man's use. The shakuhachi looks like bamboo, the koto is a log with tree rings from the Paulownia tree, and the nipples of a cat's belly is part of a good shamisen drum skin reminding one to be grateful. The timbre or sound from these unpretentious instruments is comparatively naïve, unpolished, earthy, and reflective of an unassuming, natural soundscape.

Instruments get reverential treatment. When not in use, they are stored in beautiful brocade or artistically designed covers, containers, or cases. If instruments must be retired, they are disposed of with respect and care. The shamisen receives a Shinto service followed by ritual burning. Kotos may be propped against the wall as heirloom relics. At Kyoto's Tōdō Kai headquarters, many disposed kotos grace the entire back wall of a large performance hall, exuding warmth and elegance.

When new instruments made their way from the Asian continent to Japan, the Japanese at first enjoyed every new aspect. Later, indigenous sensibilities merged with the novel. The massive gagaku orchestra became smaller, compositions close to the indigenous mode were preferred, and streamlined playing techniques better suited native aesthetics. Modifications of the biwa, koto, and sangen using available materials resulted in sturdier instruments.

One might assume that the simpler the instrument, the easier it is to play. On the contrary, novices of the shakuhachi get dizzy trying to produce a sound, ko-tsuzumi players make sad taps, and koto and shamisen students must contend with weak plinks until mastery. It can take weeks, months, or years of practice to produce good sound and to master the different techniques for timbre. Thus, the simpler the instrument, the more challenging it is to bring out its soul.

Fortunately for the simple instruments, the tuning has two modes, the IN and the YO or shade and sunshine as in yin and yang. The two modes set the tone of the music pitched to any range to accommodate the singer's voice.

4

Two Modes and Tuning of the Instruments

Purity, the premise of Shinto that applies to the aesthetics of minimalism in Japanese music, accordingly sets hogaku in two modes, the IN (shade) and YO (sun). Although the two modes sometimes are compared with the Western minor and major scales in producing happy or sad moods, the generalization falls apart for there are happy songs in the IN mode as well as sad ones in the YO mode.[1]

There are no elaborate theories as to origins of the two modes except that they came from an unknown past. When China introduced its civilized ways to Japan around the sixth or seventh century, the Japanese adopted their ideas without question or analysis. For example, the Japanese transposed the Chinese writing system to their spoken language (from which Japanese speakers suffer today), they adopted the Chinese political system that did not match the reality of Japan's society, and when they embraced the Chinese theory of music, like many imports from outside the island, the Japanese tweaked it to make it fit.[2]

China's five notes[3] *kung, shang, chio, chih,* and *yu,* like *do, re, mi* of the diatonic scale, were called *kyu, sho, kaku, chi,* and *u* when applied to the Japanese IN and YO modes. However, unlike the Chinese scale, both the IN and YO modes have six notes instead of five in an ascending and descending scale (see Figure 4.1: IN and YO Scales). The *sho* and *U* positions are semitones in the IN mode, and when the melody goes up at the U note, it is sharpened to *ei-U,* and when the melody goes down, it is a semi-tone.[4]

Most urban music of hogaku is in the practically ingrained IN mode. Even the early Heian Era *wakan-roei* (Japanese and Chinese poems) such as *Togan* written by Yasutane (934–977) and *Jisei* by Onono Yoshiki (circa 902)[5] are sung in the IN mode. However, if we look at the early songs like *Asakura*

IN Ascent   IN Descent

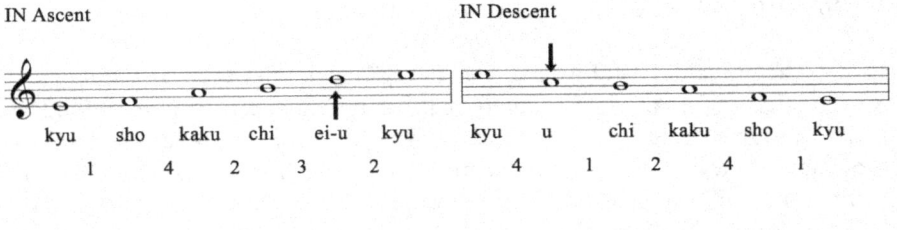

YO Ascent   YO Descent

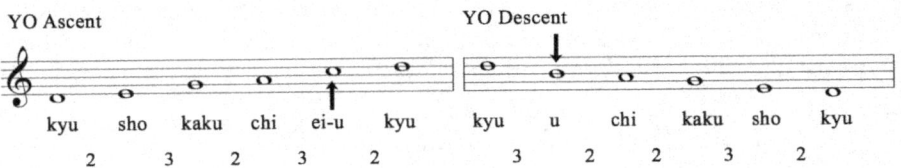

Figure 4.1: IN and YO Scale. Japanese music is modal with little sense to "key-ness." Most musicians of stringed instruments such as the koto and shamisen randomly pick a note or find one that suits the singer, and then make sure that the intervallic distance between the strings are at the desired mode. The ascending and descending scale of both the IN and YO modes, although pentatonic, has six notes.

(mentioned in Chapter 2), the Shinto wa-gon's bridges are D, E, G, A, and B of the YO mode. It is interesting to hear that the voice sings in the IN mode to the instrument's YO mode. Such juxtaposition is not unusual because it seems to be a Japanese tendency to fall back on the IN mode. In a similar experience, my American fifth graders, whose ears were accustomed to the diatonic scale, could not hear or sing the semitone in the song, *Sakura, Sakura*. After much practice they got it. Likewise, Tsugaru shamisen musicians seem to not hear or mind the mixing of two different scales in their concerts and recordings. The Tsugaru musicians seem to merrily pluck melodies in their mode as the Western band accompanies them in the Western scale.[6]

The YO mode is associated with *minyo* (folk) and with gagaku music of the *ritsu* scale, Buddhist chants of foreign origins, and some Japanese urban music of biwa, shamisen, shakuhachi, and koto music. The koto's tuning was the YO mode of the *gaku* tuning that was changed to IN mode in the late 1600s. Then in the 1800s experimentation using gagaku mode resulted in the Ascending-IN, A-IN mode. During the Meiji Era (1868–1912), koto musicians experimented with the YO mode. However, throughout Japan's musical history it seems that the IN scale dominated most songs as will be shown in the following discussion (see Table 5: Summary of the Three Modes, Names, and Their Progression on Koto Strings).

Buddhist and Noh Scale and Notation

The mode of Buddhist chants depends on whether they were imported or created in Japan.[7] The shomyo of the six Nara sects,[8] Shingon, Tendai, Zen, and the foreign chants adopted in the Jodo Shinshu repertory tend to be monotonic or in the original manner (with a Japanese accent) and in even rhythm called "raindrop beat." One example is the popular short sutra known as the "Amida-kyo," which is part of the major piece *Sambukyo* of the Jodo Shinshu sect. Each syllable takes one beat, including the spoken two syllable words like *ichi, butsu, koku,* and *doku*.[9]

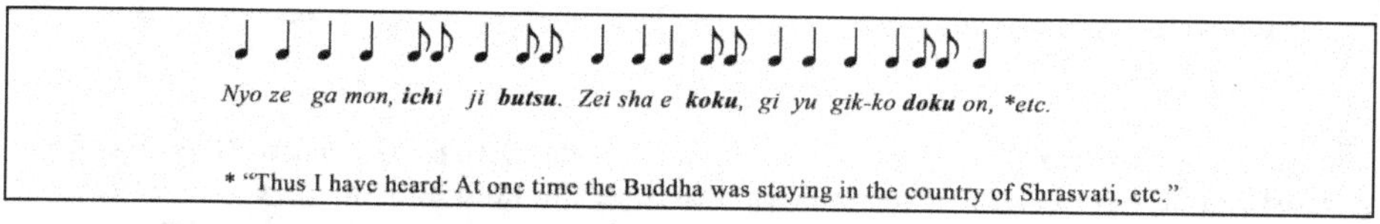

♩ ♩ ♩ ♩ ♫ ♩ ♫ ♩ ♩ ♩ ♫ ♩ ♩ ♩ ♩♫ ♩

Nyo ze ga mon, **ichi** *ji* **butsu**. *Zei sha e* **koku**, *gi yu gik-ko* **doku** *on, *etc.*

* "Thus I have heard: At one time the Buddha was staying in the country of Shrasvati, etc."

Figure 4.2: The "Amida-kyo." This chant is part of the larger Chinese *Sambukyo* of Buddha's teachings to his followers. To preserve its integrity, being foreign in origin, it is chanted monotonically and in an even tempo. This chant is a favorite among some priests for its brevity, but others find it monotonous. Chinese Buddhists recognize this chant when chanted in Japan even through the Japanese accent.

The Japanese sutra such as the *Shoshinge* followed by the *wa-san* (Buddhist poems),[10] is relatively melodic and is in the IN mode. Thus the notation next to the text with lines going up or down, straight or wavy indicates the direction of the pitch of the chants. Short or long dashes tell how long to hold the note (see Figure 4.3: *Shoshinge* Notation).

Following the *Shoshinge* chant are 6 of the 360 wa-sans. Priests who chant the *Shoshinge* twice a day can cover all 360 wa-sans in a month's time. "How do you know the melody?" I asked a priest friend. "It's indicated by the lines on the side of the kanji,"[11] he said, confirming that chanters know how far to move their voices along the IN mode. His daughter chimed in, "It's instinctive."

The wa-sans, with their Japanese-type melody and sentiments, were so popular they influenced folk music of the Muromachi Era and were incorporated into nohgaku's kyogen plays, a treasure trove of the era's popular songs.[12] One example is from the third wa-san *Ge datsu no kourin,* which begins at mid-range, goes up a bit, and ends in the lower range (see Figure 4.4). The melody of kyogen's *Hana no Sode* (Flowery Sleeves) moves similarly. The Western notation shows the jumps in intervals congruent with the IN mode.

Like the similarity of folk songs and wa-sans, the direct relationship of noh with Buddhist chants is uncanny. The scores of the Buddhist chant *Shoshinge* and noh's *Hagoromo* show that similarity (see Figure 4.5: Noh's

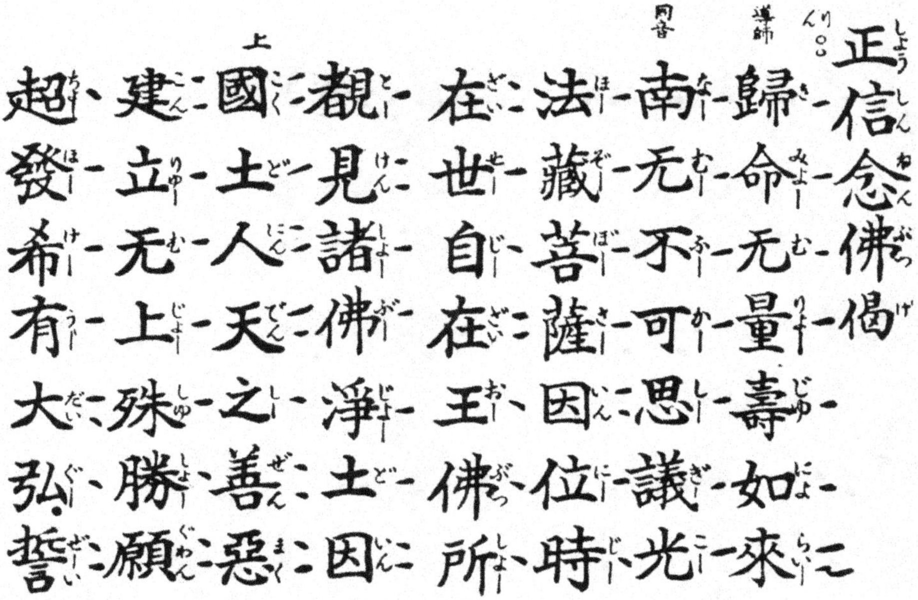

4. Two Modes and Tuning of the Instruments   71

正信念佛偈
歸命無量壽如來
南無不可思議光
法藏菩薩因位時
在世自在王佛所
觀見諸佛淨土因
國土人天之善惡
建立無上殊勝願
超發希有大弘誓

Figure 4.3: *Shoshinge* Notation (Sample). Compared to foreign chants, Japanese chants are relatively melodic and move in the familiar IN scale. The lines tell the voice to go up or down within the IN mode. Long, short, or wavy lines tell how long to hold the note or how to decorate it. Because the IN and YO modes are practically instinctive in Japanese music, the lines are adequate cues.

Hagoromo and Buddhist Chant Scores). The stylized "sesame seed" notation of the noh text duplicates Buddhist notation of lines drawn upward, downward, short or long *hiki* (dashes), or curvy for *mawashi* (melisma). At times, a kanji for up 上 or down 下 is the same as *age-uta* (voice up) or *sage-uta* (voice down). Even the vocal production is similar, grounded, and strong, and key, metered time, and exact pitch are not an issue. The lead singer sets a comfortable range.

Biwa and Sangen Tuning

The music of biwa from the Buddhist temples of the moso, Heike, Satsuma, Chikuzen, and shamisen music again is sung in the IN mode like those of the Buddhist chants. The biwa is tuned to accommodate the singer unless in an ensemble when it is pitched to other instruments. The basic biwa tuning came from the *oshiki* tuning of the gagaku biwa of A, C, E, A.

For the kojin/moso biwa, the tuning is A, D, E, E (the capital B is lower

Wa-san No. 3 *Ge datsu no kourin*

Hana no Sode

Figure 4.4: Wa-san No. 3 *Ge datsu no kourin* **and** *Hana no Sode*. **Shinran's thirteenth-century wa-sans touched the Japanese heart and were very popular. They influenced folk songs preserved during the Muromachi Era in kyogen plays. Note how both songs move along in mid-range and then end at the lower pitches.**

pitched); Heike biwa is G, b, d, g. The tuning of the Satsuma biwa that developed in the 1600s is e, B, e, f#, both in intervallic distances of fifths. In similar tuning intervals, the Chikuzen biwa with four strings is B, e, b, b. The Chikuzen biwa with five strings is e, B, e, f#, b.

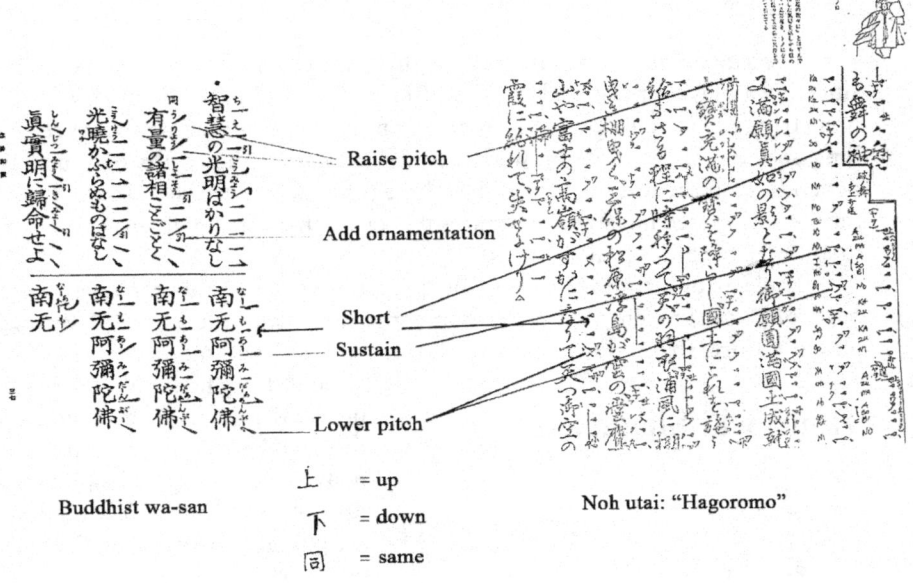

Figure 4.5: Noh's *Hagoromo* and Buddhist Chant Scores. The scores are from the Kita-ryu utai book and a service book of the Higashi Hongwanji. The juxtaposition of the two show that noh chants came directly from Buddhist chants. The up and down of "sesame seed" marks, as the noh people call the lines, serve the same purpose as the up, down, and wavy lines in the Buddhist text. Also, the vocalization and *fushi-mawashi* (melismata) are the same.

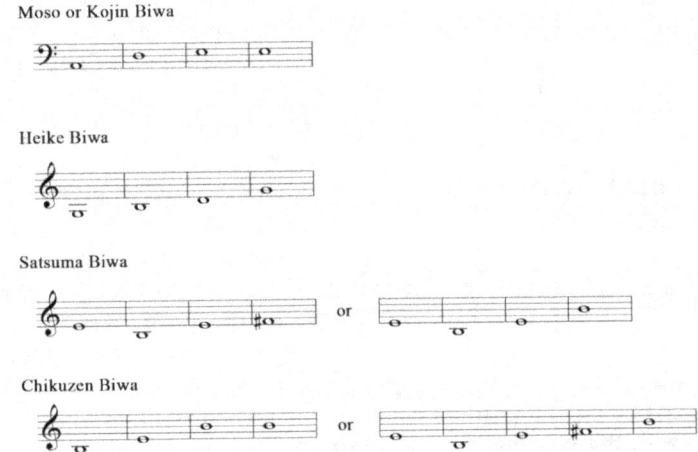

Figure 4.6: Biwa Tuning. Depending on type and number of strings, the gaku biwa is tuned according to the mode of the gagaku piece; Heike biwa uses the intervals of gagaku biwa's Oshikicho interval of G, B, D, G. The pitch of the first strings of the other schools vary to suit the voice, but the intervallic distance is constant.

The sangen tuning is similar to the biwa, which should not be surprising since biwa players reworked the shamisen for general use. The pitch of the first string of the tuning can begin on any note to accommodate the voice as long as the relative pitch between the strings is in either fifths or fourths depending on the tuning. Sangen has three tunings: the *hon joshi* (basic tuning), *ni-agari* (second string up) and *san-sagari* (third string down) (see Figure 4.7: Three Shamisen Tunings).

The various tunings allow the player to play at more convenient parts of the shamisen pole, for example, the *san-sagari* allows the player to play the third string down the pole for control and volume instead of the second string higher up the pole nearer the drum. The songs are in the IN mode unless accompanying folk songs. The pitches for both the IN and YO modes are positioned by the left fingers on the pole.

Hon-joshi Shamisen

Ni-agari Shamisen

San-sagari Shamisen

Figure 4.7: Three Shamisen Tunings. This diagram illustrates the similarity of the tuning intervals with those of the biwa. The three strings differ in size with the thickest as the lowest. Basically the tuning is in octaves with the in-between strings in fourths or fifths. The shamisen tunings accommodate playing passages at the range preferred by the singer.

Shakuhachi Tuning

The shakuhachi comes in various lengths with different pitch ranges but the 1.8 (meaning one *shaku-hachi*) is most often used (see Chapter 3: Simple Instruments). The notes are the pentatonic D, F, G, A, C and are called *ro, tsu, re, chi, ri, hi* of the YO scale. Semitones for melodies in the IN mode are made by partially covering the holes or by changing the angle of the head over the mouthpiece. Thus from the force of the blown air combined with the movement of the head, from five holes, twelve notes through two and more octaves can be attained.

Koto Tuning

The many tuning patterns across the koto are actually the progression of two modes across the thirteen strings. Key is irrelevant but the relative pitch of either the IN or YO mode matters. Unlike the *gakusoh* (gagaku koto) tuning with complicated Chinese explanations based on a twelve-note theory, the two Chinese modes of *ryo* and *ritsu* are fixed on the string with specific pitch and names like *hyojo* or *ichikotsu* tuning. Other gagaku instruments—like the ryuteki, hichiriki, and *sho*—play the melody in the specified mode. However, Japanese koto tuning can be any pitch as long as the intervals between the notes are in either the IN or YO mode.

Of the many gagaku compositions, *Ettenraku* in the hyojo tuning of the ritsu mode has direct bearing on modern koto music.[14] The hyojo tuning is the tuning of the Heian courtier's *imayo* (popular songs), *saibara* songs, Tsukushi koto, and Yatsuhashi's modern koto. As mentioned earlier, the koto was tuned in the YO mode until it was changed to the IN mode at the end of the 1600s. It is not clear whether Yatsuhashi Kengyo or his student Kitajima Kengyo changed the tuning to the IN mode. The Okinawan koto, believed either from China or brought to Okinawa by a student of Yatsuhashi, continues to be tuned to the YO scale.

In tuning, people are astonished by how quickly I can tune thirteen strings. The secret is to know which bridges to reposition from the *hirajyoshi* (peace tuning) to other tunings of the IN or YO modes. Basically it is changing the position of the pentatonic scale of *kyu, sho, kaku, chi, u* (like the *do* of the diatonic scale, *do, re, mi*) across the strings.

Hirajyoshi. In hirajyoshi, the *kyu, sho, kaku, chi, u* scale is between the fifth and tenth strings or centered on the koto. The pitch of the first string or kyu, can be any note, usually to accommodate the voice. But in ensemble with the sangen and shakuhachi, the first note is the shakuhachi's D (ro), G (re), or A (chi) depending on the piece.

The second string is the lower fifth of the first string, and the third string is a fourth lower from the first string. The fourth string is a semi-tone of the third string. The fifth string is the same pitch as the first, and the sixth string is a semitone of the fifth string.

The rest are the higher octaves of the lower strings such as 2 and 7, 3 and 8, 4 and 9, 5 and 10, 6 and 11, 7 and 12, and 8 and 13. Although electronic devices are available for tuning, the fastest and equally accurate way is to listen for relative pitch as described here.

Variations of the IN mode from hirajyoshi. The beauty of the hirayoshi is that by moving a few bridges, the IN mode is relocated on the koto in a flash. For example, to get the *kumoi jyoshi* where the kyu is on 2, 7, 12, just move strings 3, 8 to a semitone and bring strings 4, 9 up a whole note. For the *naka-*

Ritsu: Hyojo, Oshiki and Banshiki - Intervals of 2, 3, 2, 2, 3

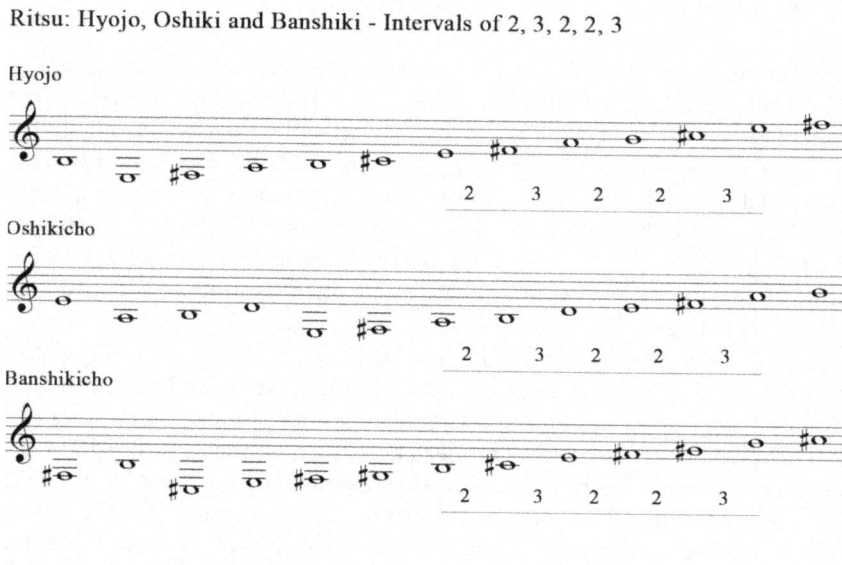

Ryo: Ichikotsu, Taishiki, Sojo - Intervals of 2, 2, 3, 2, 3

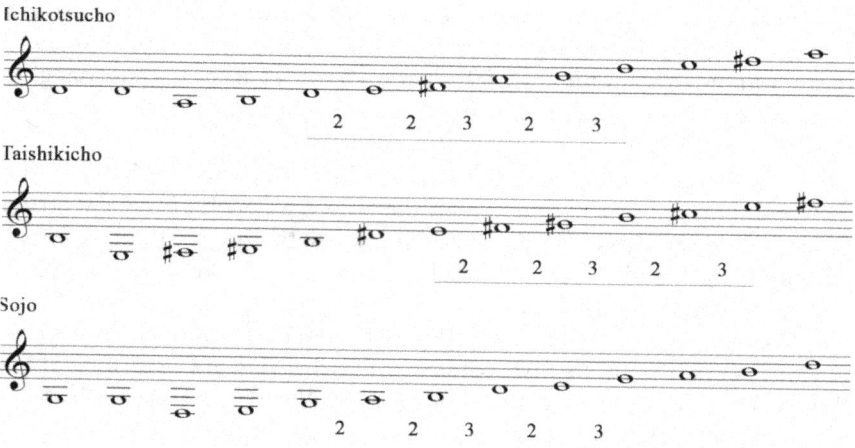

Figure 4.8: Gagaku Koto Tuning with the Location Ritsu and Ryo Modes.[13] The ritsu and ryo modes are bracketed with specific notes and have a key-ness not important in Japanese music. Of the two modes, the ritsu mode sounded familiar because its intervallic distance resembles the sound of the descending Japanese YO mode. The YO mode on the black keys of the piano starts from the two black keys plus the three black keys. The ryo mode begins from the three black keys. They sound similar, but to the attuned ear, they are not, which is why gagaku compositions in the ryo mode today are theoretical studies.

4. Two Modes and Tuning of the Instruments   77

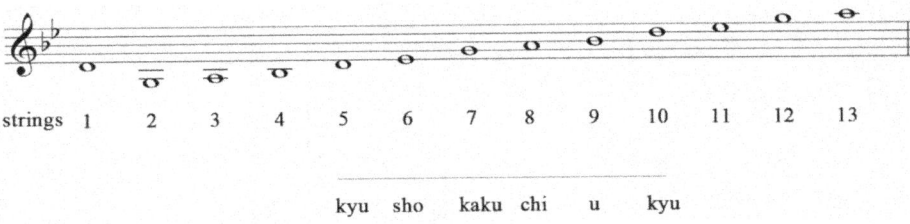

Figure 4.9: Hirajyoshi Tuning on Koto Strings. Note the *kyu, sho, kaku, chi, u,* and *kyu* on the 5–10 strings, centers the IN mode or scale in the middle of the koto, rather like having middle C in front of a piano player. From this position, the modes can be positioned across two octaves as in kumoi jyoshi or nakazora jyoshi by moving a few key bridges.

zora tuning where the kyu is on strings 3, 8, 13, again from the hirajyoshi tuning, strings 6, 11 are brought up a half tone and strings 7, 12 are made semitones. The relocation of the kyu appears to be different tuning to the koto player.

Most koto classics are in hirajyoshi, kumoijyoshi, and nakazorajyoshi. Seldom used tunings are the kyu scale between strings 4, 9 as in *Iwatojyoshi* or between strings 6, 11 as in *Akebonojyoshi*. The latter two tunings offer little pitch range differences from the *hirajyoshi* with the kyu on strings 5, 10. Some exceptions are pieces like *Aki kaze no Kyoku* and the first verse of *Mizu no Hentai* where the kyu is on the 4, 9 strings. The grid in Figure 4.10: Relationship of Three IN Tunings shows how the kyu, sho, kaku, chi, u notes move along the strings. Names of the tuning at the top identify each pattern.[15]

Variations of the tuning exist. For kumoijyoshi there is the *han-kumoi* (half *kumoi* tuning) where the third string or the thirteenth is not a semitone. A variation of the *nakazorajyoshi* is found in Kikuhara Kengyo's *Ginsekai*. The first string is tuned to the same pitch as the sixth string, and the second string is the low octave of the sixth string.

The A-IN mode. In the 1800s Yoshizawa Kengyo II experimented with gagaku koto's banshiki tuning. He modified the banshiki tuning by making its sho note a semitone which became the *kokinjyoshi* or basically the Ascending IN scale (A-IN mode in Table 5: Summary of the Three Modes, Names and Their Progression on Koto Strings). Like hirajyoshi of the IN mode, the kyu note occupies strings 5, 10 or on the center of the koto but strings 4, 9 (U notes) are brought to the ascent IN scale. *Chidori no Kyoku*, all of Yoshizawa Kengyo II's four season pieces,[16] and Tadao Sawai's *Sakura, Sakura* (with the first and second strings in the lower octaves) are examples using the kokinjyoshi.[17] If the melody descends in this tuning, the semi-note of the IN scale is produced by pressing the eighth string.

Some compositions combine two modes. Kikuhara Kengyo's *Tsumigusa* begins with *hanagumo choshi* of the A-IN mode with the kyu on strings 2, 7,

Hirajyoshi	Kumoi	Nakazora
IN mode is centered 5-10	IN mode is 2-7, 7-12	IN mode is 3-8, 8-13
1 kyu	1 chi	1 kaku
2 kaku	2 KYU	2 u
3 chi	3 SHO	3 KYU
4 u	4 KAKU	4 SHO
5 KYU	5 CHI	5 KAKU
6 SHO	6 U	6 CHI
7 KAKU	7 KYU	7 U
8 CHI	8 SHOW	8 KYU
9 U	9 KAKU	9 SHO
10 KYU	10 CHI	10 KAKU
11 sho	11 U	11 CHI
12 kaku	12 KYU	12 U
13 chi	13 sho	13 KYU

Figure 4.10: Relationship of Three IN Tunings. The chart shows that the kumoi jyoshi and nakazora jyoshi are the same IN mode and related to the hirajyoshi. They are merely the repositioning of the five note mode. Hirajyoshi is centrally located on strings 5-10. The others are placed twice across the strings beginning on strings for kumoi jyoshi 2-7, 7-12, and nakazora jyoshi 3-8, 8-13.

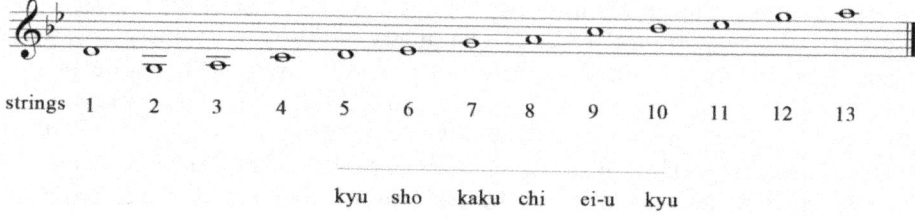

Figure 4.11: A-IN or Ascent IN Scale. The mode is centered on the koto like the hirajyoshi tuning. The difference is that the 4 and 9 strings are placed in positions for the sharpened (ei-u). The 4 and 8 strings are pressed for the descending note to get to the u pitch, the 4 and 8 strings are pressed.

11. Toward the end of the first song, the third and eighth strings are brought up a note to change the piece to a YO mode with the kyu centered on the fourth and ninth strings of the *Dai-gaku choshi*.

The YO modes. In the same manner, the YO mode marches across the strings like the IN and A-IN modes. The gagaku koto, Tsukushi koto, and even Yatsuhashi Kengyo learned the koto tuned to *nogi choshi* of the YO mode. Tateyama Kengyo invented "new tunings" (based on the progression of the YO mode across the koto strings) and wanted to create a new school from twelve of his compositions in the Natsuyama tuning like *Hototogisu no Kyoku* and *Hoshi to Hana to*. The kyu, centered on the koto, is similar to gagaku koto's hyojo of *Ettenraku*. Knowing the different tuning names helps locate the kyu note of the YO mode (see Table 5: Summary of the Three Modes, Names, and Their Progression on Koto Strings).[18]

5, 10	*Nogi choshi,*
6, 11	*Akino choshi*
2, 7, 12	*Gaku choshi*
3, 8, 13	*Natsuyama choshi*
4, 9	*Dai-gaku choshi*

From thirteen strings, three to four octaves of the IN, YO, and the A-IN modes can be attained. Tuning is made by quickly shifting key bridges, but the switch of the placement of the kyu note feels and looks like a new tuning.

Other inventive tunings. Western influences caused experimentation with tuning to go wild. Kikuzuka Kengyo's (1846–1909) tuning for the piece *Meiji Shochikubai* is G, G, D, D, C, D, G, A, d#, d, g, a, d. As elaborate as this tuning may be, the entire composition is still in the IN mode. Pressing the right strings produces the semi-tones and ascent notes (see Figure 4.12).

Another exception to the tuning pattern is Eto Kimio's *Omoide no Uta goe* (1950). He incorporates the Okinawan tuning interval on the sixth string D, G, A#, A, D#, F, g, a#, c, d#, d, g, a (see Figure 4.13).

Summary

From ancient music to the art music of the Edo Era, the music is either in the IN or the YO mode. Even when Chinese music theory was introduced to Japan, the Japanese tweaked it to their liking. Tuning through the centuries on all Japanese instruments accommodated singing that was in either of the two scales. Although an Edo Era mathematician noticed the discrepancy between Chinese and Japanese scales, his analysis went unnoticed.

The arrangement of the bridges on the koto shows succinctly that the

Mode	Name of tuning				
IN:	*Kumoi*	*Nakazora*	*Iwato*	**HIRA**	*Akebono*
A-IN:	Hanagumo	Haru no Umi	Akikaze	KOKIN	namelesss
YO:	*Shingaku*	*Natsuyama*	*Dai-gaku*	*GAKU*	*Akino*
Kyu on string	2,7,12	3,8,13	4, 9	**5,10**	6,11
String #1	(chi)	(kaku)	(sho)	(kyu)	(u)
2	**KYU**	U	chi	kaku	sho
3	sho	**KYU**	U	chi	kaku
4	kaku	sho	**KYU**	u	chi
5	chi	kaku	sho	**KYU**	u
6	u	chi	kaku	**sho**	**KYU**
7	**KYU**	u	chi	**kaku**	sho
8	sho	**KYU**	u	**chi**	kaku
9	kaku	sho	**KYU**	**u**	chi
10	chi	kaku	sho	**KYU**	u
11	u	chi	kaku	sho	**KYU**
12	**KYU**	u	chi	kaku	sho
13	sho	**KYU**	u	chi	kaku

Table 5: Summary of the Three Modes, Names, and Their Progression on Koto Strings. The table, combined from Hideko Nomura's *Koto no Shoshiki to Gakuri no Ohanashi* (pp. 125, 129), shows how the three (really two) modes march across the strings. The standard position of the kyu note on strings 5, 10 centers the scale or mode. The modes with the kyu on the 2, 7 or 3, 8, 13 strings offer more contrast in range than the kyu on the 4, 9 or 4, 12 strings. The different placement of the modes feels like a new tuning to the player. The names assigned for the various placements of the modes tell the player how to tune the koto.

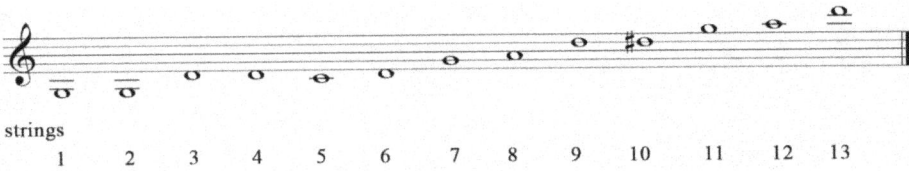

Figure 4.12: *Meiji Shochikubai* Tuning. The tuning is overwhelming at first to a novice and the effect is interesting when two or three strings of the same pitch are played at the same time. As "fancy" as the tuning may be, the composition continues to be in the IN mode. Pressing certain strings fills in "missing" notes.

Figure 4.13: *Omoide no Uta goe* Tuning. Composed in the 1950s when Western music was dominant, the tuning accommodates sequences, harmony, and harp-like Western chords. The bridges are arranged in a mixture of hirajyoshi, Okinawan, Western, and Mideast scales. Eto Kimio, the composer of this Western style piece, repeats the melody by utilizing the koto's versatility. He manipulates the strings to bring out timbre reminiscent of other world instruments.

different tuning arrangements are progressions of the two IN and YO modes that feel like a new tuning to the koto player. Even the A-IN mode is the IN mode in ascent, but to koto players it feels like a different tuning. Western scales and music can be played on any hogaku instrument, but the player must become accustomed to new sensations.

5
Singing the *Uta* (Song/Poetry)

"I don't get it. Japanese singing doesn't make sense!" exclaimed a friend who was asked to notate hogaku music. Unfortunately, he recused himself from the task in frustration. Hogaku singing is so different that I wondered if its beauty is ever appreciated by anyone. Apparently it is possible. Another friend at age 9 overheard koto playing with voice and four decades later wrote about it. "[I] could not understand the words, but the song was cadenced and sad and captured feelings that I recognized but had no prior means of expressing. Isn't it odd that music can be both new and familiar at the same time?"[1]

How does koto singing pull a listener's attention through a song? It is the voice that is a universal instrument. In hogaku music, which comes first, the melodiousness of the voice or the koto playing? According to Tomiyama, the instrumental part is composed and the uta melody is pulled along with it. In *Miyako Wasure*, the "*tsu*" of "*matsu*" (pine) in the phrase "*matsu no kokage ni*" melodically sails through many notes while the koto plays passages to meet the voice with an arpeggio at the syllable "*no*," but "*no*" is also extended to finally settle on "*kokage ni*" (its little shadow). The voice at "*ni*" is high to meet the pitch of the koto. (See Figure 5.1.)

How did the songs become a series of elongated vowels? When the gods burst into song in *Kojiki* and the *Nihon Shoki*, they must have held the syllables because all Japanese words have open vowels.[2] And it is pleasurable to sing and hold a vowel that melodically sails through many notes. Think of the beautiful rendition of the syllable "Glo—" in the word "Gloria" of the Christmas carol *Gloria in Excelsis Deo* before settling on the notes of "ia."

Because the Japanese love to sing, all instruments accompany songs. Purely instrumental hogaku pieces are foreign in origin like gagaku's and koto's dan-mono music, and Western influenced pieces like Miyagi's *Haru no Umi*. In fact Eishi Kikkawa says that the *uta* is the heart of Japanese music.[3] Its power to move listeners is in the *kotodama* (word with spirit and power),

Figure 5.1: The "*Matsu no kokage ni*" Melody of *Miyako Wasure*. The spoken words affect the pitch of the songs and the second syllable "tsu" should go down in pitch, but in this case it goes up. The purpose of the change is to connect the thought of *matsu* to Matsuko, the wife of the poet, Tanizaki Junichiro.

which brings out feelings of love, longing, happiness, and good harvest and even the islands of Japan. Two creator gods, Izanami and Izanagi sang the following untranslatable magic words as they shaped the Japanese islands.

> *Ananiyashi*
> *Ewoto ko wo,*
> *Ananiyashi*
> *Ewoto me wo*[4]

The repetitious incantation, like the rhythmic ditties of parents to infants, soothed and cajoled. When formalized, they became charms and supplications to deities, according to Ellen Dissanayake.[5] The poetic Shinto norito influenced ancient songs like *Asakura* and even the songs of *saibara*, *wakan-roei*, and *imayo*. Noh chants, biwa, shamisen, and koto singing also have similar sophisticated recitations that melodically play with a vowel sound.[6]

With the appearance of Buddhist *shomyo* (radiant songs) the influence of Buddhist chants is profound in hogaku but the underlying Shinto premise of unrolling melody with extended vowels continues to flow through all genres.

Buddhist Chants: Music of Shomyo

Of Buddhist chanting, the Rev. Mas Kodani said,

> Chanting is very different from singing. Chanting is simply talking aloud in a strong voice. When done communally, it results in rich layers of sound in which each voice is different and meant to be heard in its differentiation—yet forming a single sound. It is never soaring in feeling but rather gives the sense of being earthbound and rooted.[7]

84   Japan's Musical Tradition

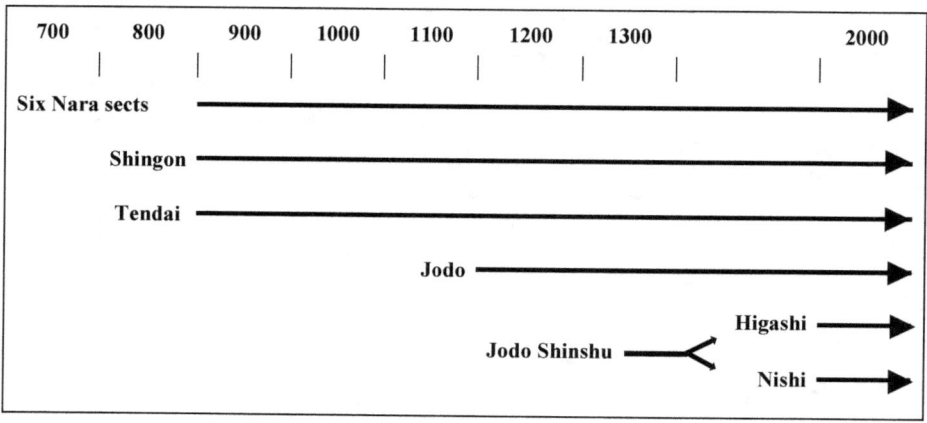

Figure 5.2: Timeline of the Appearance of the Buddhist Sects. Officially Buddhism appeared in 538. Six sects settled in the ancient capital of Nara. Their temples continue to exist with priests conducting regular services for parishioners. Not shown on the timeline is the Nichiren sect that appeared in the 1200s from the Shingon founded by Kukai in the ninth century. From Nichiren came the Soka Gakkai in the 1930s.

Like Shinto norito, vocalizing Buddhist chants comes from the *hara* (stomach, heart, with conviction) for a grounded sound with strength and depth to command respect, interest, and attention.[8] While chanting, a person is expected to learn Buddhism, the Ultimate Truth or the Buddha's words that have the power to enlighten, and to gain self-discipline transferable to other endeavors.[9]

The Jodo Shinshu[10] sect with the largest adherents has direct influence on modern music. Its political influence, by virtue of its membership, forced the Tokugawa government to split the sect into the east (Higashi) and west (Nishi) branches. Today, the branches differ slightly but share foreign and Japanese chants (see Figure 5.3: The Jodo Shinshu Okyo of the Higashi Branch). For large important services, the foreign chants *Kada* and *Sambukyo* open the ceremony. The *Sambukyo* has four subgroups of which the "Amida Kyo" is a favorite among priests (see Figure 4.2: The "Amida-Kyo"). The heart of the Jodo Shinshu sect is the Japanese *Shoshinge* by Shinran Shonin. It is the most popular chant recited on a daily basis. Filled with Japanese sentiments of gratitude,[11] it begins by thanking Indian and Chinese teachers and specifically Prince Shotoku, who facilitated the entrance of Buddhism into Japan. Being Japanese in origin, it is relatively melodic compared with the foreign chants (see Figure 4.3: Shoshinge Notation). The occasion determines the speed of the chants, slow and grave for important services or rapid when chanting by oneself or when inducting novitiates.

- Kada: opening chants by the priests (foreign)
- Sambukyo: (foreign) sutra chanted by priests only as transmitters of the teachings ascribed to the Buddha. The congregation is the receiver of the message. The rhythm and pitch/tone are to be like the steady dripping of rain.
  - Muryo-jukyo: Jo-dan: about Shakamuni's life
  - Muryo-jukyo: Ge-kan: about human suffering
  - Kam-muryo-jukyo: Meditation sutra: concerns paths to enlightenment.
  - Amida-kyo: Buddha's sermon
- Shoshinge: written by Shinran Shonin in Chinese. The congregation joins priests and people chant it daily at home.
- Wa-san (six in number) follows the Shoshinge. Wasans are poems consisting of 7,5,7,5 syllables per line. There are 360 consisting of:
  - Jodo Wasans: Gratitude to Amida
  - Koso Wasans: Gratitude to two Indian, three Chinese and two Japanese priests.
  - Shozomasu Wasans: Shinran's 58 songs written at age 85.
  - Miscellaneous: Gratitude to Prince Shotoku and others.

Figure 5.3: List of the Jodo Shinshu Okyo of the Higashi Branch. The *Shoshinge* and the wa-sans are commonly chanted at most services. At other times, important ceremonial, memorial, and funeral services include the "Kada" and *Sambukyo*. The content teaches about life as professed by the Buddha.

As mentioned previously, 6 out of 360 wa-sans follow the *Shoshinge* chant. The notation next to the words, short or long dashes going up or down, directs the voice within the IN scale. Priests and chanters embellish the notes with fushi-mawashi, similar to noh utai-singers. The wa-san and *Shoshinge* influenced popular folk songs of the era (see Figure 4.4: Wasan No. 3 *Ge datsu no kourin* and *Hana no Sode*). The earth-bound, recitation style of singing from religious chants permeated all singing and can be heard in noh, bunraku, shamisen, and koto music. One can also imagine a similar vocal style in their predecessors, such as saibara and wakan-roei.

Saibara (Horse Tender's Song)[12]

In the secular realm, the *saibara,* or folk song of horse tenderers, or romantic love ballads 5, 7 syllables per line sung by Heian courtiers are countless. Its origin is conjecture, but the story told is that a horse tenderer sings to his horse and a nobleman overhears the song and repeats it at court.[13] One famous saibara is from the *Manyoshu* poem, "Waga Koma" (My Horse). The excerpted portion in bold letters is the song. Repeating "*Matsuchi-yama*" (waiting mountain) plays on the word *matsu* (to wait) to see one's love.

WAGA KOMA	(My Horse)[14]
IDE WAGA KOMA	Go, my horse,
HAYA KU YUKI KOSE	go quickly beyond
MATSUCHI YAMA	Matsuchi mountain.
AHARE	Sadness—
MATSUCHIYAMA HARE	Matsuchi mountain hare
MATSUCHIYAMA	Matsuchi mountain
MATSURAN HITO WO	To the one who is waiting.
YUKITEWAYA **MIN**	Let us go and see.

Saibara lyrics abound in the tenth century novel *Tale of Genji*. A damsel in almost every chapter pulls out her koto[15] and sings a saibara lament. Unfortunately, saibara, as popular as it was, left us with no melody.[16] Not to be discouraged, Meiji Era (1868-1912) scholars recreated six saibara[17] using eight singers and the *saho* (left) gagaku instruments of ryuteki, hichiriki, sho, and koto, biwa, and the shakubyoshi. A lead singer began the song and others joined in, holding the vowels and ornamenting it with micro-pitches. Critics panned the effort for lacking spontaneity and shrugged it off as an exercise of ancient music revival. I suspect from the description that they copied what they knew about the existing ancient *wakan-roei* singing discussed next.

Wakan-Roei (Japanese and Chinese Poems)

According to musicologist, Akira Hoshi, fourteen *wakan* (Japanese) and *roei* (Chinese) poems survive today accompanied by the gagaku's ryuteki, sho, and hichiriki and string instruments. Before the year 784, wakan-roei had no less than 564 Japanese and Chinese poets. Fujiwara no Kinto (966-1041) compiled them in the *Wakan Roei-shu* and Fujiwara no Mototoshi (1046-1142) collected the poems in the *Shinsen-Roei-shu*.

During the reigns of Emperor Daigo (898-930) and Suzaku (930-955), four types of poems were categorized and of them *Hyo* was most popular.

- *Shi:* Chinese poems of complicated format
- *Fu:* Narrative poems
- *Jo:* Chinese prose
- *Hyo:* Message to the emperor or an official

Buddhist priests also sang wakan-roei guided by retired cloistered emperors residing in a temple. The quieting effect of the roei was good for attaining spiritual peace.[18] Time fossilized the genre giving less freedom, fixing both the vocal improvisation and instrumental accompaniment. By the fifteenth century, the *Roei Kyujishusho* collection was published with neumes like Buddhist chant markings next to the words showing how to sing the words exactly.

A leader begins the first line of the wakan-roei and others join in the second line.[19] Stephen Addiss said that "each of the fourteen surviving roei has a similar basic melody." This is because the wakan-roei follows an established format (see Chapter 6 on the format of hogaku compositions). Addiss further stated, "Having such similar melodies does not render the fourteen wakan-roei as being the same. Subtle changes in melodies and different vocal ornamentation changes them."[20] I attribute the melodic changes as responding to words with different meanings that affect mood.

Addiss further described its seemingly monotonic melody as a "resting tone," that is:

> ornamented with a slight break of the voice to a higher note and immediately back to the original tone, sung halfway through the holding of the note. This "grace note" is so subtle that it can almost pass unnoticed, but it adds a special effect to the note that helps establish it as the "resting tone" on which roei always end.[21]

Basically, the resting tone is the Japanese melody hovering on a note of the IN scale with subtle "grace notes" called *fushimawashi* (melismata, ornamentation), decorating a sustained vowel. Addiss's wakan-roei notation in a Western score reveals the formidable looking melody is clearly in the IN scale of D, E♭, G, A, C, D and in descent D, B♭, A, G, E♭, D.

Another wakan-roei sung by Togi Hideki's group is *Jisei*.[22] When one follows *Jisei* using Addiss's *Togan*[23] score, the contour is similar, as Addiss notes, because all wakan-roei pieces share a similar format.

Jisei is the famous Tanabata story of star-crossed lovers who meet once a year across the Milky Way on the seventh day of the seventh month. The second section, "*Goya masa ni akenantosu,*" begins an octave higher than the first, a range difficult for men, according to Togi Hideki, and the third section is recited or sung by a different singer. For this short lyric, it takes ten minutes to sing as the melismata extend the song. The audience pays rapt attention to this profound and solemn love song that evokes a seriousness that stills the soul. (The soloist's part is in bold.)

Lyrics to Jisei:

1. **Jisei tama tami aeri**	Two lovers, fortunate in meeting
Imada betsho ii no urami wo	Never begrudging the impending
Nobezaru ni	need to part
2. **Goya masa ni** *akenantosu*	Approaching dawn bring
3. **Shikiri ni** *ryu fu satsu*	Cold wind's incessant
koe ni odoroku	voice surprises them.

Imayo (Popular Songs), the Predecessor of Modern Koto Music

Like saibara, a majority of imayo lyrics are without melody except for two sets from the Heian court. One set is attributed to Emperor Go-Shirakawa who reigned from 1155 to 1158. He compiled imayo lyrics in *Kyojijyo* that can be sung to Mon Jidai's "*Haru no yayoi no akebono ni...*" or gagaku's *Ettenraku*. The second source is from the *Shinsho Gocho* found in a Buddhist temple. It lists ten imayo lyrics with the titles *Ettenraku-imayo* and *Etten-utai-mono*, meaning they are also from gagaku's *Ettenraku* melody.

After the defeat of the Heike clan in 1185, the victors killed all Heike men but allowed women to stay in Kyoto. Instead, many women fled to Hakata, Kyushu, with the koto among their belongings. They played imayo in their new homes, but after several hundred years and many generations later imayo began to fade from the culture. Lack of a formal school established among the women added to the difficulty of keeping imayo alive. However, Priest Kenjun (1547–1636) of Zendōji at Kurume decided to rescue the music of the thirteen-string and other seven- and twelve-string kotos. Among the different kotos, the music for the thirteen-string koto had promise because the imayo was based on gagaku's *Ettenraku*. The rescued koto music was henceforth known as Tsukushi koto. Tsukushi is the ancient name for Kyushu. Kenjun and his fellow priests became the purveyors of solo koto music and treated the instrument like Confucius's *ch'in*,[24] reserving it only for "perfect" people like priests and noblemen in religious pursuit and not for women or blind musicians. Tsukushi koto continued with the eclectic players until the 1900s when out of desperation four women were allowed to learn it to keep the school alive.[25]

Fortunately, Tsukushi koto playing did fall into the hands of a blind musician, Yatsuhashi Kengyo in the 1600s. Through Yatsuhashi, modern koto is directly linked to gagaku koto, courtier's imayo songs, esoteric Tsukushi koto, and to Yatsuhashi Kengyo. Tsukushi koto and Yatsuhashi's modern koto music is tied to the piece *Fuki* that became the basis for koto *kumi-uta* (collected songs; see Figure 6.3: Lyrics of *Fuki*). Lighter and lyrical in delivery than Buddhist and noh chants, the voice holds a vowel to melismatically sing over the koto patterned passages.

Opposite: **Figure 5.4:** Score to *Togan* (Eastern Shore). As complicated as the score looks, the singing hovers around the D and A notes of the IN scale that ascends D, Eb, G, A, C, D and descends, D, B, A, G, Eb, D. Upon hearing the wakan-roei sung slowly at formal performances, the audience is transported to a world of heartfelt solemnness (with permission from Stephen Addiss, "Singing the Wakan Roei Shu," in J. Thomas Rimer and Jonathan Chaves, trans., *Japanese and Chinese Poems to Sing: The Wakan Roei Shu* [New York: Columbia University Press, 1997], pp. 256–257).

Year		
1000	Gagaku	"Ettenraku" Banshiki tuning
1100	Court musi	"Etten-Imayo" Imayo (popular songs) set to "Ettenraku"
1100	Kyoto temple	Shinso Gocho, a compilation of Imayo lyrics set to "Ettenraku." Ten verses.
1500	Tsukushi koto	Tsukushi koto piece, "Fuki" based on "Etten-Imayo"
1600	Modern koto	"Fuki" a koto kumi-uta, sometimes called "Ettenraku" First kumi-uta based on "Fuki" of Tsukushi ko

Figure 5.5: Basis of Modern Koto from Gagaku's *Ettenraku*. Modern koto techniques clearly come from the octave patterns of gagaku koto. The first modern koto piece, *Fuki*, is traceable to the gagaku piece, *Ettenraku*. Through the years, playing techniques have improved and widened the scope for what can be played on a koto.

Biwa Singing

Biwa singing that affected noh, shamisen, and koto music came directly from Buddhist chants, specifically from the Tendai Temple. In Chapter 3: Simple Instruments, I mentioned how blind biwa playing priests came to Japan with Buddhism and had a respected position. Called biwa *hoshi* (blind priests) or *moso* (blind) biwa[26] players, by the twelfth and thirteenth centuries some hoshi played the Jishin biwa, named after a Buddhist text "*Jishin-kyo*," or the *kojin-kyo* (kitchen-kyo) and traveled from house to house to chant the sutra. After the Gempei War (1185) and the Heike clan's defeat, a former courtier named Yukinaga[27] took tonsure at the Tendai Temple and recorded the demise of the Heike court that spanned ninety years from 1131 to 1221. He taught the text to a blind priest, Shobutsu. Shobutsu passed it on to other traveling blind priests who spread the *Tale of the Heike* or the *Heike Tales*. Believing that the spirits of dead warriors resided where they had fallen, to quell them, traveling blind priests were asked to narrate one of the many tales from the Heike. The narration sounded like Buddhist chants and began with the poignant Buddhist theme about the ephemeralness of life.

Gion shouja no kane no koe	The bell of the Gion Temple
shogyou mujou no hibiki ari.	Tolls into every man's heart that all is vanity
Shara souju no hana no iro	and evanescent. The faded flowers of the *sala* trees
jousha hissui no kotowari o arawasu.	By the Buddha's deathbed bear witness to truth
Ogoreru hito mo hisashikarazu,	that all who flourish are destined to decay.
Tada haru no yo no yume no gotoshi.	Yes, pride must have its fall, for it is as
Takeki mono mo tsui ni horobinu.	Unsubstantial as dreams on a spring night.
Hitoe ni kaze no mae no chiri ni onaj	[men] must die away in the end, like a whirl of dust in the wind.[28]

5. Singing the Uta (Song/Poetry)

Having an incomplete repertoire to this popular narrative, itinerant priests began to create their own versions, much to the chagrin of people like Akashi Kakuichi. A blind son of the shogun, Kakuichi decided to standardize the texts and, because of his position, he secured permission to form a guild for blind men, the Tōdō Shoku Yashiki or Tōdōza for short.[29] Kakuichi's guild granted titles and ranks to musicians authorizing only them to perform the approved version of the *Heike Tales*. Because of Kakuichi, the status of "professional musician" was secured and reserved for blind musicians.[30]

Heike biwa players used a smaller version of the gagaku biwa and influenced the narrative style of singing. Sparse plectrum stokes accompanied the voice for pitch and rhythm. The vocalization is distinctively like Buddhist chanting, not open-mouthed, but tight, controlled, serious, and subdued.

The two types of biwa singing are *ji* (narrative) and *fushi* (melodic). The ji hovers on a note of the IN scale with cues to *age-uta* (go up) or *sage-uta* (go down) just as in Buddhist and noh chants. *Fushi* or melody emphasizes the mood and drama.

The only way to understand the music is to hear it. When comparing two renditions of the same incident, *Nasu no Yoichi* of the Heike biwa with *Ogi no Mato* (Fan Target) of the Satsuma biwa, the difference is compelling. In the story that takes place at Yashima on Shikoku Island, the best archer Nasu no Yoichi or Munekata, is ordered to shoot a fan tied to a pole of the Heike ship.

Nasu no Yoichi begins with the ji recitation, introducing Yoichi, the best archer of the Genji clan. He is described as being small in stature and carrying a short bow to match his height (perhaps emphasizing a handicap for the heroic feat he will accomplish); the narration quickly moves up and down in fifths between two notes with the biwa striking a few notes *amadera* (raindrop rhythm) for pitch cue or short arpeggios to embellish the narration. He releases the arrow (line 5) with "*'hi-fu' to zo*" (hit the mark) as the plectrum hits the biwa body. At line 8, "*hito mo mi futomomo momarete*" (circling once, twice), the fushi is melodic and very slow to add intensity to the action.[31] At the end of the piece, the fan is bobbing, floating, and sparkling on top of white waves in the red sunset. Everyone celebrates Yoichi's feat and the voice by its tone tells us how "*kan-ni-ji-tare*" (impressed) the opposition is (line 12).

Satsuma biwa's later version of *Ogi no Mato* dramatically paints vivid scenes, mood, and picture with both voice and the timbres of the biwa. *Ogi no Mato* begins with the thin string sounds setting the quiet dusk at Yashima. Suddenly, the voice describes a horseman riding through the waves and against the wind; the biwa strums strong stereotyped patterns for agitating waves at the end of line 1. The fluttering gossamer strokes of the plectrum tell us how the fan (mid-line 3) twists and flutters in the wind. Nevertheless,

    Yoichi takes and arrow and   aims. "Steadily," he releases.
1. **YOICHI - KABURA WO TOT TE TSU GAI. "YO BIDEI HYO" TO HANATSU**

    A small soldier,   but the   12 hand and 3 finger length
2. **KOHYO TO   I-U JYO   JUNISOKU - MITSU BU –SE//**

    bow is   sturdy. The arrow
3. **YUMI WA TSUYOSHI KABURA WA**

    resounds over the waters   as it flies straight onto
4. **U-RA HIBIKU HODO NI NAGANARI SHITE AYAMATAZU**

    the fan's   point from which it is   one inch   away. ffft!"   and   hits!
5. **OGI NO   KANME NI WA   ISSUN BAKARI OITE. "HI-FU" TO ZO   HIKITA RU.**

    The arrow falls into the ocean.
6. **KABURA WA UMI NI IRIKEREBA**

    The fan flies into the sky   in the   spring wind.
7. **OGI WA SORE E ZO AGARI KERU   HARU KAZE NI**

    One   time,   two times,   it turns and then silently   plunges into the sea.
8. **HITO MO MI, FUTAMOMI MOMARETE UMI E SATTO ZO CHI-TARI-KERU**

    The reddish fan   opened wide,   bobs and
9. **MINAGURE NAI NO OGI NO HIDAITARU WO**

    sparkles in the sunset   on top   of white waves
10. **YO HI NI KAKAYAITE   SHIRA NAMI NO UE NI**

    floating,   unsinking,   rocking.
11. **UKINI SHIZU MINU YURAREKU WO**

    On the sea, the Heike   hit their   gunwales,   impressed!
12. **OKI NIWA HEIKE FUNABATA WO TATAITE   KAN-NI-JI TARI**

    On land the Genji   hit their quivers
13. **KOGA NI WA GENJI-   EBIRA WO TATA-I-TE,**

    In   applause!
14. **DOYOMIKE-RI!**

Figure 5.6: Lyrics to *Nasu no Yoichi*. The Heike biwa developed in the 1200s, and biwa playing is sparse and functions to punctuate the narration. The arrow hits the fan that dances in slow motion in the air before it falls and bobs in the water. Yoichi's team and his adversary celebrate and admire the triumph of the slightly built archer.

5. Singing the Uta (Song/Poetry)

Nasu no Yoichi takes aim at the fan on the Heike ship. In solemn prayer (line 5), the narration moves in intervals within the IN mode from a note to the fifth above, and then back to the first, then up to the fourth. The arrow is shot. The biwa's triumphant pattern resounds (line 11). Melodically, the voice sings how the fan rises high up into the sky before plunging earthward with a splash into the water. The music returns to the kyu (tonic) notes to triumphantly end in the last line *"in Keri"* quietly and poignantly.

As the sun sinks over Yashima Island— from nowhere, appearing over the waves
1. I RI HI KA TA MU KU YA SHI MA GA TA SA TO NORI I RU U MI ON MO////

Crossing down-wind with intense fury riding against waves towering
2. WATARU SHIMO KAZE IDO TSUYO KU~~UCHI KOMU NAMI NO TAKAKERE BA~~

a black horse -- agitated -- the fan also shivers in the wind
3. KOMA NO WAGAKI NO SADA MARA ZU // O~GI MO KAZE NI MOTAMA RA NE BA~

round and around it turns -- impossible to take aim!
4. KURURI KURU RI UCHI MAWA RI NERAI SADAMU RU SUBEMO NA SHI ////

Yoichi quietly closes his eyes. "Please, let the waves and wind calm down!
5. MUNETAKA JIT-TO ME WO~TO~JI~TE~"KO NO NAMI KAZE WA UCHI SHI ZU ME!

Let the arrow reach the fan!" Fervently he prays.
6. OGI WO IWOTO SASE~ TA MA~ E YA!" TO. IS SHIN KO ME ~~TE~~ ZO INO RI~~ KE RU

After praying, when he opened his eyes, how strange,
7. NEN JI AOT TE MA NA KO~BA~ HI RA KE BA~ SATE MO FUSH GI YA NA

the waves and wind have suddenly subsided! Yoichi's heart strengthened,
8. NAMI KAZE HATATTO SHIZU ~~ MARI NU MUNETAKA KOKORO ~WO ISAMATACHI~

12 handspan 3 fingers long arrow he reaches for, and pulls it out [of the quiver]
9. JUNI SOKU MITSUBUSE NO KABURA YA WO TSUMAGURI SHITE ZO NUKI DASHI

Grabbing it, he places it on the bow and pulls back.
10. NIGIRI BUTO NARU SHIGETO NO, YUMI NI KUWASETE HI KI ~~~KA TA ME ~~

He takes aim carefully. "To hit the circle is sacrilege".
11. NERAI WO KIT TO ~~SADA MESHI GA. "HINO MARU IDE WA OSORE A RI"

He aims for the rivet, and "Hyo!" he lets go, and the arrow flies
12. KANAME TE WO TO KOKORO ZA SHI~~"HYO!" TO HANACHI SHI INO CHI YA WA,

"Ha shi!" The arrow falls into the ocean but the fan dances upwards
13. "HA SHI!!" TO IKITTE ~~YA WA UMI NI O~~ GI WA SORA E MA I A GA RI~~~

for a second in the sky, and then flutters downward into the sea!
14. SHI BA SHI WA CHU NI HI RA ME ITE UMI E SAT TO ~~~ ZO OCHI NI~~~~ KE~~~~RI!

Figure 5.7: Lyrics to *Ogi no Mato*. In *Ogi no Mato* or *The Fan Target,* Satsuma biwa offers a more dramatic rendition of *Nasu no Yoichi*. A peaceful sunset is broken by an archer on horseback. Appropriate biwa licks describe the horse charging into the ocean waves. The intensity rises as Yoichi prays fervently; a short lull in the sea allows the arrow to hit the target. The biwa strums a triumphant passage.

Like in Buddhist chants, the libretto is marked with notes of sage-uta (voice down) or age-uta (voice up) for pitch cues. The voice and biwa interact to make the music. Next to the lyrics, biwa techniques indicate the types of patterns to play to evoke the mood for a battle scene or the sea or a quiet beach.

Of course the music passed on by blind musicians required no notation, but in 1776 the Maeda and Hatano schools developed a writing system. The Maeda school repertory comes in three categories based on difficulty. There are 161 *hiramono* (basic pieces), 33 *narimono* (for licensed people), and *hiji* (secret pieces). For the Hatano schools, there are *hiroi momo* (battle stories and scenes) and *fushi mono* (lyrical pieces).[32] Like Buddhist chants, next to the words are clue markers like *kyoku setsu* (melodic names), *hakase* (ornamentation), and the *kan dokoro* (interludes).[33]

Around the mid-1500s, the biwa accompanied the *Joruri Hime Monogatari* (Princess Joruri) narrative about the love story between Ushiwakamaru (the childhood name of Yoshitsune) and Princess Joruri. Later, puppets added visual drama to the Joruri story, but with the introduction of the shamisen, the shamisen supplanted the biwa narrators to become part of the bunraku theater we know today. Heike and Satsuma biwa schools continued, and during the Meiji Era, or 400 years later, the new Chikuzen biwa school appeared in Fukuoka, Northern Kyushu. In a reverse role of influences of instruments, a woman, Yoshida Takeko (1871–1923), incorporated shamisen playing and singing to the biwa. (Recall that biwa musicians made it possible to play the shamisen when it was first introduced.) The biwa style created by Ms. Yoshida was polished by Chijo Tachibana (1848–1919) to become Chikuzen biwa from the Chikuzen area of Kyushu.

Noh Chants and Kyogen Songs

A good singing or speaking voice is imperative for both noh and kyogen actors to be successful. Without a good voice, a career in the arts is hopeless unless it is in the non-performance or business aspect.

Nohgaku means noh and kyogen collectively and is an outgrowth of the ninth-century temple and shrine entertainment called *sarugaku* (monkey-mimes or antics of monkeys). By the fifteenth century, there existed four Yamato sarugaku troupes and two competing *dengaku* (rice-field songs and dances). Of the troupes, the innovative Kanami Kiyotsugu (1333–1384) and his 12-year-old son, Zeami Motokiyo (1363–1443), came to the attention of 17-year-old Shogun Yoshimitsu, who invited them to reside in his palace. When Zeami was 20, Kanami died, leaving the young actor as the troupe's leader. From the influence of his formative years living with the aristocracy, Zeami took sarugaku to another plane creating the *sarugaku no noh* (sarugaku

5. Singing the Uta (Song/Poetry)

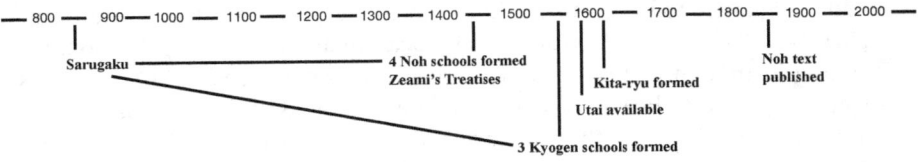

Figure 5.8: Nohgaku Timeline. Temples and shrines supported troupes of *sarugaku* (monkey-mimes), the precursor to nohgaku. Four schools and later the Kita-ryu were established with the shogun's permission. Zeami's Kanze-ryu is the oldest and largest school today. Coveted by the samurai class, noh became available to a wider audience when published noh libretto became available to the public during the Edo Era.

of skill), which differed from *hon* sarugaku (the main sarugaku) of *kyogen* (comic theater).[34]

Zeami's school, Kanze-ryu, the largest of the five Noh schools of *shi-te* (main) actors, today dominates the Hosho, Komparu, Kongo, and Kita schools. The Kita group emerged from the Kongo troupe in 1618 by permission of the second Tokugawa shogun, Hidetada.[35]

For noh performances, the prerogative belongs to the shi-te actors to hire the kyogen actors, *waki* (supporting actors) and the musicians of the nohkan, ko-tsuzumi, o-tsuzumi, and taiko. Each support unit has an iemoto (head master) who leads a school of specialized styles (see Figure 8.3: Related Schools of the Five Noh Schools).

The profound sounds of noh spoken and in song affect the soul in a primordial way like Buddhist chants, even for some Westerners.[36] Drama in noh

---

Shi-te (main actors) Kanze, Hosho, Kongo, Komparu, Kita.

Waki (support actors) Takayasu, Fukuo, Shimogakari Hosho.

Noh-kan (flute) Morita, Isso, Fujita.

Ko-tsuzumi (drum held on shoulder) Kanze, Ko Kosei, Okura.

O-tsuzumi (big drum) Kadono, Takayasu, Okura.

Taiko (stick drum) Kanze, Komparu.

Kyogen (comic relief actors) from 1500s, Okura, Izumi, Sagi (now defunct).

Figure 5.9: Schools of the Noh Ensemble. In producing a noh performance, a shi-te actor from one of the five schools chooses the waki, kyogen, and musicians from one of the three schools of waki actors, two kyogen schools, three kotsuzumi, three otsuzumi schools, and two taiko schools. Each school has its own iemoto and strict style and protocol for performances. Once the program is set, the actors and musicians rehearse a few days before the performance.

adds poignancy to life's lessons similar to Shakespearean plays. Kunio Komparu says, "The music of Noh is an invocation and a requiem, the rhythms calling forth a ghost that dances a prayer for its own repose."[37] And in this spirit, applause at the end of a noh performance breaks the almost sacrosanct atmosphere.[38] Similarly the high art music of biwa, ji-uta shamisen, and koto music leaves people quieted, humbled, and melancholy (see Chapter 1 on aesthetics). Even the comic theater leaves one lamenting and wistful (see Table 12: Relationship of Hon-sarugaku (Kyogen) and Sarugaku no Noh (Noh)).

The stylized *kotoba* (spoken words) of noh, kyogen, bunraku, and kabuki theater come from Shinto incantations. The shi-te, waki, and six to eight people in the utai-ji set the scene, reveal feelings and problems, and provide the dialogue and denouement in poetic form.

In the singing sections, there are two melodic vocal types: *yowa-gin* (softer, weaker) and *tsuyo-gin* (stronger), like pianissimo and forte of Western notation. These subjective instructions along with *shugen* (happy) and *bo-oku* (yearning, sad, recall) and to sing in *ji-goe* (natural voice) are sufficient instruction particularly when lessons are face to face. The melodies occur in IN mode just as in the Buddhist chants, with intonations that evoke feeling through the demeanor of the voice and the atmosphere created by the hayashi.

Noh also asks the audience to suspend reality and become complicit in the make-believe that takes place on stage. Professional noh troupes are all men. Even while playing female roles, the actor keeps his natural male voice. Conversely, the actors of kabuki and the *gidayu* (narrator) of the bunraku (puppet) stage produce a falsetto voice (*ura-goe*) to imitate ladies because in kabuki and bunraku realism is important.

Between the various schools of shi-te actors, stylistic differences occur. Some people will say Kanze is more elegant, while others prefer the colorful melodies of the Kita-ryu. The example of the *Hagoromo* utai of the Kanze and Kita schools shows a subtle style of the Kanze-ryu whereas the Kita melody moves relatively melodically.

The noh voice, like the Buddhist chants, should come from the *hara* (stomach, diaphragm). A slightly opened mouth with lips slightly pursed against the teeth controls the breath and allows for the focusing of the breath for diction and *fushi-mawashi* (melismata) ornamentation.[39] Think of a water hose with a narrow opening. The strong stream focuses the water to a chosen spot whereas a spray's dispersion is too broad to control. In the same way, the stream of breath through a controlled mouth opening combined with strong air coming from the diaphragm controls the fushi-mawashi and melodic flow.

The voice of *kyogen*, boisterous twin of noh, is loud as if the actor swallowed a microphone, a technique I discovered but lost through disuse. The kyogen plays are interspersed with the speech and popular songs of the Muro-

5. Singing the Uta (Song/Poetry)

Figure 5.10: *Hagoromo* Notation of Kanze with Kita. In *Hagoromo* or *Feather Mantle*, although the melody varies only slightly, the subtle elegance of the Kanze-ryu is admired by some while others prefer the more melodic style of the Kita-ryu.

machi Era. An example of a happy song in the IN mode[40] is *Okyagari Kobooshi* from the play *Futari Daimyo*. In the play, two provincial lords sing a popular song from Kyoto and physically roll over to the words "*tsui korobu*" (she flips over).

At Kyoto, at Kyoto, selling fast, tumbling dolls. When she sees a cute guy,
Kyoni   Kyoni hayaru okyagari kobooshi. Tono dani mire ba

When she sees a cute guy, she flips over! She flips over!
Tonodani mire ba   tsui korobu!   Tsui korobu!

Spoken:
Isn't that so? That is so, That is, that is, that is so!
Gatten ka? Gatten ja, gatten gatten gatten ja!

Figure 5.11: *Okyagari Kobooshi*. **The frolicsome song *Okyagari Kobooshi* or *Tumbling Doll* tells about the latest toy sold in Kyoto. The doll tumbles over when she sees a handsome guy. Kyogen has preserved many Muromachi Era popular folk songs by incorporating them into the plays, so kyogen is a good source for ancient songs.**

Kyogen songs range from frolicsome to wistful and melancholy. Two inebriated servants in *Boshibari* (Tied to a Pole) entertain each other after drinking forbidden sake. In the play *Hanago*, a philandering husband sings twelve forlorn love songs on his way home after visiting his lady friend.[41] The melody is monotonic by Western standards, but the songs in the IN scale with elongated vowels are nevertheless melodic.

The similarities of the vocal qualities of biwa, noh, and kyogen to Buddhist chants and the Shinto music are evident in the songs' primal effect meant to touch the heart.

1. The sound of a bell into the night and a parting bird do not bother me when I sleep by myself.
2. My heart tangled up like threads of a willow tree, how can I forget, the face with hair tangled up in bed
3. One spring day, flower banquet, flower banquet, once I think of it, I cannot stop thinking about it
4. I hate the one who rings bells at temples, I am in so deep love, until the dawn, when I hardly see my lover
5. When the darkness comes I feel extremely lonely; I wonder if you've arrived yet.
6. When it rains at night, who comes here wet from rain? There is no one but me who comes, but who? Whoever, it is, let the rain fall on her.
7. I hate, the time; time goes fast in the evening
8. The love letter I threw away, Hey! A carriage pulled by cows! ("ushi" for "cow" and "ushinau" for "lose" – double meaning), the letter is lost until I see you (the one I love)
9. Hanako, with her tangled hair moving, I will never forget her face; India, *shidan*, my morning! The best of three countries!
10. I need to go home quickly, as the morning has come.

Figure 5.12: Melancholy Songs from *Hanago*. Kyogen, known for comic antics, has its share of melancholy songs. A rich man, prevented from visiting his mistress, claims he must visit the shrine to clear his bad dreams. The wife allows him time to do *zazen* (Zen meditation) at home, which he agrees to if left alone. Covering his head with a kimono, he enlists his servant to take his place. On his way home from his mistress, the philandering husband sings the mournful songs listed here. At home, he unwittingly reports his escapade to his wife who has replaced the servant. The play ends with his wife raging after him across the stage and bridgeway to the exit (translation by Noriko Tsuboi Garofalo).

Gidayu (Narrator or Singer) of Bunraku (Puppet Theater)

In an incident in the early 1900s, Japanese scholars gathered to transcribe a passage of a gidayu at Ueno University. The singer sang the passage seven times and each time it varied. In desperation, one transcriber asked which version was the real passage. The singer answered, "All of them!" and stormed out in utter disgust for the lack of the transcriber's understanding of one's emotions and feelings in musical interpretation.

Although they seem worlds apart, joruri[42] or gidayu or narrative music with puppets developed from noh, which in turn came from Buddhist chants. Noh, with the shogun's patronage, was the model to emulate. Kaga no Jo, the founder of joruri, claimed noh as its parent and used its singing style and the ritual openings. He also adopted many noh plays to the bunraku stage. Later Takemoto Gidayu (who once studied with Kaga no Jo) collaborated with playwright Chikamatsu Monzaemon and made bunraku as we know it today (see Figure 6.9: Line of Subdued- and Strong-Style Singers). Hence, Takemoto Gidayu's first name is synonymous with bunraku singing: gidayu.[43]

Joruri or gidayu singers are men with large chest cavities to project great voices and to sing with the required versatility.[44] Next to the singer is a smaller musician holding the largest instrument of the shamisen family. They both sit on a rotating dais and change with another team of musicians when the scene or act changes. At times for festive scenes, an ensemble of five shamisens with an equal number of singers plays.

It is the gidayu who attracts the people, and it is common to hear from the audience at the appearance of certain singers, "*Matte imashita!*" (I was waiting for you!) Versatility is required of the gidayu. He must be melodic or gruff and imitate the voices of commoner or nobleman or warrior, woman, or child, while narrating a story. In the example "Kiyari no dan" of the *Ridgepole of Kyoto's Sanjusangendo Temple*, the story centers on a willow tree spirit who marries a samurai for saving her life from a woodcutter. They have a son named Midori (Green) and all is happy until one day the mother writhes with pain to a distant sound of a woodcutter's ax. The willow tree is felled, and its spirit as a mortal dies. When the willow log passes by the house on its way to Kyoto it stops. Only Midori can move it along. The libretto of the finale shows the singer portraying five characters: narrator, father, woodcutter, grandmother, and son over the shamisen accompaniment.

Figure 5.13: Score of Bunraku's *Kiyari no Dan*. The shamisen plays the plaintive melody of *Kiyari no Dan* or Woodcutter's Song while the narrator recounts the log's history of the spirit of the willow tree.

The Natural Voice: The Singing Style of Sangen and Koto

Usually at bunraku and kabuki performances people focus on the puppets and the actors, but at bunraku, it is the solo, gidayu singer who power the plays with his great voice. The blind ji-uta musician Tomizaki Shunsho[45] (1880–1958) came from a line of bunraku puppeteers and visited the theater often to hear the musicians. One day he and his blind student, Tomiyama Seikin I (1913–2008), went to hear a play called *The Miracle of the Tsubosaka Kannon*, a love story between a *zato* (blind musician) named Sawaichi and his wife. In portraying Sawaichi, the gidayu's great voice came from the front of his throat to sound thin and strained. This caricature shocked Tomiyama.[46]

Do I sound like that? Tomiyama realized that many blind people sang looking at the ceiling, stretching their necks out to strain the vocal chords. His mentor, Tomizaki Shunsho, said to use your natural voice and enunciate the words to give credit to lyricists.[47] Forget about the falsetto to imitate women or to set your voice unnaturally low or high to mimic other singers.[48] If one cannot reach a pitch, sing it in the comfortable octave below or above the note or in a range natural for you. Soprano, alto, tenor, or baritone is irrelevant in hogaku.

During the Edo Era and into the twentieth century, ji-uta sangen and koto music belonged to the domain of blind men who were the bona fide professional musicians or models to defer to. In fact, in the world of ji-uta shamisen and koto music, the blind musician was king.[49] They conversed with each other through the shamisen,[50] and could "see" sound and know how to add a little *sabi* (rust/patina) on the voice, like moss on a rock.

Although the blind musicians' world is said to be IN (yin, dark) as opposed to YO (yang, light), they have perfected the subdued expression and understated aesthetics from their amplified rooms made of paper on wooden frames. Seated on cushions with legs folded under, this sedentary position immobilizes the body but leaves the mind to intellectually paint musical ideas into a composition.[51] Thus, it is not unusual that my koto repertoire is 99 percent by blind musicians[52] and that the music is intellectually stimulating, challenging, and interesting. Did Johann Wolfgang von Goethe know how Nature speaks when he wrote this passage?

> Close your eyes, prick your ears, and from the softest sound to the wildest noise, from the simplest tone to the highest harmony, from the most violent, passionate scream to the gentlest words of sweet reason, it is by Nature who speaks, revealing her being, her power, her life, and her relatedness so that a blind person, to whom the infinitely visible world is denied, can grasp an infinite vitality in what can be heard.[53]

Composing for the Uta

When composing, the lyrics become the piece. Franz Schubert said to give him the words to make the melody. In a college music course, I had to count the rhythm in each stanza before creating a melody within a metered measure. The same approach with Japanese lyrics would be catastrophic. Every poem except for a few exceptions is invariably in 5, 7, 5, 7 beats per line. If all of hogaku complied with making melody to the rhythm of each line of poetry, a sine wave might result and bounce everyone off the island. Hogaku music, like marching soldiers approaching a bridge, ignores the steady rhythm to save the bridge or, as in the case of the island, to add interest in the music.

Then, how is music created when most of Japan's poems are set to the same 5, 7, 5 beat? According to Hirano and Kishibe, singing is an offshoot of poetic recitation.[54] As an example, the *Karuta* is a New Year's poetry game of the *Ogura Hyakunin Isshu* (100 waka poems by 100 poets).[55] A reader recites the waka to two teams. The team collecting the most cards wins.

After reading a few poems with the same syllabic format, a melodic cadence becomes apparent. Although the melody varies depending on the reader, basically it begins on *fa* of the diatonic scale (*do, re, mi*) and moves up to *so* for the rest of the poem, as in "A (*fa*)—(*so*) *waji shima kayou chidori no naku koe ni–*."[56] For the last two lines or the remaining fourteen syllables, the first syllable (*I* of *Ikuyo*) again begins on *fa* to move up again to *so*, as in "*I(fa)—(so) kuyo nezame nu Suma no seki mori—*."

Kishibe and Hirano also say waka-type recitation and koto kumi-uta

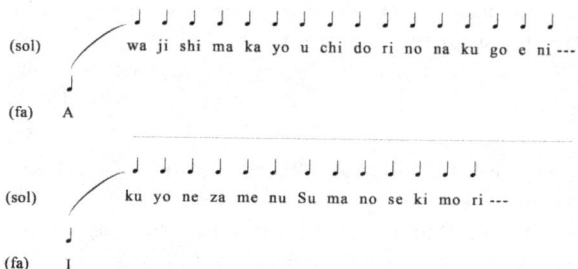

Figure 5.14: *Awaji-shima* Karuta Card Reader's "Melody." When the Karuta is played on New Year's Day, the reader melodically recites the 100 poems. Basically, in solfege the first syllable is *fa* followed by the rest of the monotonic recitation in *sol*. The last vowel in each line is extended. Karuta competitions are televised and gamers vie for the national championship. Today, schools with an iemoto teach how to read, set up, and choose the cards.

singing are connected.[57] The same *Awaji-shima* poem was set to koto's *Chidori no Kyoku* in the 1800s and a sophisticated interplay of voice and instrument appears through several octaves of the IN scale (see Figure 5.15: "Awaji-shima" Passage of Koto's *Chidori no Kyoku*). Letting the instrumental part lead, the second "a" vowel of "Awa—" is melismatically rendered to the koto's playing with the voice and koto sharing in the melody-making. The syllables come between the struck strings in order to be heard (see Figure 5.19 and the "Shio no Yama" passage). Without the koto accompaniment, the singing by itself sounds like a Buddhist chant, as was confirmed by a Buddhist priest.[58]

Critical is the context of each word, not the rhythmic stanza, to bring out mood or image such as the waka in *Chidori no Kyoku* just mentioned.

Figure 5.15: "Awaji-shima" Passage of Koto's *Chidori no Kyoku*. Compared with the Karuta reading of the waka, the vowels of the syllables are extended melodically like a sophisticated recitation. The voice interplays with the koto, and neither the voice nor the instrument's melodic tract makes sense without the other.

For example, three poems about the *hototogisu* (lesser cuckoo) in Tateyama Kengyo's *Hototogisu no Kyoku* (Composition on the Lesser Cuckoo) are rhythmically the same and can have the same melody, but in doing so an injustice would be done to the sentiment expressed in each poem. The first poem asks in the YO mode, "*Yama hototogisu, itsuka kinakan?*" (Mountain hototogisu, when will you come?) Here the voice pleads longingly in the high range. The hototogisu in the second verse is sung in mid-range, "Are you the same hototogisu?" implying, "Are you that same old tiresome bird?" In the final verse,

Figure 5.16: Example of *Hototogisu* Melody. The same word has different melodies to fit the mood. The first poem is in the upper register. The voice looks around for the *hototogisu* and wonders when will it come? The second verse feels that the *hototogisu* has overstayed its welcome and is not worth considering. The last verse in the sadder IN mode implores the bird to stay until it has no voice to sing.

sadness and regret is expressed in the IN mode for the impending departure of the hototogisu.

In other compositions, recurring words, like *uguisu* (warbler), *sakura* (cherry blossom), and *kaze* (wind), receive their own melody expressing mood, feeling, or image implicit in the moment. Musicologist Fumio Koizumi noticed that a melody assigned to a word usually follows Japanese patterns of speech. Like the word *mátsu* (pine tree),[59] the first accented syllable gets either the same note or a higher pitch. The rule applies for all words, like *chidorí* (plover), *yáma* (mountain), and *sashidé* (peninsula). The vocal examples in this book follow this rule with one exception, which is the word *matsu* in *Miyako Wasure*. The "tsu" has a higher pitch to connect the thought to Matsuko, the name of the poet's wife.

In ji-uta shamisen and koto music, the singer and instrumentalist is the same person so the vocal and instrumental parts are learned together. When music is committed to memory but forgotten, it is surprising how the lyrics can trigger recall. Hence, the satirical *Wasure Shoka* (Forgotten Song) has much truth.

Although it seems difficult to sing while playing the koto, an open-minded student has no problem coordinating the two because there is a system. For one thing, the instrumental part is consistent from school to school while the vocal part is fluid. In fact, the vocal melody not only is different between schools, variations can occur between students of the same school and even with the same singer—recall the gidayu singer mentioned earlier who sang a passage differently seven times. Such is the reality of ephemeral things.

The changes are unintentional for they come from a singer's reaction to the environment and the audience. Changes also depend on the vocalist's innate ability to execute the fushi-mawashi, or the improvisational melismata aspect that makes artists like Tomiyama Seikin and Linda Ronstadt[60] prefer performing at live concerts. Tomiyama says music is a living activity where he responds to each venue and its audience. Recorded music is like "canning" the music into a static state. Linda Ronstadt says live performances allow her to continuously perfect and strive to make the next performance better.[61]

Performers pass on their vocal ornamentation styles to their students. Consider the last words of the piece *Yugao*, "yo wa no ka ze" (evening wind) and compare Tomiyama Seikin's and Miyagi Michio's styles. Miyagi is known for ornamental high yelps, whereas Tomiyama uses a descending pattern (see Figure 5.18). The rule for hogaku is "learned freedom" in knowing what is in vogue and appropriate for the music. Kishibe wrote, "Instead of the harmonic feature, Japanese music became involved in minute tones, free rhythm, and delicate timbre, of an order higher than that achieved in Western music."[62] His statement conveys the dual idea of fluidity and preciseness characteristic of Japanese music that renders it difficult to notate in Western form.

	Wasure Shoka (Forgotten Song)	
1.	Kondo Nagasaki de	This time in Nagasaki,
2.	kawatta shoka wo narrotta	I learned a new song. It's
3.	Ato saki wa oboe nanda ga	beginning and end I can't remember
4.	naka no shoka wo wasureta	and even the middle, I've forgotten.
5.	Sa koso arubeki to kaite moratta ga	I knew I'd forget it so I had it written
6.	Sore sae deguchi de otoshita	but I dropped it at the exit.
7.	Shubi no showake mo sono tori	Even manners I dropped in the same way.
8.	Hata memboku nai	How embarrassing!
9.	yoni koko ni aware rashi	How exasperating—
10.	Shudo no kichizono sato ga	Like gays buying whores!
11.	yoi yoi kuzutsni	Talking through the night
12.	Omowase te anata no katae osarabae	Failing to recognize bargains
13.	Konatano katae osarabae	[we see] farewells between
14.	Tonosama e choki ni mo kago ni wo	Lords and mistresses in palanquins.
15.	Enorai dete amigasa wo	Umbrellas for sale, some don't buy and
16.	Kaikon de dote no kubo damari ni	some do. Puddles form here and there—
17.	ketsuma zuite hiza gashirao surimuita	I stubbed my toe and scratched my knee.
18.	Attoshiko un-non to shita!	Ouch! What do you do?
19.	"Tata ta no taisetsu bo!"	"Tata-tan, taisetsubo!"
20.	Chinba hiki hiki Kinryuzan e	Hopping on one leg, I go to Akasuka.
21.	"Yone, yone, manju wa uranaika?"	"Yone, yone cake, won't you sell?
22.	Zenya aru on yaki moshite ariyosa!	Of course I have money."
23.	Tokaku ukiyo wa omoshiroya.	This floating world is so much fun.

Figure 5.17: Lyrics to *Wasure Shoka*. Often music can be recalled by the lyrics. In this song, an Edo Era playboy learned a new song but forgot it. Taking no precaution to remember it, he likens his attitude to the carefree ways of the Pleasure Quarters, where venders sell umbrellas and cakes, and high-class lords rendezvous with mistresses (mocked by the sliding notes on the shamisen). A sudden rain leaves puddles where he slips and stubs his toe, as the shamisen passages match his mishaps. Even so, he declares that life in the Floating World is fun.

Embellishing the Songs

All instruments have standardized techniques to decorate an image or concept, like the rippling arpeggios on the koto for river, shimmering sea, splashing waves, birds chirping, flowers scattering, or wind blowing. The biwa strums across the strings for waves or battle scenes, or to make light fluttering for an unstable fan; the shamisen plucks the strings with the left hand for cries of an insect or strums rhythmically for festival-type music for dancing. The playing patterns of the techniques affect the melodic direction

Figure 5.18: Tomiyama and Miyagi Ornament. Each person is endowed with different vocal chords, so the ability to ornament a note is the individual's signature. By listening and trying the teacher's ornamentation, one learns to add melismata within one's vocal capability, through understanding the piece, and with plenty of practice.

of the voice and the voice lags, comes before, or sings together with the instrument. The goal of music is to make sure that the syllables are audible and not drowned by the sound of the instrument even while playing rapid elaborate passages.

Thus, the instrument and the voice interweave through at least two octaves in melody-making. The singing anticipates or follows the instrumental part that is composed first. If the melody of the koto goes down (*ko-rorin*), the voice follows it, or in some cases, goes before the pattern. In *Chidori no Kyoku* (Composition on the Plover) the first song begins with the proper noun "Shio no Yama," which literally means Salt Mountain. The melody of the voice is almost monotonic, holding onto the vowel sound "o" of "*shi-o-*." The koto plays *awasezume* (octaves played together) to match the pitch of the voice. The voice holds the conjunction "*no*," and the koto plays the same note, then another note with a slurring grace note is played before "*ya*" is sung which is followed by three rippling notes, then a swish sound is made for the salt spray of the beach scene. (For just three syllables already there is a barrage of timbre to describe the scene!) As the voice sings "*ma*" to complete "*yama*" meaning mountain, the koto aurally makes a "mountain" by playing a low note, then peaks to a higher pitch before moving down lower. Unless the listener is attentive, it is easy to miss the expressiveness of the words with embellishments so as to "see" the aural picture.

Figure 5.19: *Chidori no Kyoku* with "Shio no Yama" Example. Note the sparse koto tract. The voice also seems to move with only a few notes, and the notation looks complex. In actuality the voice and koto intertwine smoothly as one instrument, a skill learned during lessons.

In koto duets with a *kaede* or polyphonic independent melody line, such as in *Saga no Aki* (Autumn in Saga), the vocal melody assumes a different contour for the players of either koto. Likewise in a koto and sangen ensemble, the shamisen patterns affect the vocal part. For example, ji-uta's *Echigojishi* with four parts, high and low koto, and *honte* sangen (main), and *kaede* sangen, the four musicians have difficulty singing together as their instrumental parts affect the vocal line. An assigned singer dominates and usually it is the lead sangen player in a sankyoku ensemble.

The Appeal of Hogaku Singing

In a movie set in Japan, American Little Leaguers squinted their faces and covered their ears as their Japanese coach growled through the drinking song, *Kuroda-bushi*.[63] His *shubui* (astringent) and raspy voice that morphed out of the Shinto and Buddhist stylized grounded tradition was filled with timbre and was excruciating to Western ears. However his sincerity charmed the judges, who granted him first place, much to the surprise of his team. The Portuguese in 1543 were models of etiquette as they sat through music described as "excruciating unintelligible gutturals."[64] The human voice hits the primordial chord of people like the allure of venders' calls or the chants of Shinto, Buddhist, Catholic priests, Jewish cantors, or Islam imams. When a chorus provided the squeaking tires and splish-splash of the windshield for a Honda Civic advertisement, how many cars were sold?[65] The choir in Miyazaki Hayao's 2013 anime *The Wind Rises* evoked a primal sense of danger during the earthquake scene. Singing, which is ubiquitous in all societies, prompted some scholars to declare that it preceded speech for survival reasons.[66] The singing voice gives one's location, source for food, or the presence of danger,[67] like a hunter's yodel that can travel a great distance and get attention.

Hogaku singing intrigued Edward S. Morse (1838–1925) so much that he took noh utai lessons from the famous Umewaka. Thinking himself as musical, he was perplexed by the motion of the melody, for having a good ear for rote learning he could discern variations of the master's singing at every repetition. He concluded that noh utai was "not singing, but inflectional declamation." His friend, Professor Yatabe, "insisted that the Japanese music was superior to ours."[68] As persuasive as the human voice may be, it is surprising that the singing voice is the most contentious issue of music between cultures, within a society, between generations, and within families like parents to children.

The Japanese today enjoy singing as much as their ancestors. The karaoke machine, invented by a Japanese in the 1970s, gave ordinary people a chance to sing like professionals with an orchestral background.[69] Whether the singer is on tune or not is irrelevant; more important is the sincerity of performance, a value that is passed on and makes some karaoke singers tolerable.

Summary

Vocalization standards in hogaku apply to all singing because they came from the same source. Shinto priests must sing with conviction and sincerity. Buddhist chants have to command like thunder to capture attention and respect. These qualities were passed onto noh, kyogen, biwa, narrative, and lyrical singing where strength comes from the *hara* (stomach, diaphragm) or heart. Although singing styles are lighter for shamisen and koto music, and even lighter and more sensuous for geisha *ko-uta* (short songs), basically the words must still be heard. This is why the syllables are sung in between the notes, anticipating or following the instrumental line that is the consistent part of the music between schools. In rapid instrumental passages, the voice can be heard as the attention is on the song.

The word *uta* means both poetry and singing thus hogaku singing is poetic recitation. The open vowel of the Japanese language enables the singer to hold a vowel and ornament it with little micro-pitches, adding interest to a melody that sits on one note. Lafcadio Hearn calls the melisma "semi-demi sounds."[70] The Japanese call it fushi-mawashi. I believe fushi-mawashi is part of every world vocal tradition, East and West, popular and classical. The fushi-mawashi gives a singer his or her unique trademark. People flocked to hear Tomizaki Shunsho (1900–1960) who had a horrible voice, but great fushi-mawashi. In the United States, the unique timbre of Louis Armstrong's (1901–1971) raspy voice had indescribable charm. A good singer in any society pays attention to the words and their meaning[71] for the words trigger images and emotions. American rap music may annoy some people, but I hear it paralleling Buddhist and noh chants. The singers of both cultures monotonically narrate a story to the accompaniment of a rhythmic band. Only the content is different. Appreciating any singing style is learned.

6

The Format of Continuity in Hogaku Compositions

Many years ago I asked a Japanese friend why he thought hogaku flowed in a succession of melodies from beginning to end. As if the answer should be obvious to me, he quipped, "Why not! The water in a river is always moving along." His response reminded me of a more sympathetic comment by a protagonist in the novel *Kinkakuji* by Mishima who said,

> How strange a thing is the beauty of music! The brief beauty that the player brings into being transforms a given period into pure continuance, it is certain to never to be repeated, like the existence of dayflies and other such short lived creature beauty is a perfect abstraction and creation of life itself. Nothing is so similar to life as music.[1]

It is true. The "pure continuance" of hogaku melodies moves like water in a river, forever moving and changing and in a *jo-ha-kyu* (slow, faster, fast end) manner through life. The *jo* in music resembles our childhood when time moves at a snail's pace. The tempo picks up in *ha* at maturity when most of our activities take place, and at *kyu* the music ends quietly and quickly. Within the jo-ha-kyu of music, sections are partitioned with genre specific labels of introduction, middle, and end that are diagrammed in this chapter. In addition, the format of hogaku pieces have been influenced by historical events that reflect the structure of music being Japanese, foreign, Japanese, and then foreign as shown on the timeline on page 6.

As the timeline in the Introduction shows, the earliest music is Japanese, or indigenous Shinto norito, kagura, and ancient *uta* (songs/poetry) that set the organic format of free-flowing compositions as things in nature. Over early music, foreign Buddhist chants and gagaku music appeared around the sixth century with strict musical formats that are practiced as preserved. When exchanges with the Asian continent diminished, indigenous sensibilities re-emerged on Japanese inspired Buddhist chants and on biwa, noh, shamisen, koto, and shakuhachi music. From the Meiji Era, Western music has had extraordinary influence on Japan's music today with interesting consequences.

Basically, all music moves along in jo-ha-kyu with beginning, middle, and end. Since hogaku music morphed out of the philosophical template of Japan's religious music, the structure of Shinto norito, mi- and sato-kagura are examined first as the source of the ever-changing melodies found on Buddhist and noh chants, biwa, shamisen, and koto of the Edo Era.

Japanese Format of Early Norito, Mi- and Sato-Kagura

As discussed previously, Shinto norito and ancient songs of the Jomon period served to communicate with the kamis. Of this ancient music, Harich-Schneider said that "melodies associated with magic are prone to be long lived."[2] Priests who curried the kami's favor to ensure longevity, good fortune, and other life blessings made certain to pass the accepted format that effectuated results. Before the norito is recited, a purification ceremony is performed inviting the kami with offerings and further purification. Like an aural "letter," the priest stands before the shrine and opens with salutations, listing the kami's august status and presenting his credentials as a legitimate intermediary. After expressing gratitude for gifts received from the gods and listing the offerings decoratively arranged before the kami, the priest pleas for a specific blessing or request for good fortune upon the Imperial family, who represents the Japanese people.[3] At the close of the norito, the priest signs off humbly and retreats from the shrine. The format is a natural way of presenting a request with a beginning, middle and a quick end.

Norito's length depends on the compliments offered to the deity, list of gifts, and the reason for the request. Its cadence and sequence become apparent after listening to many noritos. The formulaic structure of the poetic and carefully chosen words became the model from which music is made to touch the heart and soul of listeners.

Kagura music. Magic imbued in kagura (music of, for, and from the gods) teaches people through elegant, simple melodies to live in harmony with the nature of things. Although some songs are *asobi* (play) for entertainments, they are nevertheless part of kagura when performed at religious ceremonies and festivals. Some mi-kagura and sato-kagura juxtapose two elements consisting of a voice or flute melody over repeating instrumental patterns.

Asakura, used for mi-kagura, juxtaposes two such forms: an ever-changing vocal melody of an extended vowel over the repeating wa-gon's melodic patterns of A B, A A B, A A B, etc. (see Figure 2.6: Score of *Asakura* with Melody Patterns). The jo-ha-kyu aspect of the music is not immediately discernible unless consciously tapping out the rhythm of the wa-gon playing.

Asakura is an example of songs with instrumental accompaniment. The repetitious instrumental passages evolved into more sophisticated passages to embellish the lyrics (see Chapter 7: Decorating the Melodic Line).

The simplicity of kagura music evokes calm and peace as found in nature. Sato-kagura's *Miko Dance Music* performed at offerings at the Izumo Shrine and in celebration of a child's *shichi-go-san* (3, 5, 7 birth years) is characterized by a three to four note flute melody that is repeated over a steady drumbeat. A stick with bells attached is held by a *miko* (shrine maiden). She shakes the bells in synchrony with the drum and occasionally breaks away from the drum's steady beats to rattle quietly as if spreading blessings over the attendees or audience. Miko dance music exemplifies the sparse aspects of Japanese music that are enhanced by the heart-felt sincerity of the performers to ensure a positive outcome (see Figure 2.7: Sato Kagura Ceremonial and Miko Dance Music).

Format of Compositions Influenced by Foreign Music

Music set by Shinto and ancient songs from Jomon times was imbued with feeling expressed in uta (songs/poems) that dominated as Azuma Asobi, Kure-mai, and Yamato mai. The Japanese also enjoyed *saibara* (folk songs) and *waka* (court) poems. When the Chinese introduced *roei* (Chinese poetry recitation), the song-loving Japanese were quick to sing them and soon added their own poems to the collection to become the genre *wakan-roei* (Japanese–Chinese poems).

Wakan-roei format. Today, fourteen wakan-roei survive. Solemnity and contemplative aspects characterize this formless sounding choral singing that actually has structure. There are three stanzas in the format that is revealed when a solo lead singer sings the first stanza of each new section. The second section begins at a higher octave than the previous section and listening for the different pitch helps locate where one is in the song. The entire piece is exceedingly slow and seems to sit in the jo and ha portion of the music, which is not uncommon even among some ji-uta performers. Musicians may feel deferential towards an audience and get into an exceedingly slow mode.

Because roei is Chinese in origin, the Japanese respect for foreign music kept its structure true to form. Therefore it is not surprising that the surviving wakan-roei pieces have the same three-part format and a similar melodic

6. The Format of Continuity in Hogaku Compositions

Part I	Part II (start an octave higher	Part III

Table 6: Format of Wakan-roei Songs. The singing sounds like a chant, seemingly monotonic with vocal ornamentations. The ryuteki and sho accompany the song. The three parts are easily discernible because a solo singer begins each new section.

contour. Listening to *Jisei* while following the score to *Togan* illustrates the point. In fact, *Jisei's* melody can be transposed over the score of *Togan* with minor differences caused by the different lyrics (see Figure 5.4).

Gagaku music. Some scholars say the *jo-ha-kyu* idea came from the Continent through Buddhism; that may or may not be the case. The strict format in music from foreign lands, however, is typical. Chinese and Korean compositions are preserved with their format intact and are categorized according to length, such as *taikyoku* (great pieces), *chukyoku* (middle pieces), and *shokyoku* (smaller pieces).[4] Instrumental music is further divided into *bugaku* (dance) and *kangen* (instrumental) music. Bugaku has no stringed instruments and accompanies dance with each instrument entering in canon-like fashion creating a lattice of sound. Kangen music with stringed instruments is of particular significance to Japanese music. The structure of gagaku pieces with melodic sections of A, B, C, etc., are repeated as in the format for shokyoku that is played more often.

> Ettenraku: AABBCCAABB
> Gakkaen: AABBCCABB
> Ittokyo: ABCA'BC
> Shukoshi: ABABCBB
> Butokuraku: ABCDCD[5]

Structurally the kangen music *Ettenraku*, a *shokyoku* (short piece), has a direct link to modern koto music particularly when played in the hyojo mode.[6] Three melodic sections A, B, C of *Ettenraku* repeat as in A, A, B, B, C, C, A, A, B, B. Jo is excruciatingly slow, rendering the melody unrecognizable. Towards the kyu section a discernible melody in the A and B passages becomes the ear-catching tune of a Buddhist gatha, *Nori no Miyama* and the popular drinking song *Kuroda-bushi*. (See Figure 6.1.)

In addition to the format, another clue to predict the music is to follow the entry and exit of different instruments. The flute begins the gagaku melody to the high tapping sounds of the shoko and kakko. The low boom of the taiko then joins together with the sho and hichiriki. The biwa and koto are the last to enter and exit with the koto having the last "plunk." (See Figure 6.2.)

Ettenraku, Hyojo Melody

Nori no Miyama

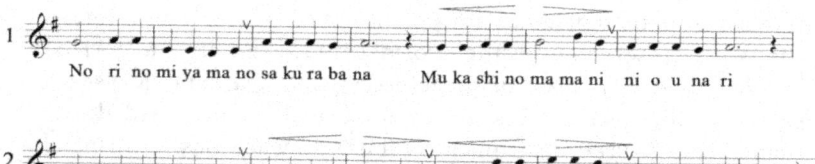

Kuroda Bushi

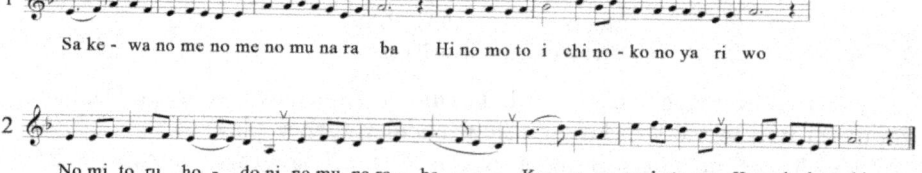

Figure 6.1: *Ettenraku* and Its Offshoots. It is hard to imagine so many different songs sprouted from this gagaku piece, such as the popular drinking song, *Kuroda-bushi*, and a Buddhist Sunday School song, *Nori no Miyama*. By lining the scores up, perhaps it will be evident.

Modern Koto's First Collected Songs

Kumi-uta. The Japanese could not resist adding their own songs over Chinese instruments, namely the koto, which explains why modern koto's kumi-uta (collection of songs) is strictly constructed. To review, the link of modern koto to *Ettenraku* comes from the Heian Era *imayo* (popular songs) that later became Tsukushi koto and then modern koto's kumi-uta music.[7]

6. The Format of Continuity in Hogaku Compositions

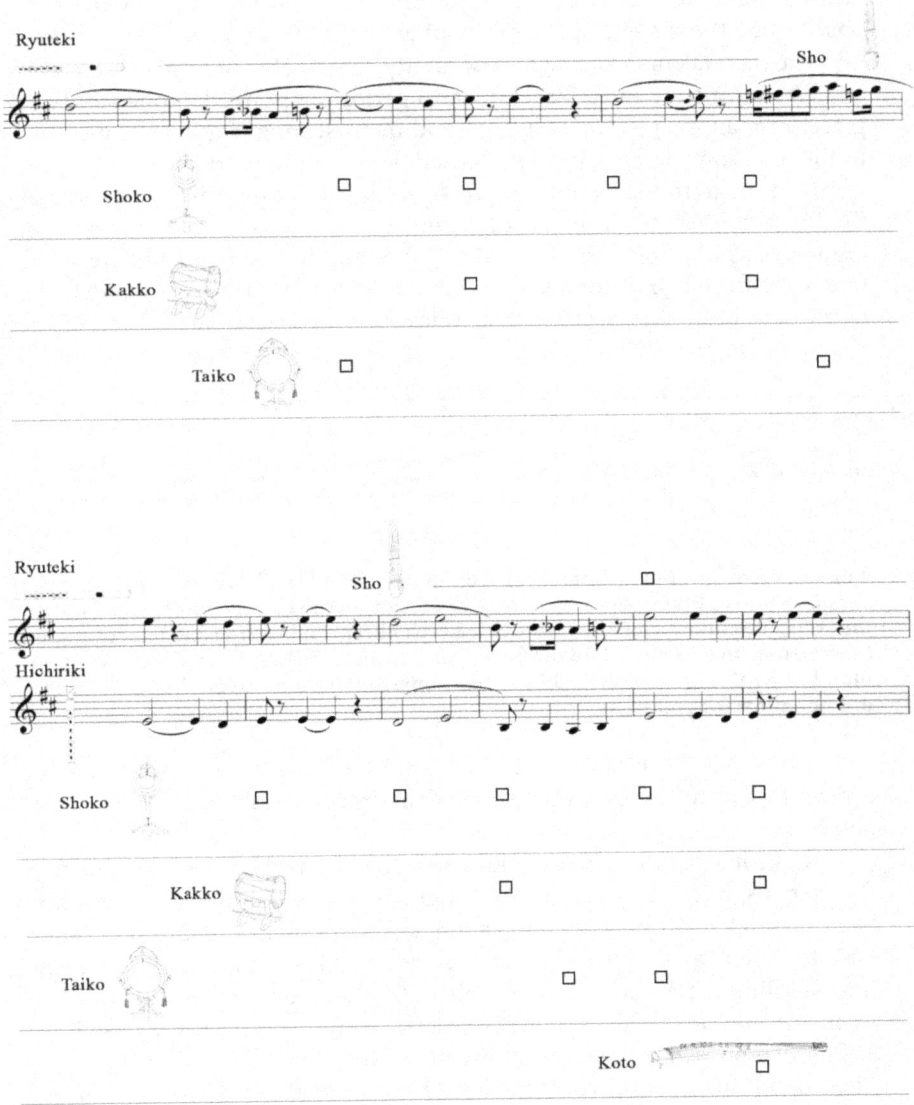

Figure 6.2: Entrance of the Instruments in *Ettenraku*. There is no excuse not to follow gagaku music. Many cues are given; one of them is the individual entrance and exit of the different instruments. The squares in the diagram indicate where each instrument plays in the score.

From the 1600s to the 1800s, thirty-one other kumi-uta koto pieces were composed using the same template of six songs with sixty-four beats per section.[8] Like the way wakan-roei songs are similarly constructed in form and melody, all kumi-uta also sound alike. How can a performer remember one kumi-uta piece from another? Tominari Seijo said the first song triggers the memory to the next song and the next as learned during childhood.[9]

The diagram for *Fuki* in progressively smaller boxes visually illustrates the jo-ha-kyu effect. Each stanza begins with a *kakezume* pattern (or K in Figure 6.3: Lyrics of *Fuki*) from the first to the third poems but from the fourth, fifth, and sixth poems the *warizume* W techniques accommodate the faster pace of the kyu section. The lyrics show precisely the location of the K and W patterns in Table 7.

Poem 1*	2	3	4	5	6
Kakezume introduces phrase	Kakezume	Kakezume	Kakezume	Warizume	Warizume

*Length indicated by length of boxes

Table 7: Format of *Fuki* (Butterbur). The shortening of the boxes indicates that the music imperceptibly speeds up. Every kumi-uta piece is similar in structure with the koto kakezume technique introducing each phrase and section and later changing to warizume to accommodate the faster pace. At first the kumi-uta pieces were popular, but by the 1800s they had lost their appeal. For composers, the strict format did not allow for creativity.

I insert an E (for end) as the cliché-phrase alerts listeners to the end of a verse that occurs at the conclusion of the Introduction and poems 1, 3, 4, and 5.

Kumi-uta pieces were so popular that this format became a requirement for every aspiring composer. However, by the end of the 1700s, the structure became uninteresting and tedious and the *so-Kengyo* (head) of the Tōdō Shoku Yashiki, Yasunaga Kengyo (d. 1779), decreed that his kumi-uta piece was the last one. But as tradition ran deep, Yamada ryu's founder, Yamada Masami, wrote *Hatsune no Kyoku* and added one more kumi-uta piece to establish himself as a composer. When koto music of the 1600s was revived in the 1800s, Mitsuzaki Kōtō (d. 1847) composed *Aki Kaze no Kyoku* (Composition on the Autumn Wind)[10] to restore both the kumi-uta and the dan-mono formats. The first half is a dan-mono that can be played with *Rokudan* with a minor tuning adjustment. The second half is a kumi-uta with six poems introduced by the kakezume pattern as in the old kumi-uta format. Could Mitsuzaki's piece be the last kumi-uta? Henceforth, other koto pieces with a collection of poems are not in the strict sense of the six songs within established techniques, but in the tegoto-mono format (see the discussion on tegoto-mono that follows).[11]

6. The Format of Continuity in Hogaku Compositions

Intro. K Fuki to iu mo K kusa no na	Fuki, as it is called, is a name of a plant
K Myoga to iu mo Kkusa no na	Myoga, as it's called, is the name of an herb.
K Fuki jisai K toku arite	The names grant good fortune,
K Myoga arasa Ktamaeya.E	of wealth and divine protection.
1.KHaru no hana no K kinkyoku	Spring flowers played on the koto in
K Kafuraku ni K Ryukaen	"Wafuraku" and "Ryukuwaen."
Ryukaen no uguisu wa	In "Ryukaen" the warbler
K Onaji kyoku wo sahe zuru.	sing a familiar melody.
2.K Tsuki no mae no K shirabe wa	Before the moon, music of the
K Yo samu wo tsuguru K akikaze.	cool night is the late autumn wind.
Kumoi no Karigane wa	Flying in formation,
K Kotoji ni otsuru K koegoe.	geese's cries echo down on koto bridges.
3.K Choseiden no K uchi niwa	Inside Choseiden
K Shunji wo K tomeri.	Spring and autumn reside.
Furomon no mae ni wa	In front of Furan gate
Tsuki no W kage oso shi. E	moonlight glide ever so slowly.
4. K Kokiden no K hosodono ni	Standing in the narrow corridor of Kokiden
K Tatazumu wa K taredare	who are they? [They are}
Oborozukiyo no naishi no kami	Oborozukiyo, the head lady-in-waiting,
Hikaru W Genji no Taisho.E	and the Shining Captain Genji.
5.K Taso ya kono K yachu ni	Who is that at midnight
W saitaru kado wo W tataku wa	knocking at my door? Even if he
tataku tomo W yomo akeji W	continues knocking, I will not answer
yoi no yakusoku nakereba E	for he has made no appointment with me.
6. W Shichi W seki no W heifu mo	The height of the seven shaku screen—
O W doraba nado ka W koezaran?	Can you not leap over?
Raryou no W tamoto mo	Won't your silk sleeves only rip away
Hikaba nado ka K kirezaran?	if you should tug hard enough?

Figure 6.3: Lyrics of *Fuki*. *Fuki* or Butterbur was composed by Yatsuhashi Kengyo (1600–1684). Only the introductory verse from *Ettenraku* occurs in this piece. The other verses from one to four are from the *Tale of Genji*. The fifth verse is possibly from Sei Shonagon's *Makura Shoshi*, and the sixth is from a Chinese story. Frequently used koto patterns are marked with K for kakezume, W for warizume, and E for the stereotypical ending.

Figure 6.4: Ending or Coda Passage for *Fuki* Verses. Most kumi-ta verses end with this coda. A listener can hear this familiar passage and be alerted that a new song will begin with either the *kakezume* or *warizume* passage.

1*	2	3	4	5	6	1	2	3	4	5	6
Dan (sections 1-6)						Uta (songs 1-6)					

*Length indicated by length of boxes

Table 8: Format of *Aki Kaze no Kyoku*. In an effort to go back to the good old days of pure koto music, the two early formats of dan-mono and kumi-uta were combined into one long piece, which did not foster any copycats. This elegant sounding composition has a quality that endures. The dan-mono section has a particularly ancient feel to it. The six poems concern the eighth-century Genso Kotei, whose infatuation with Yohiki (Yang Kei Fei) led to the demise of his kingdom.

Koto's dan-mono. The *dan-mono* (section pieces) is also foreign in origin with no singing. With fifty-two beats per section, the melodic contour of every section is a variation of the melody introduced in the first section. Only *Midare* (Ten Sections), which is called "Mix-up," deviates from the prescribed number of beats and the melodic pattern expected in dan-mono. The shortening of the boxes in Tables 8 and 9 shows the jo-ha-kyu effect in the tempo.

Titles	1*	2	3	4	5	6	7	8	9	10
Rokudan										
Hachidan										
Midare										

*Length of instrumental sections indicated by length of boxes

Table 9: Format for *Dan-mono* Pieces. Early koto pieces from foreign lands have a strict structure. The melody curves up and down like a skewed curve within 54 beats. Since the *uta* is central to Japanese music, dan-mono pieces were considered frivolous and labeled *tsuke-mono* (appendages).

Rokudan (Six Sections) is played most frequently and is practically synonymous to koto music. *Midare* (Ten Sections or Mix-up) and *Hachi dan* (Eight Sections) are played occasionally. *Kudan* (Nine Sections) is seldom played for it is basically *Rokudan* with a *kando* (connection) that links to repeating sections 4, 5, and 6 to total 9 sections, or *Kudan*. With dan-mono and kumi-uta type pieces linked to court music having Chinese origins, the koto's venture into the truly Japanese sphere occurs around the turn of the 1700s through blind musicians who played shamisen melodies on the koto. By doing so, shamisen melodies changed the direction, repertory, and techniques on the koto.

Japanese Influence on the Format of Japanese Buddhist Chants, Biwa and Noh Music

Buddhist chant format. Buddhist sutras from the Asian continent are chanted on the same pitch in an even tempo and differ from the Japanese sutras like *Shoshinge*, which is melodic. Composed by Shinran Shonin the *Shoshinge* has 120 lines of text that move up and down the IN scale. The words unroll in an indigenous sense of the flowing river water. In the overall jo-ha-kyu sense of the chants, mini-jo-ha-kyu occurs within each section.

The head priest begins *Shoshinge* by striking a hollow resonating bell setting the pitch and tempo. He chants the title of the sutra. The tempo depends on the occasion, faster and lighter for oneself or for inducting a novitiate, or measured and very stately for funerals and memorial services. Lines 1 through 92 move in jo-ha-kyu; at line 93 the chant goes back to the jo-tempo (slow), and the priest rings the bell again to set the pitch and tempo for the last section that also moves in jo-ha-kyu. The bell at the end of the sutra evokes the mantra, "*namu amida butsu*" repeated six times. Immediately following are six wa-sans[12] or the melodic waka-type songs interspersed with four or six repetitions of the "*namu amida butsu*" mantra.

The sutras of different Buddhist sects are led similarly with a presiding priest signaling the tempo to the congregation by sounding the hollow or high metallic bell. Usually, percussive instruments accompanied the songs that were sung by the masses. Musical instruments such as the koto and biwa were not accessible to the commoners as the koto belonged to courtiers and the biwa was the providence of the biwa-hoshi who were associated with temples and sang about the Gempei War.

Biwa music format. Modern biwa music came directly from blind priests who chanted the sutra with the instrument. Upon learning the narration of the *Tale of the Heike*, the format and chant-like singing style of the Japanese Buddhist sutra affected the format. The music begins with *ginsho* (declamation of the title of piece, like the title of a Buddhist sutra), and then moves to the body of the piece, the *rosho* (recitation) and then the *eisho* (aria) similar to the melodic wa-sans, and ends with the coda.

Biwa singing, as mentioned in Chapter 5 regarding *Nasu no Yoichi* of Heike biwa and *Ogi no Mato* (Fan Target) of the Satsuma biwa style, combines both narrative and lyrical aspects. Although Satsuma biwa is dramatic in style compared with Heike biwa, the structure of both styles is similar with the lyrics moving the drama in jo-ha-kyu.

Noh music format. The subject of many noh plays is from the biwa repertory based on heroes and heroines of the Heian Era. Noh, however, boasts of jo-ha-kyu in every aspect of its theater, beginning with the order of the program, the performance on stage, position on the bridge and stage,

	Jo	Ha	Kyu	Jo	Ha	Kyu	Jo	Ha	Kyu
Bell begins line 1 by the priest.	Congregation joins in for 92 lines. At the end of ¾ of the text and on line 93, the bell is rung			On line 93, the bell rings to reset to a faster pace and higher pitch.			*Bell: Namu amida butsu* is repeated 6½ times	6 different *wasans* with 6 or more mantras in between. Priest rings to finish.	

	Jo		Ha			Kyu
"Nasu no Yoichi"	Ginsho: Declamatory		*Rosho*: Recitation in pitch		*Eisho: Aria*	Coda
"Ogi no mato"	Ginsho: Declamatory		*Rosho*: Recitation in pitch		*Eisho: Aria*	Coda

Table 10: Format of the Buddhist sutra (*Shoshinge*) and Biwa Music. The biwa-hoshi music and *Shoshinge* share the same chant-like quality and format of Buddhist music. Like Buddhist sutra chanting, the piece is named and then moves through the text in jo-ha-kyu, slowing down at the very end with a coda.

phrase of a chant, and rhythm of the instruments.[13] Other theaters like bunraku and kabuki also follow this overall structure set by this respected theater.

With so many components to the noh play from actors, *utai-ji* (chorus), to the hayashi, how can the musicians know what and when to play?[14] Fortunately, similar to kagura music, the instrumentalists need only to learn patterns for five basic passages in addition to other special passages necessary to enhance a particular play. Basically the five passages are[15]:

1. Prelude and Entrance music
2. Transition music
3. Descriptive mood or action music, such as for a battle scene
4. Dance music
5. Exit music

The noh play begins *jo* (slow) with the appearance of the *waki* (secondary character); the hayashi of flute and drums plays the entrance music to set the patterns. The waki makes a self-introduction to set the scene and provide the reason for being at a particular location. He then retires to the waki pillar

6. The Format of Continuity in Hogaku Compositions

(right front).[16] The entrance music plays again for the *shi-te* (protagonist) which picks up speed for the *ha* section of the play. The shi-te makes a self-introduction after the bridgeway on stage by the shi-te pillar. The two characters converse and the protagonist reveals his true identity—he is a god, a ghost of notable person of the area—(there may be descriptive mood or dance music) while the *utai* (chorus) aids the shi-te in song and dance. When the shi-te leaves the stage to change costumes, the musicians play transition music. In most noh plays, a kyogen actor appears and explains in the vernacular what has transpired. The kyogen's monologue has no instrumental accompaniment but when the protagonist reappears, the instruments pick up the action at the *kyu* section. In the denouement the shi-te, usually freed in the Buddhist sense, leaves the stage to the exit music. The musicians exit quietly; they had all brought a drama with music of "brief beauty ... pure continuance ... never to be repeated."[17]

Kunio Komparu charts the shortest noh play, *Shojo*, about a sáke elf who imbibes sáke and ends up doing a tipsy dance. Five types of music (as listed earlier) correspond with the action on stage. The Japanese is in bold italics with the translation and action in the noh play immediately beneath. Additional elements, such as an extra dance or plot lines and the kyogen actor's explanation of the play, lengthen the play (see Table 11).[18]

Jo		Ha					Kyu	
Shirabe	*Nori-bue*	*Nanori*	*Machi-utai,*	*Sagari-ha*	*Kake ai*	*Issei*	*Jo or Chu no mai Shi-te*	*Kiri*
Prelude by instruments	(flute) Waki entrance music	Waki's self-intro (flute/2 drums)	Waiting song	Shi-te's entrance music	Exchange song	Preparing to dance	Dances (Taicho drum)	Finale

Table 11: Format of a One-Act Noh Play. Having sections differentiated to denote the activities of the drama, the overall format is jo-ha-kyu. The play begins with the introduction of the character and purpose, and then gradually moves faster through the drama to its finale, ending quietly.

In addition to being part of a noh play, in between the noh dramas, delightful kyogen skits provide comic relief. The format of kyogen plays is similar to the noh plays as the two theaters are like twin theaters, coming from the same zygote (see Chapter 5, endnote 34). However, only a handful of kyogen plays have a hayashi or a chorus accompaniment. The actor's job is to make all illusions with his actions, words, songs, and onomatopoetic sounds. Preserved in kyogen are typical Japanese Muromachi Era folk songs where melodies driven by the lyrics are rarely repeated through the entire song (see Figure 5.11: *Okyagari Kobooshi* and Figure 4.4: Wa-san No. 3 *Ge datsu no kourin* and *Hana no Sode*). Through the songs and satirical nature of kyogen plays, man's foibles are exposed and pompous lords, *yamabushi* (mountain priest), demons, and supernatural beings are deflated to mere mortals. At the end, the characters run off, yielding to the human condition that is forever unresolved.

	Hon sarugaku Kyogen	Sarugaku no noh
Format	Jo-ha-kyu, enter character, states problem, tries to resolve problem, chase off stage	Jo-ha-kyu, enter waki, shi-te enters, the two converse, the shi-te leaves, kyogen retells problem, shi-te enters as true self, finds peace, exits.
Stage & costume	Minimal props, characters are identified by costume	Minimal props, characters are identified by costume
Story line	The human condition, the foible of ordinary people and the pompous	Heroes and heroine of the Heike downfall, characters from the *Genji Tales* and popular Japanese and Chinese legends
Characters or categories of plays	Servant (Taro Kaja), priests, Provincial lords, blind men or priests, women, son-in-law, demons, con men	God, warriors, women, deranged people, supernatural
Songs	Popular songs of the Muromachi Era, some with hayashi	Poetic libretto, with chorus and hayashi accompaniment setting the scene, emotion, action.
Resolution	*Aware*, (pathos) of human condition	Buddhist understanding that attachment brings problems

Table 12: Relationship of Hon-sarugaku (Kyogen) and Sarugaku no Noh (Noh). The two theaters are similar in format, intent, and production but not content. Kyogen plots bring gods and demons to the human level and reveal human nature with all its foibles. The plays may be boisterous or poignant, but they are truthful. As kyogen plays are not serious, noh actors looked down on kyogen actors. Even noh connoisseurs take intermission during a kyogen play.

Nohgaku addressed the upper samurai class, and new theatrical ventures like bunraku and kabuki emulated it, which explains why Japanese theaters are similar in format and vocalization. But the biggest difference of the Edo Era theaters is the shamisen introduced in the mid–1500s. The shamisen became the sound of the common Edo man only after blind biwa musicians made the instrument manageable to play with a repertory based on commoner songs.

Japanese Format on Lyrical and Narrative Music of the Edo Era for Shamisen and Koto

Kumi-uta of sangen/shamisen.[19] The remodeled Chinese *sansen* was interchangeably called *sangen* or *shamisen* and its first major repertory, the *kumi-uta* (collection of songs), came from the songs of the people. Thus structurally it is freer with as many as one to fifteen songs in a piece, so unlike the restricted six songs per section of the court-based koto kumi-uta.

Ishimura Kengyo (d. 1642) with student Torazawa Kengyo (d. 1654) compiled the first seven *honte-gumi* (main collection) and later Yanagawa Kengyo (d. 1680) expanded the genre with *hade-gumi* (flashier collections),[20] *ura gumi* (back collection), and *hi-gumi* (secret collection). The songs describe the activities of ordinary people; thirty-one sangen kumi-uta survive today.[21] Sangen kumi-uta begins with three-note introductory notes of the tuning like Tsugaru shamisen music.

Type	Collection	Compositions
Main	HONTE-gumi	7 pieces by Ishimura Kengyo (d. 1642) and Torazawa Kengyo (d. 1654)
Flashier	HADE-gumi	7 pieces by Yanagawa Kengyo (d. 1690)
Other	URA-gumi	7 pieces by Yanagawa Kengyo
Secret	HI-gumi	10 pieces by others

Table 13: Types of Sangen Kumi-uta. Each instrument has its proprietary compositions. For the sangen, their *kumi-uta* (collection of songs) belongs to them. Today thirty-one exist composed by the early founders and their successors. The list is divided into *hon-te* (main), *ha-de* (flashier), *ura* (back), and *hi* (secret) pieces. Secret pieces are reserved for promising students.

The title for sangen kumi-uta pieces comes from one of the poems that is not necessarily thematically related. Ishimura's first kumi-uta piece, *Ryukyu gumi* (collected songs from Ryukyu/Okinawa) does not mention Ryukyu (Okinawa) in any of the verses.[22] Some people surmise the songs came from the Ryukyu, or that Ishimura's mother was from Ryukyu. The jo-ha-kyu effect of each verse is shown in the following diagram with progressively shorter boxes. The first verse is about love with the moon, the second is about love and pine trees, then the third is about the joys of love and the fourth about love's trials, but suddenly the fifth and sixth verses change topic to an umbrella and selling wood. The incongruous collection of songs may have provoked some composers to create compositions with one long song on one topic, as this is what eventually happened.

Sangen lyrical format of naga-uta (long songs), ha-uta, and tegoto-mono. The sangen kumi-uta evolved into one long song called naga-uta. *Naga* (long) *uta* (songs) became the basis for *ha-uta* (popular songs) where they are structurally the same. The music unrolls like Shinto ritual music

Song 1	2	3	4	5	6
Lover is like the full moon	Love like wind in Shiga pine	I am happy	Love is like twisting mountain	Umbrella	Wood for sale

Table 14: *Ryukyu gumi* Format. Like the koto kumi-uta with six songs, the shamisen collection also has unrelated lyrics but differs with compositions having an unlimited number of songs, some as many as fifteen.

and ancient songs where each word and its meaning shape the melody. The result is a composition with unfolding melodies from the beginning to the end.

The term naga-uta is problematic because the same word *nagauta* applies to music created by sighted musicians associated with kabuki. In Japanese, it is distinguished by the second kanji, *uta* (song), which is 歌 or 唄. The hyphenated Kansai[23] lyrical or ji-uta naga-uta uses the first kanji for uta as in 長歌 and the Edo narrative music, *nagauta* (without a hyphen) uses the other kanji for uta as in 長唄.[24] Of the musical styles, naga-uta is refined and nagauta is flashier and appealing and fortunately not as confusing as the presence or absence of a hyphen!

But to confuse the issue (again), ji-uta naga-uta of Kansai originated in the Kanto or Edo region in the 1680s. Sayama Kengyo,[25] a blind musician from the Kansai (Kyoto/Osaka) region, composed the first naga-uta while in Edo from the popular song *Katabachi*. *Katabachi* was taken to Osaka to become the model used by Nogawa Kengyo (d. 1717) to compose *Ne no Hi*. *Ne no Hi* became the prototype for other naga-uta compositions known for high-quality, up-lifting praises of Japan's scenery and fine products. Today fifty naga-uta exist with only ten to fifteen played with any frequency (see the top half of Figure 6.5).

In naga-uta pieces, the voice and sangen begin together. The popular naga-uta *Kurokami* is an example (see Figure 7.4 for the lyrics). The instrumental *ai-no-te* (short instrumental interlude) punctuates the song occasionally to enhance the mood. In an intuitive way, each composition is recognizable by its tuning, hints of recurring theme-like patterns, and overall mood or atmosphere led by the lyrical theme.

Sangen ji-uta naga-uta pieces were so popular that it was not long before blind musicians transposed them onto the koto and by doing so Ikuta Kengyo founded the Ikuta-ryu koto style.[26] The combination was a marriage with the koto as the complacent bride to the dominant shamisen and henceforth, every new composition of *naga-uta* (long songs), *ha-uta* (popular songs), and later the *tegoto-mono* (instrumental interlude) became part of koto music.[27] Only kumi-uta pieces are proprietary to the respective instruments.

Naga-uta topics are celebratory, of longevity, prosperity, scenery

- *Ne no Hi* by Nogawa Kengyo: Emphasis on eternity, pine, Imperial reign, peaceful waters, fledgling cranes, nests, turtle, blessed place, parent tree over small pine tree, glorious sight of smoking chimneys (people cooking)
- *Sarashi* by Fukakusa Kengyo: Scene of linen bleaching in the Uji River with yards of cloth looking like the milky way. Area scenery is extolled like the Sahi mountains, Suruga's Fuji, and waves on Kojimagaska, Fushimi, Takeda, Yodo and Toba
- *Tamagawa* by Kuniyama Koto: Scene of Ide Castle with mention of seasonal flowers like the yamabuki for spring, white unohana for summer, hagi in autumn. The moon and snow make the winder scene. Also mentioned are singing plovers, bleaching of cloth, and six other rivers.
- *Miyama jishi* by Kikuoka Kengyo: An auspicious piece that refers to the lion and Kagura dances and seasons like Ise Shrine at spring, Isuzu river, Sekidera and fireflies at summer, Tobaguchi for maple leaves, and Asama mountains with snow capped Mt. Fuji.
- *Echigojishi* by Minezaki Koto: Lists specialties from the Echigo area like their charming dialect, net fishing at Naoezuno, lovers at Itouwo River, their famous sheer white fabric and the auspicious lion that is found with the peony flower, a sign of happiness.

Ha-uta topics are varied from serious to comical and come from different sources

1. Upbeat lyrics "Kyoku Nezumi," "Egao," "Wasure Shoka"
2. Narrative from gidayu of Bunraku theater
3. Narratives from Eikan-bushi, Handayu, and Shigedayu of Bungo bushi
4. Saku-momo Narratives of Aku-mono (vulgar) and Odoke-mono (comical)
5. Zukushi pieces that thematically concerns one subject
    - "Matsu zukushi" (Pines) lists all famous pine trees in Japan and their significance. These pieces are played as openers to insure an auspicious performance.
    - "Tsubaki zukushi" lists Japan's famous camellias.
    - "Taki zukushi" lists waterfalls
    - "Machi zukushi" concerns famous places in Osaka
    - "Ko zukushi" (Incense perfume) lists various incenses. Ko-zukushi pieces are performed at memorial services.
    - "Shiri zukushi" about "ends and end suffixes" including the de rierre that is music of questionable taste
    - "Heso no Jukkai" (Ten navels). As more women learned how to play the koto and shamisen, such music became unsuitable. One will recall that ji-uta composers were blind men

Figure 6.5: Naga-uta and Ha-uta Lyric Topics. Forty-one naga-uta pieces exist today. Listed are those played most frequently. Notice that the topics praise the country, goods, and places noted for scenic beauty. Ha-uta pieces number in the hundreds and range from celebratory topics to tea house escapades, including even vulgar subjects.

During the late 1980s, I met avant-garde kotoist Sawai Kazue who said that all classical music today was once popular music of the past. She is correct, for in looking back in history at Heian Era saibara, wakan-roei, and imayo, biwa, noh, sangen kumi-uta, and narrative genres (to be discussed here) were all once popular songs. Ha-uta of the Edo Era is no exception. The word came from *hayari-uta* (popular songs), which was shortened to ha-uta. Its inspiration came from *shibai-uta* (stage drama) of the Genroku Era (1688–1704).

Jo	Ha	Kyu
Naga-uta (long song) and *ha-uta* melody changes throughout the piece with the mood of the lyrics		

Table 15: Format of Naga-uta and Ha-uta Music. Identifying whether a piece is naga-uta or ha-uta is difficult. In both, the words direct the course of the music that moves in jo-ha-kyu. The difference appears in the choice of lyric topic.

Ha-uta is hard to discern from naga-uta because they share the same format, singing style, and instrumentation. The big giveaway is the topic of the lyrics (Figure 6.5: Naga-uta and Ha-uta Lyric Topics). Naga-uta lyrics praise the country, regional specialties, and scenery while ha-uta lyrics are about any subject from fun comic songs and questionable topics to sad tear-jerkers about the plight of yujyos (prostitutes) and geishas. The composer who set the trend towards sad, morose songs was Utagi Kengyo (mid–1700s) with *Na no Hana* (Mustard Flower), a short beginner's piece taught before learning *Kurokami*. When I learned *Na no Hana* as a child and later learned *Mama no Kawa* (see Figure 6.6: Lyrics to *Mama no Kawa*), I enjoyed singing the words "*nano ha ni cho mau*" (butterflies dancing on the mustard flowers) and "*kawaii, kawai no karasu*" (cute, cute crows). I only learned much later that the song was a metaphor of a *kawaisoo* (pitiful) yujyo's life as she went from one customer to another.[28]

These sad ha-uta songs written from the 1750s to the 1800s were cathartic because the miserable condition of the prostitute's life was a reflection of the commoner's intolerable condition caused by famine and economic hardship.[29] Instead of easing the situation, the Tokugawa government dealt harshly by imposing stricter sumptuary laws and higher taxes. A rich merchant's wife was forbidden to flaunt a luxurious kimono that outdid that of a noblewoman's kimono. Precious silk that could be made into sumptuous kimonos was woven coarsely to look like humbler fabric. The government censored writing and publishing. Social mobility was frozen, including any opportunity to better oneself through marriage outside of one's class. Some poor farmers

6. The Format of Continuity in Hogaku Compositions

1. Yume ga ukiyo ka	Is this a dream or reality?
2. Ukiyo ka yume ka	Or reality, or a dream?
3. Yume cho wo sato ni	"Dreamland"
4. Sumina gara	is where I live.
5. Hito me wa koi wo	My affection flows
6. Omoi gawa	like a river.
7. Uso mo nasake mo	Lies, sympathy,
8. Tada kuchisaki de	come merely from my lips.
9. Ichi ya nagare no	The destiny of
10. Imose no kawa wo	one night stand lovers
11. Sono mizu kusaki	is like moving water—
12. Kokoro kara	of uncommitted hearts.
i. (tegoto)	(interlude)
13. Yoso no kawori wo	The fragrance of another
14. Eri sode guchi ni	on his sleeves and collar
15. Tsukete kayo waba	lingers as he visits.
16. Nan no ma, ma,	I joke, "My, my,
17. Kawai, Kawai no	how cute, very cute!"
18. Karasu no koe ni	like a crow's call—
19. Samete kuyashiki	awakening me
20. Mama no kawa	to this river of life.

Figure 6.6: Lyrics to *Mama no Kawa* (River's Life Course). *Mama no Kawa* was composed by Kikuoka Kengyo and Matsuno Kengyo in about 1830 and used in the opening scene of the play *Tsubosaka*. A *yujyo* must go to one customer after another. She is requited when she accepts her course in life that flows onward like the water in a river.

sold daughters to prostitution when trapped in an untenable economic situation. Even as the lyrics of ha-uta are outdated by today's standards, these pieces endure and appear on concert programs because of their excellent compositional construction. The pieces are *Yuki* (Snow; Figure 1.2), *Mama no Kawa* (River's Course), *Kaji Makura* (Rudderless Pillow), and *Sue no Chigiri* (The Broken Promise), among others. The songs end with resignation and Buddhist acceptance and redemption because there was no other recourse from the trapped feeling.

The topics of ha-uta's lyrics held widespread appeal as they were authored by a variety of people, including playwright Chikamatsu Harima, novelist Ihara Saisaku, the occasional *tsujins* (frequenter of the Pleasure Quarters), and *geishas* (*gei* is art, *sha* is performer).[30] The late musician Kunie Fujii (1930–2006) particularly liked *Kusunoto* by Kubi Nobu, a Gion geisha.[31] Her lyrics, she said, have a gentler perspective about love unlike the contrived situation written by men.[32] Geishas sing *ko-uta* (short songs) in a lighter sensuous style and also naga-uta and ha-uta composed by blind musicians for it was at the teahouses of the Pleasure Quarters that entertainers converged.

The aristocracy, lords, and samurai had their highfaluting noh and gagaku music—but some samurai were known to sneak off to enjoy the activities at the Pleasure Quarters.

UKIGUSA WA	Floating grass
SHIAN HOKA NO	mindlessly
SASOU MIZU	flows with the water.
KOI GA UKIYO KA	Is love, the Floating World or
UKIYO GA KOI KA	is the Floating World, love?
CHOTO KIKITAI	I want to ask
MATSU NO KAZE	the wind in the pine,
TOE DOKO TAEZU	but here is no answer—[even from]
YAMA HOTOTOGISU	the mountain little cuckoo and the
TSUKI YO WA	moonlit night.
MONO NO YARUSENAKI	I am at loss but
SHAKU NI URESHIKI	I am happiest
OTOKO NO CHIKARA	with a strong man who
JITTO TE NI TE WO	gently holds my hands
NAN NI MO IWAZU	without saying anything—
FUTARI SHITE	just the two of us
TSURU KAYA NO MINO	under the mosquito net.

Figure 6.7: Lyrics to *Kusunoto*. Unlike lyrics written by a man who imagines a woman's feelings, *Kusunoto* is by the geisha Kubi Nobu who longs to know what love is. The simplest gesture of sitting beside her man is what makes her warm and happy.

As different types of ji-uta music paraded through the Edo Era beginning with kumi-uta, naga-uta, and ha-uta, I call attention to the fact that each style appeared fifty years before it became the dominant format. For example, the ha-uta appeared around 1750 and peaked in the early 1800s with the piece *Yuki* (Snow). The tegoto-mono format also appeared before ha-uta peaked and then become the standard format. The tegoto-mono format lasted through the first half of the twentieth century.

Format of the tegoto-mono (instrumental interlude). By the 1800s the tegoto-mono pieces took hold (no doubt as an extension of the *ai-no-te* instrumental interlude) during a song or from *gin no shirabe* (silver interlude) of the koto kumi-uta.[33] For blind composers the extended instrumental interlude was a playground to explore and intellectualize musical ideas. If a piece did not have a tegoto, another composer inserted it later.[34]

The overall tegoto-mono format is jo-ha-kyu with three sections: *mae-uta* (song at the beginning), followed by the tegoto-mono (instrumental interlude), and ending with the *ato-uta* (continuation of the song). The

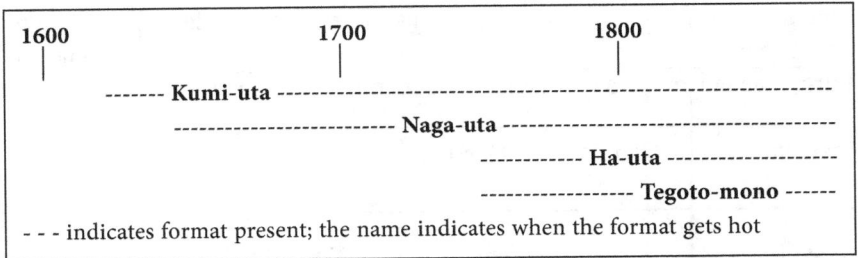

Figure 6.8: Appearance of Different Formats of Ji-uta Music. Ji-uta pieces are specifically the work of blind musicians of the Kansai area. From the kumi-uta format, experiments with new formats such as naga-uta, ha-uta, and tegoto-mono appeared fifty years before they became popular and peaked.

mae-uta is longer by at least two-thirds to three-quarters than the ato-uta. Within each section, mini-jo-ha-kyu exist like in the Buddhist chant, *Shoshinge*.

This versatile format allowed for many permutations (see Table 16: Various Permutations of the Tegoto-mono Format). The jo can begin with an introduction or directly with the mae-uta that accelerates to the ha tempo. Within the mae-uta there can be an *ai-no-te* (short instrumental interlude), sometimes called *tsunagi* (connector).

When the tegoto section starts, it can start right in or there may be a *makura* (pillow, or introduction to the tegoto), followed by the main body of the tegoto (see example 5 of Table 16). The tegoto can also have its own coda, *chirashi* (scattering), or go right into the ato-uta (again, see example 5). Often the chirashi is *omoshiroi* (fun, interesting).

Some tegoto is cordoned off into *dans* (sections) with two to five dans (see examples 3 through 8 of Table 16). Dan-awase pieces are composed so that different dans can be played together for a polyphonic effect (see examples 4 and 6 of Table 16). Sometimes the tegoto has a *naka-uta* (mid-song; see example 6 of Table 16). Some pieces have a second instrumental part called *kaede* (polyphonic embellishment) in addition to the main melody. Variations depend on the imagination and feeling of the composer.

Tegoto-mono pieces can be as short as three minutes, like *Sato no Ko* by Tomizaki Shunsho, or as long as thirty minutes, like *Yae Goromo* by Ishikawa Kōtō and *Shochikubai* by Mitsuhashi Kengyo. Yaezaki Kengyo specialized in adding the koto to many sangen pieces such the two just mentioned.

The versatile tegoto-mono format allowed for remarkably sophisticated compositions. The usual ensemble is one sangen with the main melody, and one koto accompanying it. The shakuhachi was added later to add the *san*

1. Mae uta (front song)	Tegoto (instrumental interlude)		ato uta (end song)
2. Intro, mae uta	makura (pillow) main tegoto chirashi		ato uta
3. Mae uta	Dan I Dan II Dan III		ato uta
4. Mae uta	Dan I Dan II (Dan awase) Dan II Dan I		ato uta
5. Intro mae uta	makura Dan I Dan II chirashi		ato uta
6. Intro mae uta	Dan I (naka uta) Dan II Dan II Dan I		ato uta
7. Mae uta	makura DAN I, II, III, IV, V		ato uta
8. Mae uta, tsunagi, naka uta	makura Dan I, Dan II, Dan III		ato uta

Table 16: Various Permutations of the Tegoto-mono Format. This structure of song, instrumental interlude, and continuation of the song dominates the koto repertory. A piece can be three to thirty minutes long when connections, two or three sections, introductory passages, a mid-song, and other elements are inserted in the basic structure. This format offers creative freedom to composers.

(third) instrument to become the *sankyoku* ensemble. Some compositions are composed for one sangen and two koto lines as in *Shochikubai*. *Echigo-jishi* has two sangen lines and two koto lines with each instrument having its own kaede (polyphonic embellishment) melody played around the main melody like a torsade necklace.

For music with so many independent melodic tracks, it is expected that every musician will know his part thoroughly—like the performers of the noh—so that during rehearsal references to the lyrics or to a specific section bring everyone together.[35] In putting sangen or several koto parts together, I often wondered if the tegoto-mono pieces were for the composers' pleasure or for the fun of the performers. I also wondered if listeners are able to discern and appreciate the complexities that are so much fun to play.

At the turn of the 1800s some musicians were unimpressed with multi-track compositions that twisted around the main melody and called it muddled music. Yoshizawa Kengyo II and Minezaki Kōtō went a step further and threw out the lead twang of the shamisen and composed pure koto pieces.[36] The deed was so outrageous by the standards of the day that the Tōdō Shoku Yashiki ostracized the two composers.[37]

Format of shakuhachi music. Shakuhachi has two categories of music: *hon-kyoku* (main pieces) and *gai-kyoku* (outside pieces). Hon-kyoku are exclusively for shakuhachi. Rather meditative in its flow, shakuhachi pieces unroll like a musical stream of consciousness. The piece *Shika no Tone* (Distant Cry of Deer) was analyzed for "themes" but such an exercise was futile. Gai-kyoku generally follows the sangen and koto music (discussed earlier), so as to add timbre to the sankyoku ensemble.

Japanese format on shamisen's narrative music used for theater. When the shamisen was first introduced, the powerful Tōdō Shoku Yashiki guild forbade blind musicians to teach and associate with sighted musicians for fear of degrading their art. Sighted musicians, however, learned enough shamisen techniques to strike out with their own -*bushi* (song) and rose or fell from the Edo scene like rock stars. Some styles were reworked to ji-uta music, adapted for bunraku and kabuki theater, or became part of a separate style of koto playing and were thus saved for posterity. Their music, coming from previous forms, also follows the jo-ha-kyu with ever-changing melodies as discussed in the next section.

Format of Narrative and Bushi (Song) Music for the Stage

Music of bunraku and kabuki are treated outside and separately from *utai-mono* (lyrical music) of ji-uta blind musicians but sighted musicians' *katari mono* (narrative music) and *bushi* (song style) came from the example set by blind musicians. At first, sighted musicians relied on the ji-uta style, but they soon added their own spin to songs that became recognizable depending on whether they came from the Kansai or Kanto regions. Kansai is known for the elegant music associated with the Kyoto/Osaka area that was Japan's cultural center until the mid-twentieth century. Kanto is the Edo area of present day Tokyo, noted for its rough frontiersmen who built the new capital. Music and art reflected the atmosphere of the two regions.

Narrative shamisen music also maintains the jo-ha-kyu of an aural scroll format. New music styles morphed from musicians who changed the Edo Era music (see Figure 6.9: Line of Subdued- and Strong-Style Singers). The shamisen line begins with its innovator, Ishimura Kengyo (d. 1642), who

Kamigata/Kansai	Kanto (Edo area)
Osaka (subdued)	Flashier, stronger
Kyoto (subdued, quieter, elegant)	Aragoto (warrior type)

Table 17: Regional Differences of Shamisen Music. People of the Kansai area of Kyoto and Osaka prefer elegance and understated expressions in their art. Kanto (the Edo area) was a frontier town where louder, stronger bravura expressions were preferred. Regional differences add variety and appeal to different musical tastes.

taught his student, Torazawa Kengyo (d. 1654), who taught Sawazumi Kengyo. Sawazumi Kengyo taught the sighted Minekiya Chizaburo (d. 1623) and Hikita Awajinojo (1632–1684).

The clue to who is the blind or sighted is the title in the names. Blind musicians are Kengyo or Kōtō, and *tayu* or *dayu*[38] and *jo* after or within the names are sighted musicians, such as Sugiyama Tangonojo[39] and Satsuma Joun. Sugiyama Tangonojo and Satsuma Joun replaced blind musicians in narrating *joruri* (narrations) for theater and led the way in developing two different styles of singing, one subdued and the other strong.

Strong style of singing. Satsuma Joun (1593–1671) of Edo is known for his impressive, strong flashy style. His student, Inoue Harimanojo (1632–1685) of Osaka, created Kimpira-bushi which is a strong flashier style that later became *Geki-bushi*. The impressive *Ozatsuma-bushi* is known for its even grander type of singing[40] suitable for the *aragoto* (heroic) style of Edo kabuki. In the story of today's bunraku music, Inoue Harimanojo (1632–1685) taught Uji Kaganojo (1636–1711) with whom Takemoto Gidayu (1651–1714) had studied for a short while. Uji Kaganojo wanted to be a noh actor, but the goal was beyond his reach since he was not born into a noh family. Nevertheless, he created a new style of joruri, arguing that it was noh with puppets because each season began with the same ritual dances of *Okina* and *Sambaso*. He also reworked new historical love dramas into the same five sections as in a noh drama and incorporated songs from the Heike biwa and *kowaka-mai* (popular and folk song). In this manner, noh was Kaganojo's initial influence but his innovations spawned a new theater that became popular around 1675.

Uji Kaganojo's fiercest competitor was Takemoto Gidayu[41](1651–1714), whose fame and fortune skyrocketed after teaming up with playwright Chikamatsu Monzaemon (1653–1725). The duo became synonymous with Osaka's puppet theater beginning in 1684. Noh plays and ancient legends adapted to bunraku attracted audiences, but the pièce de résistance was the dramatized

6. The Format of Continuity in Hogaku Compositions

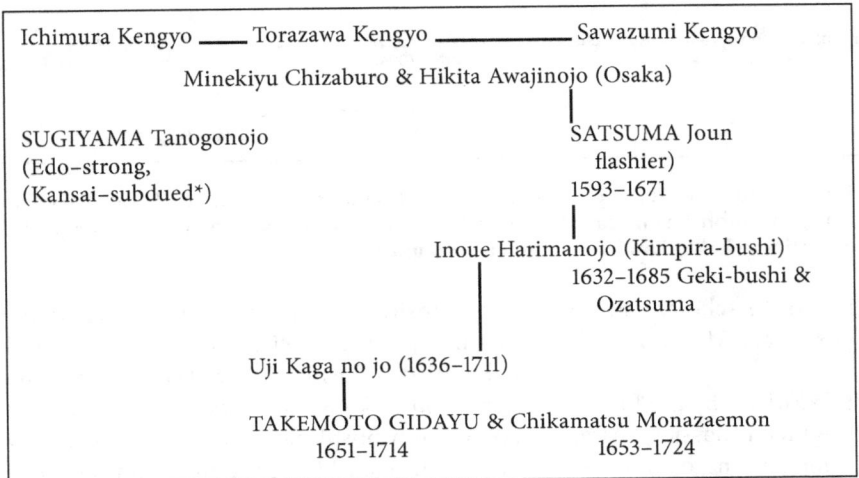

Figure 6.9: Line of Subdued- and Strong-Style Singers. Most people are not aware that bunraku and kabuki music originated with blind musicians of the Kengyo title. Sighted musicians split off into the subdued- and strong-styles with Sugiyama Tangonojo and Satsuma Joun, from whom emerged the legendary Takemoto Gidayu.

tabloids of actual events, like the *Love Suicides of Sonezaki, Love Suicides of Amijima,* and *Woman Killer and the Hell of Oil.* Takemoto Gidayu's strong singing style dominated bunraku to the point of calling the singing style gidayu.

For one play, many singers change places on a rotating dais between *dans* (acts/sections). A day's program begins with celebratory plays and then the classics. Today certain acts are performed like "Heitaro juke yori Kiyari no dan" (Heitaro and the Woodcutter) from *Sanjusangedo Munagi no yurai* or four acts from *Kokusenya Gassen,* especially "Senritake Toragi no dan" where a tiger appears, much to the audience's delight.[42] The best place to sit in a bunraku theater is near the musicians' dais. One can see the singer's every breath, facial expression, and even sweat.

Subdued style of singing. The term "subdued" for a singing style may sound unpromising, but the Japanese like *jo-hin na* (refined), understated music that has *aji* (good taste) and *sabi* (patina). The subdued style grew with Sugiyama Tangonojo. From him, the new bushi genres emerged to take the names of the originators, such as Hizen-bushi, Handayu-bushi, Katoh-bushi, and Itchu-bushi.

Masumi Katoh (1684-1725), creator of Katoh-bushi, was the son of a fish wholesaler of Nihonbashi who learned from Handayu. In 1717, at age 33, using a shamisen with narrower sao (pole), he split off from Handayu's school and began the custom of narrating behind screens in people's houses. Accord-

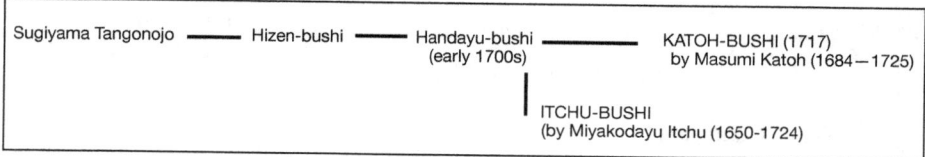

Figure 6.10: Early Line of Subdued Style of Shamisen Narrative Music. This line leads to Katoh-bushi and Miyako Itchu-bushi and includes many popular pieces essential to kabuki and Yamada-ryu koto music.

ing to the scholar Akira Hoshi, compositions by various Katoh-bushi composers are *Matsu no Uchi* by the first successor, *Mizu Jyoshi* by the second successor, *Yoru no Amigasa* by the third successor, and *Sukeroku Yakari no Edo Zakura* by the fourth successor. *Sukeroku* is one of kabuki's *Juhachi ban* (Eighteen Classics). After the sixth Katoh-bushi successor, there are no new compositions, only preservers. Yamahiko Genshiro is the eighth Katoh-bushi player. Katoh-bushi and Itchu-bushi have been incorporated in Edo nagauta and are the basis of Edo Yamada-ryu koto.[43] From Katoh-bushi and Itchu-bushi other offshoots of Tokiwazu, Tomimoto, and Kiyomoto emerged. Together with Kineya line of nagauta, it is hard to imagine kabuki and its buyo offshoot without them.

In America, we have performers considered outrageous and offensive. Edo Era Japan had Miyakoji Bungonojo (1660–1740). It was said his singing style instigated lovers to commit double suicide (see Figure 6.11: Later Line of Subdued Narrative Singers). His origin is traced to Kansai's Yamamoto Tosanojo (d. 1700), famous for his crying style. Tosanojo taught Okamoto Bunya in the 1680s and passed his sad style singing to Miyakodayu Itchu (1650–1724), founder of Itchu-bushi around 1704.[44] Miyakodayu Itchu's style was *jo-hin-na* (refined), or graceful, dignified, and *shibui* (astringently mature). His famous pieces are *Kyo Sukeroku* and *Yatsuhyakuya Shichi*, often performed on the kabuki stage. Itchu-bushi and Katoh-bushi combined in 1717 and became known as Azuma Joruri (Eastern narratives).

After Miyakodayu Itchu, we finally arrive at his notorious student from Kyoto, Miyakoji Bungonojo (1660–1740). In 1734, Miyakoji Bungonojo premiered the song *Nagoya Shinju* (Double Suicide of Nagoya) based on a true 1733 incident. The song became an overnight sensation. Young people swooned to hear him and even imitated his clothing, topknot hairstyle, and swagger. So sensuous was his singing, a popular saying arose that if the performer's clothing matched the performer's vocal style then Katoh-bushi singers would wear *kamishimo* (very formal shoulder wings), Geki singers would wear *hakama* (formal culottes) or a business suit, Handayu bushi singers would wear *haori* (informal jacket), gidayu singers

```
Yamamoto Tosanojo (d. 1700)
    |
Okamoto Bunya (1680s)
    |
Miyakodayu ITCHU (1650–1724) 1680 (Sukeroku play); style suitable for dance;
    portrays emotions
                1720 Miyako Bungonojo (1660–1740)
                        1747 TOKIWAZU Mojidayu (d. 1781) (Seki no to
                            Fuyumauba, Modorikago); male dance pieces
                            1748 TOMOMOTO Chikuzannojo (d. 1764);
                                more refined Tokiwazu; female dance pieces
                                and michiyuki
                                    1814 KIYOMOTO Enjudayu; lighter than
                                        Tomimoto; incorporates folk songs
```

Figure 6.11: **Later Line of Subdued Narrative Singers.** This branch brought about Itchu-bushi and the notorious Bungonojo, who in turn brought out the styles of Tokiwazu, Tomimoto, and Kiyomoto music often found accompanying buyo and kabuki plays.

would wear work clothes, but Bungo-bushi singers would wear nothing at all.[45]

In 1739, the government banned Miyakoji Bungonojo from performing, saying his songs were dangerous. His association with the deposed Muneharu of the Owari branch of the Tokugawa clan in 1730 may have been the real reason, since his disciple Miyakoji Mojitayu (d. 1781) continued to perform Bungonojo's songs.

From Miyakoji Mojitayu, three important shamisen styles emerged to supply music for the kabuki stage and *buyo* (dance). Mojitayu in 1747 changed his name to Tokiwazu Mojitayu and started the Tokiwazu line of shamisen players. Mojitayu's student, Tomimoto Buzendayu (1716–1764), also a student of Miyakoji Bungonojo, broke away in 1748 and began the Tomimoto School, a refined rendition of Tokiwazu music that appealed to women students. When Tomimoto Buzendayu died, his 11-year-old son became iemoto under the tutelage of Tomimoto Itsukidayu (1727–1802). In a rift of iemotos, the son broke away to begin the Kiyomoto line of shamisen players, taking the name Kiyomoto Enjudayu. Since the different styles are offshoots of the previous styles, all share a similar format unrolling in jo-ha-kyu (see Table 18).[46]

A very popular style that emerged during the Edo Era is the *nagauta*, which is attributed to Sayama Kengyo. Sayama Kengyo taught Kisaburo, the

Tokiwazu Shamisen

Jo		Ha		Kyu	
Maku aki	*Oki-uta*	*Hon-ban*	shamisen tuning in *hon, ni-agari, sansagari*	*Chirashi*	*Awari*
Curtain opener	Intro to piece	Main narration		Coda	End

Kiyomoto Shamisen

Jo		Ha		Kyu	
Oki	*Hanamichi*	*Kudoki*	Dance	*Chirashi*	*Dan-giri*
Intro	Bridge entrance	Speech, songs, and narrative		Coda	End

Table 18: Tokiwazu and Kiyomoto Shamisen Format. These two styles are offshoots of Miyako Bungonojo and so the format of their music follows a similar path. Only the terms differ.

first of the many Kineya line around the Genroku era (1688–1704). Nagauta music is a potpourri of song styles like kabuki plays and dance. It begins with the noh chant in the *oki* (introduction) section. The introduction is followed by the strong and grander Ozatsuma style that is interspersed with a stereotypical flashy shamisen interlude. Following the shamisen interlude is the lyrical nagauta style of singing of the *michiyuki* (travel section). Dialogue, lyrical-type singing, and dance music with a taiko drum build the drama. At the end, there is the recognizable *dan-giri* (coda). The lyrics move the story

Oki	Michiyuki	Mondo	Kudoki	Odori, Taiko-ji	Chirashi	Dan-giri
Intro	Enter	Dialogue	Lyrical	Taiko enters	Buildup	Coda
	Travel		Romantic song	Dance		

Nagauta shamisen for kabuki: "Suehirogari" form, also applies to "Kanjincho," "Renjishi," etc.

Table 19: Format of Naga-uta Shamisen Music. Naga-uta music borrows and melds different genres to relate a story or to use as dance music. Their stage presence is most impressive. Many singers and shamisen players sit on an elevated red dais across the back of the stage while the hayashi (drums and flutes) are seated on the floor below them.

and follow a jo-ha-kyu form (see Table 19) similar to a noh play with introduction, entrance of the actors, main plot with dialogue, songs and dances, and the end. *Suehirogari, Kanjincho* (Subscription List) and *Renjishi* (Lions) are popular examples.

The kabuki actor's success depends on his musicians from Tokiwazu's, Tomimoto's, Kiyomoto's, and Kineya's nagauta schools. One can tell which group is accompanying the actors by the color of kimono and where the musicians sit on stage. Tokiwazu musicians wear orangish-brown *kamishimo* (shoulder wings) and use a red music stand and sit opposite the *hanamichi* (runway) on a platform stage right; the Kiyomoto musicians wear green kamishimo and use a black music stand and sit on the right; the gidayu singers wear grayish kamishimo and sit to the right on an elevated dais similar to their location at the bunraku theater. The nagauta ensemble is the flashiest of all. They wear kamishimo in colors to match the theme or mood of the play (even pink kamishimo with cherry blossoms for *Musume Dojoji*) and sit on a red elevated dais that stretches across the entire back length of the stage. The shamisen musicians are to the left of the singers. The noh bayashi, or percussion section, sits below them on red cloth.

At times all three groups play for kabuki plays such as *Kumo no Ito* and *Adachigahara*. Called *sanpo-kakeai* (three narrative interchange), there are six Tokiwazu who sit in front of the *kuromizu* (hidden stage) by the hanamichi; two gidayu musicians sit stage right, and twelve nagauta musicians sit across the length of the stage.[47]

Yamada-ryu koto. As mentioned earlier, the -bushi styles of the Edo Era exist today because they were integrated into bunraku, kabuki, buyo, ji-uta, and in Yamada-ryu koto in Edo. Edo in the 1600s was a frontier town with no koto players. To fill the void, the *so-Kengyo* (chief Kengyo) of the Tōdō Shoku Yashiki, Yasumura Kengyo (d. 1790), sent Hasetomi Kengyo to start a school. His first student was a physician, Yamada Shokoku, who adopted a talented 15-year-old blind masseur who became Yamada Kengyo (1757–1817). With his great singing voice and a knack for music, the adopted son formed the Yamada-ryu of koto. The difference between Ikuta-ryu compositions and Yamada-ryu is that Ikuta-ryu music flows with ever-changing melody from beginning to the end. Yamada-ryu does not hesitate to repeat melodic sections that came from narrative Katoh-bushi and Itchu-bushi music. In an unwritten rule, Ikuta-ryu people do not play Yamada-ryu music although Yamada-ryu share some Ikuta-ryu repertory. Yamada-ryu players performed in Edo and regions north of it, and Ikuta-ryu players stayed mainly in Kansai. Today the boundaries no longer hold and many Ikuta-ryu players have migrated to Tokyo in the twentieth century.

Matsu kaze	A B B A' C' B C A		
Chikubushima	A B B' B B B" B'	B B' B C B" A	A' B B' B C B' A'
Shichi Fukujin	A B C A' D B		
Kogo no Kyoku	A A B A A	C C A D D B D B B	B' A A A B A

Table 20: Format of Some Yamada-ryu Compositions. Yamada Kengyo appealed to his audience by transposing Edo narrative theater music to the koto. Thus, as in narrative music that accompanies dances or scenes, sections are repeated. Such repetition does not occur in Ikuta-ryu music of the Kansai area.

Use of Stories and Lyrics by Different Genres

Creative artists are always in search of themes and stories from other genres to reinterpret. In the West, we see different interpretations of Shakespeare's plays, Broadway musicals, popular songs, and opera. In Japan, plays from the respected noh theater are a rich resource. The noh play *Ataka* is kabuki's *Kanjincho*; noh's *Shunkan* is also part of bunraku and kabuki plays; *Dojoji* of noh is the kabuki dance play *Musume Dojoji* and *Shin Musume Dojoji* of ji-uta music. Noh's *Gion, Saigyo Zakura, Chikubushima, Sakuragawa* are ji-uta, and the list goes on.

The nagauta shamisen music of the Kineya line borrows from everywhere and reworks music for popular appeal. *Echigojishi* is an example (see Figure 6.12). Originally a folk song sung by traveling *goze* (blind women musicians) from the Echigo region, ji-uta musicians popularized it. In 1811, the nagauta took the ji-uta rendition for kabuki dance music and wove a narrative with references to Echigo's northern dialect, a lion curled into a peony, and the lion dance. An *enka* (popular song) was inserted for good measure. For a festive finale, another ji-uta piece, *Sarashi* (Bleaching), was added. Here dancers wave yards and yards of white cloth in the air in an impressive display. *Echigojishi* is so popular that it is an ideal kabuki dance showcase for foreign audiences. Westerners will recognize its melody in the first act of Puccini's *Madama Butterfly*.

Another example of reinterpretation of a popular piece is noh's *Takasago*, a folk story about two old wedded Takasago and Sumiyoshi pine tree spirits. Although physically apart, they represent connubial bliss. The excerpted part of the noh utai sung at weddings and other new endeavors describes a journey, a boat ride passing familiar scenes to Suminoe (see Figure 6.13).

When seeing the journey portion on a noh stage, three priests step into the center of the stage into an imaginary boat. The actors are absolutely motionless as they chant to the hayashi's flute and drums telling the audience

6. The Format of Continuity in Hogaku Compositions

Bold = **quotes** from the original ji-uta pieces of both "Echigoshiji" and "Haya Sarashi"

1.	Utsu ya taiko no ne mo sumiwatari	Sound of the taiko all around
2.	"Kakube, Kakube" to mane karete	calling, "Come, Kakube, Kakube
3.	"Inagara misuru Shakkyo []	Come see the Stone Bridge!
4.	Ukiyo wo watau fu ga mono	It's easy to cross to the Floating world
5.	Utau mo mau mo hayasu mono."	where there's songs, dances, & drums
6.	Hitori tabi ne no kusa makura	Traveling alone with grass for pillow,
7.	Oraya nyobo wo homeru jya naiga	my dear wife—I praise not
8.	Mama mo taitari mizu shigoto	her cooking rice and cleaning up.
9.	Asa yoru, tabi no tanoshimi wo	All day, the pleasures of travel makes
10.	hitori emi site-e-e- kita—ri keru	my grin break into a smile.
11.	Echiji gata okuni meibutsu sama zama aredo	Specialties from Echigo? I've got them
12.	Inaba namari no kata goto majiri usa ni naru koto no ha wo no tayori ni todo kete hoshiya. Ojiya chijimi no dokoro yaraga	like mixing the sound of the word, Shira "white rabbit," showing my dialect. Kari Geese, be my mailer to her. Give her my pledge of love
13.	mie suku kuni no narahini	so translucent
14.	Enno wo musube shi aniya san anijya nai mono.	forever to my wife,
15.	tsuma jya mono	but not to my brother.
16.	Kuruka kuruka to hamae dete mireba no	Will she come to the beach and see
17.	Hoi-no hama no matsukage	the small shadow of the pine tree
18.	otoyama sarasa yatokakeno	and hear the roar of the big pine
19.	Hoi natsu ka to kana suita suisen	I shall wait for my wife, my
20.	sukareta yanagi no Hoino kororo seki chiku	beloved willow. My heart beats like
21.	kihaya momijisa yatokakeno	trees in autumn, burning red in love.
22.	Hoi matsukatona shinku jinku mo okesa bushi	Hoi, waiting is like going up and down.
23.	Nantara guchidahe **botan wa motanedo**	While fretting, look at the peony, it's the
24.	Echigojishi wa Onoga sugata o hana to mite Hani ni saitari sakase tari sokono okesa ni	Echigo lion figure curled up in its place. Flowers blooming,
25.	inakoto ri hare	let it blossom.
26.	Nemare nemarazu machi akasu gozare hanashi	Fretful sleep until morning
27.	Maseu zo kon komatsu no kokage de matsu no	let's sit down and talk under pine shade
28.	Hano you ni kon komaya kani ://	of many little details.
29.	**Hii te utau ya shishi no kyoku**	They are playing drums and flute
30.	**Mukahi Koyama no shichin dake**	of lion dance music from Koyama's
31.	**eda fushi souhete kiri o**	purple-leafed bamboo joints cut

32. **komaya kani jiyshichi ga muro**	neatly in a row. A 17 year old maiden
33. **no koguchi ni hirune shite**	naps at the entrance and
34. **Hana no sakaru o yume ni mete sourou**	dreams of a flower in its prime.
35. (Sarashi)	
36. **Miwatase ba miwatase ba** nishi mo higashi mo	When I look beyond, beyond, [I see]
37. Hana no kao izure nigiwafu hito no yama, hito no yama	flowers all round with countless people
38. Uchiyosuru uchiyosuru menami inami no taemanaku	or waves of men and women lookin
39. Sakamaku mizu no omoshiro ya, [ ] omoshiro ya.	like whirling water, how fun, how fun
40. Sarasu hoso nute ni kuru kuru to.	waving thin towels around and around,
41. Iza ya! kaeran onoga sumika he.	Iza ya! I don't want to go home.

Figure 6.12: Lyrics to *Echigojishi* ji-uta and nagauta. Artists borrow from each other. To attract people's attention, kabuki actors concocted a story, inserted a popular song, and then interwove ji-uta music about itinerant lion dancers from Echigo. At the end, they added another popular ji-uta music, *Haya Sarashi*, for an impressive cloth waving finale. Content from the original ji-uta pieces of *Echigojishi* and *Haya Sarashi* are in bold.

that they have hoisted the sails and are riding the tide in the moonlight. Awaji Island is silhouetted by the waves and as they go past Naruo, they finally they reach Suminoe. The priests step back as if disembarking from a boat. At Suminoe, the Sumiyoshi god appears and showers eternal good fortune on everyone.

The journey section also is rendered in the *ko-uta* (short song) style of geishas and the formal koto tegoto-mono style. The ko-uta version is accompanied by the smaller nagauta shamisen and the lighter singing style has a slight sigh or seductive slur. A tsuzumi taps softly at the mention of *nami* (wave; see line 4 in Figure 6.13).

The koto rendition in tegoto-mono format is for two kotos, the main koto and the *kaede* (other hand) koto tuned to a lower range. The singing style is lighter than noh but more serious than the ko-uta. The first four lines consist of the *mae-uta* and at the mention of *nami*, the kotos make swish sounds for waves, showing how lyrics affect the melodic embellishment (see lines 1 through 4 in Figure 6.13). A polyphonic instrumental interlude follows. The last two lines form the ato-uta that ends quickly (see lines 5 and 6 in Figure 6.13).

Through all of the interpretation, the jo-ha-kyu is evident. In addition, the symbolism attached to *Takasago* is compelling enough that any mention of the play or portion of the play triggers eternal happiness and good wishes

6. The Format of Continuity in Hogaku Compositions 141

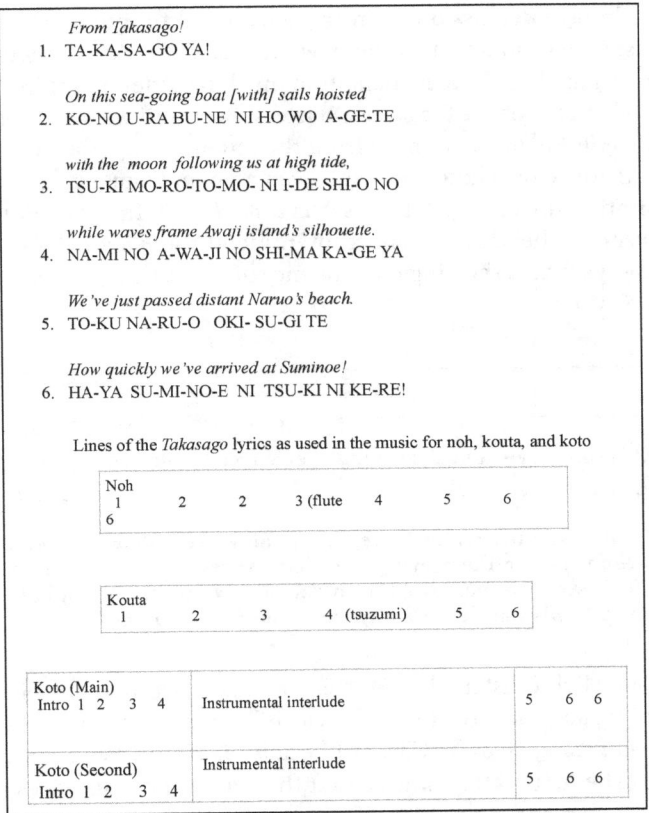

Figure 6.13: *Takasago* Journey Section of Noh, Kouta, and Koto. Although propitious words are not mentioned in this segment of the lyrics, the travel segment of the noh utai is sung at any auspicious occasion, such as weddings, for the mention of *Takasago* conjures the right sentiments associated with the legend and noh play. Different genres also interpret the lyrics within their respective styles, paying heed to the word *nami* (waves).

beyond music alone. Paintings of pine trees representing the Takasago story and calligraphy of the journey section decorate lacquerware, ceramic plates and bowls, handkerchiefs, fans, gift cards, scroll paintings, fine tea sets, and serving trays for gifts to herald good fortune.

New Musical Forms from the Meiji Era

The Meiji Era set off the dissolution of the Tōdō Shoku Yashiki, leaving blind musicians in a lurch but free to experiment with tuning, lyrics, and format without repercussion from the once watchful guild. The most successful instrument to adapt to the new era was the koto. The tegoto-mono format dominated, and experimentation involved different tuning and lyrics away from laments of the Pleasure Quarters. Beautiful waka poems from the *Kokinshu, Shin Kokinshu* to those from the reigning Imperial family became appropriate for female koto students. Even a poem from a grade school text was inspiration for Miyagi Michio's *Mizu no Hentai*. In between the verses, Miyagi inserted the *ai-no-te* (short interlude in the *mae-uta* songs) similar to Yamada-ryu pieces showing the influence of his association with a Yamada-ryu koto player.

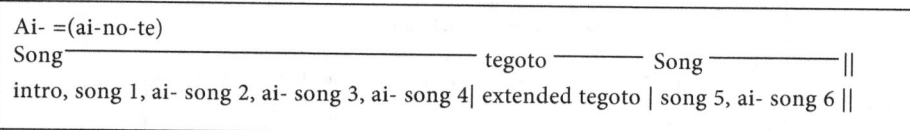

Figure 6.14: *Ai-no-te* Insertions in Tegoto-mono Pieces. Short instrumental interludes between verses in Ikuta-ryu pieces help express or give time to contemplate the lyrics. This style was borrowed from Yamada-ryu music. Miyagi Michio's *Mizu no Hentai* and Tomiyama Seikin's *Miyako Wasure* are examples.

Miyagi Michio listened to Western bands to learn about melody, harmony, tempo, and the ABA format. As a child, one of my favorite pieces was Miyagi's *Hanazono* (Flower Garden) because it was so Western. It came in two parts. The first section sings about the colors and fragrances of flowers to the koto's descending ripples. The second part changes pace and tuning and the voice sings about butterflies dancing over the flowers to the koto's happy waltz. When a koto group from Japan played in San Francisco in the 1930s, the exotic quality of the hogaku pieces was praised, but *Hanazono* was criticized for being blatantly Western sounding. When I played this piece before musicologist Dr. Marta Robertson at Gettysburg College to illustrate how Miyagi adapted Western music, she sat up straight and asked in a concerned voice if the circus-like waltz-time playfulness was a parody of Western music. Taken aback by her comment, I realized that Japanese and Japanese American audiences reacted differently to the piece from non–Japanese audiences. When I played *Hanazono* for Japanese American audiences, they liked it, but the non–Japanese audience reception was lukewarm because they probably preferred to hear something very "Japanese" sounding.[48]

Another of Miyagi's pieces, however, successfully crossed the Western barrier. *Haru no Umi* (Sea at Spring) with Debussy-like passages was recorded by renowned flutists Pierre Rampal and James Galway, and by different orchestras with koto or harp. Often I play it with a flutist, and I have played it with two orchestras.[49] It's fascinating to hear different combinations of Western string and wind instruments play *Haru no Umi* (check YouTube).

A	B	A
Sea Section	Activity at sea	Sea Section

Table 21: ABA Format of *Haru no Umi*. With the introduction of Western music, the ABA format became the standard for most koto music composed in the Western manner with a melody accompanied by chords. The famous *Haru no Umi* by Miyagi Michio is no exception. The A section describes the lapping waves and soaring birds, and the B section describes the activity at sea of the rocking boats and fishermen pulling in their catch.

Other koto composers who followed Miyagi's lead in Westernizing koto music were Nakashima Utahiko, Sakamoto Tsutomu, and Hisamoto Genshi, and later, Hiromu Handa, Eto Kimio, Tadao Sawai, and others. The jo-ha-kyu element has diminished along with the extended vowels of words. In its place is the ABA format. Today, in the twenty-first century, is there any composer capable or interested in composing in the classical hogaku manner? Is hogaku at the cusp of being replaced by Western music similar to how scholarly works must be written in English to be universally accepted and read?[50]

Summary

To expect to understand Japanese music from the Western perspective is like expecting that a large square Japanese cushion should fit in a round Western hatbox; the corners must be folded inwards to make it fit. It is like Karl Popper's "Of Clouds and Clocks."[51] Hogaku is "cloud" and Western music is "clock" and they are philosophically incomparable. Western music is based on pitch and harmony, but hogaku's musical flow is dictated by the lyrics. Each word is like a brush stroke that connects the lines and colors on a scroll painting. Hogaku's aural scroll moves through time in an overarching form having jo-ha-kyu with signposts to section off different places in a composition. How the words and instruments interact to make music is the topic of the next chapter.

I concur with scholars who say that appreciation for hogaku or any new music comes with familiarity. An American shakuhachi student[52] with extensive experience playing the saxophone said hogaku melodies do make sense after a lot of practice and repetition. The music has its own logic and when one finds it, one experiences an epiphany—enough to make one exclaim, "Aha!" If hogaku sounded exactly like Western music, like *Hanazono,* then it would sound disappointingly un-Japanese.

7

Decorating the Melodic Line

The surfaces of Japan's earliest Jomon pottery resemble basket fibers mimicking familiar things in nature. Today modern man converts plastic to look like glass, wood, cloth, clay, metal, and other everyday materials for daily use. Although clay cannot mimic the properties of plastic, clay was fashioned into utilitarian vessels for cooking, storage, religious regalia, musical instruments, and other objects. The Jomon pottery designs were at first replications of basket fibers and later became designs of familiar plants, fauna, fire flames, or waves made with bumps, grooves, pressed coils, appliqués, and other techniques.

Could the decorations on Jomon pottery apply to the way music is ornamented? I was surprised to learn that the formidable designs on the impractical looking pottery were actually variations of a few simple techniques fashioned into complicated-looking designs (see Chapter 2: Ancient Music and Its Properties).[1] In playing the koto, I saw parallels in how a few techniques on the strings decorate the melodic line. In the natural soundscape of the Jomon people, inspiration for decorating music must have come from nature. Listening to a bird sing, its twitterings are variations of many subtle timbres. Similarly insect cries display different timbres throughout the late summer and autumn.

I decided to assign my college students to tape record a September evening when insects were out in vocal splendor.[2] At first students considered insect cries as noise but they soon learned to hear a rhapsody of crickets and katydids, some ringing in bell-like spiraling tones calling for mates, others providing heterophonic chirps in short sawing sounds while others chimed along monotonously in basso continuo.[3] Even as cars rolled past or people's footsteps crunched dried leaves, these unwelcomed pieces of "music" decorated the symphonic surrounding. The ancient Japanese similarly heard birds, insects, frogs, and the call of a deer or bear, the crack of a tree limb, and the roar of river and of wind and used these sounds to decorate their music.

In hogaku, the decoration of a melodic line from nature's examples is accomplished in three ways.

- Contrasting instruments, as heard in *Asakura,* miko dance music, gagaku, noh, and sankyoku ensemble
- Timbre manipulated by the techniques and patterns of each instrument, such as on the biwa, shamisen, koto, shakuhachi, and the voice
- Heterophony using two or more independent instruments decorating the single melody line

Decoration with Contrasting Instruments

Introduced to Japan were thirty-four gagaku instruments with low and high pitches like the violin family of the Western orchestra. The Heian Era Japanese preferred different high-pitched instruments and chose eight of them to enjoy their distinct timbre.[4] In the kangen pieces, like *Ettenraku,* each instrument enters at a different time (see Figure 6.2: Entrance of the Instruments in *Ettenraku*). First to start is the clear tones of the ryuteki (flute) followed by the reedy and strident hichiriki and the organ-like sound of the sho. In the meantime, the low boom of the big taiko takes command while the high-pitched rolling knocks of the kakko and the metallic clunk of the shoko add contrast in the percussion section. The biwa of the string instruments plays, and the koto is last to enter with its stereotyped plunk-like sounds. The instruments exit in the same order with the koto having the last word (see also Chapter 3: Simple Instruments).

The noh costume visually describes the intent of gagaku music. In Figure 7.1, the warrior *Kiyotsune* appears in a soft silken inner white kimono that has both abstract and realistic flowers. From the left shoulder, a stiff blue brocade kimono with zigzag designs dominates and covers part of the purple *hakama* (trousers). A partially opened fan, a stylized ghostly mask, and black wig complete the costume. With its balanced mixture of textures, colors, and varied designs, the costume is visually stunning and so commands attention.

Like the contrasts in the noh costume, the music of noh is a contrast of sounds with several elements: the chorus, two drums, flute, and kakegoe. The chorus enters from the side stage as three musicians (flute, o- and ko-tsuzumi) step along the bridgeway to the stage proper. Once situated, the o-tsuzumi player growls the *kakegoe* (shouts to define the rhythm), "Yo—" followed by a sharp whip-like whack on the o-tsuzumi. The ko-tsuzumi player answers with "Ho" and hits rounder tones on his shoulder drum of any of the *chi, ta, pu,* or *pon* sounds. The kakegoe shouts of "Yo-o! Ho!" or "yoi" or "Iya!"

Figure 7.1: Noh Actor in Kiyotsune Costume. Here Kiyotsune is playing his flute to calm his heart before his suicide in a hapless battle. The costume of different textures and designs reflects a warrior of noble birth. The photograph is of Richard Emmert, professor at Musashino University and director of theatre of Nohgaku, taken at Kita Noh Theater in 2002. Professor Emmert performs worldwide and has composed music for noh in English and Spanish (courtesy Richard Emmert; Kita School Photo Department, Abiko Photos).

between striking the drums communicates rhythm and timing to the ensemble. How fast or slow to make the tempo depends on the character on stage and is set by the kakegoe. "Yo-o-i" can be an elongated growl or a quick yelp. A good example is the *mitsuji* (three note) pattern. It is strong and forceful for a heroic character like Benkei, or gentle and quieter for the fair and demur Matsukaze. Figure 7.2 shows the interaction of the kakegoe with the ko-tsuzumi pictured as a triangle (*ta*) and unfilled circle (*pon*), and the larger o-tsuzumi shown with the filled circle.[5] Although the drum rhythm is within eight beats, this "metered beat" is Chinese and Western in concept. More often noh rhythms fall into organic random beats, which is Japanese. The patterned phrases or cells have names and repeat as many times as necessary to accompany the play or dance.

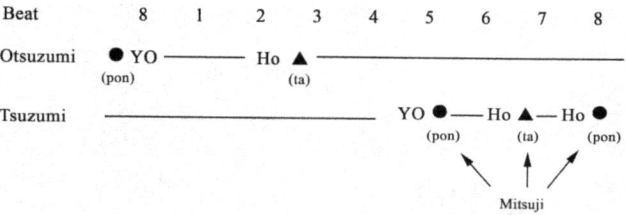

Figure 7.2: Mitsuji (Three Pattern in Tsuzumi) for Two Drums. The interplay of the *kakegoe* (vocal timing) with two drums hitting the skin softly (triangle with the nemonic *ta*) or with strength (filled circle, *pon*) sets the scene for either feminine or masculine characters depending upon how strongly the pattern is played. The o-tsuzumi begins with *pon*, followed by voice, "Yo" and "ho" followed by a lighter *ta* on the drum. The ko-tsuzumi continues with the kakegoe "Yo" followed by a loud *pon*, then the, "Ho" with a quick light tap *ta* and the "Ho" *pon*!

Soaring above the drumming and chorus is the nohkan in *hyoshi-ai* (controlled) beat for dance numbers. The *ashirai* (non-controlled beats) accompany the actor when he introduces himself or exits. The nohkan has no absolute pitch but can ring sonorously or piercingly depending on the desired atmosphere. Like the drums, the nohkan has its own solfege or *shoka* (onomatopoetic solmization).[6] The shoka specifies melodic cells for fingering consisting of two to five notes (see Figure 7.3: Nohkan Fingering and *Choka*).[7] The fingering pattern is learned within a pattern because the "hi" pitch in the second cell (below) is different from the "hi" pitch in the fourth cell. The flutist learns the melody cells (like the drum's mitsuji) with names like Nakano-takane, Takane hishigu, and Banshiki-gaku, and plays them when called for.

Noh experts like Kunio Komparu and Akira Tamba, among many, have diagrammed the motion of the drums, songs, and flute in tablature form, but the consensus is that noh music defies notation. When actors and musicians

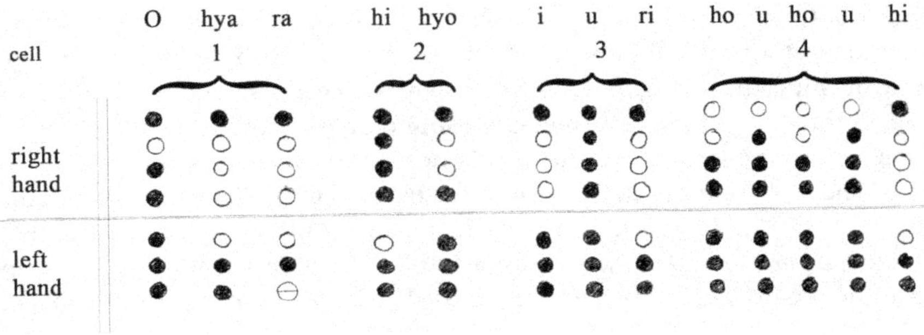

7. Decorating the Melodic Line

cell	O hya ra 1	hi hyo 2	i u ri 3	ho u ho u hi 4

Figure 7.3: Nohkan Fingering and *Choka* (Solmization). Each instrument, such as the koto or shamisen, has its own solemnization that calls out techniques. Choka calls out which finger pattern is to be used, and the nohkan player learns the notes within a unit or pattern.

get together for rehearsal, it is to talk through the play or walk through the parts because players already have their parts memorized. At performance time, the actor and musicians give everything to the performance to achieve the *hana* (flower) or the near divine.[8]

The noh-bayashi[9] is also part of the nagauta shamisen ensemble and adds contrast to kabuki and buyo (dance) performances. However, in addition to the basic noh-bayashi cells, the hayashi player must be acquainted with the shamisen melody for often the tsuzumi plays the same melodic rhythm of the shamisen, as in *Suehirogari*, *Echigojishi*, and *Renjishi*.

Kabuki's *Renjishi* (Auspicious Lions) has an interesting hayashi interlude that intrigues Westerners. The interlude projects the concept of *ma* (space) by playing a ritardando of the previous note and letting the pitch resonate until it fades. In *Renjishi*, the organic taps between the o-tsuzumi and ko-tsuzumi are echo-like, suggesting an expansive canyon or an eerie stillness before a storm or a prelude to something eventful.[10] When two auspicious lions appear, the hayashi, shamisen, and singers burst into celebratory music for the dance finale. The lions swing their long manes around in circles for several minutes until the recognizable *dan-giri* (coda) pattern signals the end of the performance. The music with multiple timbres adds to the festive scene of the colorful kabuki dance.

Decoration or Timbre from Biwa

Biwa. The biwa timbre is vast ranging from thin mosquito-like whines to aggressive whacks. The sympathetic buzzing of strings called *sawari* (drone) gives the biwa character. Its appealing sound is produced from the four *chu* (bridge/fret) that come in varying heights, sizes, and widths where one can get a note, vibrato, and bent notes produced by pressing, pulling, and pushing the strings midway between two bridges. The left hand also plucks the strings for *hajiki* (plucking) sound or for dramatic effect, abruptly stop a vibrating string with the *utsu* (stops) technique.

The timbre produced from the biwa's triangular fan-like *bachi* (plectrum) is also vast. The top point of the bachi plays down on one string and then hooks upward for *sukui* (scoop) for a subtle change in sound. The bachi tip also slides across the strings in arpeggios. The long edge or facet of the bachi when played in quick rapid succession makes a scraping sound for shimmering waves or a trembling, spinning fan. Most dramatically, the bachi hits the *haraita* (body of the biwa) for a loud whack sound to punctuate a thought or emphasize a battle scene.[11]

Timbre decorates a melody that sits on one note. This quality perplexes Japanese composers with Western training who have difficulty capturing the essence of hogaku instruments. When Toru Takemitsu (1930–1996) composed *November Steps* for biwa, shakuhachi, and Western orchestra, he chose to display the respective colors instead of trying to mix or blend them with the Western orchestra.[12] The result is an orchestral piece of extraordinary color and intense mood from both Eastern and Western traditions.

Decoration or Timbre from Sankyoku Instruments

This ensemble of three instruments—sangen/shamisen, koto, and shakuhachi—utilizes the timbre-laden capacity of each instrument. Played together, the instruments polyphonically decorate around a basic melody to form an aural torsade in a refinement of high artistic sophistication.

Timbre on the sangen/shamisen.[13] The strings on the shamisen are played with a bachi held in the right hand. The fingers on the left hand stop the strings along the pole for pitch and even pluck a string for added timbre.

Which hand is the more important, the left or the right with the bachi? The answer came from Kyushu's Sakamoto Jinoichi (1856–1926).[14] Inebriated at a party, he placed the sangen on his lap, held a sake cup in his right hand, and sang *Kurokami* (Black Hair, see Figure 7.4: *Kurokami* Lyrics), a popular song for buyo and kabuki geza (background).[15] His left fingers danced along the *sao*, stopping the strings for pitch, plucking, and hitting the strings for effect and sliding down the pole for slurring grace notes.[16] He played 70 percent of the piece with his left hand.

Then what is the function of the shamisen bachi? Volume.[17] Sound is amplified when the string and drum are struck simultaneously with the bachi.

KURO KAMI NO	Black hair
MUSUBORE TARU	layered and tied
OMOI OBA	are like memories of
TOKETE NETA YO NO	our night together
MAKURA KOSO	sharing a pillow.
HITORI NERU YO NO	But tonight, sleeping alone is with
ADA MAKURA	a wretched pillow [placed]
SODE WA KATASHIKU	on kimono folded to a sleeve's width.
TSUMA JYA TO YUTE	You called me your love—.
(interlude)	
GUCHI NA ONAGO NO	I'm a dejected woman and
KOKORO WO SHIRA DE	no one knows of my heart!
SHIN TO FUKETARU	Stealthily night deepen—
KANE NO KOE	the temple bell calls!
YUBE NO YUME	Last night's dreams
KESA SAMETE	fades with the dawn—
YUKASHI NATSUKASHII	those wistful
YARU SENAYA	melancholy dreams
TSUMORU TO SHIRADE TSUMORU	mindlessly layer like
SHIRA YUKI	white snow.

Figure 7.4: *Kurokami* Lyrics. One of the earliest ji-uta naga-uta by Koide Ichijuro (circa 1800), this popular piece is played at any mention of black hair. The lyrics are attributed to Rennyo Shonin, the eighth patriarch of the Jodo Shinshu sect. They tell about the uselessness of attachment and longing for such thought prevents one from seeing the beauty of life's passing, such as the falling snow.

When an upward stroke is made, it is like the biwa's *sukui* (scoop) making two different sounds from one string, thereby adding interest to a note. Notation provides hardly any textual clues, as in the score for *Kokaji* (Little Fire).[18] A change of pace from the lyrical portion to the festive rhythmic interplay of the shamisen, hayashi, and the kakegoe is hard to notate, especially in Western notation.

The shamisen score is equally daunting. One might wish for a universal notation system, but each instrument and school have their own notation. For shamisen notation, there are three lines for three strings. The numbers on the lines indicate the note and finger position. The important timbre cue is ス for *sukui* or scoop, /\ *hajiki* or pluck, or arrow for slurring down the pole.[19] Tiny *kana* (syllabic writing) are the *kuchi-jamisen* (mouth shamisen/ onomatopoetic solmization), which are important for phrasing.

Timbre on the Koto. The koto is a "timbre box" that can be played to sound like any stringed instrument in the world—piano, harp, harpsichord, sitar, mandolin, ukulele, guitar, steel guitar, balalaika, and even a violin if the koto is bowed (which is seldom).[20] Koto techniques rooted in gagaku koto's

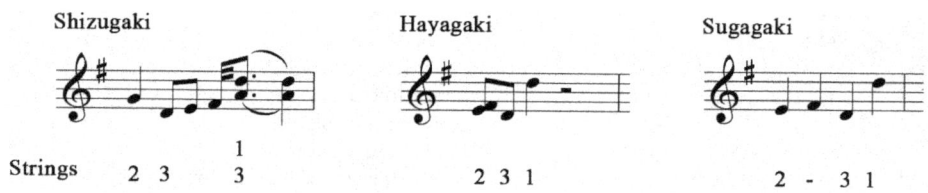

Figure 7.5: *Shizugaku, Hayagaki,* and *Sugagaki* Octave Patterns of the Gaku-soh. Modern koto techniques come directly from gagaku koto, just as the kumi-uta came from its music. With time, the rhythm of the patterns changed, but the early patterns are discernible.

shizugaki, hayagaki, and *sugagaki* (see Figure 7.5) decorate the melodic line and embellish lyrics.

Three ivory *tsume* (plectra) and the bare left hand make timbre. The Ikuta-ryu's squared plectrum uses the corners, tops, sides, and tips on the right thumb, index, and middle fingers. Yamada-ryu tsume is oval shaped and because of its rounded tips, a player sits perpendicular to the koto whereas the Ikuta-ryu player sits at an angle or parallel to the bridges' alignment.

Fingers do not pluck the koto but press against the strings at about 2.5 inches from the *kaku* (unmovable bridge), delivering a strong sound. A mellower tone rings out playing at the strings midway between the kaku and the *ji* (moveable bridge; see Figure 3.9: Parts of a Koto).

As with other instruments, the teacher sings the koto *shoga*[21] (onomatopoetic solmization) at lessons to indicate pitch, fingering, phrasing, and clues to interpreting the phrase. For example, for the thumb, the shoga *ko-ro-rin* is for three notes that flow down the strings in descent, but the shoga *chi-tsu-te* means that each string should be emphasized in descent. In other words, the shoga for the same fingering pattern tells of the intent and importance of the three notes.

Figure 7.6: Thumb Pattern Score *Kororin, Chi tsu te, tsu te.* The fuss here is that when koto shoga is ignored, particularly in koto classical pieces, and the three descending notes played without any consideration for the intent contained in the shoga, the music loses its meaning.

The thumb plays the *sukui* (scoop found in biwa and shamisen) in two motions. The downward press of the string is *tsu,* and then scooping it is *ru* or *tsu-ru*. When the two sounds *tsu* and *ru* on one string are played in succession, it is *tsu-ru, tsu-ru, tsu-ru* as found in the shamisen part of *Kokaji*.

The index and middle fingers play the lower octaves while the thumb hits the higher octave.[22] Rarely used are the formal names for the octave patterns called *kakezume*, *warizume*, and *uraren* that came from gagaku koto. The shoga (in parentheses after the formal name) for *kakezume* (*kara kara ten*) is like gagaku's *shizugaki*. Modern koto has the *awasezume* (*shan*) when simultaneously playing the low and high octaves. When alternating the low and high octaves, the low octave is *ton* followed by the high octave *ten*.

The *kakite* or *kakizume* (*sha-sha*) plays the adjacent strings[23] twice in succession and finishes with the thumb (*ten*) or *sha-sha ten*. When only one *sha* is played on the lower strings and finished by the higher octave, the shoga is *sha-ten*.

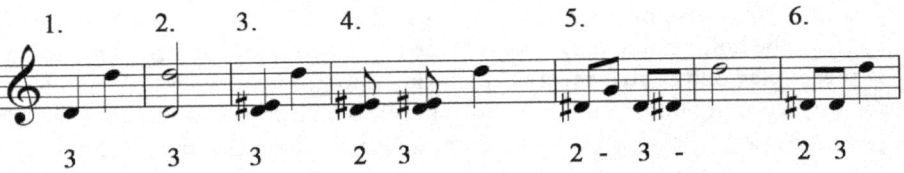

Figure 7.7: Octave Patterns for the Modern Koto. The koto octaves patterns decorate hovering notes, thereby tantalizing the listeners with different sounds. There are six main octave patterns. (1) Playing the lower octave followed by the thumb on the higher note, as in the shoga *ton-ten*. (2) Third finger and thumb play the low and high notes together (*awasezume*). (3) Third finger plays two adjacent lower strings in one stroke followed by the thump in the higher octave (*kakite*). (4) Second finger plays two adjacent strings immediately followed by the same strokes of the third finger that is finished by the thumb (*warizume*). (5) Second finger plays two adjacent strings separately while the third finger follows. The thumb completes the octave (*kakezume*). {6} A variation of kakezume except the second finger plays one string and the third finger plays two strings separately with the thumb playing the octave (*han kakezume*).

In addition to octave patterns, the koto player produces other timbre for effect. The backs of the second and third plectra trickle down the string for arpeggio called *ura-ren* (*sa-ra rin*). The thumb finishes the pattern with the shoga *ra rin*. The *nagashi zume* (*ka-ra rin*) is a robust clear arpeggio that starts with the thumb *ka-* at the highest string before sliding down the strings in a glissando to end with *-ra rin*. In the opposite direction, the *hiki ren* (*sha rarin*) is a glissando up the koto with the middle finger.

Chirizume (*shu*) is a pendulum-like swing with the third finger's plectrum that slides past the first two strings. Short light swishes using just the tops of the second and third plectra make a quick *shu, shu* sound. The *surizume* (also *urasuri* with the shoga *zuu-zuu*) is a back and forth zipper-like sound produced by the second and third fingers sliding the length of two strings. Some people wonder if these sounds are musical, but for koto music they are perfect for evoking wind, splashing waves, and even for settling down.

The left hand is as equally busy as the right hand. The left hand moves bridges, plucks strings, and also presses the string for a new pitch as in *osae (tsun)*. Pressing a vibrating string makes a slurring grace note as in *ato osae (tsu-n-)*. Subtle bends of a note, like *hiki iro* (pull string) or *yuri iro* (wavy) or vibrato, are made by pulling back and forth quickly on the string behind the bridge. The left index fingernail placed under a string and played with the right hand makes buzzing sounds called *keshi zume (ten, ten)*. The left hand dampens the string for staccato sounds and produces harmonics when placed lightly at mid-point of a string. A mellow and harp-like sound results when the left hand plucks the strings.

Contemporary players bring out timbre on the koto by using anything other than the tsume, such as a bottle or stick. They even pound on the strings or on the koto's sides, top, or underside like a percussion instrument. Some pieces play on the strings left of the bridges to produce a mesh of sounds.

Shoga or onomatopoetic solmization reveals interpretation of the music transmitted at lesson time. The shoga tells how the techniques line up like words in a phrase to make sentences, paragraphs, chapters, and an entire composition. To illustrate this concept, koto's *Rokudan* a *dan-mono* (section piece) with no song is a good example[24] (see Figure 7.9).

The *Rokudan*'s first section is a melodic study in the subsequent sections. Composed in fifty-two[25] beats per section, the first section begins with a *kando* (introduction) of notes d, G, and then d/G (together) with the shoga: "*te-n ton shan.*" The *shan* is two strings struck together by the middle finger. The pitches are d, G, d and the final c has a little color with the added G note or d/G.

Rokudan's melody clearly hovers around a few notes of the IN mode, but the techniques add interest and timbre. In measures 17–22, the shoga of "*sha sha te tsu sha sha te tsu ton ko rorin*" is a mixture of octave patterns combined with "*ko ro rin*" by the thumb. When the octave patterns are removed, the melody is B, B, b, a, B, B, b, d, E, e, c, b, E.[26] As you can see, the melody hovers around the B and E of the IN mode. The left hand bends and adds vibrato to enrich the melodic line.

For expression, one rule of hogaku is that every note is important and should be played distinctly.[27] Dynamics in the Western sense do not apply, particularly since hogaku does not use metered measures.[28] However, the shoga indicates that the top note of **ko**rorin, or **chi** tsu te **chi** tsun- te (measures 46–48) should be emphasized. A note is also accentuated by the *ato osae* (pressing after the string is played like the **tsu**-n) or with the *hiki* (bent note) in the first note of *Rokudan*. As mentioned previously, implicit in the

7. Decorating the Melodic Line

Thumb:
1. Each string is played individually.
2. Sukui (*tsu ru*) is first playing down on a string (*tsu*) then scooping upward (*ru*).

Arpeggio techniques:
1. Uraren (*sararin*): The inside corner of second finger plays a slight tremolo and then trickles down the koto followed by the third finger. The thumb finishes the pattern by playing the last two "target" strings.
2. Nagashi zume (*ka-rarin*): The thumb starts at the top strings and lightly moves down the koto to end on the last two "target" strings with emphasis.
3. Hikiren (*ka-rarin*): In the opposite direction, the third finger plays two lower strings and trickles up the strings to play the last two top strings.

Scraping slides sounds:
1. Chiri zume (*shu*): The second and third fingers arc in a pendulum swing and swishes the first and second strings.
2. Surizume: (*zuu,zuu*): The insides of the second and third fingers rest on two strings and slide forward and backward like a zipper.
3. Urasuri (*shu*): The tops of the second and third fingers swish lightly across two strings.
4. Nami gaeshi is a combination of urasuri (tops), chiri zume (side), and uraren (trickle down the koto with backs of tsume. This techniques usually describe waves.

Left hand: In addition to plucking the strings for a harp-like sound, the left hand presses, or tugs at the strings for subtle decoration. Among them are
1. Osae (*tsun*) press string for another note.
2. Ato osae (*tsu-n*) pressing a vibrating string after it is played for a slurring grace note.
3. Kake osae (*chi-tsun*) two strings pressed in succession.
4. Oshi awasezume (*ryan, ryan*) two strings played together with one stringed pressed to the same pitch of the higher string.
5. Hiki-iro, yuri-iro are subtle sounds created by pulling and tugging on a strins behind the bridge after it is played.

Figure 7.8: Other Koto Techniques. The list is a partial example of koto techniques followed by its shoga in parentheses. The variety of timbre produced on the koto is up to the imagination of the composer. See also Figure 7.7 for the koto octave patterns.

shoga is the important phrasing telling which notes to emphasize to affect the feel of the music, rhythm, and tempo.

Like the *shoga* for koto and the *kuchi-jamisen* (mouth shamisen) for shamisen, other instruments also have their respective onomatopoetic solmizations for phrasing and pitch that are teaching tools at lessons.

Shakuhachi. Shakuhachi is the third instrument of the sankyoku ensemble that is popular around the world. Its timbre ranges from mellow and

Figure 7.9: Score of *Rokudan* (First Section). The shoga for *Rokudan* is sung during lessons to aid in hearing techniques, phrasing, and the strings to play. Without the shoga, calling out the string number does not make sense as an aid to remembering the music. Like words in a sentence, shoga (in parentheses) calls out koto words as they line up to make a phrase, sentence, paragraph, chapter, and ultimately, a composition. I have underlined the octave patterns of warizume (*sha, sha, ten*), the kakite (*sha, ten*), alternating ton-ten of low to high octave that connects the blocked in *kororin* (three notes down) patterns. In other words, the octave and thumb patterns interconnect to make melody.

pleasant to breathy, particularly in its *honkyoku* (main repertory) proprietary to the shakuhachi. The clear shakuhachi tones accompany *gaikyoku* (outside) pieces with koto and sangen. It replaced the *kokyu* (bowed shamisen) in the ensemble because of its stronger contrasting properties.

In the Kinko-school, students learn gaikyoku pieces first to acquire the basic techniques before advancing to the subtle techniques required of the honkyoku. Changing the angle of the head or compressing the lips across the mouthpiece for *meri* (lower pitch) and *kari* (overblow for higher pitch) require much practice. It is tricky to manage the chromatic scale that has a two and a half octave range, for the fingers must cover either the top or bottom half of the holes for semitones. The list of specific techniques suggests the skills a shakuhachi player must learn, such as the *nayashi* (portamento pitch raised half tone), *suri-sage* (portamento to high pitch, low pitch), *oru* (bend the note), *muraiki* (explosive air burst), *kasaiki* (breath sound blowing outside the mouthpiece), *tamane* (fluttering tongue), *sorane* (aerier breath than normal), *korokoro* (tremolo), *karakara* (lighter tremolo), *sutebyoshi* (repeated single note), *yuri* (vibrato), plus others.[29] In all cases, a teacher facilitates learning playing techniques along with the attitude required to play the instrument with conviction and sincerity which is an attractive feature of shakuhachi music.

Heterophony Decorates a Melody

The function of the *kaede* (other hand) for koto or shamisen is to decorate around the main melody with two interweaving polyphonic melodies like a rolling melody like the *orugoru* (music box), which Ichiura Kengyo imitated.[30] The kaede is mostly associated with ji-uta sangen and Ikuta-ryu koto music and often involves two kotos, one tuned high and the other low. These compositions are challenging because they require a thorough understanding of the composer's intentions especially since there is no downbeat as in a metered score. Once put together, they are satisfying and fun. By contrast, the Yamada-ryu koto and the nagauta shamisen play the same melody and decorate the music with the respective timbre of the instruments.

For some koto pieces, a continuous *sukui* (scooping) pattern called *ji*[31] or *tsuru-shan ji* (ostinato accompaniment) or *tate no ire-te* accompanies the melody. Famous examples are *Chigo Zakura* and *Shin Sugomori*. The *tsuru-shan ji* of the second koto rhythmically brings out the melody of the main koto.

At times passages from existing music bring out atmosphere. The *gaku-no-te* or gagaku koto's *shizugaku* or *han-kake* technique played with the main melody evokes an ancient atmosphere. At the mention of the shrine of Benzaiten (goddess of music) in Yamada-ryu's *Enoshima no Kyoku* and Ikuta-ryu's *Haru No Enoshima*,[32] the second koto plays the *gaku-no-te* to give an ethereal effect. In the *ai-no-te* (short interlude) of the *mae-uta* (song at the beginning) of Miyagi Michio's *Haru no Yo*, the *gaku-no-te* brings out feelings of ancient koto playing.

Sometimes two separate compositions are composed and played simultaneously. Called *awase* (put together) or *uchi-awase* (played together) pieces, a good example is Tateyama Kengyo's *Hototogisu no Kyoku* that is played with *Hoshi to Hana to*. Another is *Rokudan*[33] played with Ikuta-ryu's *Aki Kaze no Kyoku*[34] or with *Aioi no Kyoku*.[35] Yamada-ryu also has many pieces using *Rokudan* to add interest.

Summary

Harmony in the Western musical sense came to Japan during the Meiji Era.[36] Before then, contrasting instruments, timbre from the instrument, and polyphony of several instruments added tantalizing interest to the melody line. Gagaku music and noh employ different instruments to create a texture of contrasting sounds. For music of the biwa, shamisen, koto, and shakuhachi, the inherent textures and manipulating the instrument with techniques subtly ornament a melody line. These instruments are best heard in solo presentation.[37] The sankyoku of three instruments form a torsade-like decoration by using contrasting instruments with their individual timbre to enhance a melody line as exemplified in a symphony of nature's musicians.

Timbre producing techniques have names like ballet's pirouette, arabesque, or plié.[38] At lessons the informal shoga for koto or kuchi-jamisen for shamisen calls out pitch, techniques, and phrases. Like nature's musicians who do not sing in a metered measure, hogaku music unfolds using patterns of the instrument to connect in order to make a phrase, sentence, paragraph, chapter, and ultimately a composition.

8

Why We Are Able to Hear Ancient Music Today: The Iemoto System

The exposed crisscrossing rafter poles of the ancient Ise Shrine stand serenely above the bustle of worshippers and tourists. I was there in 2013 during the recurring twenty-year dedication of the sixty-second iteration of the new shrine. Even then I imagined that the cycle of rebuilding the next shrine was already set in motion as it had been in the past. Cypresses were being selected to be hewn from the forest, seasoned, planed, and made ready for carpenters to assemble another replica adjacent to the existing shrine to be dedicated twenty years hence. How is it possible for generations of woodcutters and craftsmen to keep Amaterasu's abode exactly as originally constructed?

The answer resides in the deep Japanese tradition of refreshing the memory of each generation to extend longevity, while paradoxically expressing the Shinto precept for purity and cleanliness in the Japanese aesthetic and preference for newness. Starting anew—like beginning the New Year or a new enterprise or a new grade in school with new clothes, books, and pencil box—is serious. The process of renewal allows perpetuation, and longevity is a testament to a family's endurance, to beating the odds against life's fickleness. It's a way of fighting decay.

The responsibility of ensuring the family longevity rests on the family head; he passes the family trade, art, or skill directly to his son. Today, he is known as the *iemoto*, from ie (house), and moto (foundation, base, or head master), a word tagged during the Edo Era (1600–1868). The meta-concept of iemoto goes back to ancient times, to respecting the hierarchical relationship between kami and man, superior and inferior, and parent and child. However, the concept of the iemoto can leave the modern Japanese nonplussed because the word evokes an archaic hierarchical system that seems out of sync with their self-image of living in a modern democratic society. Nevertheless, old Japanese habits persist. Like the quip about two Londoners at a bus stop forming a queue, when two Japanese strangers meet, they initiate the proper etiquette of hierarchy by exchanging name cards to assess job, position, and age so they know how relate to each other. The ingrained behavior from ancient times of building relationships in the iemoto group is one powerful reason why we are able to hear ancient music today.

To clarify at the onset, the iemoto entity is not a utopia dreamt up by a philosopher like Thomas More's *Utopia* or like Samuel Butler's *Erewhon* or like Plato's *The Republic*. Neither is it a government imposed "behavior law" pressuring society to obey. It grew from the grass roots of people in the Shinto environment. Later Buddhism, Confucianism, and Taoism affected individual and group behavior, and then through the centuries, patterns for making good relationships became institutionalized in the iemoto groups. The iemoto paradigm reveals how the iemoto grooms followers and the next head to continue the family enterprise into the future.

An iemoto's enterprise is a desired commodity that people want as a career, as a way to make a living, or as a way to gain status in society.[1] Concomitantly, the iemoto wishes to protect his enterprise through a type of enterprise copyright by inculcating his charges to a "kin-tract,"[2] a portmanteau for kinship and contract promoting a tight-knit family-like relationship. Face-to-face lessons build emotional ties of loyalty, trust, and belief in the iemoto's values that are as strong as mesons that hold together the nucleus of an atom.[3]

Among the countless iemoto-headed groups, there are four basic types: (1) the Imperial sanctioned straightforward lineal iemoto, or the direct father-to-son transmission; (2) the quasi-lineal[4] iemoto groups that imitated the direct lineal father-to-son transmission but had no government recognition;

~ 200 ~ ~ ~ 1200 - - -1300- - -1400- - -1500- - -1600- - - -1700- - - - -1800- - - - -1900- - -				
Lineal	**Umbrella**	|	**Quasi-lineal**	**Dendritic**
clan chief	Todoza	noh	narr. shamisen	tea, flower, uta, koto
guild heads			theater	

Figure 8.1: Timeline of Iemoto Type and Their Appearance. Ensuring the longevity of a family's trade or skill has Jomon roots. Beginning with the coveted family position that served the clan chief or emperor, heads of families passed the trade, skill, or art to sons. Other families with specialized skills imitated the exclusiveness practiced by the houses with Imperial sanction. Later as non-relatives apprenticed to an iemoto, umbrella organizations and iemoto with pyramid schemes developed. Students were "adopted" into the family with the certification and name change to authenticate their relationship with the iemoto's trade.

(3) an umbrella organization that accommodates different heads with interrelated skills; and (4) a dendritic configuration developed during the Edo Era with one iemoto and many licensed teachers to mind branch schools so as to accommodate more students (see Figure 8.1: Timeline of Iemoto Type and Their Appearance).

The four types overlap and share the same attribute of having one authority figure who is the director and decision-maker of the group. The members of all four types share a strong volition to join the iemoto's realm and compete with others in the group. In turn, the group competes with other groups. There is also a system of inclusion and exclusion in place in the four types of groups. For example, before or after each hurdle, there are certificates, titles, and name and rank changes as recognition for each promotion. But the chief and sole purpose of the iemoto in the four types is to perpetuate the art, trade, skill, or enterprise as originally conceived. A creative iemoto innovates to ensure the continuity and freshness of the group. In the following discussion of the four iemoto configurations, variations occur in the inclusion and exclusion system of the group. It all depends on the finances or income of the organization, the personality of the iemoto, and the changes in events and social conditions. In the overall picture, each iemoto enclave or organization is an economic and educational group protecting its enterprise and copyright.

Direct-Lineal Iemoto

In the direct iemoto configuration, only one son succeeds the father. He is the only person privy to the family *hi-den* (secrets) of the skills, values, and standards of the house exactly as practiced in the past. In the ancient clan society, the emperor appointed experts to serve the Imperial court and the community.[5] Imperial appointments included the Mononobe or warrior family and other experts (see Figure 8.2: Ancient and Edo Era Guilds). The suffix "-be" indicates that the family belongs to a *be* (guild) or *tomo* (corporation).[6] Some heads have successfully maintained the family line from mythological times, such as the Shinto priests who are the Kamibe. The Urabe (diviners) and Imibe (abstainers) conducted recitations and offerings for many centuries. Uzume,[7] who enticed the Sun Goddess out of the cave, is from the Sarume family of mikos (shrine maidens).[8]

The family of carpenters responsible for the Ise Shrine goes back to the reign of Emperor Temmu[9] (678–686 BCE). The court musicians of the Togi and Ono gagaku families appointed during the Nara (701–794) and Heian Era (794–1185) continue to serve the court today. From the years 1200 to 1868, shoguns appointed heads of schools like the five noh shi-te schools with the related schools, schools of tea, flower, martial, and other arts.

Third Century "Be" or Guilds and Edo Era Families
(Note the "Be" ending each name.)

Amabe	fisherman	Kataribe	storytellers	Tanabe	rice field
Akazomebe	dyer	Mononobe	arm	Tamatsuribe	jewelers
Ayabe	broade	keepers		Umakaibe	horse
Fumibitobe	scribe	Nakatomibe	medium	grooms	
Hasebe		Oribe	weavers	Urabe	diviners
	potters	Osabe			
Imibe	abstainers		interpreters		

Edo Era Families to the Shogun

Iami family	Tatami makers
Goto Shozaburo	Gold mint
Gotyo Nuidonosuke	Dry goods
Daikoku Joze	Silver mint
Yagyu Taimakami Munemori	Swordsmanship
Ogasawara	Horse & archery

Figure 8.2: Ancient and Edo Era Guilds. The names of actual guilds during Jomon and Edo eras demonstrate that a prototype iemoto system existed and served the ruling family and community needs. To ensure the head status of the family trade, each iemoto trained his son from an early age and passed the secrets only to him. The guilds provide an insight of the occupations needed to make a society function.

Shi-te (main actors) Kanze, Hosho, Kongo, Komparu, Kita
Waki (support actors) Takayasu, Fukuo, Shimogakari Hosho
Noh-kan (flute) Morita, Isso, Fujita
Ko-tsuzumi (drum held on shoulder) Kanze, Ko Kosei, Okura
O-tsuzumi (big drum) Kadono, Takayasu, Okura
Taiko (stick drum), Kanze, Komparu
Kyogen (comic relief actors) from 1500s, Okura, Izumi, Sagi (now defunct)

Figure 8.3: Related Schools of the Five Noh Theater. The shi-te or protagonist's role is often considered the carrier of a noh play, however, a noh performance includes the waki and kyogen actors and musicians on drums and flute. Each group of actors and musicians train in their specialized schools with an iemoto. Every school strives for excellence so that when they come together for a noh performance, they fit perfectly together like puzzle pieces.

A fifteenth-century Buddhist monk, Ikenobō Senno, became the iemoto of the classical flower arranging school and today the school has its forty-fifth headmaster, Ikenobō Sen'ei. Murata Shuko inspired the school for the Way of Tea that Sen Rikyu devised and celebrates fifteen generations of iemotos.

Family longevity is cachet in Japanese society. A charismatic iemoto with exceptional skill and impeccable conduct that is recognized by a community sustains the family enterprise. No doubt many iemotos have faded away with changes in society, but among the survivors the head is like an admired *hito-gami* (living god), placed on a pedestal and looked upon as a person to emulate.

Quasi-Lineal Iemoto

Creative commoners followed the direct-lineal iemoto practices of the aristocracy in a quasi-lineal iemoto fashion. They include puppeteers and gidayu musicians of bunraku and kabuki actors, and lines of narrative shamisen musicians. Without official government sanction, they nevertheless passed trade secrets and skills to their sons in the manner of the direct-lineal iemoto. However, they allowed non-family members to join the group after passing their stringent course of study.

The iemoto, who is also a teacher, must transmit the high standards he has acquired. As a teacher, Confucius says, "Know your station" and thus the teacher as *loco parentis* afflicts upon his charge corporal[10] and verbal punishment "to point out the wrong to correct the wrong."[11] Harsh treatment reflects the teacher's positive assessment of a student's potential. In Tanizaki Junichiro's novelette *Shunkin Monogatari*, Shunkin scarred a child's face with a shamisen bachi. Confronted by an enraged father, her retort was that it was her duty as a teacher to maintain high standards. Tomiyama Seikin's childhood teacher, Tominaga Keikin, spared no rod. Crying on his trek homeward, Tomiyama Seikin vowed to quit forever, but the teacher's wife cajoled him into returning. Harsh treatments include being hit with a fan, kept up without sleep, and thrown in the snow. Even a chef of Chinese ancestry during his training at a fine Japanese restaurant in Honolulu boasted of being insulted during his training in Japan with, "*Baka! Nani shite iru no?*" ("Stupid! What are you doing?") He was also kicked and pinched with the caution to "get it right!" But he valued the strict training that prepared him with high and exacting standards.[12]

With stories of such abusive training, why would anyone want to train with an iemoto's group? Volition. Volition wells up from within a student desiring to acquire the iemoto's skill, identity, and status for a livelihood. Student volition must be intense, for like leading a horse to water, without desire, the iemoto would be wasting his time.

The iemoto or teacher is equally selective of potential disciples. The student must feel in his heart as he approaches each lesson, "*Narawasete itadakimasu*," meaning, "I humbly *receive* the learning." The founder of the Suzuki Method of teaching the violin, Shinichi Suzuki, insists that children beg to learn how to play the violin. Woodblock artist Keiji Shinohara had to wait six months before the master even acknowledged his daily presence. One day he joyfully accepted the task to run an errand for the master, a request that signaled the master's recognition of his earnestness. After a year he was rinsing brushes, and then finally, printing one color on simple pictures. After ten years, Shinohara had acquired valuable printing skills, but he had endured long hours of tedious repetitive work in order to absorb those skills and the spirit behind woodblock printing.

A child born to an iemoto's immediate family begins as a toddler to learn informally the nuances of the art as naturally as learning to walk or talk.[13] Other children begin lessons from the age of six on the sixth day of the sixth month. The arts acquired at an early age are more likely to become ingrained and naturally a part of the person.

Many quasi-iemotos follow the standards set by the respected noh iemotos who refer to the Motokiyo Zeami (1363-1443) lessons on attaining performance status written in the *Kyu-I* (Nine Steps; see Table 22: Kyu-I: Upper, Middle, and Lower Levels). Like a modern educational psychologist, Zeami recommends face-to-face lessons in order to transmit the art precisely. Novices start at the middle level (Level 6) and not at the bottom of Level 9, as one might imagine. When the novice reaches Level 5, he can either fall backwards in skill from overconfidence or move onto Level 4 and upwards. By Levels 3 and 2, the performance has depth, and at Level 1, the performer leaves the audience speechless and breathless. At the lower levels of the *Kyu-I*, a student is beyond hope of attaining any greatness. If by misfortune a student chooses a mediocre teacher, attaining the upper level becomes inaccessible because habits acquired from initial exposure are hard to correct.[14]

Zeami also mentions the *hana* state of performance. Hana literally means flower but in Zeami's definition, it stands for performance beyond words or as Rimer and Mazakazu translate it, "peerless charm."[15] A performer reaches

Upper level:	Middle level:	Lower level:
1. Peerless charm	4. True Flower	7. Strength and delicacy
2. Profundity	5. Broad Mastery	8. Strength and crudeness
3. Tranquility	6. Early Beauty (Begin Here)	9. Crudeness and leadenness

Table 22: *Kyu-I*: Upper, Middle, and Lower Levels. Zeami had the mind of an education psychologist. He understood the ability of students from the lowest, most crude and undisciplined level to the highest level that is beyond praise. He notes that learning should start at Level 6 as anything below is wanton behavior. Training with a good teacher is also key to achieving the highest level. (Based on information from Thomas J. Rimer and Yamazaki Masakazu, trans., *On the Art of the No Drama: The Major Treatises of Zeami* [Princeton: Princeton University Press, 1984].)

hana at different times of his life. A child actor is adorable like a flower bud, a young adult full of vigor is hana at another level, and an aged actor is like a fresh flower on a craggy old tree. A hana level performance leaves the audience humbled, awed, and welling tears.

The hana level comes from hard work or suffering, as in Zen training. Stories about self-inflicted hardship abound, like a gidayu singer who practiced with a broken rice bowl over his stomach to feel pain created by a sword in a bunraku play. One singer perched from a five-story rafter to improve his voice. *Kangeiko* (practicing in the extreme cold) in mid-winter was believed to help technique and voice for shamisen and koto playing. Yamase Shoin (1845–1908) awoke at 4:00 each morning and played for two hours for thirty days. The koto plectrum band froze on his fingers and was removed by first warming the band with a warm sweet potato lest the skin be torn away. The list of the suffering of artists to attain greatness is long.

Umbrella Iemoto

An umbrella-type iemoto group oversees many iemotos of related skills. The ancient Tōdō Shoku Yashiki (or Tōdōza for short) from 1330 to 1872 managed the occupations of blind men, including masseurs, poets, sword experts, acupuncturists, and musicians. Through this organization, musicians became the government-sanctioned *professional* musicians who earned an income through music.[16] The guild functioned outside the Edo shogunate government, banished wayfaring members,[17] and dictated what and how to compose music.[18] The musicians kept the Tōdōza and the noble Koga[19] family solvent during the economic crises of the Edo Era and lent money, creating suspicion about the purpose of the group. As an umbrella organization, the Tōdōza administered and financed itself by selling certificates, ranks, and titles recommended by the members who headed their own schools.

Kakuichi, the blind son of the Ashikaga shogun in the 1330s formed the Tōdōza, placed the ninth-century prince Hotoyasu Shinnyo as the patron saint, and devised the Rules and Regulations with the four titles of Kengyo, Kōtō, Betto, and Zato[20] and sixteen grades and seventy-three steps. Figure 8.4 shows the ranks, grades, steps, and fees required. Members paid fees from 5 to 19 *ryo* or a total of 719 ryo to move to the top. *Tsubu iri* (skippers) could bypass the grades in-between, showing that wealth was a big factor in how quickly one could move through the grades. As noted on the chart, each rank also wore a special insignia or different colored clothing. At the top, the *so-Kengyo* wore red, received a fan from the Koga[21] mentor, and ruled over all Tōdōza members.

The Tōdōza was a national organization for blind men only. A separate

STEPS	RANK & CLOTHING	GRADE	FEES
1	Uchikake (tentative member)		4 ryo
2			3.5 ryo
3			.25 ryo
4	ZATO	Grade 1	4 ryo
5	White cloth		4 ryo
6	4 Grades		4 ryo
7	18 Steps (1–18)		20 ryo
8		Grade 2	6 ryo
9			6 ryo
10			30 ryo
11	White hakama	Grade 3	4 ryo
12	(from Step 11)		4 ryo
13			20 ryo
14		Grade 4	22 ryo
15			6 ryo
16			3 ryo
17			6 ryo
18			25 ryo
19	Kōtō	Grade 1	3 ryo
20	Koromo with hat		17 ryo
21	8 Grades		10 ryo
22	35 Steps (19–53)	Grade 2	10 ryo
23			6 ryo
24			4 ryo
25		Grade 3	.25 ryo
26			.25 ryo
27			.5 ryo
28			6 ryo
29			5 ryo
30		Grade 4	5 ryo
31			5 ryo
32			5 ryo
33		Grade 5	.25 ryo
34			.25 ryo
35			.5 ryo
36			4 ryo

Above and opposite: Figure 8.4: Tōdō Shoku Yashiki. This chart shows the four titles: Zato, Kōtō, Betto, and Kengyo. From the Zato entry level, a blind man has seventy-three steps and sixteen grades to get to the top. He does so by paying the appropriate fees (shown in italics). His status in the guild is indicated by clothing. Those at the lowest grade wear white cloth and later white *hakama* (trousers). At the Kōtō level, a hat is added. When a person earns the Betto rank, he can wear a purple *koromo* (jacket). The Kengyo wears a golden *koromo*. The guild essentially certified and authenticated a blind man's salable skills as masseur, acupuncturist, poet, or musician. Of the different occupations, the musicians held the highest status and kept the guild lucrative and powerful. (This chart by Mari Kono is translated from Giichi Tanaka, *Gendai Sankyoku Tenbo*, vol. 3 [Osaka: Shakuhachi Nihon-sha, 1973], p. 55.)

STEPS	RANK & CLOTHING	GRADE	FEES
37			5 ryo
38			25 ryo
39		Grade 6	.5 ryo
40			.5 ryo
41			.25 ryo
42			8 ryo
43			10 ryo
44			14 ryo
45		Grade 7	.5 ryo
46			.5 ryo
47			1 ryo
48			8 ryo
49			10 ryo
50			14 ryo
51		Grade 8	10 ryo
52			10 ryo
53			30 ryo
54	BETTO	Grade 2	10 ryo
55	Purple koromo with tail	(No Grade 1)	10 ryo
56	10 Steps (54–63)		30 ryo
57		Grade 3	20 ryo
58			10 ryo
59			10 ryo
60			30 ryo
61			45 ryo
62			10 ryo
63			10 ryo
64			30 ryo
65	KENGYO		No fee
66	Gold koromo		No fee
67	10 Steps (64–73)		No fee
68			No fee
69			No fee
70	SO-KENGYO		No fee
71	Red clothing		No fee
72	4 Steps (70–73)		No fee
73			No fee

organization sponsored by the provincial lord of Echigo in northern Japan formed a group for blind women called *goze*. The goze installed the Princess Sasami, daughter of the Saga Emperor (809–823), as their patron saint and Benzaiten, goddess of music, as their guide. Their specialty was folk songs with tsuzumi or shamisen accompaniment. Being from Echigo, known for winters with deep snow, they traveled in the warmer season in groups and sang songs of the Echigo area at houses of lesser lords and at bathhouses. Blind ji-uta musicians immortalized Echigo products, songs, and the lion dance the goze introduced in the piece *Echigojishi* (see Figure 6.12 for the *Echigojishi* lyrics).

The guilds of the Tōdōza and goze authenticated blind people's employable skill to make a livelihood. Blind musicians were part of village life. Old screen paintings depict them playing the shamisen at a house or at picnics, or traveling in a group to the next venue. The goze lived by strict codes, such as remaining celibate. Since the two guilds were separate with different goals, the biwa and koto belonging to the blind men did not fall into the hands of the goze.

The blind men of the Tōdōza equally abided by strict rules. Since they did not beget blind sons to pass their art music to, they devised the *yurushi seido* (release system) or a list of pieces to pass before getting permission to learn another set of pieces. Every performance group from gagaku, noh, biwa, etc., also have their own required course of study. The yurushi system was a brainchild of the ninth century Kukai, the founder of the Shingon Sect to impress upon Saicho, his rival, and upon anyone else the seriousness of maintaining the purity of the Buddhist liturgy.

The yurushi system kept the purity of the compositions and the commodity of music out of the hands of any self-proclaimed musician who might corrupt a piece.[22] Also, the yurushi system produced income from both blind and sighted pupils who had to "earn the privilege" to learn new pieces. After each grade, a graduation-like ceremony of *shono* (sake exchange) took place. A *maki* (scroll) listed the pieces learned from the yurushi list with the amount of gratuity paid and the certification granted. Even the blind Tomizaki Shunsho (1879–1960)

First main series: *Yaegasumi, Rosai, Sagoromo*

After the three pieces above were completed, nine more are taught:
Mushi no koe, Sarashi, Tamagawa

Only after the three pieces have been completed, six more are taught:
Azuma jishi, Sumie no Tsuki,
Matsukage no Tsuki, Momiji zukushi, Sode Shigure, Sanak no aki.

Second series is called *Geiko Mittsu mono* (Practice three)
Saigyo Zakura, Echigojishi, Zangetsu

Third series or *Oku Mittsu -mono* (Back three)
Samushiro, Kagurazome, Okina

The last three pieces are called *San yaku*
Meisho Miyage, Shochikubai, Nebiki No Matsu

Figure 8.5: List of Yurushi Mittsu Mono (Release System). The yurushi mittsu mono was adopted by the teachers of the Tōdōza to keep music standardized and proprietary to the composer. Somewhat like a copyright, a person had to patiently go through a course of study before being allowed to learn popular pieces. *Shochikubai* was called the equivalent of a million-dollar piece because people flocked to learn it. *Nebiki no Matsu* by the same composer was called the miso money piece as it sounded similar to his million-dollar piece, but not as appealing.

learned the yurushi pieces after learning fifty-one naga-uta pieces. For the next set of pieces, he memorized six to seven *hundred* ha-uta compositions.

The payment to learn yurushi pieces was two hundred times the monthly tuition. One popular piece, *Shochikubai*, was nicknamed *sembiki mono* (million-dollar piece) for its compositional excellence. When learned, a *maki* (scroll) listed the name along with other names who pledged not to forget the piece and not to teach the piece to unqualified people. They promised to perform the piece only in a proper setting before a proper audience. Anyone deviating from the promise incurs the wrath of the local, regional, national, and universal gods, also listed on the scroll, thus forbidding instruction of outsiders and even relatives who do not have proper lessons and training. The yurushi list kept the integrity of the music passed by rote.

How strictly the yurushi seido is practiced depends on the iemoto. Today popular *yurushi* pieces are less tightly held to the chest; what was once popular in the past has changed. Also, there are recordings and published music scores. But, some proprietary pieces are available only through the composer or his school, like a copyright. Some composers, like Tomizaki Shunsho, release their compositions to the public upon death.

In 1872, the Tōdōza as an organization became extinct but the name, Tōdō, continues. The meaning of Tōdō changed in significance through the centuries. During the Heian Era, Tōdō meant biwa players of the gagaku ensemble. Later, the word pointed to "blind biwa players," and still later, "blind Heikyoku musicians" or blind biwa players singing the *Heike Tales*. By the 1330s, so during Akashi Kakuichi's time, it meant simply "blind men." Today the name refers to an umbrella organization for iemotos of sankyoku musicians of the shamisen, koto, and shakuhachi. Osaka's Tōdō Ongaku Kai (Tōdō Music Group) and the Tōdō Kai of Kyoto are two organizations using the Tōdō name. They require payment for membership, certificates, professional ranks, and titles.

Dendritic Iemoto System

Within and outside of the umbrella organization, iemotos head their own enclave in a dendritic or branch-like manner with lieutenant teachers who are licensed. The dendritic configuration sprouted during the Edo Era (1600–1868) as did the word iemoto. Until the Edo Era, the iemoto came from the aristocracy. But, the Tokugawa government recognized three commoner class experts of *noh-utai* (noh singing), flower arranging, and *chado* (Way of Tea). These newly minted iemotos could associate with the masses without repercussion. They kept their headquarters in Kyoto to protect their high status by being near the seat of nobility. The iemoto's son or trusted *jiki-deshi* (direct student) taught important aristocracy and provincial daimyos. However, with the rising moneyed merchant class desiring to improve themselves, the *natori*[23] or *shihan* (master teacher)[24] came from the same commoner class and could teach new students of the merchant class. The *natori* is literally *na* for name and *tori* for taking, a link to the iemoto's art. Figure 8.6 shows the iemoto at the head with his jiki-deshi of shihan or natori under him; beneath the teachers are students, some at the natori level.

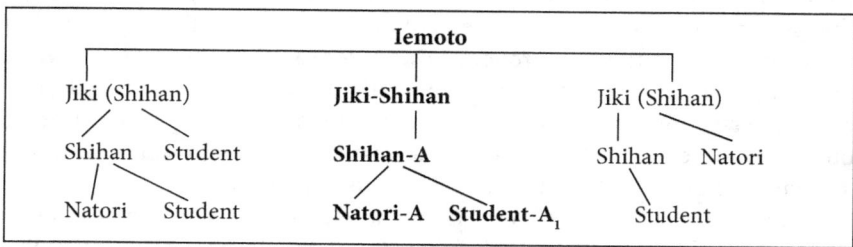

Figure 8.6: Branching of the Iemoto Dendritric System. Each student has the potential to form a branch of the iemoto's school by moving up the ranks and becoming a shihan (certified teacher). The jiki-deshi is the immediate student of the iemoto (headmaster) and those with the shihan have their own students. Each student is nurtured into the iemoto's realm and earns the natori (stage name) before becoming a teacher. The shihan transmits personally the values and attitude of the headmaster and each shihan communicates with the iemoto through the immediate teacher.

In order for lessons to be like the direct experience of the lineal iemoto, lieutenant teachers provided the father-to-son type of interaction by forming an emotional channel to the iemoto. For example, in Figure 8.6, the bold type Student A_1's teacher is shihan A, who communicates to the Jiki-deshi (shihan), and who in turn talks to the iemoto. How can students at the bottom of the branch feel a close tie to the iemoto? In my and other students' experience, the feeling is real and fostered vicariously through the immediate teacher's admiration and experience. In addition, there are opportunities to observe the iemoto first hand at performances and to meet him personally.[25]

The trigger that fosters loyal relationships and trust is *en* (fate, interconnection). *En* in the Japanese scheme of things is chance or chance meeting, fate, or destiny.[26] *En* has billions of permutations because the chance of two people meeting is infinitesimal. Like students in my university class with many course offerings, they chose mine, and I happen to be teaching because of many alternatives that got me there because of *en*. Thus *en* is a very serious matter. *En* sparks the *aidagara* (human relationship) that also sets off the feelings of *on* (benevolence) tinged with responsibility in a hierarchical vertical relationship like that of a parent to a child, a teacher to pupil, and any person in a superior position to one in an inferior position. Parents feel *on* toward a child and provide all they know. The child cannot return the quality of *on* bestowed upon him or her except to reciprocate *on* (*on gaeshi*). The saying is that, "The *on* of a parent is deeper than the ocean and higher than the sky." The only recourse for reciprocating *on* is to do one's best in all aspects of life. Even if one is limited in innate talent, working to one's fullest potential gains admiration. Thus, the concept of an overachiever is nonexistent.

ON = 恩	On gae shi = 恩 返 し
Bestowing benevolence	Reciprocating the ON or benevolence

Figure 8.7: Kanji for On and On-gaeshi. It is interesting to note that the "on" kanji has the *kokoro* (heart, spirit) as part of it. "On" evokes the feeling of responsibility, the feeling of benevolence, or a feeling that swells in the heart when a person is charged with responsibility, like a parent to a child. Over the *kokoro* kanji is the *dai* (big) in a box which is said to be a man resting on a quilt. He is relying or depending on someone in supplication and trust. Thus, "on" is obligation and benevolence towards others, and *on-gaeshi* is the desire to reciprocate "on" by doing one's best, as the reciprocation will be different because of rank and status.

On and *on-gaeshi* in the purest sense is unselfish, idealized, unconditional giving, often perverted to *giri* (duty, obligation). When giri is unfulfilled, there is *haji* (shame).[27] Giri and haji sadly are the realities of the human condition and are the source of conflict in noh, bunraku, kabuki, plays, stories, and songs. But putting human failings aside, *on* in the purer sense is the aspirational ideal.

Importance of Name as Identity to an Iemoto Group

A musician, a dancer, or an artist without an iemoto is like an orphan for the artist is without foundation or credence. The iemoto is the brand name and the authenticator of the artist's skill, art, or commodity. As a student advances, a change in name known as the *natori* (name-taking) includes him in the iemoto's realm.[28]

What's in a name? Like kotodama, it is believed that a name holds a person's fortune. In koto, Yatsuhashi Kengyo (1614–1685) first had the name Yamazumi Kōtō, then Kaminaga, and finally Yatsuhashi Kengyo. An association through name to a prominent person or family brings good fortune.[29] In kabuki, actors took the name of a famous predecessor to emulate his aura. Nakamura Kanjuro became Nakamura Kanzaburo. Similarly kabuki descendants of Ichikawa Danjuro I took his name so that today, there is a Danjuro XII. In ji-uta music, Tomiyama Seikin retired in the year 2000 and relinquished his name to his son, Kiyotaka, to become Tomiyama Seikin II, a name with cachet. Tsugaru shamisen player, Takahashi Chikuzan's student took his name to keep Tsugaru shamisen music alive, and students of the narrative shamisen genres receive the surnames of Takemoto, Kineya, Tokiwazu, Kiyomoto, and others to continue the styles. The public sees power behind the time-tested brand name, and power it has indeed. Like Martha Graham for dance, Harvard for university, Julliard for music, and even McDonald's for hamburger, the iemoto's name has weight like any valued brand name.

Taking the iemoto's name depends on the school. With Tōdōza's dissolution in 1872, blind musicians had no organization to shelter them. Some artists banded to form a sankyoku organization called Tōdō Ongaku Kai, or the Tōdō Kai of Kyoto, that administered the ranks and certification. However, each artist like Kikuzuka Kengyo (1846–1909) formed his own dendritic system with branches of schools with an inclusionary *natori* or name-taking system. Usually, the first syllable of the iemoto's first name forms the first syllable of a disciple's name. The late Tomiyama Seikin I's ji-uta disciples have the Sei (pure) prefix like Seijo, Seiritsu, Seishi, Seiei, Seiyu, Seigiku, Seiko, Seiho, and so on. Later, the Tomi- prefix forms the last name when disciples complete the advanced kumi-uta and dan-mono course. Thus, there is Tominari Seijo, Tomio Seiritsu, Tomita Seiho, Tomii Seiko, Tomihara Seigiku, Tominori Seiyu, and so on. For ji-uta musicians of the Osaka region, the names have a Kiku-, Naka-, Yone-, Tomi- and other prefixes.

Students in the United States may also apply to the iemoto in Japan for a brand name and authentication. Among *buyo* (dance) students, the iemoto's last name identifies the school such as Onoe, Fujima, or Hanayagi. In Virginia, the *jiki-deshi* (direct student) of Onoe Kikunojo II is Onoe Kikuyuki, a shihan, who bears the Kiku-prefix of the iemoto showing the direct tutelage. Her natori students have the "yu" part of her name indicating that they trained with her. They are Onoe Yuzuki, Onoe Yuka, Onoe Yubuki, Onoe Yuriki, Onoe Yurina, etc. Should any natori transgress any agreement of the school, Kikuyuki can recommend expulsion, to which the iemoto acquiesces because of the trust he has for his shihan. In fact, every branch of any iemoto acts autonomously because of the loyalty and trust the shihan earned from the iemoto.

By examining the names of the performers on a program, one can draw

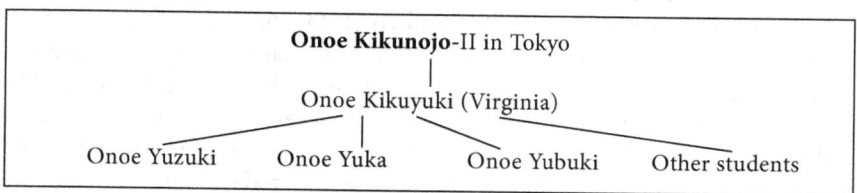

Figure 8.8: Onoe Kikuyuki's Natori and Students. The iemoto's reach is beyond Japan's border. The name gives authenticity to Onoe Kikuyuki's dance group in Chantilly, Virginia. As a jiki-deshi of the iemoto, she has several students who have the natori degree and the privilege to use the Onoe name with their stage name.

lines to determine which students studied with which teacher. However today, some teachers do not link their students through their names, thinking it old-fashioned. Kotoists who studied with Sawai Tadao and Kazue identify their styles by crediting their training with the Sawai Koto Academy.

In the stratified society[30] of the Edo Era, social mobility was impossible, but people of different social ranks could mix in the iemoto's realm and even become a teacher and gain status. In the tea and flower-arranging world, only men could earn the teacher's license until the Meiji Era. Teaching positions became available to women when new types of work opened to men in international business and manufacturing. In addition, modern medicine eradicated blindness leaving few males to pursue koto and shamisen music, their default profession.[31]

Today the respect accorded iemotos and teachers, both men and women, continues.[32] The society is cognizant of the hard work and precise study required to becoming a master of the classical Japanese arts. As younger students learn hogaku, replacing older musicians like the newly rebuilt Ise Shrine replaces the previous Ise Shrine, how much of the hogaku music passes on as originally composed? A study of the koto piece *Rokudan* provides insight.

Probably introduced from the Asian continent to Hakata,

```
1500s                    Tsukushi koto
                              |
                              |
1600s                    YATSUHASHI ryu
                              |
                              |_____
                              |                   OKINAWA ryu
1700s                     IKUTA ryu              /
                              |                 /
                              |_____        /
                              |        \      /
1800s                         |     YAMADA ryu
                              |        /    /
                              |       /    /
1900s      Sanada Shin        |      /    /
                  _____|_____/____/
                       Roku-dan USA
```

Figure 8.9: *Rokudan* from Various Regions, Schools, and Eras. This chart based on my observation and experience shows that *Rokudan*, which is passed by rote, has kept its fidelity from the 1500s to the present. *Rokudan* has been taught at different schools, from Tsukushi, Yatsuhashi, Ikuta, and Yamada to their modern offshoots, and in different locations, such as Kansai, Kyushu, Okinawa, and the United States and elsewhere in the world. It is note for note the same piece as originally conceived. Even the Okinawan rendition played in the YO mode is the same music. Save for minor rhythmic differences here and there, if representatives from the past or from different schools and different locations got together and played the piece, it would not be a problem.

Kyushu, around the 1300 or 1400s, *Rokudan* in the YO mode was played by expatriate courtiers and then transmitted to Tsukushi koto players in the 1500s. Yatsuhashi Kengyo learned it in the 1600s and taught it to other musicians,[33] one of whom transposed the piece to the IN mode to be played by the Ikuta-ryu. By the 1800s it had passed to Yamada-ryu koto. Primarily transmitted by rote and played by different and independent schools separated by geography and time, I learned *Rokudan* by rote in the mid–1900s in the United States and taught it to my students in the 2000s. When I heard the different renditions of *Rokudan* separated by mode, different regions, time, schools, and particularly the rendition by Sanada Shin who is a descendent of the Yatushashi Kengyo's school, I found that everyone played the same *Rokudan* note for note save for a few insignificant differences. Its musical integrity is preserved by thousands of layers of teachers just as Shinto, Buddhist, and noh chants and all other musical endeavors have been similarly replicated because of the behavior and values institutionalized in the iemoto and its system.[34]

Still, the iemoto's position has always been tenuous for he or she is human. In the past, an emperor or shogun could dissolve an iemoto's domain with a single decree. Today a misplaced goal or ego of an iemoto can bring down an entire school and thus, many schools must have faded into oblivion. Also, to become an iemoto today seems easier than centuries ago. It is a matter of self-proclamation as long as there are enthusiastic disciples to perpetuate the school.[35] A gifted disciple can split off to form a new school.[36]

The popular belief and criticism is that the iemoto system is stifling. Again, this depends on whether the iemoto has an open or closed mind. Because performers are human beings, innovations and interpretation occur constantly but in the classical arts, it is in subtle ways noticeable only to the cognoscenti.[37] Although some Japanese artists wish to disassociate themselves from the iemoto label, inadvertently they fall into the iemoto pattern whether they want to or not for it holds their copyright to control the art they create.[38]

The unique element offered in the iemoto system is that one does not have to reinvent the wheel. Zeami's *Kyu-I* points out that a student need not flounder at the lower levels if he begins at the Level 6 where proper guidance will bring out early beauty. One learns the tools of the trade and proper techniques instead of groping on an instrument without any basis. Proper training eliminates any nightmare of trying to make music without the basics.[39] Thus, a creative person takes off from the higher launching pad provided in an iemoto's studio.

Summary

The iemoto system is not an abstract utopia idealized by an august philosopher. It is a practical apprenticeship system that fosters continuity of the skill, craft, or art. Only one person succeeds as headmaster and is privy to the house trade secrets. The bonds of kinship are triggered by *en*, the chance meeting of two people, which mobilizes the feeling of *on* (benevolence) from which the senior feels responsibility towards the junior person. An emotional bond or "kin-tract" has a religious basis. Often referred to as folk sense or wisdom, the early formation of the iemoto is evident in the clan societies of the Jomon people.

All iemoto groups share the attributes of authority, volition, inclusion and exclusion, and continuity. The different iemoto configurations are direct lineal, quasi-lineal, umbrella, and dendritic groups. To ensure that loyalty, values, and skills pass precisely, each configuration allows for crucial face-to-face instruction.

The iemoto includes or excludes people through name changes after passing a rigorous course of study. Like any institution, the iemoto provides individual identity, a standard of accountability for excellence, and a way to relate and work collectively towards goals benefitting oneself and society. The premise to work together comes from the Buddhist karmic idea, Confucius' morality of obedience, and the Shinto belief of anoyo/konoyo and the interconnectedness and sentience of everything.[40]

The criticism of the iemoto system is that individuality and creativity are suppressed.[41] Working together can be difficult because students must check and suppress their ego if they wish to acquire a skill from a master and perform their best for the sake of the group. Like schools of fish or flocks of birds, a common goal (a repulsive imagery to our Western sense of individualism) in the larger scheme of things assures survival, strength, and continuation of the skill, art, trade, or species.[42]

A gifted person, a star performer of a hogaku group, shines for the entire school. Creative individuals within a group have brought Japan to the modern world with innovative goods and art works. The famous Toraya,[43] a Kyoto candy company, instead of languishing in Japan has expanded to New York and Paris to spread Japanese confections around the globe. The Nintendo Corporation that invented the classic Karuta (100 Poetry) game in 1889 is now a big producer of video and high tech games. Manufacturers like Toyota, Honda, Panasonic, Sony, and others are successful because of the link between top management and shop workers to create products for the common good.[44]

In other words, as archaic as the iemoto system may be, the work ethic fostered in the iemoto paradigm has kept Japanese ancient classical music alive for the world to hear with fidelity. It will be our good fortune if the iemoto system continues with new students to supply hogaku musicians forever, like the trusted carpenters of the Shrine of Ise.

9

The West, Hogaku Today and the Future

In the previous chapters, I laid out the commonalities of hogaku's aesthetics, scale, structure, and the use of voice and timbre on unassuming instruments to decorate the unfolding melody. Thanks to the iemoto system, unwritten hogaku music remains alive through performers from whom we hear, identify with, and relive the emotions of our ancestors in the lament for the deposed emperor in the Yuraku castle or the sorrow of the parting lovers in *Jisei* of the Tanabata story. We can also imagine the magnificent cherry blossoms of Yoshino and feel the same joy at spring with the first songs of the *uguisu*.

Some poets and lyricists have even glorified places they have not visited and described the majesty of Mount Fuji or the beauty of Enoshima as in the koto piece *Haru no Enoshima* (Enoshima at Spring), in which it is idealized as a heavenly island in the sky. Today, Enoshima is a hangout for young bathers who reach the island via a concrete causeway and climb to the summit on a noisy escalator. A tenth century poet of the first poem of *Chidori no Kyoku* imagined a beautiful expansive spot wherein resided the chidori at "*sashide no iso*," but in reality it is tiny spot hidden in Yamanashi-ken mountains.[1]

Through music, the pride of Edo Era commoners exalts everyday products or beautiful scenery while others are of raw emotions of unrequited love, loneliness, and hopeless situations. Because the music is word-based, it taps known and rare sources for legends, stories, and historical events that are retold in almost every genre, including noh, bunraku, kabuki plays, and today's manga and anime,[2] thereby exposing the Japanese to familiar recurring themes. Through music we meet people from the past and react similarly to beauty, feelings of nostalgia, and love because hogaku contains the emotional history of the Japanese people.[3]

The Quest for Novelty

The Japanese characteristically like novelty. New instruments from the Asian continent were adapted and made their own. In the sixteenth century when the Jesuits brought Western music, Father Organtino Gnecchi wrote, "Everybody is in the highest degree eager to learn our music and to play our instruments; and if we only had more organs and other musical instruments, Japan would be converted to Christianity in less than a year."[4] His prediction came to naught when in 1639, Christians and foreigners were ousted and Japan slammed the doors behind them. Between the mid-1600s and mid-1800s during an interval of relatively minimal foreign influence, hogaku thrived on its own terms. Even then, the Nagasaki port reserved for only Dutch traders was a sieve. Scientific and medical information, books, and many curios such as the *orugoru* (music box) entered Japan. The orugoru found its way to kabuki's *geza* (backstage music) and gave the idea of the *kaede* (other hand, or polyphonic part to the main melody) to the blind musician Ichiura Kengyo, who composed a high tinkling kaede to *Oranda Manzai* (*Holland Manzai*).

Japan's leaky closed doors by the 1830s allowed a fife and drum corps into Kyushu and pushed the Kagoshima daimyo to organize a similar band. Later in 1853, Commodore Matthew Perry brought two military bands to impress the Japanese. Count Eulenburg in 1860 stunned the public with his blaring forty-piece marine band marching down the streets of Yokohama. Soon thereafter Japan opened its doors to the world and welcomed marching bands, the French bugle and signal corps, and military brass bands along with Western goods and ideas.

Why Japan Adopted Western Music

At this point, the Japanese sense of etiquette came into play. One rule of etiquette is to be sensitive to the comfort of your guest—in this case, to be attentive to the needs of foreign visitors. A second rule of etiquette is to be "correct" in the eyes of others and not appear "strange." In their endeavor to belong to the world community, particularly at ceremonies, the Meiji emperor suggested that court musicians learn how to play Western instruments to entertain foreigners. No other nation has acted reciprocally, but it was not unusual for the Japanese to adopt Western music for the comfort of its visitors. Also, historically Japan had adopted and included other music from foreign countries, such as gagaku from China and Korea.[5]

In addition, the Meiji oligarchy knew that in order for Japan to participate in the international sphere, she would have to modernize, meaning to

Westernize. The Iwakura Mission (1871) traveled around the world to explore how to accomplish this. Aside from technological and political ideas, the mission was impressed with the education of children, namely how they sang sweetly in unison. The well-established hogaku curriculum with iemoto-licensed teachers did not fit the oligarchy's goal and the songs were hardly suitable for little voices.

In a decision that mirrored the establishment in year 701 of a foreign music department, the Meiji government formed the Institute of Music in 1879 to create a new national music and to train primary teachers for the public schools. The first director, Izawa Shuji (1851–1917), headed the project and enlisted Luther Whiting Mason (1818–1896) the superintendent of the Boston Public School music program from 1864 to 1896. In Boston, Mason had devised foolproof lesson plans and charts for inexperienced music teachers.[6] When invited to Japan, he took Scottish songs in the pentatonic scale upon which the Japanese added their lyrics emphasizing good moral character. One such song is *Hotaru no Hikari* (Light of the Firefly)[7] set to the tune of *Auld Lang Syne* with words to study hard by the light of the firefly and light reflected off snow or in any condition. Thus, Western music planted in the ears of young children from the late 1800s had by World War II nurtured generations of Japanese versed in Western music[8] leaving hogaku as a strange novelty in its own land.[9]

The West and Gagaku

With the reinstatement of the emperor to political power and interest in Western music, it was not all a happy time for the biwa. The biwa was "grievously injured by the Restoration"[10] for it sang of the virtues of past samurai heroes when Japan wanted to modernize. Gagaku musicians fared better, and the musicians were reassembled from near and far to perform Imperial ceremonial music and to entertain foreign dignitaries. By 1961, the Imperial household sent Suenobu Togi (1932–2009) to teach gagaku at the University of California at Los Angeles, a position he held until 1993. After Emperor Hirohito's death, the world heard segments of gagaku music during the televised enthronement in 1989 of his successor, Emperor Akihito.

Gagaku music became very popular through Hideki Togi (b. 1960), considered a renegade by purist gagaku members but a champion by the Japanese public. A rage in the early 2000s, his group included two women, his mother on the sho and his sister on the ryuteki. He also rearranged the seating of the gagaku group to feature the *hichriki* (his instrument) in front and composed and mixed gagaku music with Western instruments.[11] Influenced by the Beatles' music, he enjoyed playing hichiriki transpositions of *Hey Jude* and *Yesterday* accompanied by a jazz band.[12] His creations and innovations called attention to and breathed new life into the ancient ensemble. Togi said, "I love gagaku, so I want to share it with everyone."[13]

Sukeyasu Shiba came from the Koma clan that provides gagaku music for the Kofukuji and Kasuga Taisha of Nara. Shiba revived gagaku instruments and scores that were tucked away at Nara's Shosoin. He brought to light an old biwa score found in the margins of a receipt book from the year 747. Additionally he reacquainted the Japanese with the *U* or bass sho, *genkan* (round moon lute), *o-hichiriki* (bass *hichiriki*), a *hokyo* hanging metal xylophone-like instrument, *haisho*, and others (see Chapter 3: Simple Instruments). His group, called Reigaku, performs on the restored instruments.

The West and Noh

The restoration of the emperor meant the noh groups suddenly lost the centuries of shogun support. To sustain themselves, actors took odd jobs like selling charcoal and their gorgeous costumes and stage props.[14] Oddly enough the noh's rescue came from the Empress Dowager, the Prince of Wales, President Ulysses S. Grant, and Minnie Hauk. In 1879, Grant praised noh and remarked to Iwakura about the importance of preserving it.[15] Similarly in 1894, Camalia Mignon Hauck known as Minnie Hauk (1851–1929), a premier soprano from New York, wrote,

> Our German and Austrian dramatic entertainments are of recent origin when compared with those in your country, and your Society has done well to preserve these remains of the ancient past and tradition. We had thought that we in Europe were the first to create operas, but now that I know that the art existed in Japan before we even became civilized, I am struck all the more with admiration. I am nothing short of amazed at how early music and the art of singing developed in Japan.[16]

The general public was invited to join the exclusive Noh Society and attracted Japanese scholars such as Tsubouchi Shoyo of Waseda,[17] who formed in 1904 the Society for the Study of Noh Literature to explore its development, influence, drama, and music in relation to Buddhism.[18] Noh connoisseurs appeared with foreigners such as Earnest Fenollosa who translated noh plays in 1879. E. S. Morse studied noh utai with Umewaka, a noh master, and explained his problems in producing the voice, learning the score by rote, and acquiring an appreciation and aesthetics for Japanese which Morse's friend, Professor Yatabe insists is superior.[19] Noh continues to intrigue people[20] and many Western scholars specialize in noh.[21]

The West and Shamisen

While Meiji Era school children learned about Western music, late nineteenth-century woodblock prints depict riotous party scenes at the Pleasure Quarter. A Western man dances a jig to shamisen music[22] and in another, a geisha dressed in Western clothes plucks a violin with a shamisen bachi while holding it sideways on her lap.[23] The lowly kabuki theater finally became more widely accepted after the Imperial family gave it audience. The narrative shamisen provided most of kabuki's music. The art ji-uta shamisen continued with the koto, but the folk-based Tsugaru shamisen became popular after a movie about blind Takahashi Chikuzan's life and also caught the attention of the West with its fast-paced bluegrass-type pickings of the Yoshida Bros and Agatsuma. They combined the youthful blend of percussive beats and fast melodies with rock or jazz bands. In a similar vein, the AUN J classical group formed a modern age band using hogaku instruments of koto, shamisen, shakuhachi, *yoko bue* (flute), and *narimono* (percussion).

Music of Koto

With the dissolution of the Tōdō Shoku Yashiki, blind musicians of ji-uta sangen and koto also lost government support but were freed from the restraints of the powerful guild. Some musicians performed for vaudeville-type shows and others joined the religious order called Fuso Kyo Ninko Kyokai that later became the Nippon Tōdō Ongaku Kai. In 1904, Kikuzuka Kengyo (1846–1909) reorganized this group into the Tōdō Ongaku Kai (Tōdō Music Organization) headquartered in Osaka. The group opened the exclusive domain of koto and shamisen music to the public, published scores, and fostered research of other genres of koto, including the Yamada-ryu of the Tokyo region. They also held four public concerts annually as a way to disseminate the Meiji shinkyoku or new koto compositions of the Meiji Era. The pieces experimented with new tuning and new techniques, such as left-hand plucking.[24]

The koto's appealing harp and guitar-like sound became the first Japanese instrument to successfully cross into Western music. From here, koto music diverges in two paths, the classical Japanese and the Western types of music. The leading composers of the classical style were Kikuzuka Kengyo (1846–1909),[25] Tateyama Noboru (1876–1926),[26] Kikuhara Kengyo (1877–1948),[27] Tomizaki Shunsho (1880–1958),[28] and Tomiyama Seikin (1913–2008).[29] Their new compositions follow the tegoto outline: song, instrumental interlude, and song. The lyrics by contemporary poets in Tomizaki Shunsho's *Haru no Enoshima* and *Manzai Raku* hint of Western influence in chords in fourths instead of octaves. Tomizaki's disciple, Tomiyama Seikin of Tokyo also continued the established style with his compositions *Akatsuki no Uta*, *Shuno-ten* (1958), and *Miyako Wasure*. *Miyako Wasure* in classical tegoto format incorporates Western chords and left-hand plucking, and his *Shoka no Ogawa* for beginners is an exercise of all koto techniques with a touch of Western chords and sequences.

Meanwhile in the Japanese colony of 1907 Korea, Miyagi Michio at age 14 (1893–1956) composed his first work, *Mizu no Hentai*, in the classical tegoto format. Playing it before Ito Hirobumi, the Resident-General of Korea,[30] this dazzling piece was exactly what Ito was looking for to impress Westerners. He promised to take Miyagi back to Tokyo, but Ito's assassination delayed the trip. Ten years later Miyagi returned to Japan where he continued to compose koto music in the Western manner with singable Western-type melodies set to chordal accompaniments. His 1929 signature piece, *Haru no Umi* (Sea at Spring), composed in collaboration with Yoshida Seifu (1890–1950) met with international acclaim.[31] By 1925, Miyagi was heralded as the "*Nihon no unda tensai sakkyokuka*" or "Japan-born genius composer" by the Tokyo newspaper *Nichi Nichi Shimbun*, which featured him in a series of four articles.[32]

The koto purists thought Miyagi cheapened and compromised the koto, a criticism that reached my ears in Los Angeles as a child. The public's opinion of Miyagi was different. He was a hero because his music crossed over to the West.[33] Miyagi also invented a seventeen-string bass koto for orchestral type pieces that ranged from bass to soprano. Other people invented the twenty-one- and the thirty-one-string kotos[34] that accommodate the diatonic scale. Prominent composers include Hisamoto Genshi, Nakashima Utahiko, and Sakamoto Tsutomu, however, it was Tadao Sawai (1937–1997) and his wife, Kazue Sawai (b. 1941), who caught the attention of the Western world with their album *J.S. Bach Is Alive and Well and Doing His Thing on the Koto*, released in 1971. Later, Sawai's transpositions of Vivaldi's *Four Seasons* and Mozart's *Eine Klinenachtmusik* were played on American classical radio stations in the 1980s. Today their disciples win koto contests in Japan and play in New York, California, and Hawaii, spreading the Sawai renditions of modern koto music.

The shakuhachi, in the meantime, garnered a worldwide following of students because of its versatile and pleasant sound. Many non–Japanese have mastered the *honkyoku*, and Western composers also write new compositions.[35]

The West and Japanese Composers of Western Music

I am not aware of any composer today who composes hogaku in the classical manner, which brings us back to the question of why Japanese composers with Western training compose characteristically Japanese music. In other words, why does their "Western"-type music sound Japanese? Is there any influence of hogaku upon them today? The active showcase for Japanese composers is the New York–based Music From Japan, Inc., headed by Naoyuki Miura (b. 1938)[36] since 1975. Its purpose is to introduce contemporary Japanese composers to the United States. Early in his enterprise in 1980, a symposium held at the John F. Kennedy Center for the Performing Arts in Washington, D.C., had Japanese and American composers, critics, and scholars facing each other to discuss the music from Japan. The Japanese composers wanted recognition that they have joined the world in music, but the Americans wanted to know about Japanese music and the exotic quality that makes Japanese music different. The perplexed Japanese sat silently for their training was Western in scope and the symposium continued with the two sides talking past each other. The Americans did not get their answer, but the Japanese had the opportunity to display their music to a Western audience in the Kennedy Center Concert Hall.

Twenty-eight years later at a meeting in Baltimore, Maryland, at a Music of Japan Today: 2003 Festival and Symposium,[37] those present raised the same question, "What is Japanese music?" The Japanese participants said that it is impossible to pinpoint what is typically Japanese because of the regional differences between Kansai and Kanto or Okinawan and Hokkaido and all the places in between. American and Europeans may also claim regional differences of French, German, English, Italian music, and so on. So trying to define what is typically Japanese also belies what is typically Western. Some of the composers present at the Kennedy Center symposium of 1980 also participated at Baltimore.[38] In Baltimore the musicians surmised that the question of "What is Japanese?" might become irrelevant in the future. Joji Yuasa (b. 1929) pointed out that young Japanese composers (trained in Western music) strive to feel and create music from their "cosmology." Akira Nishimura (b. 1953) continued that the question is odd and has no meaning because each composer goes his own way. Younger ones in time will have more freedom.

But does the recurring question of "What is Japanese music?" arise because musicians of the two worlds look at each other and have different expectations because of their obvious racial and cultural differences?

The conference members did capture one central difference between the two types of music. They agreed that Western music is anthropomorphic-centric, while Japanese music is nature-centric and a human activity.[39] For example, Tokuhide Niimi (b. 1947) is awed and inspired by trees that are the longest living thing on earth. Although trees do not speak, he listens for their voices as they are part of nature.[40] The titles of many Japanese composers' works evoke nature, like *Winter Shadows, Rain, Calling Autumn,*[41] *Bird in*

Colors, Bird in Grief, Bird in Wind,[42] or feelings, like *Solitude*,[43] *Reminiscences II*, and *Profoundly*.[44]

Another fundamental different between Japanese traditional music and Western music is how they are defined within temporality. European music has metered or countable time. In contrast, the human breath governs the timing of Japanese music, so it is organic with a sense of continuity. The Japanese are unencumbered by structure because music can unroll with different melodies unhindered by the use of motifs. In one example where nature is the source, Mamoru Fujieda (b. 1955) placed electrodes on plants to compose melodies using the movement of the growing leaves.[45]

Is the music "Japanese" because the Japanese and non–Japanese composers write for a hogaku instrument or evoke Japanese topics? Joji Yuasa used three quiet poems by Basho[46] for koto and shakuhachi piece because artists commissioned him. Although he prefers the notes of a well-tempered scale, he sometimes incorporates the shakuhachi or koto because Western instruments can't change timbre. Joji Yuasa admitted that he knows Western instruments better. Likewise, the Reigaku gagaku ensemble performed the works of composer Kazuo Kikkawa (b. 1954) at the Kennedy Center. There, I asked if he wrote often for gagaku instruments. His knee-jerk response was a vehement, "No!"[47] He preferred writing for Western instruments.[48]

Although Tokuhide Niimi wrote thirty pieces for hogaku instruments and the twenty-string koto, he found composing for them difficult, saying that the techniques and notation for the instruments is different. Akira Nishimura confessed, "I don't really know how to compose for them [hogaku instruments]," and pointed out that most of the Japanese instruments came from China except the *wa-gon*. Nishimura added that Chinese instruments have more techniques. Their shakuhachi has seven holes whereas the Japanese instrument has five holes. The Chinese biwa has more frets whereas the Japanese biwa has fewer frets and uses a bigger bachi. Japanese instruments have one perfect voice and each instrument has different techniques to affect rhythmic construction. Even a note such as the "A" pitch is different on the shakuhachi and koto, said Nishimura.[49]

If we review the commonalities of hogaku from Chapter 3: Simple Instruments, we find the Japanese used simple instruments made from natural materials with no mechanical parts. So, do contemporary Japanese composers prefer to write for Western instruments because they are "simpler" to write for because they have one voice and less variability than Japanese instruments?

Is music by Japanese composers "Japanese" because they use the Japanese scales? With Western ideas, the Japanese composers have a wider range of scales to create a variety of atmospheres and at times use the IN or YO scales for a Japanese effect. In addition, singing that dominated hogaku is now set to the wayside except for popular Western-type songs. However, contemporary Japanese composers do not hesitate to use timbre or "noise" for ethereal, eerie, or agitating sounds for effect.[50]

Ideas for music in ancient times came from the kami, and composers told tales about visiting shrines for divine inspiration. I wondered if Japanese composers today also sought similar guidance, and I asked this question at the Baltimore conference. Joji Yuasa said he composes from a deep part of the self, of who he is, from his culture and language, all of which defines his way of thinking and sensitivity. He writes from his sphere or in other words, "I am composing for myself." He also added that he writes for human beings, not for cows. Tokuhide Niimi said he composed for himself with an imagined audience but not specifically Asian or European. "We are musicians, but that's not the purpose. Good music lets me live, keeps me alive. I like to keep that attitude." Niimi added, "I think only humans understand music." Akira Nishimura said, "I write for my life. I want to live life perfectly, enjoy my life, and compose for my life." Teizo Matsumura (1929–2007) noted, "The highest state of composition would be to write freely and naturally with the composer's mind open."[51] He wrote for koto, shamisen shinobue, and biwa. After hearing and studying the koto piece, *Rokudan*, he wrote *Poeme* (1969) for koto and shakuhachi. Compositions by professional composers are interesting but extremely difficult to play because the notes deviate from the familiar techniques of playing the instrument.

By contrast composers who play and know the instrument are better at utilizing its techniques and timbre. Tadao Sawai brings out the koto's full colors and exploits virtuoso sounding techniques. His disciple, Hideaki Kuribayashi, continues with a Philip Glass–like repetition using different koto patterns. Togi Hideki, who plays both gagaku and Western instruments, successfully melds the innate qualities of the East and West. Similarly the Yoshida Brothers with the Tsugaru shamisen mix rock elements with the fast-paced Aomori tuning and spirit. The AUN J classical band of hogaku instrumentalists employs innate techniques to bring out fast-paced melodies that appeal to today's audience.

Today, classical hogaku music is deemed old-fashioned—a paradox for a society that values longevity in brand names and family line. The long-playing NHK television series *Nihon no Geino* features classical Japanese arts and among the programs are children playing the koto. The television hosts were quick to praise the virtuoso modern players over the classical hogaku player, inadvertently and subconsciously skewing the bias of audiences. Even at koto contests, the modernists excel with impressive techniques that accentuate the drabber colors of the hogaku classics.

Ironically, European music of the same classical period of hogaku composers attracts the modern Japanese, although they claim their own classics to be "old fashioned." To the converse, the American and Russian[52] audiences find quintessentially Japanese music like *Rokudan* interesting and even avant-garde sounding. Shakuhachi students of Yodo Kurahashi prefer to study *honkyoku* pieces or the meditative Zen sounds of Edo Japan. Whenever U.S. performances by Music from Japan features hogaku instruments, the audience is larger in anticipation of hearing Japanese music on Japanese instruments.

The Future

Changes have occurred in compositions using hogaku instruments. For one thing instrumental music without voice now dominates. Music also incorporates both Japanese and Western scales and at times juxtaposes the two scales, as in Agatsuma's *tsugaru* shamisen with a Western band.[53] New techniques accommodate melodic units and Western harmony. Contemporary music also fits a metered measure. In addition, Western instruments such as flute, violin, viola, clarinet, and the entire orchestra accompany most all hogaku instruments and even accompany Buddhist chants.

Audiences preferring the quiet sedate music have waned along with the patience needed for time-consuming, introspective musing. In place of refined elegance is *kawaii* (cute), evoking pleasant feelings of warmth and smiles. Japan excels in cute things—perhaps video games hold cute music? New virtuoso-type contemporary music is louder and faster. The ever-increasing speed and volume reminds me of the science fiction story *The Nine Billion Names of God*.[54] Tibetan monks hand wrote tediously the name of each god. When completed, it will be the end of the universe. To speed the process, they rent a computer from the West. As the two computer installers depart for their plane to take them back to civilization, they look up in the night sky and notice that the stars were fading one by one. In regards to contemporary music, is it faster and louder portending a crescendo that ends in deep silence? Is Max Richter's[55] *Sleep* a step in that direction? *Sleep* lasts eight hours with pages of whole notes meant to quiet the unconscious in order to put audiences (or even the musicians) to sleep.

Let us return to the question what makes the music of Western-trained Japanese musicians different from that of non–Japanese composers? There must be a subliminal influence from the environment or musical mitochondria powering their musical creations. Although Japan has attained modernity in high-rise buildings, cars, trains, planes, and cell phones, with 99 percent of the people in Western clothes and listening to Western music, sandwiched between Western façades are ancient temples, shrines, castles, rivers, mountains, trees, sumo, and recurring poetry contests, annual games like the

Hyakunin Isshu poetry and hogaku music played on New Year's Day. Cultural references to mythology, legends, and beliefs give meaning to daily activities, food, confectionery, and festivals at countless local, regional, and national shrines. The mix of culture from the past and modern worlds feed Japanese artistic endeavors.

I am sure that hogaku instruments will endure with new compositions, but I am concerned about its classical repertoire. Jazz and popular musicians with a classical background have a stronger foundation for their music. Similarly hogaku musicians with a classical background also have better command over their instruments and music.[56] But the question is: Is there a need for hogaku's *classical* music in a society dominated by Western music? Similar to storing seed banks of various plants and learning about the world's cuisine to enrich our diet, a variety from the world's music is like having a good cultural gene pool. One cannot anticipate how or which idea will prove useful. The ancient art of gigaku[57] disappeared, but the lion dances at processions at celebrations and huge colorful masks and costumes stored at temples and museums are the cultural capital that have inspired, of all things, Japanese anime and video games to the delight of world gamers who found new intrigue and interest in Japan studies.[58]

In an unrelated but relevant example, a South African production of the *Magic Flute* using African marimba, drums, dances, costumes, and customs to present Mozart's familiar arias was a delightful reinterpretation of the opera.[59] Mozart's original score anchored the performance and likewise, hogaku can add richness to experimental music like *Chidori* for women's voices by Gary Davison sung to koto's *Chidori no Kyoku*.

If we trace back to the beginning of hogaku, each genre of pre-Western hogaku developed and enriched Japan's cultural capital from the basis of Shinto norito. The magic endowed in the words formed Japan's uta-centric music. Even as the gagaku ensemble brought new instruments, the uta of Buddhist chants touched Japanese sentiments to influence biwa music that became fodder for noh plays enjoyed by the shogunate. Shamisen and koto music continued to echo the emotional concerns of the Tokugawa Era commoner class in a quintessentially Japanese manner.

In the story of hogaku, the music from the Asian continent helped develop a rich sophisticated music over Japan's indigenous premises. Now that Western music dominates in Japan, how strongly will the ancient DNA permeate through Japan's future musical hybrids? Only time will tell. Today with English being the universal language, Japanese literature and scientific papers must be in English to gain recognition.[60] In the same manner, must Japanese music and instruments henceforth be Western in scope to attract an audience? If the past is any indication, my hope is that the future music of Japan will be a hybrid as vigorous and interesting as the hogaku that developed between the eighth and twentieth centuries. Historically the Japanese have integrated the best of other cultures without losing what is quintessentially Japanese, thanks to the aesthetic depth set by their Jomon ancestors. One clear goal of Japanese music is that music should touch the heart, and this attribute fortuitously is universal.

Epilogue

Formerly, I was confident about the iemoto system's power to continue hogaku music, like the families of gagaku, noh, bunraku, and kabuki. However, my doubts grew in 2011 when Mia Saidel[1] and I journeyed to Japan to see its status today. We visited koto makers, string makers, shopkeepers, teachers, performers, memorials, and gravesites. Three decades earlier I had visited Mr. Imai of Tokyo who made kotos from start to finish. Expecting to see a shop with a single craftsman, I found several men had banded together to form a "factory" because "a *kojin* (independent person) cannot make a livelihood."[2] Even the largest factory I visited in the 1980s in Fukuyama, Hiroshima, had dissolved. The few remaining craftsmen gathered to form their own company, but the *shacho* (boss) confessed that he is not encouraging his son to take over because of the diminishing number of koto players.[3]

The koto makers knew happier times in the 1980s and 1990s when high school koto clubs competed locally, regionally, and nationally as encouraged by the Monbusho (Ministry of Education), making the demand for kotos so high that they said even Yamaha Piano got into the act and commissioned a factory in China to produce cheap kotos.[4] But after the contests, the students, like athletes in school sports, abandoned the instrument. Only those students from families specializing in hogaku continued to play the koto.[5]

Fewer koto players affected the need for string makers. In the past there were hundreds of string factories along Lake Biwa but now there are less than five. Music publishers, small hogaku shops, and department stores that sold hogaku regalia also closed. Ando Masakazu, kotoist and retired professor at Tokyo Geidai, questioned his prospective students' major, cautioning them, "You can't make a living [in hogaku]."[6] It was also sad to see the stars of the koto and ji-uta world with fewer and fewer concert gigs and students.

Mia's and my attention turned to the Kyoto gravesite of famous composers like Yaezaki Kengyo (1776–1848), a prolific composer for the koto of sangen compositions. We found it shunted to a corner of a concrete driveway of a Kyoto Temple. As for Yatsuhashi Kengyo's memorial at Konkai Komyoji, there were no mementos from musicians and only a few prayer sticks left by a successful candy company with the same name. At Tomonoura Museum built facing a circular harbor in Fukuyama of Hiroshima Prefecture where Miyagi Michio's *Haru no Umi* was inspired, his statue and exhibit room had not a single visitor save us. Such was the status of hogaku and its instruments as observed in 2011. I envied the accolades given on the other side of the world to Mozart's and Beethoven's tombs decorated with garlands of live flowers.[7]

The Japanese schools and the mass media treat hogaku as an oddity similar to the way American textbooks introduce foreign music. Although the Monbusho in 1971 made videos of prominent artists for use in schools,[8] the average Japanese music teacher is ill-prepared to teach the subject as the teachers are products of the Monbusho's historical choice and emphasis on Western music.[9] Earlier in the 1950s, the government awarded the status of Living National Treasure to hogaku specialists with an annual stipend. The title however had the unintended consequence of making artists similarly unapproachable as *hito gami* (living gods) and some raised their tuition to match their new status. Instead the government might do better to consider giving hogaku musician prime time media exposure and awarding generous scholarships to students wanting to study with them.[10]

Generally people in Japan hear hogaku music only when it is broadcast nationally on New Year's Day.[11] In Japanese movies hogaku is rarely heard except in biographies of hogaku musicians such as the koto in two old movies called *Okoto to Sasuke* and *Shunkin Monogatari*,[12] and the Tsugaru shamisen in *Life of Chikuzan*. I was surprised to hear that the Japanese public was astonished to hear the biwa as late as 1964 in a movie called *Kwaidan*.[13] Assuming that Japanese movies will have complementary music, my American friend craving for a dose of good Japanese music went to see the 1983 movie *Makioka Sisters*. Instead, he was bombarded with Handel.[14] Even at a 2014 pre-public showing of an Ise Shrine documentary, piano and Western music set the quiet scenes of the quintessential Japanese shrine when the wa-gon would have been more mysterious and appropriate.[15]

Fortunately, the internet makes it easy to access a variety of foreign music on its own terms.[16] The challenge is to hear and train our ears with patience. Once our brain learns the schema, it can anticipate and tame the "noise" to become pleasing—an axiom suitable for any type of learning.[17]

As Japan tries to assume a Western identity, the attraction of Japan to some people is its refined aesthetics based on themes of nature that follow the maxim that "less is more."[18] The "less is more" idea pervades The Way of Tea, which is simply boiling the water, whipping the tea, and drinking it. Likewise *ikebana* (flower arranging) with three major points of *shin, soe,* and *tai* (heaven, earth, man) is merely placing flowers in a vase as found in nature. Poetry expresses deep emotion with only five to seven syllables in three to five lines, and the melodic line of music is linear—simple yet complex.

Since the Meiji Era, the Japanese are guided by the values and standards of the West. Kensuke Shichida of southern Japan and Yasuyuki Yoshida of Yoshida Brewers[19] are very well acquainted with this Japanese trait. Their sake business, overwhelmed by Western wine, whiskey, and beer, is leaving them in the wake. To reawaken the taste for sake the brewers are on a mission to introduce sake to the world. They surmise that when sake, is accepted and proclaimed globally, the Japanese will then turn inward and rediscover Japan's national drink.[20]

Perhaps hogaku should employ the same tactics as the sake brewers. When outsiders of Japan value and appreciate hogaku, then the Japanese may reassess its value.

Glossary

age-uta vocal instructions to go up a pitch (sage-uta, go down) in Buddhist, biwa, and noh chants

aidagara human relationship

ai-no-te short instrumental interlude in songs

Ainu indigenous inhabitants of Japan believed to be descendants of the Jomon people

amadera choshi raindrop rhythm found in Buddhist chants, biwa, and shamisen music

ama-no-iwafue stone flute of the Jomon site found during the Taisho period (1912–1926), stored at the Hakodate Municipal Museum

Amaterasu Sun Goddess who heads the Shinto pantheon

anoyo the invisible other world as opposed to konoyo, this world

aragoto heroic style or rough macho style of Edo kabuki acting and singing

Asakura song about Emperor Yuryaku's (456–479) castle sung with wa-gon

ashirai percussion tempo in freer beats of the introductory and exit songs of noh actors

asobi play, a word for secular music used for entertainment. Asobi is categorized today under gagaku music or as "ancient" music. Azuma asobi are songs from eastern Japan

Asoka Indian Prince of the third century who spread Buddhism throughout Asia

ato-uta song at the end (as opposed to mae-uta or song at the beginning) of the tegoto format

a-ware pathos

awasezume koto technique of playing the low and high octaves simultaneously with the thumb and middle finger

Azuma asobi ancient songs from eastern Japan

bachi plectrum, fan-shaped for both the biwa and shamisen. Biwa bachi is large and made of wood. Shamisen bachi is smaller made of ivory, water buffalo horn, tortoise shell, or plastic.

banso accompaniment to singing

-bayashi hayashi. In compounds, the "h" gets a "b" sound as in noh-bayashi.

be guild, or tomo, corporation of ancient times. Be is usually a suffix identifying that a person belongs to a certain guild, like Kamibe is kami, or god, and be, of the guild.

Benzaiten (Benten) goddess of music, arts, and letters with a biwa in her hand. Originally from Persia, she became India's Sarawasti and then Benzaiten of Japan

biwa lute from Persia played with a fan-like biwa bachi. Used in several genres, including the gagaku, moso, Heike, Satsuma, and Chikuzen

bugaku court dance with huge masks and elaborate costumes and music of a gagaku ensemble without strings

bunraku theater with puppets and narrators who can trace their style to Takemoto Gidayu of Osaka

-bushi song, or song type or style of song, usually preceded by an adjective, Itchu-bushi, Naniwa-bushi, Kato-bushi, etc. (Somewhat similar to different styles of music like blues, country, jazz.)

bushido way of the warrior; includes a Zen Buddhist influence

buyo dance, usually classical dance of the kabuki theater and ji-uta music

chado Way of Tea or Tea Ceremony, as developed by Sen Rikyu (1522–1591)

ch'in a small, quiet seven-stringed Chinese instrument associated scholars who played it for spiritual enlightenment. Combined with the shitsu, the duet exemplifies "Kin-shitsu aiwa," or love and harmony as in connubial bliss.

Chikuzen biwa smaller biwa held sideways like the shamisen developed by Ms. Yoshida Takeko in the late 1800s; Tachibana Chijo codified its repertory and techniques

chinkon-sai spirit pacification ritual of Shinto

chirashi scattering or coda of the instrumental interlude of the tegoto format

chu bridge or fret on the biwa

chukyoku middle length pieces of gagaku music; taikyoku are great pieces in about eight movements, whereas shokyoku are shorter pieces

daikin large inverted bell used in Buddhist ceremonies

dan steps or sections

dan-awase section played with another dan or section of music to create a heterophonic melody line

dan-giri stereotype musical passage at the end of a piece; the coda in nagauta pieces

dan-mono koto pieces without song divided into sections with 52 beats per section

dendritic iemoto system iemoto with branches of the school headed by shihan or licensed teachers

dora gong used in some Buddhist sects

ebi shrimp, symbol of longevity

Ebisu Japanese god depicted with fishing pole and *tai* (seabream) among the Seven Gods of Good Fortune

eisho aria part of biwa music that is followed by the coda; ginsho (declamation of the title of the piece) begins the piece followed by rosho (recitation) and then the eisho

Emperor Daigo (898–930); emperor of the ninth and tenth centuries

en chance meeting, destiny, fate

enka popular songs, Japanese blues popular during the 1900s

Enryakuji Tendai temple on Kyoto's Mount Hiei founded by Saicho in 806

Fujiwara Sadotoshi biwa player who returned from China 839–840 with secret pieces such as *Ryusen* (Running Spring) and *Takobuku* (Hitting Wood) that were lost during the Heian Court's demise

Fuke sect shakuhachi playing priests created by the government for ronin (masterless samurai), dissolved in 1871

fukiawase priests or teachers of shakuhachi who taught non-priest students

fushi melody that emphasizes mood and drama

fushi-mawashi melismata, ornamentation of a vowel melodically with curlicues, grace notes, or micro pitches; Lafcadio Hearn calls them "semi-demi sounds"

fushi mono lyrical pieces for biwa players, also called narimono and hiji or hiramono of 161 basic pieces

Futotama god who directed the goddess Uzume to dance and entice Amaterasu out of the cave

gagaku elegant music introduced from China around the eighth century

gagaku biwa or gakubiwa biwa with four frets played with a small shakushi (rice scooper type) plectrum

gagaku-ryo Foreign Music Department formed in 701 to study Chinese, Korean, and Manchurian music for entertainment and ceremonial purposes

gaikyoku outside pieces for shakuhachi; pieces of the sankyoku repertory in an ensemble of koto, shamisen, kokyu, or shakuhachi

gaku-no-te gagaku koto techniques of shizugaku or han-kake played polyphonically with a main koto melody

gaku-so gagaku koto with thirteen strings

geido Way of the Art

***Genji Monogatari* (*Tale of Genji*)** novel by the eleventh century Murasaki Shikibu about court life

genkan round moon lute introduced with gagaku instruments and stored in Shosoin

geza background music of the kabuki theater drama

gidayu narrative music; from the singer Takemoto Gidayu of the bunraku theater

gigaku miscellaneous performing arts of dance, song, drama with huge masks introduced during the sixth through seventh centuries to foster Buddhism

ginsho declamation of the title of a biwa piece followed by the rosho (recitation), eisho (aria), and coda

giri duty, obligation based on social rules

hachimaki cloth towel tied around on the head to perform a task

haikai haiku poet

haji shame

hajiki plucking strings of shamisen or biwa with the left hand

hakama culottes worn over kimono

hakase note marking, biwa ornamentation

hana flower; epitome of a noh performer; also depending on context, hana means sakura (cherry blossom)

haniwa terracotta clay figures of people, animals, houses, transport wagons, and utensils buried in the Tumulus of Kofun period third through sixth centuries

Hanyashingyo The Heart Sutra from the *Prajnaparamita*. The shortest sutra, popular among pilgrims of the Shingon and Zen sects

haori kimono type jacket worn over kimono or with hakama to complete formal attire

happi short informal kimono-like cotton jacket for work or play

hara stomach, diaphragm. Implies to sing with strength, heart, with conviction

haraita wooden body of a biwa often whacked with the bachi to punctuate or emphasize fight scenes

ha-uta popular songs, hayari-uta of the late 1700s and early 1800s concerning the activities of the teahouses abbreviated to ha-uta

hayari-uta popular songs that became ha-uta of the ji-uta genre

hayashi a collective term for the noh ensemble consisting of tsuzumi (shoulder drum), O-tsuzumi (big drum), taiko (stick drum), and the nohkan (flute); also used in nagauta kabuki music. In compounds, hayashi is pronounced –bayashi.

Heian Era 794–1185, noted for the artistic pursuits of courtiers

Heike biwa smaller version of the gaku biwa, with its main repertory comprising *The Tale of the Heike*, the 90-year demise of the Heian court

hichiriki reed wind instrument of the gagaku ensemble; the O-hichiriki bass hichiriki introduced with the ensemble is stored in Shosoin

hiden secret or the secret pieces of various genres reserved for the successor iemoto

hiki dash found in Buddhist and noh notation next to a kanji indicating to extend the note

hirajyoshi IN mode tuning for koto with the scale centered on the fifth and tenth strings from which other tunings are easily made

Hirano Matsuri large festival held by the Hirano Shrine in Kyoto

hito-gami living god

Hitoyasu Shinno (844–886) blind fourth son of Emperor Nimmyo (810–850) who played the biwa; his mother created the titles of Kengyo and Kōtō as a memorial upon his death at age 42; he became the patron saint of the Tōdō Shoku Yashiki

hitoyogiri　bamboo flute with one joint or 1.1 feet in length with five holes, precursor to the shakuhachi

hogaku　pre-Western Japanese music including gagaku and Buddhist chants; pre-Western music of the Edo Era mainly koto, shamisen, and shakuhachi

hokyo　hanging metal xylophone-like instrument introduced with gagaku instruments

hon-joshi　term for the main, basic tuning for both biwa and shamisen

hon-kyoku　main repertoire, proprietary music of a genre such as biwa, shamisen, koto, kokyu, shakuhachi

hon-sarugaku　main sarugaku that became kyogen as opposed to sarugaku no noh that is refined

honte　main part of two-part music for koto or sangen; kaede is the second part

hoshi　blind Buddhist priests; also, blind Buddhist priests who play the biwa

Hyakunin Isshu　One Hundred Poetry Collection used for the New Year's game, Karuta

hyojo　tuning of gagaku belonging to the ritsu mode; others are oshiki and banshiki

hyoshi-ai　controlled beats for the dancer in noh as opposed to ashirai

ichikotsu　tuning of the ryo-mode from China's gagaku ensemble

iemoto　ie for house and moto for foundation; also the grand master of a family line of artists or any endeavor

iemoto seido　iemoto system; a pyramid economic apprentice scheme headed by an iemoto to teach artistic skills through licensed teachers to many students. The system appeared during the Edo Era; quintessential Japanese apprentice system where the crucial secret skill is passed only to the successor.

iki　sexy aesthetics of Edo Era bourgeoisie imbued with sensuality; similar to sui, merchant class sensibility of Osaka

Ikuta-ryu　koto school named after Ikuta Kengyo who is credited for combining ji-uta sangen with the koto to form an ensemble of the two instruments

imayo　Heian Era popular songs from the masses, Buddhist songs, or the nobility; the nobility sang imayo to gagaku pieces known as *Ettenraku-imayo* or *Etten-utai-mono* with Japanese lyrics

IN　shade, somber mode. The IN mode has semitones at the sho and u positions; When a melody ascends, the u is sharpened (ei) and when the melody descends, the u is in the semitone

Inari　fox deity; messenger of the gods; guardian of rice, houses, trade, and foundries, who appears to help a forger make a sword in *Kokaji*

ingaku　vulgar music as opposed to gagaku, which is elegant music

Ingyo Emperor　(374–454); nineteenth emperor, Nintoku Tenno's fourth son

Irare no Kure Koto Hiki　southern Chinese by birth who brought from Korea's Kure Kingdom two arts: gigaku (song and dance) and the koto in 467

Ise Shrine　Shinto shrine in Mie Prefecture dedicated to Amaterasu

ishibue Jomon Era stone flute also called the ama-no-iwafue made of lava-like rock

Ishimura Kengyo a blind musician of the late 1500s who remodeled the snakeskin sansen to cat and dog skin. Also created the first sangen *honte-gumi* (main collection) called *Ryukyu-gumi*. Some people think he may be Naka Koji.

Itchu-bushi style of narrative singing founded by Miyakodayu Itchu (1650–1724)

Izanagi and Izanami two creator gods of the Japanese pantheon

Izumo Shrine enormous wooden shrine given to Okuninushi by Amaterasu. Each October the Kamiari Matsuri takes place wherein all of Japan's kamis congregate (hence, October is Kaminashi month).

jamisen Okinawan shamisen with snakeskin drum

ji 1. downward mesh of sound along the strings of the wa-gon; zan is the upward stroke; the ori and tsume are other wa-gon patterns; 2. bridge of a biwa; 3. moveable bridges of the koto; 4. Joruri narrative portion as opposed to fushi, which is the melodic part; 5. Ostinato type accompaniment called *tate no ire-te* played by the lead player

ji-goe natural voice devoid of falsetto

jiki-deshi students who take lessons directly from the iemoto

Jimmu-tenno great-grandson of Ninigi-no-mikoto, headed the Yamato clan of ancient Japan

Jisei wakan-roei song about the Tanabata lovers who meet once a year across the Milky Way on the seventh day of the seventh month

jishin earthquake; there's a folk saying "jishin, kaminari, kaji, oyaji" (earthquake, thunder, fire, and father/boss) about the four things to fear

ji-uta lyrical art music created by the blind musicians of the Kyoto/Osaka area on the sangen and koto

jo-ha-kyu jo (slow), ha (fast), kyu (faster) phenomenon found in the structure of music, poetry, and theater; mini-jo-ha-kyu also occur within each subsection

jo-hin-na refined quality that has grace, dignity, and maturity

Jomon Era (13,000–250 BCE); named after rope designs (jomon) on pottery

Joruri Hime Monogatari narrative story about Princess Joruri and Ushiwakamaru (childhood name of Yoshitsune)

kaede literally means "other hand"; sometimes called share-biki (decorative sound) by some schools; polyphonic embellishment to koto and shamisen pieces

kagura music of, for, from the gods consisting of mi-kagura for the emperor, and sato-kagura for the general public. Music for religious occasions

kagura-bue flute used in kagura

kakegoe 1. shouts by drummers of the noh or kabuki bayashi; 2. refrain by participants in song and dance

kakezume koto octave technique; characteristic openings of koto kumi-uta

kakko two-headed drum played with two sticks; the lead instrument in gagaku music

kaku elevated permanent bridge at the head and tail of the koto for the strings; ryu kaku for the head and unkaku for the tail

Kakuichi or Akashi Kakuichi; blind son of the Shogun who standardized the Heike texts and formed a guild for blind men called the Tōdō Shoku Yashiki, or Tōdōza for short

kami god, spirits

kamidana shrine or altar for the kami found in many Japanese homes or enterprises

kami koma top bridge on the shamisen pole near the pegs

kamishimo formal stiff winged shoulder attire worn over kimono

kando introduction of koto dan-mono pieces

kangeiko practice in mid-winter to improve technique and skill

kangen instrumental music of the gagaku ensemble

kanji Chinese ideographs that combine smaller units of strokes to mean a word or sound

karuta New Year's poetry game of the *Ogura Hyakunin Isshu* (Hundred Waka Poems by a Hundred Poets)

Kawachi district in Osaka

kawaii cute

kawaisō pitiful

Kengyo highest title in the Tōdō Shoku Yashiki; the others are Kōtō, Betto, and Zato

Kimpira-bushi strong flashier style that later became Geki-bushi and Ozatsuma-bushi; created by Inoue Harimanojo (1632–1685) of Osaka

kin-tract portmanteau for kinship and contract where human relationship is based on emotional ties

kinuta pounding sound of autumn to make silk pliable, or what is called a fulling block where two people sit opposite of each other to hit cloth with sticks to soften fabric

kirigirisu crickets of the autumn scene along with matsumushi (pine/waiting bug) and suzumushi (bell bug)

Kiyomoto shamisen playing and singing style grew out of the Tomimoto style

Kofun or Tumulus Era (250–538) noted for keyhole shaped burial mounds eulogizing the Imperial family

Kojiki written chronicles (712) of Japan's origins, also the *Nihon Shoki* was written later (720)

kojin independent people or businessmen

Kokugaku Shinto and Japanese classics studies initiated by scholar Motoori Norinaga (1730–1803)

kokyu bowed shamisen-like instrument resembling the Chinese erhu

koma horse, bridge. On the shamisen, the *koma* is placed on the drum and the *kami koma* (top horse/ bridge) elevates the top thinner strings nearest the pegs of the *sao* (pole)

Komyo wife of Emperor Shomu (724–749) of the Nara Era; she stored her husband's treasure at Shosoin

konoyo this world; anoyo is the other world

ko-rorin numonics for three descending notes in koto

koto thirteen-stringed long hollow instrument with moveable bridges played with three plectrum on the right hand

Kōtō second highest title after Kengyo of a Tōdōza member, the others being Betto and Zato

komabue Korean flute

kotoba spoken words in Shinto, bunraku, and kabuki theater

kotodama words with spirit and power; words to invoke magic; powerful words to bring good fortune, disaster, etc.

ko-tsuzumi smaller drum held on the shoulder and an o-tsuzumi (larger drum placed on the lap) are played as one instrument. Also called tsuzumi.

ko-uta 1. short songs; 2. songs associated with the geisha

kowaka mai dances used in noh plays

kuchi-jamisen mouth shamisen is the onomatopoetic solmization of the pitch and techniques when learning the shamisen

Kukai or Kobo Daishi, ninth century founder of the Shingon Buddhism at Koyasan

kume-uta military songs of Jimmu Tenno Era believed to have no Continental influence, or Yamato-uta

kumi-uta compositions of collected songs proprietary to the koto or shamisen

Kuroda-bushi song from gagaku's *Ettenraku* with lyrics extolling the victory of the Kuroda clan; also popular as a drinking song

Kurokawa noh noh performed by farmers of Yamagata-ken for the Kasuga Shrine matsuri

kuse mai dance of the Heian Era used in noh

kyogen 1. comic performance between noh plays; 2. performance during the noh play with explanation of what has transpired; 3. word meaning a play or drama

kyoku setsu melodic names for biwa melodies

kyotaiko large sutra drum struck with drumstick for Buddhist chants

kyu 1. first note of the scale kyu-sho-kaku-chi-u, like "do" of the Western do-re-mi diatonic scale; 2. fast.

Kyui Nine Steps, treatise by Motokiyo Zeami (1363–1443) spelling out the steps to learn noh

mae-uta song at the beginning of the tegoto format which is usually longer than the ato-uta song at the end

maki scroll that lists names of those who completed a set of pieces

makoto sincerity required in performance

makura literally "pillow"; an introduction to the instrumental interlude of the tegoto format

Makura no Soshi Pillow Book by Sei Shonagon who wrote about court life in the late 900–1000s

mamori o-mamori, fortune sold at shrines and some temples

Man'ichi famous biwa playing priest who passed his skills to Manse-in and Myotoku-In.

Manyoshu Collection of Ten Thousand Pages, anthology of poems compiled by Otomo no Yakamochi in 760, with mixed authorship of courtiers, commoners, peasants, men, and women

matsumushi pine/waiting bug mentioned in autumn poems along with suzumushi (bell bug) and kirigirisu (cricket)

matsuri ritual or religious festival celebrating the local, regional, or national Shinto kami

mawashi curlicues made with the voice as in fushi-mawashi

medetai felicitation, congratulation

meigen bowed-string used in exorcism until the Heian times

meiwaku to cause problems to others

michiyuki lyrical travel music in kabuki nagauta drama

mi-kagura celebrations for the emperor as the sole audience

miko Shinto shrine maidens

mikoshi portable Shinto shrine carried by people during matsuri festival

minyo folk songs

mitsuji a noh drum pattern for the tsuzumi and o-tsuzumi named after three beats

mnemonic an aid to retain melody

momiji maple leaves or autumn colors of leaves

Monbusho Ministry of Education, Culture, Sports, Science and Technology of the Japanese government

moso biwa blind priest–musicians of Jishin biwa named after a Buddhist text *Jishin-kyo* or the kojin-kyo (kitchen-kyo)

Murakami Emperor sixty-second emperor, who reigned 946–967 CE and fostered the arts during the Heian Era

Murasaki Shikibu author of the eleventh century novel, the *Tale of Genji*

Muto clan clan that ruled the Shonai Province in the thirteenth through sixteenth centuries and introduced in 1463 Kyoto noh actors to farmers who began Kurakawa Noh

nabe-mono boiled food known to be a cuisine from Jomon times consisting of boiled fish and vegetables

naga-uta long song (with a hyphen) is (長歌) pointing to lyrical music of the Kansai area composed by blind musicians first on the ji-uta sangen

nagauta long song (長唄), narrative music for kabuki drama and buyo (classical dance) with nagauta shamisen accompaniment

Naka Shoji blind musician of the late 1500s believed to have remodeled the snakeskin sansen to cat and dog skin sangen/shamisen and created its artistic repertory. Also some think he is Ishimura Kengyo.

Naniwa ancient name for Osaka. Naniwa-bushi are songs from the area

namu amida butsu mantra of the Jodo Shinshu sect

narimono percussion instruments

natori literally na for name and tori for taking; receiving a stage/family name from the iemoto

neo braided twine on the shamisen's drum that hooks into the extended sao beyond the drum to hold three strings

Nihon Shoki (720) written chronicles concerning Japan's origins, also *Kojiki*

Ninigi-no Mikoto led an expedition northward and established the Yamato region in the Nara-Ise area

ninjo natural human feelings, sentiments, versus giri of duty, obligation of society

Nirvana Symphony 1958, by Mayuzumi Toshiro (1929–1997)

noh sarugaku no noh, theatricals of the skills of song, dance, and drama developed by Kanami and Zeami in the fifteenth century

nohgaku collectively noh and kyogen; theatrical outgrowths of the ninth century sarugaku (monkey-pleasure/antics of monkeys)

nohkan noh flute made of eight to twelve tubes of a female bamboo are inserted into another to give it a slightly conical shape

norito invocation, sacred spell, or incantation addressed to the kami performed by a priest; senge-tai are words from the kami; sojo tai are prayers addressed to the kami that end with "mosu" or "Thus I humbly speak…"

Nyohachi cymbals used for Buddhist rituals of certain sects

Ogawanomiya third son of the Emperor Gokomatsu (1377–1433)

o-hichiriki bass hichiriki, introduced with the gagaku ensemble around the ninth century. It was later stored in Shosoin because the higher sounding hichiriki was preferred.

oki introductory section of nagauta pieces followed by the strong and grander Ozatsuma (stronger) style of narrative singing

Okuni originally a shrine maiden who formed the first all female kabuki troupe in the 1600s

omiya Shinto shrines, the "o" is honorific; miya is "shrine"

on benevolence/responsibility, on-gaeshi is reciprocating on

on-gaeshi reciprocating "on," reciprocating benevolence

ongaku sound pleasure, music, a general term encompassing any type of music

ori one of four wa-gon patterns; also tsume and two strums called zan (up) and ji (down)

orugoru music box from Holland

o-tsuzumi big drum of the noh-bayashi held across the lap and hit with fingers covered with papier mache tips on the third and fourth fingers of the right hand; it is played with the ko-tsuzumi. Also called *o-kawa* (big skin/drum).

Pillow Book *Makura no Soshi*; Sei Shonagon writes about court life in the late 900–1000s

reigi tadashii good mannered

roei songs translated from the Chinese and later Japanese songs accompanied by gagaku instruments

Roei Kyujishusho collection of Wakan-roei songs

ronin master-less samurai

rosho recitation that succeeds ginsho (declamation of the title of piece) music followed by eisho (aria) and coda of biwa music

ryo/ritsu modes of gagaku music from China; the ryo-scale is ichikotsu, sojo, and taishiki; the ritsu scales are hyojo, oshiki, and banshiki

ryu dragon and prefix for the parts of the koto ryu-to (dragonhead) and ryu-o (dragon tail)

-ryu school, style, as in Ikuta-ryu

ryuteki gagaku flute from China

sabi rust or patina; an aesthetic favoring simplicity and restraint as opposed to loud brilliance; likened to moss on a rock; often combined with wabi which is similarly simple and quiet

Sadatoshi a court biwa player who learned biwa in China around 805

Saga Emperor (reigned 809–823), initiated the changes in gagaku ensemble

saho left or Chinese (Togaku) gagaku music; those of uho (right) are Komagaku or Korean and Manchurian in origin

saibara folk songs by horse tenders; noblemen sing saibara at court; saibara may be a corruption of the word "saibari" of kagura

Saicho (767–822), founder of Tendai sect on Mount Hiei, posthumously called Dengyo Daishi

sakura cherry blossom, also hana (flower)

sangen also called shamisen with the "mi" added to assist pronunciation; a three-stringed instrument introduced from China in the mid-1500s, played with a bachi (fan-like plectrum)

sangen/shamisen are the same instruments, but the ji-uta players prefer to call the instrument sangen

sangen tuning hon joshi (basic tuning) with variations of san-sagari (third string down), and ni-agari (second string up)

sankyoku ensemble consisting of three instruments, the sangen (shamisen), koto, and shakuhachi (in place of the kokyu)

sanpo-kakeai 3 group musical exchange such as 6 Tokiwazu musicians, 2 gidayu, and 10–12 nagauta musicians usually for kabuki plays

sansen Chinese name for the popular three-stringed instrument, sangen or shamisen

sao pole of the shamisen

sarugaku monkey mimes of dances and songs popular during the Heian Era to become hon sarugaku (main sarugaku of kyogen) and sarugaku no noh

sarugaku no noh sarugaku (monkey mime) of noh (skill). Kanami and Zeami developed sarugaku no noh to an art in the fourteenth through fifteenth centuries through the patronage of Ashikaga Yoshimitsu. It is often called noh for short.

Sakagami a noh play about Semimaru, a blind biwa player

sakaki branch held by Shinto priests in ceremonies believed to be infused with life's energy

sankyoku an ensemble of three instruments, sangen/shamisen, koto, and shakuhachi

sasa bamboo leaves

Satsuma biwa biwa from Kyushu developed in the 1500s with a larger bachi for playing

sawari medium inverted metal bell used in Buddhist ceremony; sympathetic string vibrations on the biwa and shamisen

scale/mode kyu, sho, kaku, chi, and u coming from the Chinese kung, shang, chio, chih, and yu.

seken world of ancestors, spirits, and descendants

sembiki mono million-dollar piece, or a revenue producing popular piece like *Shochikubai*.

semi cicada

Semimaru renowned biwa player immortalized in the noh play *Sakagami*

semmyo Shinto chant that addresses the throne; norito, addressing a deity

settaku percussive instrument used for pacing Zen chants

shacho boss of a business or group

shakubyoshi two long flat sticks making sharp whacks to punctuate the vocal line

shakuhachi bamboo vertical flute of 1.8 length or approximately 1 foot 8 inches, with five holes

shakushi rice paddle or rice scooper shaped plectrum

shamisen *see* sangen/shamisen; sansen

shamisen kumi-uta collected songs proprietary to the sangen with introductory three notes of its tuning, like the introduction of Tsugaru shamisen music

shibai-uta stage drama songs of the Genroku Era (1688–1704)

shibui aesthetics of matured astringency, graceful, dignified, and jo-hin-na (refined)

shihan teacher, lieutenant teacher of the iemoto

shimenawa sacred rope used to designate a sacred area or object like a shrine, tree, rock, etc.

shinobue thin flute used in folk music

Shinran Shonin (1173–1263), founder of the Jodo Shinshu sect

Shinsen-Roei-shu collection of wakan-roei by Fujiwara no Mototoshi (1046–1142); see also *Wakan-roei shu*

shi-te main actor; protagonist of a noh play

shitsu large twenty-seven-stringed koto made of Paulownia found in China and usually played in combination with the ch'in

sho mouth organ of the gagaku ensemble made of seventeen bamboo pipes of different lengths

Shobutsu blind priest who learned the narration of the *Tale of the Heike* to transmit to other blind priests

shochikubai sho (pine), chiku (bamboo), and bai (plum); symbols of the New Year

shofu singing or calling out shakuhachi notes and techniques similar to shoga for the koto and kuchi-jamisen for the shamisen.

shoga onomatopoetic solmization for the koto. Sung in pitch, the shoga calls out koto techniques, melodic passages, phrasing, and notes to emphasize; Shoga came from *kuchi-jamisen* (mouth shamisen)

shoko small metallic gong on a stand struck with two sticks to make a high clunk sound in the gagaku ensemble

shokyoku short pieces of the gagaku repertory. The others are taikyoku, longer pieces with about eight movements and chukyoku, pieces of middle lengths

Shomu Emperor (724–749), of the Nara Era, who constructed the Todaiji Temple in Nara

shomyo chants/sutras of Buddhism

Shoshinge chant by Shinran Shonin followed by six of Shinran's 350 wa-san

Shosoin storehouse of Todaiji in Nara

Shotoku Taishi (574–622), regent of Empress Suiko (592–628) pivotal in accepting Buddhism to Japan

shugen happy style of noh singing contrasted with bo-oku or the sad, yearning style

shugyo austere training or the single-minded, self-sacrificing pursuit of The Way

Sofuren (Missing My Love), a saibara mentioned in the *Heike Monogatari*, "Kogo no Tsubone" chapter

soh no koto specifically the thirteen-stringed koto; its prototype was developed in China's Shin Dynasty (220–206 BCE)

so-Kengyo chief Kengyo of the Tōdō Shoku Yashiki, identified by his red clothing

Sokkyoku Taiisho book by Yamada Shokoku of Edo on koto techniques based on Ikuta-ryu

solfege singing of notes

solmization for teaching where each note of a scale is associated with a particular syllable

sui/iki fashionable, sexy

sukui scooping motion with plectrum for effect on stringed instruments, such as the biwa, shamisen, and koto

Susanowo Storm god, born from Izanagi's nose

Suzaku Emperor emperor of the tenth century (930–955)

suzu bells on a stick usually used by Miko shrine maidens

suzumushi bell bug, referred to in poetry to denote autumn along with the kirigirisu (cricket) and matsumushi (pine/waiting bug)

tai sea bream symbolizing felicitations and congratulations, coupled with the god Ebisu

taiko two-headed drums of folk origin, tied with flaxen ropes to a small stand and played with two drum sticks

taikyoku great pieces of gagaku music with about eight movements, the chukyoku (middle pieces) and the shokyoku (smaller pieces)

Tale of the Heike attributed to Yukinaga who had taken tonsure at Tendai Temple and taught Shobutsu the narration of the Heike clan's demise

tamashi soul or sentience

tanka tanka and waka poems are interchangeable. They have five lines with 5, 7, 5, 7, 7 syllables per line

tate no ire-te or ji an ostinato type accompaniment played by the lead player

tegoto-mono a three-part format comprised of a song, an extensive instrumental interlude, and the continuation of the song

Tendai sect founded on Mount Hiei by Saicho with Enrakuji in the ninth century

Todaiji Nara temple built by Shomyo and dedicated in 752; famous for its giant Buddha

Togan (*Eastern Shore*) a wakan-roei song

Tokiwazu shamisen style that grew out of Miyako Bungonojo (1660–1740)

Tomimoto shamisen style that grew out of Tokiwazu

tombo dragonflies, believed to be the spirit of the dead

tomo corporation, or "be" meaning guild

tonkori Ainu koto 30 centimeters long, with a flared end

toraijin Chinese and Korean immigrant of early Japan

Tozan-ryu shakuhachi school invented by Nakao Tozan (1876–1956), who collaborated with koto's Miyagi Michio to popularize new Western-type music on the two instruments

tsubu iri someone who skips grades and steps by paying a higher fee for the Tōdōza course for title and rank

Tsuguyama Kengyo (d. 1697), early kotoist, student of Sumiyama Kengyo

Tsukiyomi   god of moon came from Izanagi's right eye

Tsukushi koto   esoteric style of koto playing founded by Priest Kenjun of Kyushu in the 1500s

tsume   plectrum of the koto made of ivory; wa-gon playing pattern along with ori, zan (up), and ji (down)

tsuru   crane symbolic of longevity and voice of authority

Tsuyama Kengyo   (d. 1836), invented the Osaka style of sangen with a larger drum and bachi; style dominates ji-uta music of Osaka; Kyoto musicians use Yanagawa Kengyo's shamisen

tsuyo-gin   stronger, forte joyful style of singing as opposed to yowa-gin, softer, weaker, pianissimo style of noh singing

tsuzumi   two-headed drums, often called ko-tsuzumi, the smaller of two noh drums; o-tsuzumi is the larger

U   bass sho of the gagaku ensemble

uchi-awase   two different independent pieces played together

uchi/soto   inside/outside

uguisu   bush warbler harbinger of spring with a distinctive song, "ho—hokekyo!"

uho   right, or Komagaku, music of Korean and Manchurian origin; saho (left) is Chinese music

uji   ancient clans

uke   round box drum upon which Uzume danced to entice Amaterasu out of a cave

Urabe   family of ancient fortune-telling priests named Nakatomi and later given the last name Fujiwara

ura-goe   falsetto voice used by kabuki actors to imitate women

uta   poems or songs

utai or noh utai   noh chants or songs

utsu   stopping a vibrating string for effect

wabi   rustic, patina, refined sense of aesthetics usually in conjunction with sabi (rust)

Waga Koma   (*My Horse*) a saibara from a *Manyoshu* poem, sung at court

wa-gon   indigenous Japanese six-string koto made of Paulownia wood and played before the emperor

waka   court poems of 5, 7, 5, 7, 7 syllables per line: sometimes called tanka

wakan-roei   wakan (Japanese) and roei (Chinese) poems sung by courtiers and accompanied with gagaku instruments of ryuteki, sho, and hichiriki and string instruments

Wakan Roei-shu   a collection of poems by Fujiwara no Kinto (966–1041); see also *Shinsen-Roei-shu* by Fujiwara no Mototoshi (1046–1142)

waki   side or supporting actor in a noh play

waki pillar   Right front pillar of the noh stage. There are four pillars of the square noh stage used as a guide seen through masks. The shi-te pillar is approached first from the bridge. Opposite of the shi-te pillar is the fue (flute) pillar where the flutist sits; opposite the waki pillar is the metsuke (sighting) pillar.

wa-san Buddhist poems by Shinran and Rennyo Shonin with Japanese sentiments

yamabushi mountain priest, ascetic, sorcerer, medicine man, identified with pompoms, small black caps, and carrying a conch shell and small bells

Yamada-ryu koto founded by Yamada Kengyo (1757–1817), using the text and music of the Edo kabuki stage; made the koto the dominant instrument over the nagauta shamisen

Yamato synonymous with Japan, originally a kingdom in southern Nara before the fifth century

Yamato clan clan from Jimmu-tenno, great-grandson of Ninigi-no mikoto, who headed the original clan of ancient Japan

Yamato-e style of painting that distinguishes it from Chinese ones with Japanese scenes and themes of famous places, seasons, simple lines for facial features, and bird's eye view of interior of houses and landscapes.

Yamato Era (300–710), is collectively the Kofun, Asuka Era (552–645), and Early Nara and Nara Eras (646–710; 710–794)

Yamato spirit expresses pure Japanese sentiments devoid of Chinese influence

Yamato-uta songs of Jimmu Tenno's era with no Continental influence; see also kume-uta (military songs)

Yanagawa Kengyo developed the Kyoto style Yanagawa-ryu sangen

Yang Kei Fei or Yohiki consort to Genso Kotei, the Chinese emperor who lost his kingdom because of her beauty

Yayoi people newcomers who introduced a rice culture and began a new era called the Yayoi Period (250 BCE–250 CE)

YO sun mode as opposed to the IN mode (shade)

yogaku Western music

yokobue horizontal bamboo flute

yowa-gin softer, weaker, pianissimo voice in noh versus tsuyo-gin (stronger, forte, joyful)

yugen mysterious, suggestive, hidden beauty

yujyo prostitute

yukata cotton informal kimono

yurushi mono release pieces; a list of pieces required before being granted the privilege to learn a new set of popular pieces

yurushi seido permission system granted when a person passes the prerequisites of the yurushi mono pieces.

zan up stroke, on the wa-gon; the opposite is ji the downward mesh of sound

zokkyoku miscellaneous pieces of lowlier style; any music outside gagaku

Chapter Notes

Preface

1. Comments of Hiroyuki Iwaki in Matthias Kriesberg, "Japan's New Generation of Composers," *New York Times*, February 6, 2000, p. 30.
2. Denise Patry Leidy, "Buddhist Art in a Secular Space: Case Studies from the Metropolitan Museum of Art," lecture at American University, March 27, 2015.

Introduction

1. Conversation with Yuriko Shiga on July 8, 2003.
2. So Sugiura, "Basic Knowledge about Pure Hogaku, Traditional Japanese Music," Japan Foundation, Performing Arts Network Japan, January 19, 2005.
3. *Hagoromo* (Feather Mantle) is about an angel that swims in Lake Biwa leaving her feather mantle on a pine tree. A fisherman finds the magical robe and is about to take it home. She implores him to return it to her for she cannot return to the heavens without it. When he does, she rewards him with song and dance, and showers good fortune over the land. She spirals up and disappears into the sky.
4. Gagaku should not be confused with *gigaku*, a miscellany performance act to interest converts to Buddhism that was introduced during the sixth century.
5. Jess M. Stein, *Random House College Dictionary*, rev. ed., New York: Random House, 1980, p. 248.
6. Mistakenly, the headline, "Hatsuko Kikuhara, 102; Master of Japanese Folk Music," by Mark Magnier, *Los Angeles Times*, September 16, 2001, claims that she is a folk musician. Madame Kikuhara was Japan's highly acclaimed *ji-uta* classical musician on the shamisen and koto. She was named Living National Treasure in 1979. She studied ji-uta music by rote since the age of 3 from her father and grandfather within the iemoto system. Madame Kikuhara taught privately in Osaka and at Osaka College of Music.
7. The kabuki dance *Musume Dojoji* is transmitted exactly from one performance to another with allowances for artistry. Any movie of a performance can be edited with another performance and not miss a beat or step and will be exact in every aspect, including the scenery, costume, dance movement, and music.
8. Machlis and Forney analyzed four *kakezume* notes of *Fuki*, a solo vocal piece, with the four-note motif of Beethoven's *Symphony No. 5*. The analysis describes two different unrelated premises. Of *Fuki*, they said the notes are "freely conceived and lacks metrical accents. Each phrase of sixteen beats is based on the opening four measures, but no two are identical; rather, a kind of variation form is at work, with each repetition subtly shifting pitches and rhythms, then dividing beats in dotted figures and adding octave leaps. Note too the use of sequence and the widely disjunct movement of the melody." From a Western perspective, the analysis might be correct, but *Fuki* becomes a musical oddity. Joseph Machlis and Kristine Forney, *The Enjoyment of Music*, 8th ed., New York: W.W. Norton, 1999, p. 194.

Chapter 1

1. Michael Cooper, ed., *They Came to Japan: An Anthology of European Reports on Japan*,

1543–1640. Berkeley: University of California Press, 1981, p. 4.

2. Although the aesthetics of Tea are associated with Zen Buddhism, the principles espoused here did not suddenly appear with Zen Buddhism. Shinto premises were melded with Zen.

3. The first two principles—wa (harmony) and kei (respect)—are Chinese; the latter two—sei (purity) and jaku (tranquility)—are Japanese, according to Kishibe Shigeo, *The Traditional Music of Japan,* Tokyo: Ongaku no Tomo sha, 1984, pp. 14–17.

4. Way of Tea touches upon the entryway, garden, architecture, tatami room arrangement, flower arranging, paintings, calligraphy, poetry, ceramics for tea bowls, water containers, bronzeware tea kettle and equipment, bamboo craft for the tea scoop and whisk, charcoal making, ash arrangement, fragrance of incense, kimono wearing, way of walking, sitting, sipping, fine cuisine, confectionery, tea powder, conversation, and music.

5. Today the trend of music is faster and with louder compositions which include passages showing off the virtuosity of the performers. The NHK World show *Blends* features new music on hogaku instruments.

6. When I was entering Gettysburg Battleground to get to Gettysburg College, I thought I was being attacked. The gunshots I thought I heard were from a CD by a modern composer whose transition from quiet shakuhachi music suddenly hit the drums like gunshots.

7. At a *noh* performance of the Nohgaku Kyokai with Katayama Kuroemon and Shigeyama Sensaku at the Japan Information and Culture Center of the Japan Embassy in Washington, D.C., March 22, 2004, I was requested by the performers to instruct the audience to hold their applause until everyone left the stage. The performers wanted to ensure that the disrupting atmosphere would not be created here in America.

8. Some young hogaku musicians attuned to audience expectation of today gesticulate to their music by moving their bodies, heads, and waving their hands and arms like Western musicians playing the piano or violin, or like rock bands swinging to the music.

9. Kabuki's Danjuro spent a week of austerities at Shinshoji before the 1703 opening of the kabuki show *The Avatars of the Narita Temple Fudo.* In Laurence R. Kominz, *The Stars Who Created Kabuki: Their Lives, Loves and Legacy,* Tokyo: Kodansha, 1997, pp. 79–80.

10. See Chapter 9 and *Kyu-i.*

11. Edward S. Morse, *Japan Day by Day, 1877, 1878–79, 1882–83,* vol. 2, Boston: Houghton Mifflin, 1917, pp. 394–395.

12. Edward S. Morse, p. 401.

13. Lafcadio Hearn, "A Street Singer," *Kokoro: Hints and Echoes of Japanese Inner Life,* Rutland, Vermont: Charles E. Tuttle Co., 1980, p. 41.

14. Ai Kawakami, Kiyoshi Furukawa, Kentaro Katahira, and Kazuo Okanoya, "Sad Music Induces Pleasant Emotion," *Frontiers in Psychology* 4 (2013): 311. The authors' research used Japanese subjects and ironically compares their responses to pieces in the major and minor scales of Western music.

15. We can measure Japanese movies according to the number of handkerchiefs required. *Twenty-Four Eyes, Burma no Tategoto,* and the anime *Wing Rises* are some examples.

16. Lecture series on "Music of Japan" for the International Conservatory of Music, a two hour, 10 session series from November 1980 to May 1981.

17. At an orientation for recruits to Japan, I spoke about the aesthetics of hogaku and played *Chidori no Kyoku.* A young lady wept at the ending and said she felt the loneliness. JET orientation in August 1988 at Meridian House, Washington, D.C.

18. Murasaki Shikibu and Royall Tyler, trans., *Tale of Genji.* See koto's *Chidori no Kyoku,* second song.

19. By novelist Tanizaki Junichiro (1886–1965).

20. The Western calendar was adopted during the Meiji Era in 1872.

21. Akehiro Shirai and Kazuhiro Aruga, *Nihon no Nanajuni Ko wo Tanoshimu* [Enjoying the 72 Seasons of Japan], Tokyo: Toho, 2013.

22. When compiling Mieko Yoshikami's book *Sarasoju* by Minojo, published 1998, she preferred to categorize her poems by the seasons. Categorizing by location was suggested instead since she had lived in mainland United States, Hawaii, and Japan, and had traveled to Europe but she opted for the traditional seasonal categories. Like the Rev. Akira Kubota's *Houki Ini Kashu,* published spring 2001, many poetry collections are privately published for the author's immediate families.

23. The *sho* or *matsu* are the Chinese and Japanese pronunciation for pine tree. The two ways to pronounce a word are separated with a slash, with the Chinese first as *chiku/ta-ke* for bamboo, *bai/ume* for plum. When the three are combined, it is easier to say *shochikubai,* instead of "*matsu, take, ume.*"

24. The *Takasago* utai of the noh play is sung at weddings or at any new endeavor. The journey segment on a boat mentions Japan's familiar coastline before arriving at Sumioe where the Sumiyoshi god appears to shower

good fortune (see the translation of *Shin Taka-sago*).

25. "*Yo no naka ni Taete sakura no Nakariseba Haru no kokoro wa Nodoke karamashi.*" (If in this world, cherry blossoms did not exist, our hearts at spring time will be carefree, peaceful.)

26. Sei Shonagon writes about a special excursion to write poems about the *hototogisu*. With so many distractions en route, the inspiration cooled to write about them (pp. 104–109). In *Pillow Book of Sei Shonagon*, vol. 1, trans. Ivan Morris, New York: Columbia University Press, 1967.

27. "*Tsuki mireba, chijini monokoso kanashi kere. Waga mi hitotsu no aki ni wa aranedo,*" by Onoe Chisato.

28. "*Yamazato wa aki koso koto ni wabishikere. Shika no naku ne ni me wo samashi tsutsu,*" by Minobu Tadamine. This is also true of the shakuhachi music, *Shika no Tone* (Distant Cry of Deer).

29. Yoshizawa Kengyo II's *Chidori no Kyoku*. Second poem: "*Awaji-shima kayou chidori no naku koe ne, ikuyo nezame nu Suma no sekimori.*"

30. "*Shira yuki no tokoro mo wakarazu Furi shikeba iwao ni saku hana tokoso mire.*"

31. Mitsuzaki Kōtō's *Aki Kaze no Kyoku*'s lyrics are about the Chinese beauty Yang Kei Fei and the Emperor Genso Kotei of the Tang Dynasty.

32. *Ginsekai* by Kikuhara Kengyo is the winter piece from his four seasons work. The others are *Tsumi Gusa* (spring), *Kumo no Mine* (summer), and *Monaka no Tsuki* (autumn).

33. Ebisu is the only god of Japanese origin among the Seven Gods of Good Fortune who consists of Ebisu (Japanese), Benzaiten (Indian), Daikokuten (Indian), Bishamon (Indian), Fukurokujo (Chinese), Hotei (Chinese), and Jurojin (Chinese).

34. John Tierney in "A Generation's Vanity, Heard Through Lyrics" in the *New York Times*, April 26, 2011, p. D1, discusses changes in lyric content of American popular songs from 1980 to 2007. Tierney shows a trend towards narcissism in songs, replacing lyrics that valued connections of love with words of anger, like hate or kill.

35. Although Zen Buddhism is credited for Japanese aesthetics, Buddhism at its core is averse to make judgments of whether things are beautiful/ugly, good/bad, right/wrong, smart/dumb, etc. Things are "as they are" and therefore life is "as it is."

36. Helen Keller, *The Story of My Life*, New York: Grosset and Dunlap, 1905.

Chapter 2

1. *Kojiki* is the *Record of Ancient Matters*, 712, and the *Nihon Shoki* is the *Chronicle of Japan*, 720. They were printed after Chinese writing was introduced.

2. Other societies that worshipped the sun are the Aztecs of Mexico, the Incans of South America, the Egyptians with Ra, the Greeks had Apollo, and the Hindi worshipped Surya.

3. Tatsuo Kobayashi, *Jomon Reflections: Forager Life and Culture in the Prehistoric Japanese Archipelago*, Chapt. 8 (Oxford: Oxbow, 2004).

4. E. M. Satow, "The Shintau-Temples of Ise," in *Transactions of the Asiatic Society of Japan, III*, Yokohama, 1874, p. 117. The *hito futa miyo itsu muyu nana ya koko no tari momo chi yorodzu* is another counting system from one to ten, etc.

5. I am reminded of the PBS children's program *Mr. Rogers' Neighborhood* that aired from 1968 to 2001. A trolley moved the audience from this land to a place of make-believe.

6. Takeshi Umehara, philosopher. Lecture on "Forest Culture and Japan" for the International Research Center for Japan Studies on June 27, 1991.

7. The Meoto Iwa is found at the Futami Okitama Shrine in Futami, Mie-ken.

8. Makoto Takemitsu, *Nippon Tanjo* [Japan's Birth], Chapt. 3, Tokyo: Bungei Shunju, 1991.

9. Kobayashi, p. 92.

10. Kobayashi, p. 85.

11. Kobayashi, p. 89; for a complete list of food, see pp. 234–235.

12. Kobayashi, p. 16.

13. Diorama exhibits at the Niigata Prefectural Museum of History.

14. Tatsuo Kobayashi, *Jomon Reflections: Forager Life and Culture in the Prehistoric Japanese Archipelago*, Chapt. 6: "Settlement and Society" (Oxford: Oxbow, 2004), pp. 99–135.

15. Author's visit to Sannai Maryuama in Aomori, Japan, on May 15, 2015.

16. The modern equivalent of duality continues as red versus white as in the New Year's Kohaku Utakakuksen (Red/White Song Contest) or the Japanese propensity to separate work from play, things for children and adults, duties of men and women, and so on.

17. Tatsuo Kobayashi, *Jomon Reflections: Forager Life and Culture in the Prehistoric Japanese Archipelago* (Oxford: Oxbow, 2004), pp. 132–133.

18. Jomon people favored equality and remembering descendants was not worshipping ancestors.

19. Neither of the religions requires strict

allegiance and loyalty, thus some Japanese claim both.

20. In contrast, Jodo Shinshu Buddhists ascribe to no superstitions, magic, or miracles and these families have only a Buddhist altar. This is one of the first tenets announced by the Rev. Masanobu Kubota when guiding University of Maryland Study Abroad students, January 2004 at the Honzan (main temple) in Kyoto.

21. Takeshi Umehara, philosopher, lecture on "Forest Culture and Japan" for the International Research Center for Japan Studies on June 27, 1991. The ritual dance Sambaso stamps the earth to awaken seeds in the soil.

22. Kobayashi, p. 166. The numbers 3 and 7 are also magic numbers in Western fairytales.

23. Takeshi Umehara believes Shinto took hold during the Mid-Jomon Era (3500–2500 BCE).

24. Masafumi Ono and Tsutsumu Takashi, eds., *Jomon Bijitsukan Shashin* [Jomon Museum Photos] (Tokyo: Heibon sha, 2013), pp. 190–191.

25. Early Yayoi immigrants' remains were found in the Yoyoi district of Tokyo, assimilated with the majority Jomon people.

26. Takeshi Umehara. *Nihon no Shukyo no Tokushitsu to Imi* (Characteristics and Meaning of Japanese Religion), 1987, p. 104. Both groups share the same concept of anoyo and konoyo, even after being separated for over a thousand years.

27. Makoto Takemitsu, *Nippon Tanjo* [Japan's Birth], Chapter 3 (Tokyo: Bungei Shunju, 1991).

28. The *Shinsen Shojiroku*, published in 815 by order of Emperor Saga, listed 1182 families, including 404 as divine, 335 as vassals, and 326 as of foreign origin. From Jun Kubota, *Iwanami Nihon Koten Bungaku Jite*, Iwanami Shoten, 2007.

29. Donald L. Philippi, trans., *Kojiki*. Chapt. 92 (Tokyo: Tokyo University Press, 1968), pp. 257–258.

30. John Noble Welford, "Flute Music Wafted in Caves 35,000 Years Ago," *New York Times*, International section, June 25, 2009, A12.

31. The Ainu dance and sing around an object at religious ceremonies, as seen on You Tube.

32. According to archeologist Tatsuo Kobayashi, *Jomon Reflections*, pp. 45–49.

33. Many Jomon pieces at the Niigata Prefectural Museum of History exhibit a design variation as the design moved around the pot.

34. Tatsuo Kobayashi, *Jomon Doki wo Yomu* [Reading the Jomon Pots] (Tokyo: Yokoyama, 2012), pp. 72–73.

35. Neil MacGregor, *A History of the Word in 100 Objects* (New York: Viking Penguin, 2008), p. 59.

36. Taro Okamoto first saw Jomon pottery at Ueno Museum and was overwhelmed. Picasso remarked similarly about Western man's art upon seeing French cave paintings. To the contrary, Tadanari Mitsuoka says in *Ceramic Art of Japan* (Tokyo: Japan Travel Bureau, 1956), p. 19, that "their designs after all belong to the savage design peculiar to primitive art, and give modern people the impression of the grotesque." In addition it is handmade in contrast to the wheel thrown Yayoi pottery of uniform simple elegance, of a higher level.

37. Professor Yatabe and other cognoscenti of hogaku claim it to be superior to Western music. Comment of Professor Yatabe in Edward S. Morse, *Japan Day by Day, 1877, 1878–79, 1882–83*, vol. 2 (Boston: Houghton Mifflin, 1917), p. 408.

38. Joseph M. Kitagawa's "Preface" in Donald L. Philippi, *Norito: A Translation of the Ancient Japanese Ritual Prayers* (Princeton: Princeton University Press, 1990), p. xxx.

39. Sir Ernest Satow in "Ancient Japanese Ritual," cited in Joseph M. Kitagawa's "Preface" in Donald L. Philippi, *Norito: A Translation of the Ancient Japanese Ritual Prayers* (Princeton: Princeton University Press, 1990), p. xxviii.

40. The Urabe received the last name Nakatomi and later Fujiwara.

41. See the website *Encyclopedia of Shinto Number 9. Texts and Sources* for an extensive list.

42. Eta Harich-Schneider, *The Music of Japan: Record V, Shinto Music,* comments on the notes (London: Oxford University Press, 1973).

43. Joseph M. Kitagawa, in Donald L. Philippi, *Norito: A Translation of the Ancient Japanese Ritual Prayers* (Princeton: Princeton University Press, 1990), p. xxv.

44. Takeshi Umehara, philosopher, in lecture on "Forest Culture and Japan" for the International Research Center for Japan Studies on June 27, 1991.

45. Joseph M. Kitagawa, in Donald L. Philippi, *Norito: A Translation of the Ancient Japanese Ritual Prayers* (Princeton: Princeton University Press, 1990), p. xxx.

46. Shigeo Kishibe, *The Traditional Music of Japan* (Tokyo: Kokusi Bunka Shinkokai, 1969).

47. Hisao Tanabe, *Japanese Music* (Tokyo: Kokusai Bunka Shinkokai, 1959).

48. Hisao Tanabe, p. 10. Japanese people generally make light of their primitive past because of their unsophisticated ways and living like primitive people. They prefer the new, clean, civilized ways.

49. How obsolete are Shinto practices when the majority of Japanese parents take children at ages 3, 5, and 7 years to the local shrine and people of all ages participate in Shinto festivals and pray for good fortune, work, passing exams, and good marriages, etc.? Many Japanese scholars acquiesce to what the Western world regards as "civilized people."

50. Twentieth century Japanese musicologists continue to be influenced by Western ideas and minimize anything Japanese. The same criteria apply to ceramic art. Jomon pottery is discredited as primitive, savage, grotesque. Tadanari Mitsuoka, *Ceramic Art of Japan* (Tokyo: Japan Travel Bureau, 1956), pp. 18–19.

51. Foreign music is esteemed and the Japanese' own music is relegated to the wayside. Although some Japanese consider their music superior, the mass acquiesces to the outsider's opinion.

52. Any online source on festivals in Japan will provide a Matsuri guide with date, location, and reason for the festivals, sometimes with photographs.

53. John K. Nelson, *A Year in the Life of a Shinto Shrine* (Seattle: University of Washington Press, 1996), p. 108.

54. Nelson, p. 50.

55. Tangentially, the amateur Kurokawa noh performances by farmers of Yamagata Prefecture is purported to be close to Shinto roots. Their noh chants resemble more—the spiraling Shinto norito than Buddhist chants. It is a reasonable supposition because early *sarugaku* has folk roots and was part of *dengaku* (field performances) and Shinto shrine performances.

56. Donald L. Philippi, *Norito: A Translation of the Ancient Japanese Ritual Prayers* (Princeton: Princeton University Press, 1990), p. 2.

57. Donald L. Philippi. The norito text of the *Hirano* Festival, pp. 32–33, is identical to *Kudo Furu Aki*, pp. 34–35. Kyoto's Hirano Festival is held in the fourth and the eleventh months for blessings on the Imperial court.

58. Donald L. Philippi, Joseph M. Kitagawa's remarks, p. xxvii.

59. Donald L. Philippi, Joseph M. Kitagawa's remarks, p. xxxvi.

60. Lyrics in *ji-uta* pieces such as in *Manzai* and *Egao* list many products in gratitude as in norito.

61. In Japanese letters today, the important request or message is towards the end.

62. Listen to Shinto norito on YouTube.

63. Similarly people enjoy Catholic liturgies, Jewish cantors, Islamic clerics, and the voices of Buddhist priests.

64. Eta Harich-Schneider, *A History of Japanese Music* (London: Oxford University Press, 1973), p. 579.

65. For complete details, see Benito Ortolani, *Japanese Theater: From Shamanistic Ritual to Contemporary Pluralism* (Princeton: Princeton University Press, 1990), pp. 17–22.

66. The singing is like *Two Stars* of the Wakan Roei (see my Chapter 5 on singing).

67. There are many Jomon figures with wide open mouths seeming to call in "Ohhh!" as in Shinto rituals.

68. Often early Japanese are pictured with something in their hands like a fan. A Shinto priest will hold a wand with strips of white paper, fan, or tree branch believed to be imbued with the kami's power.

69. Mi-kagura sung *Asakura* recorded by Eta Harich-Schneider, *A History of Japanese Music* (London: Oxford University Press, 1973).

70. The wa-gon plays during the sake exchange during weddings at the Meiji Jingu in Tokyo, as seen on YouTube. Note the distinct *zan* (up strum) and *ji* (down strum), and the A sections.

71. Eight beats of noh music become a moot point as many noh pieces disregard the "eightness" of the beats. Naturalness is the rule and noh pieces have no symmetry, more like Japanese gardens and unlike the symmetry of English or Italian gardens.

72. Performed by the Reverend Ogawa on record with Eta Harich-Schneider's *A History of Japanese Music* (London: Oxford University Press, 1973).

73. Harich-Scheider, *A History of Japanese Music* (London: Oxford University Press, 1973), p. 288.

74. Adding Korean and Chinese instruments to ancient songs is similar to adding guitar, piano, and Western instruments to today's Japanese melodies.

75. The miko comes from the family of Sarume no Kimi of professional court shamans of ancient kagura. Yoshinobu Inoura and Toshio Kawatake, *The Traditional Theater of Japan* (New York: Weatherhill, 1981), p. 20.

76. *Mikoshi* are portable shrines. At Himeji Castle in Hyogo Prefecture, a matsuri called *Nada no Kenka* (Fight of Mikoshi Shrines) is held in October. A fight is staged among portable shrines held by men.

77. See clips of *Hirano Matsuri* by Hankisu on YouTube.

78. Similar gatherings at the Fourth of July, Memorial Day, and Labor Day parades occur in different American communities.

79. *Kojiki*. Donald L. Philippi, trans. (Tokyo: University of Tokyo Press, 1969), p. 222.

80. It is like Buddhist temples adding the organ.

81. I am reminded of a cousin in Hiroshima who is now a guest conductor of many orches-

tras. On a visit in the fall of 1982, he said he was leading a Western type band for the matsuri.

82. This music is heard in the David Westphal and Peter Grilli video *Shinto: Nature, Gods and Man in Japan,* New York: Japan Society with Togg Films, #197. It is also played at an Izumo Shrine scene in the Doug Humphrey video *Buddha in the Land of the Kami,* on Films on Demand, Digital Educational video, April 1, 2009.

Chapter 3

1. Tomiyama Seikin and Kinzaburo Imai, eds., *Seikin Ji-uta Shugyo* (Tokyo: Geino Hakkyojyo, 1966), pp. 111–112. Tomiyama found going up 785 steps to Kompira Shrine in Shikoku in the old-fashioned way with two men carrying him in a palanquin was more convenient than a motorized car that required paved roads.

2. Clay pot drums amplify stomping under the noh stage. Kunio Komparu, *The Noh Theater: Principles and Perspectives* (New York: Weatherhill/Tankosha, 1983), pp. 147–148.

3. Percussionist Tsuchitori Toshiyuki (1959) performed in 1989 at Mount Yatsugatake, the site of the Jomon center, recreating rhythms. In Tatsuo Kobayashi, *Jomon Reflections: Forager Life and Culture in the Prehistoric Japanese Archipelago,* Chapt. 8 (Oxford: Oxbow, 2004).

4. Hakodate Municipal Museum was founded during the Taisho period (1912–1926). The ishibue was made of lava-like rock and was 14 cm in length and 6 cm in width at the widest point.

5. Scholars Teranaka Tetsuji and composer Hirose Ryohei blew into the stone flute, "The Oldest Japanese Flute?" *The East* 12, no. 2 (1976).

6. The nohkan also is the aural curtain for bunraku, kabuki, and other theater openings.

7. In the second verse of *Kuroda-bushi,* the sound of the thirteen-string koto is "*Mine no arashi ka, matsu kaze ka, koto no ne ka?*" (Are they sounds of the storm on the mountain peak, wind through the pines, or the sound of the koto?) Unlike the Western "pure" sound without overtones, pure in the Japanese sense would be what is found in nature with raspiness or wispiness or that with natural timbre.

8. *Kojiki.* Donald L. Philippi, trans., p. 323.

9. Made of rolled clay tubes using the coil-built technique, simple, unvarnished figures made by Hajibe potters from fifth through the seventh centuries. Used as religious symbols, they accompanied the deceased.

10. Harich-Schneider, 1973, pp. 16, 17.

11. The instruments found in the mounds are also listed in the *Nihon Shoki.*

12. *Nihongi: Chronicles of Japan from Earliest Times to AD 697,* trans. W.G. Aston (Rutland, Vermont: Tuttle, 1972), p. 326. The procession is like Korean funerals today.

13. The words gigaku and gagaku sound similar but gigaku is dancing and singing and uses huge masks. Gagaku is instrumental music, ostensibly religious music from the continent.

14. Buddhism did not supplant Shinto; they existed together.

15. *Traditions of Jodoshinshu Hongwanji-ha* (Los Angeles: Senshin Buddhist Temple, 1982), p. 29.

16. Shiba Ryotaro, trans. Akiko Takemoto, *Kukai: The Universal Scenes from His Life* (New York: ICG Muse, 2003), p. 121.

17. Similar government action again takes place in 1872 to include Western music in the schools.

18. A poetry collection of *Ten Thousand Leaves* expressing indigenous sentiments compiled in the eighth century of work by poets from as early as 347 to 759.

19. Sueyasu Shiba restored many bass instruments of the gagaku to re-explore the past. Miyagi Michio developed lower pitched instruments like the *jushichi-gen* (seventeen-string bass koto) because of Western music.

20. Shigeo Kishibe. *The Traditional Music of Japan* (Kokusai Bunka Shinkokai, Tokyo, 1969), p. 16.

21. For details on the gagaku instruments, see websites on specific instruments.

22. For some reason, the left is more important than the right in ancient politics and government appointees. It may also be that Amaterasu emerged from Izanagi's left eye.

23. When I played a gagaku video in a class I was teaching, students could not appreciate the hichiriki. When the students of a Study Abroad program heard gagaku outdoors at Kyoto's Heian Jingu on a cold January day, the students asked, "What is that beautiful instrument?" The hichiriki is perfect to pierce the expansive outdoor environment where gagaku is often played.

24. The ryuteki player also plays the komabue (Korean flute) for bugaku (dance) music, and the kagura-bue for Shinto music.

25. For detailed and insightful information on the biwa or any gagaku instruments, see Biwa-gagaku Project at ccrma.stanford.edu/groups/gagaku/strings/biwa.html.

26. Koto strings come in a package of 13 and are about 10 to 12 feet long. They come in different weight sizes called mommne or 3.75 grams for each string. Number 17 string is 64 grams, number 18 is thicker, and number 25 momme is used for gagaku koto. Number 17, 17.5, and 18 are for the modern kotos.

27. Ryoichi Hayashi, *The Silk Road and the Shoso-in* (New York: Weatherhill, 1975), pp. 54–55.

28. Hisao Tanabe, *Japanese Music* (Tokyo: Kokusai Bunka Shinkokai, 1959), pp. 21–22. Semimaru is immortalized in the noh play *Sakagami*. In the play, Sakagami visits her brother at Afusaka (Osaka) Gate where he recites poetry about the passersby of his hermitage.

29. Shigeo Kishibe and Kenji Hirano, *Nihon Ongaku no Ayumi* (Tokyo: Chikuma Shobo, Hogaku Taikei, 1970–1972), p. 5.

30. Giichi Tanaka, *Gendai Sankyoku Tenbo*, vol. 3 (Osaka: Shakuhachi Nihon-sha, 1973), pp. 50–55. These titles became the ranks in Tōdō Shoku Yashiki, established in 1330, and some have been continued through the twentieth century.

31. Also from the temple in the 1200s, shomyo became peppier and rhythmic and influenced the music for pleasure like *haya-uta* (popular songs) that also emanated from the temples. Performances like *sarugaku* (monkey mimes) and *dengaku* (field dances) performed by dengaku *hoshi* and sarugaku *hoshi* (*hoshi* meaning priests) were popular. Sarugaku also became noh which also shows its temple origins with Kanami and Zeami. (The "ami" part of their names denotes that they were priests.)

32. Later, the noh-bayashi became part of the shamisen *nagauta kabuki* ensemble.

33. Akira Tamba with Patricia Matore, trans., *The Musical Structure of No* (Tokyo: Tokai University Press, 1981). And Kunio Komparu, *The Noh Theater: Principles and Perspectives* (New York: Weatherhill/Tankosha, 1983).

34. When I first saw noh in Tokyo, I missed the sound of stringed instruments associated with stage dramas until I realized that the biwa and koto had different functions and that the shamisen was not introduced until the sixteenth century.

35. Today, concrete basins are constructed beneath the stage for the same effect.

36. Katada Kissaku can play the *Shojoji* song on the ko-tsuzumi. Any demonstration on ko-tsuzumi on YouTube shows this feature.

37. Tamba, *Musical Structure of No*, p. 155.

38. The Japanese add extra syllables to foreign words, so tacos become "ta-ko-su" and MacDonald's becomes "ma-ku-da-no-zu" and so on.

39. The shamisen's rise coincided with political events. The country was at peace after the turbulent warring years (1482–1558). Each shogun—Oda Nobunaga (1534–1582), Toyotomi Hideyoshi (1537–1598), and Tokugawa Ieyasu (1543–1616)—supported the arts, particularly the tea ceremony, paintings, calligraphy, and the *noh shimai* (dance) and *utai* (song). But with Tokugawa Ieyasu, Japan closed its doors from the 1630s and foreign trade was limited to the Dutch at Nagasaki; Christians were ousted; no Japanese could leave or re-enter the island under penalty of death. With no internecine wars, merchants and farmers had expendable income to spend at the pleasure quarters.

40. Some say Naka Shoji and Ishimura Kengyo are the same person but the two names are usually mentioned as to the remodeling of the sansen. Shigeo Kishibe and Kenji Hirano, notes on *Nihon Ongaku no Ayumi*, VictorVP3005 (Tokyo: Chikuma Shobo. Hogaku Taikei Furoku), p. 10.

41. Tomizaki Shunsho (1881–1969) introduced the innovation to the larger concert halls of Tokyo.

42. London Philharmonic Orchestra's CD, *The Greatest Video Game Music*.

43. University of Maryland features music of *Pokemon X and Y*, *Final Fantasy*, *Kingdom Hearts*, and *World of Warcraft: The Wrath of the Lich King*.

44. The Yoshida Brothers and Agetsuma made Tsugaru shamisen popular worldwide.

45. "Kokyu" in Fumio Koizumi, Yoshihiko Tokumaru, and Osamu Yamaguchi, eds., *Asian Musics in an Asian Perspective* (Tokyo: Heibonsha, 1977), pp. 187–189.

46. It is not unusual for young musicians like Yatsuhashi to invent instruments. Miyagi Michio created the seventeen-string bass koto and the eighty-eight-string koto and modified the fan-like koto plectrum to a straight edge.

47. *Chidori no kyoku* is accompanied by the kokyu played by Yokoi Mitsue on the recording *Sokyoku, Jiuta no Sekai* (Nippon Columbia, 1991, COCF 7896–900).

48. A *shaku* is a unit of measure of about 11.9 inches or 30.3 centimeters.

49. Program notes of "Brilliance of Bamboo: the 40th Anniversary of Mujuan," by Yodo Kurahashi, October 25, 2014.

50. Comments of Yodo Kurahashi, June 25, 2015. The Tsugaru shamisen player, Takahashi Chikuzan, became famous after a movie that documented his life. He performed in 1986 for the Japan America Society in New York, Washington, D.C., and Baltimore.

51. David Wheeler of Colorado brought several plumbing pipes with five holes for students to experience the shakuhachi at Gettysburg College, April 10, 2000.

52. Yodo Kurahashi of Kyoto teaches students in Texas, New York, Maryland, Colorado, California, Pennsylvania, and in Europe. There are countless students up and down the West Coast, Europe, and Asia.

53. *Kanji* is a Chinese pictograph or ideo-

graph that combines smaller units of strokes to mean a word or sound.

54. The number of string factories in 2012 consisted of only four places. We visited the Marusan Hashimoto Company, which makes silk and polyester strings for koto, shamisen, biwa, and the ukulele.

55. Pianist Virginia Lum of Bethesda, Maryland, bought a koto in the 1980s and kept it under her piano. When opened after 30 years, the tension on the strings had held and it was playable.

56. Eto Kimio's *Omoide no Utagoe* (Songs of Nostalgia) is a good example. A melody is repeated using different timbre making the koto sound like a harp, guitar, pizzicato of a violin, mandolin, steel guitar, and of course, koto.

Chapter 4

1. The folk song *Hakata Obi* in the IN mode tells of a girl who came to town wearing her hakata obi but left with a lover.
2. Discrepancies between Chinese or Japanese scales were neglected until a mathematician during the Edo Era made note of it, but even then the non-analytical Japanese disregarded the differences. In the same manner, the Japanese today continue to apply Western theories to Japanese music in a manner of trying to fit Cinderella's step-sister's foot into Cinderella's shoe.
3. The Chinese like the five-ness of things like five colors, five flavors, five-year plan, five musical notes, etc.
4. A good example is last line "*mini yukan*" of the popular song *Sakura, Sakura*, the syllable, "*mi*" is sung at the ei-u note in the IN ascent. Likewise, the koto's *Rokudan* accommodates the ei-U note by pressing strings 4, 9 of the *hirajyoshi* tuning.
5. "Jisei" is performed by Togi Hideki in the video *Togi Hideki Concert* in Heian Era attire.
6. Listen to Agatsuma Hiromitsu in his CD, *Beams*, and to the Yoshida Brothers.
7. Buddhist chants came from India, China, Vietnam, and Manchuria.
8. The six Nara sects are Hosso, Kegon, Ritsu, Jojitsu, Kusha, and Sanron, introduced in the sixth and seventh centuries.
9. Roughly translated, the line says, "Thus I have heard: At one time the Buddha was staying in the country of Shrasvati."
10. Shinran Shonin (1173–1263)
11. Meeting with the late Rev. Dr. Mokusen Miyuki of Los Angeles and his daughter Noriko Miyuki, October 11, 2015.

12. I asked kyogen actor Nomura Mansaku about the source of the kyogen songs while attending the Classical Performing Arts Friendship Mission of Japan, Asian Performing Arts Summer Institute held August 3 to September 8, 1981, by the University of California, College of Fine Arts in Los Angeles. He confirmed that they were Muromachi Era folk and popular songs.
13. Kishibe, p. 21.
14. The *banshiki* tuning influenced koto pieces by Yoshizawa Kengyo II in the 1820s with his *Chidori no Kyoku* and his four seasons pieces. The melody of *Ettenraku* for the *ryuteki*, *hichiriki*, and *sho* for the two modes are found in my Chapter 7 on decoration.
15. Hideki Nomura, *Koto no Shoshiki to Gakuri no Ohanashi* (Nagoya: Shogenshu Hanbu, 1973), p. 119.
16. Yoshizawa Kengyo II (1808–1872) thought he was inventing a new tuning; however, it is a variation of gagaku's Banshiki tuning. Yoshizawa's new pieces took poems from the tenth century *Kokin-shu* from which kokin-choshi got its name.
17. For *Chidori no Kyoku* the second string is raised to the same pitch as the seventh string. In Sawai's *Sakura, Sakura*, the first string is the octave of the fifth string.
18. Hideki Nomura, *Koto no Shoshiki to Gakuri no Ohanashi* (Nagoya: Shogenshu Hanbu). I combine information from pages 120 and 129.

Chapter 5

1. Words of Peter Hansen, Esq., Warrenton, Virginia, recalling when he heard koto music and singing while playing with my son. From an email November 10, 2015.
2. Dr. Harriet Natsuyama said in her study of *woshite* (pre-Chinese Japanese writing) that when the vowels of a, i, u, e, o are pronounced deliberately with feeling, the effect is awe-inspiring and exalting. Interview, December 5, 2017.
3. Eishi Kikkawa, *Nihon Ongaku no Rekishi* (Osaka: Sogen-sha, 1965), p. 8.
4. Eishi Kikkawa, *Nihon Ongaku no Rekishi* (Osaka: Sogen sha, 1965), p. 9.
5. Ellen Dissanayake, *Art and Intimacy: How the Arts Began* (Seattle: University of Washington Press, 2000). These ditties are characteristic of religious incantations of Ainu, indigenous Taiwanese, and other world tribes.
6. The Shinto vocal cadence is characteristic of Kurokawa noh which was introduced in 1463 to the farmers of the Yamagata area. These farmers perform noh at the Kasuga

shrine as transmitted from the fifteenth century during noh's early days. Modern audiences in Tokyo, Kyoto, and Osaka marvel at Kurokawa noh's Shinto-like chants rather than Buddhist chants.

7. The Rev. Masao Kodani, editor, *Senshin Buddhist Temple* (Los Angeles: Senshin Buddhist Temple, 2001), p. 79.

8. *Traditions of Jodoshinshu Hongwanji-ha* (Los Angeles, Senshin Buddhist Temple, 1982), p. 81.

9. The 1958 *Nirvana Symphony* of Mayuzumi Toshiro (1929–1997) attracted much attention as a Western interpretation of a Japanese tradition using a soloist, chorus, and orchestra. Beginning with a direct transcription of temple bells that dissipates, recedes, and returns, the voices sing with the dense cacophonous chromatic effect while a solo voice sings out, not with the weighed down vocal control of the Japanese style but in the open-mouthed style of a baritone or tenor, resonating like an operatic singer. The *Nirvana Symphony*, considered to be Mayuzumi's greatest composition, is reminiscent of Frederic Chopin's *Fantaisie-Impromptu I* in C-sharp minor (Op. posth. 66), which is a tribute to Beethoven's *Moonlight Sonata*. Is Mayuzumi's *Nirvana Symphony*, which reflects his Western musical training, meant to praise Buddhist chants in its reinterpretation?

10. This sect has less appeal to Westerners for unlike Zen, Shingon, and other sects, it has less interesting exotic rituals and strict practices. Jodo Shinshu emphasizes knowing oneself and having a disposition of gratitude.

11. Columnist David Brooks wrote an op-ed titled "The Structure of Gratitude" in the *New York Times* on July 28, 2015. He hit upon the basic premise of Shinran's gratitude espoused in the Jodo Shinshu sect.

12. The *bara* part of *saibara* means *horse*. However, according to musicologist Akira Hoshi, the word *saibara* may be a corruption of the word *saibari* of kagura. *Nippon Ongaku no Rekishi to Kansho* (Tokyo: Ongaku no Tomo-sha, 1971), pp. 310–311.

13. The custom even today is for guests to sing to entertain the honored guests after eating at private gatherings, banquets, wedding parties, etc.

14. Akira Hoshi, *Nippon Ongaku no Rekishi to Kansho* (Tokyo: Ongaku no Toma-sha, 1971, p. 22).

15. The koto has accompanied the saibara since the year 859.

16. Akira Hoshi wrote that when a saibara called *Sofuren* (Missing My Love) was mentioned in the "Kogo no Tsubone" chapter of the thirteenth-century *Heike Monogatari*, it caused excitement. Could it be the same *Sofuren* of a known gagaku piece about a lotus pond of a Chinese prince? The kanjis used for the title *Sofuren* are different, but they could have been changed to fit the love story. No one is sure. *Nippon Ongaku no Rekishi to Kansho* (Tokyo: Ongaku no Toma-sha, 1971), pp. 55–56.

17. Akira Hoshi, *Nippon Ongaku no Rekishi to Kansho* (Tokyo: Ongaku no Toma-sha, 1971), p. 23.

18. Eta Harich-Schneider, *A History of Japanese Music* (London: Oxford University Press, 1973), p. 229.

19. Choral singing requiring Western type harmony was not introduced until the Meiji Era (1868–1912).

20. Stephen Addiss, "Singing the Wakan Roei Shu" in J. Thomas Rimer and Jonathan Chaves, trans., *Japanese and Chinese Poems to Sing: The Wakan Roei Shu* (New York: Columbia University Press, 1997), p. 255.

21. Stephen Addiss, p. 255.

22. *Jisei* is available on video, Togi Hideki's *Gagaku* (TOCT-24293).

23. Stephen Addiss, pp. 256–257.

24. Priests and scholars played the six-string ch'in, a quiet instrument with soft strums. It was symbolic of scholars and philosophers because of its contemplative quality. The koto, treated like the sacred ch'in, required lustration and cleansing of the air before approaching it. Later, the purification ritual became more important than playing it.

25. One of the four women may have been Murai Rei (1887–1958) who taught Miyahara Chizuko (b. 1938). Ms. Miyahara plays *Ettenraku* or *Fuki* on the video *Nihon no Koto to so no Ongaku*.

26. Recording by Eta Harich-Schneider, *The Music Anthology of the Orient*, vol. 4: *Buddhist Music*, UNESCO Collection, Moso Biwa by the Rev. Gyoshun Ogawa of Kwanzeonji of Kyushu, August 7, 1957.

27. Hiroshi Kitagawa and Bruce T. Tsuchida, trans., *Tale of the Heike* (Tokyo: University of Tokyo Press, 1975, p. xvi).

28. *The Tale of the Heike*, Hiroshi Kitagawa and Bruce T. Tsuchida, trans. (Tokyo: University of Tokyo Press, 1975), p. 5.

29. Somewhat in competition with blind musicians in Kyushu, the Tōdōza became a national authorizing center for a blind man's employable skill, be it masseur, shampooer, acupuncturist, poet, sword expert, or musician.

30. Blind women musicians were called *goze*. They sang folk songs of the Echigo area with a shamisen. See my Chapter 8 on the iemoto system for more information.

31. Slowing the music or slow motion action is commonly used to show intense excitement.

Noh's *Shari* is an example in noh. In the movie *Kwaidan*, the crashing sound after the walls collapse dramatizes the panic of a man who discovered that he had spent the night with his wife's ghost in *Kurokami* (Black Hair).

32. Haruko Komoda, "The Musical Narrative of the *Tale of the Heike*," Chap. 4, in *The Ashgate Research Companion to Japanese Music* (Burlington, VT: Ashgate, 2008), pp. 99–100.

33. Haruko Komoda, Chapt. 4, p. 98.

34. *Nohgaku* is often referred to as twin theaters. I liken it to the 1988 movie *Twins* starring Arnold Schwarzenegger and Danny DeVito. Their scientist father tampered with an ovum, making twins, one tall, handsome, and virtuous and the other short, homely, and amoral. Noh is longer, sophisticated, serious, and kyogen is short with delightful antics.

35. J. Thomas Rimer and Yamazaki Masakazu, trans., *On the Art of the No Drama: The Major Treatises of Zeami* (Princeton: Princeton University Press, 1984, p. xxv).

36. I am reminded of Shirley Marneus, director of Theater at California Institute of Technology in the 1980s, who enjoyed the indefinable affect noh utai had on her.

37. Kunio Komparu, *The Noh Theater: Principles and Perspectives* (New York: Weatherhill, Tankosha, 1983), p. 168.

38. See Chapter 1, note 17.

39. A video of a professional noh singer had a grounded voice while four ladies in a sample lesson sang with their mouths wide open as accepted in Western singing but with unsuccessful results.

40. IN mode in the ascent.

41. Hiroshi Koyama, *Nihon Koten Bungaku Taikei 43: Kyogen Shu*, vol. 2 (Tokyo: Iwanami Shoten: 1983), p. 449.

42. Joruri is from the play "Joruri-hime" (Princess Joruri.) The word joruri became synonomous to storytelling narratives, which is distinquished without the capitalization.

43. Similarly, Gidayu is Takemoto Gidayu's name, but gidayu without the capitalization means the bunraku style of singing as developed by this great singer.

44. Women gidayu singers appear in amateur recitals.

45. Shunichi Fujita, *Tomizaki Shunsho Geidan: Ji-uta Sokyoku, Sangen no Hanashi* (Tokyo: Nihon Ongaku-sha, 1968), p. 29. Tomizaki became blind at age 4 and, coming from a performance family, he was destined to be a puppeteer, gidayu singer, or a shamisen player. Being blind, he learned ji-uta music, a career for blind people.

46. Tomiyama Seikin and Imai Kinzaburo, eds., *Seikin Ji-uta Shugyo* (Tokyo: Geino Hakkojyo, 1966), pp 47–48.

47. These words were repeated by Tomiyama Seikin to his disciples Tominari Seijo and Tomio Seiritsu. Comments to me by the two musicians, November 14, 2015.

48. Tomiyama Seikin and Imai Kinzaburo, eds., *Seikin: Jiuta Shugyo* (Tokyo: Geino Hakkojyo, 1966), pp. 72–73.

49. They can be identified by the titles granted to them by the Tōdōza guild. The suffix of *Kōtō* or *Kengyo* after a name is indicative. Sighted musicians have the suffix *–jo* or *tayu* or *dayu* such as Takemoto Gidayu of the Bunraku Theater.

50. Shunichi Fujita, *Tomizaki Shunsho Geidan: Ji-uta Sokyoku, Sangen no Hanashi* (Tokyo: Nihon Ongaku-sha, 1968), p. 14.

51. Some interesting pieces are *Aki no Koto no Ha* (the one and only piece by Nishiama Kengyo), *Chidori no Kyoku, Mama no Kawa, Yaegoromo*.

52. The only pieces in my repertoire by sighted composers are by Tadao Sawai or my Western composer friends.

53. Johann Wolfgang von Goethe, in Andrea Wulf, *The Invention of Nature: Alexander Von Humboldt's New World* (New York: Vintage, 2016), epigraph.

54. Shigeo Kishibe and Kenji Hirano, notes on *Nihon Ongaku no Ayumi* (Tokyo: Chikuma Shobo. Hogaku Taikei Furoku, 1970–1972), p. 9.

55. The Portuguese may have introduced playing cards in the 1500s, which was re-gamed with poems. The University of Virginia Library's Japanese Text Initiative offers translations of the 100 Poems.

56. See my Chapter 8 on the iemoto system. There is a tendency to form schools around an expert who is recognized for his or her "correct" way of reading and playing. Even folk and *enka* singers have their schools and licensed teachers.

57. Shigeo Kishibe and Hirano Kenji, notes on *Nihon Ongaku no Ayumi* (Tokyo: Chikuma Shobo, Hogaku Taikei Furoku (Series), 1970–1972), p. 9.

58. The Rev. Dr. Mark Unno mentioned the chant-like quality of koto singing at my koto presentation at the University of Mary Washington, April 16, 2014.

59. Fumio Koizumi, *Nihon Dento Ongaku no Kenkyu I*, p. 20. There are some exceptions. The one I know about is Tomiyama Seikin's *Miyako Wasure*. In the first verse, "Matsu no kokage," the second syllable is higher, probably to bring out the poet's wife, Matsuko. See my Figure 5.1: The *"Matsu no kokage ni"* Melody of *Miyako Wasure*.

60. Singer Linda Ronstadt talks about the "sheen" or "resonance" she lost in her voice as

a result of Parkinson's disease. She describes notes that dance around sympathetic frequency of many vibrations per second where she can do mystical things with her voice to bring out emotions. Interview on the *Diane Rehm Show*, July 29, 2014.

61. Linda Ronstadt interview on the *Diane Rehm Show*, July 29, 2014.

62. Shigeo Kishibe, *The Traditional Music of Japan* (Tokyo: Kokusai Bunka Shinkokai, 1969), p. 11.

63. *Bad News Bears Go to Japan*, Paramount film directed by John Berry and starring Tony Curtis, 1978.

64. S. J. Lourenco Mexia, "Their Music," in Michael Cooper, ed., *They Came to Japan: An Anthology of European Reports on Japan, 1543–1640* (Berkeley: University of California Press, 1981), pp. 256–257. Also Britten Dean titles his Japanese music paper as "'Howling' Music" in *Monumenta Nipponica* 40, no. 2 (1985): 147–162.

65. Honda Choir Advertisement on YouTube, November 11, 2007. Uploaded by Blue Monday 1983. In 2006 Honda released its choir advertisement.

66. Daniel Levitan, *This Is Your Brain on Music* (New York: Dutton/Penguin, 2006).

67. Paul Vitello, "Peter Marler, Graphic Decoder of Birdsong, Dies at 86," *New York Times*, July 28, 2014, p. 16.

68. "Ours" meaning Western music as the author is Edward S. Morse, *Japan Day by Day*, vol. 2 (Boston: Houghton Mifflin, 1917), p. 408.

69. Daisuke Inoue of Kobe invented the karaoke machine in 1976. Karaoke is *kara* (empty), *oke* (short for orchestra) or orchestra minus the singer to supply the melody.

70. Lafcadio Hearn, "A Street Singer," *Kokoro: Hints and Echoes of Japanese Inner Life* (Rutland, Vermont: Charles E. Tuttle, 1980), p. 41.

71. Comments of Billie Holiday on NPR interview, npr.org/2010/11/19/131451449/billie-holiday-emotional-power-through-song.

Chapter 6

1. Yukio Mishima, *Kinkakuji* [The Temple of the Golden Pavilion], Ivan Morris trans. (New York: Alfred A. Knopf, 1959, Berkeley Medallion, 1971), p. 160.

2. Eta Harich-Schneider, *A History of Japanese Music* (London: Oxford University Press, 1973), p. 283.

3. In Japanese letters, the protocol is to place the most important item at the end.

4. See Rose/Kapuscinski, Gagaku Project-CCRMA 2010, Stanford University for details on gagaku music.

5. From "Orchestration in Gagaku Music" by Rose/Kapuscinski, Gagaku Project-CCRMA.

6. The piece is also played in the ichikotsu mode, sounding familiar, yet different like the koto piece *Rokudan*. Originally it was in the YO mode which the Okinawan koto continues to play, but the piece in the IN mode dominates on Honshu.

7. On the video *Koto on Monogatari* (IKPR 2004,Toshiba-EMI, Victor Entertainment), Miyahara Chizuko (1936) plays *Fuki* as learned from the last Tsukushi kotoist, Murai Rei (1887–1958).

8. Machlis and Forney analyze the four (really five) *kakezume* notes of *Fuki*, a vocal music, with the four-note motif of Beethoven's *Symphony No. 5*. The unrelated premise of both musical styles reveals nothing about *Fuki*. Joseph Machlis and Kristine Forney, *The Enjoyment of Music*, 8th ed. (New York: W.W. Norton, 1999), p. 223.

9. Comments of Tominari Seijo to the author, November 13, 2015, at rehearsal for her concert at the Freer Gallery of Art, "Making Musical Waves: Legacy of Yatsuhashi," November 14, 2015.

10. The lyric is about Genso Kotei, the Chinese emperor who lost his kingdom because of the beautiful Yohiki, or Yang Kei Fei. For a Chinese feel to the piece the tuning is in the A-IN scale or the ascent IN mode (see Tuning).

11. Kumi-uta loosely means a collection of songs. However, *Chidori no Kyoku* and the four seasons pieces by Yoshizawa Kengyo II, *Yaegoromo* by Ishikawa Kōtō and *Miyako Wasure* by Tomiyama Seikin—all in the tegoto-mono structure—at times are called "kumi-uta" as their lyrics are collections of poems.

12. So popular were the wa-sans, they influenced folk songs of the Muromachi Era. See Kyogen songs, Figures 4.4, 5.11, and 5.12.

13. Kunio Komparu, *The Noh Theater: Principles and Perspectives* (Tokyo: Weatherhill, 1983), see chart on p. 28.

14. Recall that the hayashi musicians are *tsuzumi* (shoulder drum), *o-tsuzumi* (big drum), *taiko* (stick drum), and the *nohkan* (flute) player.

15. Kunio Komparu, *The Noh Theater: Principles and Perspectives* (Tokyo: Weatherhill, 1983), pp. 203–208.

16. There are four pillars to mark the stage. The first is the shi-te pillar, where the shi-te usually in mask stops and then turns to face the metsuke-pillar (eye pillar) on the front left of the stage. The waki-pillar is on the right front of the stage where the waki sits, and the flute pillar for the flute player.

17. Yukio Mishima, *Kinkakuji*, p. 160.

18. Kunio Komparu, pp. 286–287. He has an excellent diagram of how the jo-ha-kyu is structured in the units of a noh play.

19. Sangen and shamisen are interchangeable, but ji-uta musicians prefer to use sangen. I will use them interchangeably, but use the term hamisen when talking about kabuki, bunraku, and other narrative genre.

20. Tomiyama Seikin I's rendition of the delightful *Hayafune* (Fast Boat) is particularly engaging. See website.

21. To keep alive Yanagawa Kengyo's pieces, members of Kyoto's Tōdō Kai meet twice a week to practice them. Comments of Ms. Ooki, executive of Tōdō Kai, Kyoto, June 2012.

22. It is surmised that the songs came from Ryukyu or that Ishimura's mother was a Ryukyuan.

23. Kansai is Kyoto and Osaka area. Kanto is Edo, or Tokyo.

24. Akira Hoshi, *Nippon Ongaku no Rekishi to Kansho* (Tokyo: Ongaku no Tomo-sha, October 10, 1971), p. 75. According to Yodo Kurahashi, the two kanjis were interchangeable until Kikuhara Hatsuko made the distinction, which the media and other musicians followed. Interview, August 10, 2015.

25. Sayama Kengyo's student began the Kineya line of Edo Nagauta music.

26. Yatsuhashi's student, Kitajima Kengyo could have proclaimed a new school of the new ensemble but, out of respect for Yatsuhashi Kengyo, he withheld this declaration. After Yatsuhashi's death, it was Ikuta Kengyo who proclaimed the school.

27. Until the twentieth century, the koto styles were associated with either sangen's Yanagawa-ryu or Nogawa-ryu showing the dominance of the shamisen in the ensemble instead of the koto innovator's names, like Ikuta ryu, Tsuguyama ryu, or Yamada ryu.

28. These songs of adult content were short and ideal for beginners.

29. It is no wonder that the Mombusho of the Meiji Era adopted Western music for the public schools. Many art songs of the time were inappropriate for children.

30. Geishas were originally men who performed on drums and sang at the teahouses. Women replaced them and became the Edo Era entrepreneurs who cultivated the art of entertainment by being highly skilled in music, dancing, and good conversation. Unlike the *yujyo* (prostitutes), they were not banned in the 1950s as they were performers. See Liza Dalby's book *Geisha* (Berkeley: University of California Press, 1998).

31. The blind musician Minezaki Kōtō set *Kosunoto* to music.

32. The exaggerated feelings of women are found in *Yuki, Mama no Kawa, Kaji Makura, Sue no Chigiri*, etc.

33. Some early kumi-uta, such as *Ougi no kyoku* by Yatsubashi Kengyo, had a 64-beat section without song played between sections 4 and 5, or played simultaneously with section 5, possibly a precursor to the tegoto-mon format.

34. The four seasons pieces (*Haru no Kyoku, Natsu no Kyoku, Aki no Kyoku*, and *Fuyu no Kyoku*) by Nagoya's Yoshizawa Kengyo II (1808–1872) became popular after Matsuzaka Kengyo (1854–1920) inserted the tegoto. Nagoya koto players continue to play it without the tegoto to be true to Yoshizawa's intentions.

35. Even with written music, the scores on the shamisen, koto, and shakuhachi are different so that similar lyric or section references are made.

36. Minezaki Kōtō composed *Aki Kaze no Kyoku* and *Godan Ginuta*, and Yoshizawa Kengyo II is famous for *Chidori no Kyoku* and his four seasons pieces.

37. Their brave deed was tantamount to a divorce from the shamisen that opened the path for pure koto music that raged during the Meiji Era (1868–1912) and thereafter. Some people are convinced that the new koto music was so gorgeous that jealousy prompted their demise.

38. *Tayu* becomes *dayu* for pronunciation, like Gidayu is easier to say than Gitayu.

39. Tangonojo Hoshi, borrowing among different disciplines.

40. The Ozatsuma style, created in 1721, was given to Kineya Saburosuke IV in 1826 when no iemoto was available to take over.

41. Takemoto Gidayu's style of singing became known simply as gidayu (after his name). Thus gidayu means narrative style of singing for the puppet theater and is not capitalized.

42. For the play, *Gion Sairei Shinkoki*'s two acts, "Kinkyoku no dan" and "Tsuma saki nezumi no dan," are performed.

43. Akira Hoshi, *Nippon Ongaku no Rekishi to Kansho* (Tokyo: Ongaku no Tomo-sha, 1971), p. 68.

44. Akira Hoshi, pp. 68–69. In 1707, his song style combined with puppets and later became dance music for Edo kabuki's Ichimura and Nakamura families from 1715 to 1722.

45. Shigeo Kishibe and Kenji Hirano, *Nihon Ongaku no Ayumi* (Tokyo: Chikuma Shobo, Hogaku Taikei Furoku (Series)), 1970–1972. Notes to the recording, p. 9.

46. For a detailed description of the Kiyomoto format and structure, see Alison McQueen Tokita's *Kiyomoto-bushi: Narrative Music of the Kabuki Theatre* (Kassel, Germany: Bärenreiter, 1999), p. 116.

47. Interviews with dancer Hanayagi Shifu of Osaka, November 2014 and August 30, 2016.

48. In a similar vein, at an Indian sitar concert, I would prefer to hear what is quintessentially Indian and not a Japanese or Western melody played on it.

49. The orchestras were the National Symphony Orchestra in 1977 and the Washington Symphony Orchestra in 1996.

50. Minae Mizumura, *The Fall of Language in the Age of English* (New York: Columbia University Press, 2008).

51. Karl Popper, *Objective Knowledge: An Evolutionary Approach* (Oxford, United Kingdom: Oxford University Press, 1975).

52. Robert Bernhardt, a student of shakuhachi who practices *gaikyoku* with me, on September 1, 2016.

Chapter 7

1. Tatsuo Kobayashi, *Jomon Doki wo Yomu* [Reading the Jomon Pots] (Tokyo: Yokoyama, 2012), pp. 72–73.

2. Students in Music 112: Two Music(s) of Japan, Gettysburg College, 1998–2009. The Japanese hear insects as musicians. See also Lafcadio Hearn's "Insect Musicians" in *Exotics and Retrospectives* (Boston: Little, Brown, 1916).

3. Yoshida Susumu (1947) studied European music in France and returned to Japan looking high and low for quintessentially Japanese music in spirit and sound. He settled on a chorus of *semi* (cicada) whose on-tune, off-tune, arhythmic drone-like Buddhist chanting evoked the *a-ware* (pathos) prevalent in hogaku.

4. The bass *sho* and *shitsu* (large koto) and other instruments were stored for safekeeping in the Shosoin, but they have been recently restored by Shiba Sukeyasu.

5. Akira Tamba, *The Musical Structure of No* (Tokyo: Tokai University Press, 1975), p. 86.

6. It is choka for the nohkan, or solfege-like shoga, for koto, kuchi-jamisen for shamisen, shoga for biwa, etc. They call out specific techniques or patterns like a ballet dancer's pirouette, arabesque, or plié.

7. Akira Tamba, *The Musical Structure of No* (Tokyo: Tokai University Press, 1975), p. 155.

8. Kunio Komparu, *The Noh Theater: Principles and Perspectives* (Tokyo: Weatherhill, 1983), pp. 165–166.

9. Hayashi becomes bayashi in compounds for pronunciation.

10. I am reminded of Beethoven's *Sixth Symphony, The Pastorale,* with the quiet before the storm.

11. Examples of the sounds described here can be heard on the recordings of *Nasu no Yoichi* and *Ogi no Mato* (see my Figure 5.6: Lyrics to *Nasu no Yoichi* and Figure 5.7: Lyrics to *Ogi no Mato*).

12. See YouTube, *November Steps*, Takemitsu project, with Seiji Ozawa conducting, Feburary 2, 1967. When challenged to write for hogaku instruments, Toru Takemitsu brought out the positive aspects in respect for the artistic quality of both cultures. Likewise Lori Laitman and Winifred Hyson wrote a Western melody for flute and clarinet respectively for the piece, *Rokudan*. Gary Davison (b. 1961) composed *Chidori* for women's chorus and with the swell of voices brought out another texture to koto's *Chidori no Kyoku*.

13. Sangen and shamisen are interchangeable but ji-uta musicians tend to use sangen.

14. Shunichi Fujita, *Tomizaki Shunsho Geidan: Ji-uta Sokyoku, Sangen no Hanashi* (Tokyo: Nihon Ongaku-sha, 1968), pp. 10–12, describes the fantastic left-hand skill of Sakamoto Jinoichi.

15. *Kurokami* is taught to beginners. As an 8-year-old, I debuted this piece with my teacher, Nakashima Chihoko, on the *sangen*. The lyrics did not make sense until I was an adult. I had some trepidation about teaching it to my young 9-year-old koto student Mia Saidel, but it paid off when at college her interest turned to Tamasaburo, who danced to *Kurokami*. She knew the piece and was delighted to have learned it long ago.

16. The terms are *hijiki* (left-hand plucking) and *utsu* (hitting a note on the pole).

17. A small pick is used for quiet practicing by geisha and nagauta players.

18. The *Kokaji* story is about the Inari fox god appearing in autumn to help a swordmaker forge a sword for the Emperor that is called "Kogitsune Maru" or Little Fox. The hayashi drums enhance the high jumps showing the supernatural quality of the fox as he applies his magical powers.

19. People are inventing other ways to notate shamisen and even have provided computer programs.

20. The Korean seven-string *ajaeng* is bowed with forsythia wood or a horsehair bow.

21. The koto's shoga was called *kuchi-jamisen* (mouth shamisen) since the teachers also played the sangen. Sangen music was transposed to the koto. Lately koto's kuchi-jamisen is called shoga.

22. Chinese music seems to play the high octave first followed by the lower octave.

23. The adjacent strings often are not harmonious.

24. Having no singing, it was *tsukemono*

(appendages) or incidental music and taken less seriously. Musicologists think their origins were part of *zokkyoku* (*solo* koto) dalliance in the Hakata, Kyushu area where it was easy access for foreigners during the middle centuries. It may be connected to Okinawan koto music which consists of many dan-mono *sugagaki* pieces, also believed to be of *zokkyoku* origins.

25. The music within strict fifty-two beats for dan-mono or sixty-four beats of kumi-uta came from a Chinese format. The Japanese prefer spontaneous forms and broke away with naga-uta, ha-uta, and tegoto-mono formats which have more freedom.

26. When a Western orchestra transfers the hovering notes of Japanese music, the entire orchestra plays the same note which sounds weighted and heavy. Try playing *Rokudan* on a piano! Also, in the reverse, Western classics on hogaku instruments lose the intended flavor.

27. In the metered measure of Western music, the first note gets the emphasis. Dynamic does not apply to koto scores, which have uneven phrases. When I was a child, a shakuhachi player coached a koto player to add dynamics to a classic, *Aki no Koto no Ha*. The resulting interpretation was strange, and the performance was deemed mediocre.

28. In this context, one can hear stylistic differences between *Rokudan* played by a classical specialist versus one who plays predominantly Westernized koto music using the written score.

29. See Christopher Y. Blasdel, *The Shakuhachi: A Manual for Learning* (Tokyo: Ongaku no Tomo sha), 1988.

30. The music box came from Holland, and the piece *Manzai* with the high *kaede* is called *Oranda Manzai* or (*Holland Manzai*).

31. "Ji" has many meanings (see my Glossary).

32. Piece by Tomizaki Shunsho.

33. Both pieces are by Tateyama Kengyo (circa 1890s).

34. Piece by Mitsuzaki Kengyo (d. 1853).

35. Piece by Kikuoka Kengyo (1850–1926).

36. Jesuits in the sixteenth century did introduce Western music, but the effort to train the masses to harmony did not occur until the Meiji Era. To hasten the process, children were given a harmonica and later a harmonium.

37. Koto concerts with 10, 20, or even 100 players is an imitation of the Western orchestra with massive instruments and the construction of large concert halls in the twentieth century.

38. Pirouette is to spin on one foot, arabesque is to have one leg straight behind the back, plié is to bend the knee, per atlantaballet.com/resources/ballet-terms-and-positions.

Chapter 8

1. Esyun Hamaguchi, *Nihon Rashisa no Saihakken* [Rediscovery of Japaneseness] (Tokyo: Nihon Keizai Shinbun sha, 1977).

2. According to anthropologist Francis Hsu, the Chinese, Korean, and Scottish societies value blood kinship so the secondary group is clan or kinship based. In the caste system of India and Pakistan, integration between the groups is unthinkable. The West has contract agreements as in marriage that allow unrelated people to join secondary groups such as clubs, schools, political parties, or workplaces.

3. Meson is the concept of the Japanese physicist, Akira Yukawa, Nobel Prize, 1949.

4. Japanese sociologists call it imperfect-iemoto, but I call it quasi–iemoto for it imitates the rules and regulations of the sanctioned iemoto's group.

5. It is like the British Royalty's Royal Warrants to suppliers of products with the Royal crest and words saying, "By appointment to her Majesty, the Queen," or Duke of Edinburgh or Prince of Wales.

6. G. B. Sansom, *Japan: A Short Cultural History* (Stanford: Stanford University Press, 1987), pp. 40–41.

7. Note the "me" as suffix. The "be" (guild) becomes "me" for pronunciation.

8. Herbert Plutschow, *Japan's Name Culture: The Significance of Names in a Religious, Political and Social Context* (Kent: Japan Library, 1995), p. 70.

9. Yamatohime no mikoto, daughter of Suinin Emperor (29 BCE–70 CE) founded the location for the Ise Shrines with the approval of Amaterasu per the *Nihon Shoki*.

10. Nowadays, corporal punishment and verbal abuse is kept at a minimum but such conduct depends on the teacher.

11. Words of Uchida Anshin, noh teacher of Kita ryu during lessons. Using a fan, he would hit students on the knee so they would remember to lift it higher.

12. Chef Victor Jian of Jinroku Restaurant in Honolulu, October 16, 2010, in answer to my question,"How did you become a Japanese chef?"

13. This is the basis of Suzuki Shinichi's (1898–1998) Mother Tongue Method exposing the child early to music so that it is second nature.

14. An accomplished artist at the upper level is able to move through all levels. Kanami, Zeami's father, was purported to be one of a few actors who could move through all levels and maintain his superiority.

15. J. Thomas Rimer and Yamazaki Masakazu, *On the Art of the No Drama: The Major*

Treatises of Zeami (Princeton: Princeton University Press, 1984).

16. Music playing was considered a hobby among the well-to-do since Heian times. Earning money was reserved for the professional realm.

17. Yoshizawa Kengyo II, composer of *Chidori no Kyoku*, was banished for daring to compose a piece without the sangen. His mentor, Mitsuzaki Kengyo, was also banished.

18. Between the 1600s and 1700s, the requirement of koto composers was to write a kumi-uta, which had a very strict form. By the 1800s, composers were released from the straitjacket by Yasumura So-kengyo (d. 1779) of the Tōdō Shoku Yashiki who forbade any more, claiming his kumi-uta to be the last.

19. After the fall of the Heike, noble families languished without any governmental duties. The Muromachi shogun encouraged noble families to sponsor arts and trade. The Koga family had a blind son, Jogen, who played the biwa and became the hereditary sponsor of the Tōdōza.

20. The titles of Kengyo and Kōtō were bequeathed to deserving blind musicians after Hitoyasu Shinno's death. His mother lobbied for it in his memory. The Betto and Zato grades were added by Kakuichi.

21. The noble Koga family continues to be titular heads of Osaka's Tōdō Ongaku Kai.

22. Shinnai shamisen music, once considered high art music, was downgraded when street singers played it. To this day, it has not shaken off this association.

23. Depending on the school or iemoto, the natori can teach.

24. Silk producers and weavers found time and money to study flower arranging. Some became teachers. Matsunosuke Nishiyama, *Edo Culture, Daily Life and Diversions in Urban Japan, 1600–1868* (Honolulu: University of Hawaii Press, 1997), p. 48.

25. The iemoto of Urasenke School of Tea circulated to speak to every person attending the reception held at the Hays-Adams Hotel in Washington, D.C., September 2015, according to Robert Bernhards, a tea and shakuhachi student. He was honored to meet him.

26. *En* can also be *Que sera, sera*, God willing, stars being in position, or even a perfect storm condition.

27. Ruth Benedict describes the Japanese as having a shame culture in *Chrysanthemum and the Sword: Patterns of Japanese Culture* (New York: Houghton Mifflin Harcourt, 1946).

28. Like wearing a designer's brand name in front of a shirt, t-shirt, or dress to show you have good taste or the means to afford the brand name.

29. Changing names occurred often depending on profession and location, and as rewards granted by the emperor. Herbert Plutschow, *Japan's Name Culture*, Chapt. 2 (Kent: Japan Library, 1995).

30. The samurai, peasants, and artists were at the top; merchants were at the bottom.

31. Miyagi Michio, Tomizaki Shunsho, and Tomiyama Seikin, among others, followed the traditional blindmen's occupation.

32. When introduced as a koto teacher, I am astonished when some Japanese immediately bow in deep respect.

33. In the 1700s some took it to Okinawa to form the Okinawa-ryu.

34. The fidelity of Mozart's music was recreated from a 200-year-old instruction sheet. A musician was to sit upright and to use small finger movments. The elbows were held against the body "with forearms sloping down and hands askew." This method helps the player change chords and scales quickly compared to today's methods. Rachel Nuwer in "Playing Mozart's Piano Pieces as Mozart Did," *New York Times*, Science section, July 20, 2015.

35. Four Japanese—Tani Innosuke, Sano Shinmijiro, Inokuma Genichiro, and Aoyama Yoshiro—went to Paris to study Henri Matisse's (1869–1954) style of painting and came back to Japan to claim to be four iemotos of the Matisse style of painting.

36. Suzuki Mie, a certified teacher of the Bando School of Dance, choreographed folk dancing for local school groups. Considered beneath the dignity of the Bando School of Dance's classical style, she had to dispense with the folk dances or leave the school. With many ardent followers and the attention of NHK television, Suzuki Mie left and created the Suzuki Mie School of Dance.

37. Nomura Mansaku of Kyogen stirred the reflection of his lord in the sake dish in *Boshibari* while commenting on the lord's greediness. Kanze Kiyokazu in the *Hagoromo* dance came forward on one knee to offer treasures to the world. Sawai Kazue's *Midare* reinterprets the piece in the manner of the *Star Spangled Banner* by singers at American football and baseball games.

38. Among those who distain the iemoto system, Suzuki Tadashi of SCOT claims proprietary rights to his avant-garde theater. According to his letter dated April 1990, he required anyone wanting to teach his theater style to enroll in his workshop and be certified. His action confirms Matsunosuke Nishiyama's assertion that all modern groups pattern themselves after the iemoto system whether they want to or not.

39. One koto teacher without proper train-

ing encouraged her university students to find their own playing technique, which is philosophically contrary to the premises of the iemoto system. None of her students achieved any prominence.

40. The *en* in Shinto is "rooted in the instinctive being of human nature feeling itself in communion with the living forces of the world ... wherein gods or spirits, animals and trees, even rocks and streams are believed to be in living communion with man." Esyun Hamaguchi, *Nihon rashisa no saihakken*, p. 109. Matsunosuke Nishiyama, Esyun Hamaguchi, and Noboru Haga, "Iemoto Seido to Nihon no Shakai [Iemoto World and Japanese Society]," *Rekishi Koro* [History Journal] 4, no. 4 (1978): 12. Buddhism sees the karmic life cycle of things, a natural continuity, in forming broader fellowship, for it includes the *seken* (world) that in turn includes ancestors, descendants, family, communities, and unknown people by chance encounter. In Hamaguchi, p. 107.

41. Matsunosuke Nishiyama in *Edo Culture: Daily Life and Diversion in Urban Japan, 1600–1868* (Honolulu: University of Hawaii Press, 1977), p. 208, blames the iemoto system with individualized lessons for not fostering teamwork for choral music. He fails to recognize that choral singing requires Western harmony, which was not introduced until the Meiji Era. It is ironic that the Japanese, often criticized for being too groupish, are criticized here for being too individualistic.

42. Among scientists doing malaria research, a large team of fifty or more scientists work together to solve problems from various aspects. *DeMystifying Medicine* lecture at National Institute of Health, March 2, 2015.

43. Founded in Kyoto in the sixteenth century by Kurokawa Enchu.

44. W. Edward Deming's (1900–1993) ideas on quality control are credited for Japan's economic turn after World War II. Because Japan's society already advocated working together, his 14 Points, such as communication with everyone, on the job training, and create trust, were easily instituted.

Chapter 9

1. Comment of Yodo Kurahashi on his search for sites mentioned in music.

2. The Pokemon "Ghost of Maiden Peak" episode (1998) refers to Bunraku's "The Battles of Coxinga." In Coxinga, Komutsu watches her husband Watonai depart for China. I am reminded by her of two ancient stories: China's *Wife Watching Mountain* and Japan's *Scarf-Waving Mountain*. In both stories, the women turned to stone while waiting for their husbands.

3. John Tierney in "A Generation's Vanity, Heard through Lyrics," *New York Times,* April 26, 2011, discusses how we can hear changes in young Americans' attitudes and emotions through popular song lyrics. In the 1980s Americans heard music that was more interconnected and positive. By 2011, the lyrics related to anger and antisocial behavior with narcissistic attitudes.

4. Harich-Schneider, p. 457.

5. The Sanjo Minister wrote, "The music in the repertory of the court musicians is in the first place Japan's original music, but also includes some from China and the Korean kingdoms. We have repeatedly adopted music from other countries; this was a natural human development. Now the situation is the same with respect to European music. Not only in the army and navy, but also at court ceremonies and banquets we need the music of the West. We therefore advise that the reijin [gagaku musicians] should make themselves acquainted with this material as its use is increasing, and they should fulfill their duties comprehensively. We wish therefore to give a command to the reijin and reiin to learn the music of the West immediately. ... We think it will be less expensive if we employ the teachers of the navy band," from Harich-Schneider, p. 535.

6. Lesson plans and collections of Mason's works are in the Performing Arts Library of the University of Maryland, College Park.

7. The translation of the lyrics to *Hotaru no Hikari* is on Wikipedia.

8. Mia Saidel's grandmother, Mrs Koji Miyagawa, asked me why I had learned the koto. I responded, "Because my parents wanted me to learn about Japanese culture." I asked her why she became a piano teacher. Mia's grandmother said, "Because her mother wanted her to know about the culture of the victors after losing the war to the United States."

9. Shakuhachi player Yodo Kurahashi mentions that because children today have not seen a shakuhachi, it is to his advantage. Up until about 2000s, Japanese students laughed and made light of the instrument and paid little attention to his explanations, but today, the shakuhachi is a curiosity and students are willing to listen and learn. A comment made August 10, 2015.

10. Toyotaka Komiya, ed., Donald Keene and Edward G. Seidensticker, trans., *Japanese Music and Drama in the Meiji Era* (Tokyo: Obunsha, 1956), p. 334.

11. Hideki Togi played the piano and electric guitar and listened to the Beatles and Eric Clapton.

12. My university students were dubious of the *hichiriki* playing Beatles songs.
13. Yuri Kageyama, "From Imperial Court to Food Court: An Ancient Japanese Music Finds a Crossover Champion," *Washington Post*, April 24, 1999, C10.
14. Umewaka Minoru (1828–1909) took odd jobs; Matsuda Kametaro became a ferryman.
15. Grant saw *Mochizuki, Tsurigitsune*, and *Tsuchigumo*, which are still favorite performances for newcomers.
16. Toyotaka Komiya, ed., Donald Keene and Edward G. Seidensticker, trans., *Japanese Music and Drama in the Meiji Era* (Tokyo: Obunsha, 1956), p. 17.
17. Tsubouchi Shoyo translated all of Shakespeare's plays.
18. Toyotaka Komiya, ed., Donald Keene and Edward G. Seidensticker, trans., *Japanese Music and Drama in the Meiji Era* (Tokyo: Obunsha, 1956), pp. 111–112.
19. Edward S. Morse, *Japan Day by Day*, vol. 2 (Boston and New York: Houghton Mifflin, 1917), p. 408.
20. My friends Peter Hansen and his son, Pierce, expressed to me May 3, 2015, how much they enjoy the voice-driven music of hogaku. They like the strong groundedness of its tones. Also, Shirley Marneus, director of theater at California Institute of Technology, could not get enough of noh singing.
21. Noh scholars are Monica Bethe, Karen Brazell, and Richard Emmert, to name a few. Richard Emmert with his Nogaku Theater (founded in 2000) performs and conducts noh workshops all over the world. He also composes and arranges noh plays in English and Spanish.
22. Issen Yoshikazu, *Foreigners Having a Party at the Gankiro Tea House at Pleasure Quarters in Miyozaki, Yokohama*, January 1861.
23. *Picture of a Mercantile Establishment in Yokohama, Edo period*, 1861 by Sadahide (1807–1878). Collection of William and Florence Leonhart, Washington, D.C.
24. The left-hand pluck was discarded during the Heian Era with the clean-up of gagaku music.
25. Kikuzuka composed *Ganjyo no Matsu, Meiji Shochikubai, Mittsu no Keshiki*, and *Aioi no Kyoku* to be played with *Rokudan*, among many others.
26. Tateyama wanted to create a new school using his Natsuyama tuning based on the YO mode. Among his famous pieces are *Hototogisu no Kyoku* played with *Hoshi to Hana to* and *Kongo Seki*.
27. Kikuhara Kengyo wrote *Tsumigusa, Kumo no mine, Gin sekai*, and *Monaka no Tsuki*.
28. Tomizaki composed thirty-two pieces, among them *Sato no Ko, Haru no Enoshima, Manzai Raku*, and *Yomogifu* (lyrics by Tanizaki). He released all rights to his works.
29. Tomiyama's compositions include *Shoka no Ogawa, Akatsuki No Uta, Shunoten*, and *Miyako Wasure*.
30. Ito Hirobumi was prime minister of Japan four times previously and assassinated by a Korean dissident in 1909.
31. Pierre Rampal and James Galway recorded *Haru no Umi*. Andre Kostelanetz (1901–1980) conducted this piece with kotoist Yuize Shinichi at Carnegie Hall, and also in 1977, with the author and the National Symphony Orchestra at the Kennedy Center for the Performing Arts.
32. Eishi Kikkawa, *Kono Hito Nari Miyagi Michiyo Den*, Chapt. 63 (Tokyo: Shincho Shappan, 1962), pp. 393–400.
33. Japanese Americans in particular identified with Miyagi's music. But in my experience, serious Western musicians preferred to hear quintessential koto music.
34. Nosawa Keiko plays the twenty-one-string koto, and Miyashita Susumu plays the thirty-one-string koto.
35. Composer Marty Regan (b. 1972) has composed many shakuhachi and koto pieces.
36. To showcase the works of contemporary Japanese composers, Music from Japan, Inc., headed by Naoyuki Miura, introduced several composers, such as Sato Shin and Joji Yuasa (1929). Textbook lists include Toru Takemitsu (1930–1996), Akira Ifukube (1914–2006), Teizo Matsumura (b. 1929), Toshiro Miyazumi (1929–1997), Toshi Ichiyanagi (b. 1933), Teruyuki Noda (b. 1940), Shin-Ichiro Ikebe (b. 1953), Akira Nishimura, and Tokuhide Niimi.
37. Music of Japan Today, 2003 Festival & Symposium, April 2–6, 2003, UMBC, Baltimore, Maryland.
38. Japanese composers present at the Symposium were Joji Yuasa, Tokuhide Niimi, Akira Nishimura, and Toshi Ichiyanagi.
39. Niimi, UMBC conference, April 5, 2003.
40. Tokuhide Niimi's comment at the Baltimore conference.
41. Akemi Naito, *Strings and Time* (New York: Composers Recording, CRI CD 771).
42. Takashi Yoshimatsu (b. 1953), *Saxophone Concerto "Cyber-Bird,"* Op. 59 (Colchester, England: Chandos Records, 1999), LC 7038.
43. Akemi Naito, *Strings and Time* (New York: Composers Recording, CRI CD 771).
44. Joji Hirota, *The Gate* (Real World Records, 72438-47740-2-8, 1999).
45. *Patterns of Plants*, works of Mamoru Fujieda, Yoko Nishi (ALM Records, ALCO-52). Ironically his name means *fuji* (wisteria) *eda* (branch).

46. Matsuo Basho (1644–1694) is a famous haiku poet of the Edo Era. Yuasa chose three of Basho's quiet poems.

47. In the hierarchy in music of what is popular today, hogaku is considered old-fashioned and not as advanced as Western music. Kikkawa's response conveyed that he was a composer of advanced knowledge since he could write for Western instruments.

48. Response of the composer at a Reigaku performance at the Kennedy Center for the Performing Arts, September 9, 2004.

49. Response of Akira Nishimura to my questions at the Music of Japan Today, 2003 Festival and Symposium, April 2–6, 2003, UMBC, Baltimore, Maryland.

50. I am reminded of Peter Grilli's 1997 film *Film Music of Toru Takemitsu* that features how Takemitsu set mood in various movies using timbre of instruments rather than melody.

51. Teizo Matsumura, *Poem*, 30CM-428, December 1988.

52. Tominari Seijo and Tomio Seiritsu are requested to play the classical music of koto and sangen for their annual visits to Moscow in the past ten years.

53. Hiromitsu Agatsuma in *Agatsuma Beams* (Los Angeles: Domo Records, Toshiba-EMI, 7 9401 73013 27, 2003). Many of the performances on YouTube show this effect.

54. Arthur C. Clarke, *The Nine Billion Names of God* (New York: Harcourt, 1967).

55. Max Richter, a British composer, premiered *Sleep* music in Berlin from midnight to 8:00 a.m. in the fall of 2015. A physically difficult piece, it requires concentration especially to play twenty-five pages of whole notes. The goal is to put everyone to sleep. "Trouble Sleeping? A Composer Wants to Help," National Public Radio, September 3, 2015.

56. Hayashi tsuzumi drummer Katada Kissaku dabbled with jazz but relies on his classic repertory; kyogen actor Nomura Mansaku likes to improvise but thinks about it seriously before actually presenting it on stage.

57. Gigaku is dance, music, and theater from the Asian continent, sixth through seventh centuries. Koma Chikazane (1172–1242) wrote *Kyokunsho* for future reference. Masks and costumes are stored at Horyuji, Todaiji, and Waseda University's Tsubouchi Shoyo Museum.

58. In the past, students wanted to learn Japanese for business purposes. Today, it is to understand anime and video games.

59. The *Magic Flute* (Impempe Yomlingo) by the Isango Ensemble with music transposed by Mandisi Dyantyis as seen at Center Stage in Baltimore, Maryland, October 17, 2014.

60. Minae Mizumura, *The Fall of Language in the Age of English* (New York: Columbia University Press, 2008).

Epilogue

1. June 28–July 11, 2011. Mia Saidel was my koto student from age 7 until she entered college. The "Koto Journey" was financed by Andrew Saidel as part of Mia's essay for college. Toshiko (Riko) Saidel accompanied us.

2. Comment of Mr. Kazuhiro Tanikawa, a koto specialist in Setagaya-ku, Tokyo, June 30, 2011.

3. The *shacho* is Fujii Yoshiaki who began at age 20 making koto legs.

4. The poorly made Chinese kotos were known to break and injure students. Subsequently they were banned from all of Japan.

5. Ms. Masayo Ishigure of New York and all of AUN J's Classical Orchestra come from families of hogaku musicians.

6. Interview with Professor Masakazu Ando, July 2, 2011.

7. I am reminded of the Yurushi seido (Release System) mentioned in my Chapter 8 on the iemoto system. The system includes a promissory note to treasure the music or else "incur the wrath of the gods." Matsuri festivals are held so as not to ignore the kami.

8. The Monbusho provided videos of *Rokudan* and *Haru no Umi* for grade 6, *Godan Ginuta* and *Shiki no Nagame* for grade 7, *Ettenraku* and *Kanjincho* for grade 8, and *Shika no Tone* for grade 9.

9. The son of shakuhachi musician Yodo Kurahashi reported to him that the video course was boring.

10. Some hogaku artists prefer that the government keep out of hogaku affairs. One elderly recipient refused what she considered the meaningless Living National Treasure award but relented when she found out that a stipend came with it. But she was in need of students.

11. Countless times Japanese nationals have come up to me after a performance to exclaim that it was the first time they have seen a koto live! The latest incident was on November 13, 2017, at a lecture and recital I gave at the University of Mary Washington in Fredericksburg, Virginia.

12. *Okoto and Sasuke*, 1935 film directed by Yasujiro Shimazu starred Tanaka Kinuyo. The film featured the hogaku classics mentioned in the novel *Shunkin Monogatari* by Tanizaki Junichiro. The 1954 version of the same story, *Shukin Monogatari*, starred Kyo Machiko and was directed by Daisuki Ito. It featured Miyagi Michio's modern compositions which were incongruous with the period of the novel. *Life of*

Chikuzan, 1977, directed by Kaneto Shinto, featured the life of Takahashi Chikuzan (1910–1998) and his music.

13. *Kwaidan* (怪談, Kaidan, Ghost Stories), a 1964 film directed by Masaki Kobayashi with music by Toru Takemitsu (1930–1996), the first story "Earless Hoichi" was about a blind biwa player.

14. The *Makioka Sisters* (細雪, Sasameyuki, Snowflakes), a 1983 film directed by Kon Ichikawa based on a novel by Tanizaki Junichiro. The novel is about changing Japan through ji-uta music such as *Kurokami* and *Cha-ondo* that Tanizaki had studied. The movie instead changed the musical focus to a kimono shop. My friend is Tim Healy, director of the International Conservatory of Music, in Washington, D.C.

15. In questioning the director Masaaki Miyazawa why he did not use Japanese instruments to evoke the serene settings of the topic, he seemed puzzled—no doubt a product of the Japanese school music curriculum. His pre-debut showing of his film *Umi Yama Aida: In Between Mountains and Oceans* featured the Ise Jingu, held at the National Archives, Washington, D.C., April 11, 2014. Although the AUN J Classical Orchestra played during the introduction of the film, their contemporary style could have matched the hallowed scenery and theme.

16. NHK has featured many young hogaku players of koto on the *Nihon Dento Hour*.

17. Daniel J. Levitin, *This Is Your Brain on Music: The Science of a Human Obsession* (New York: Plume, Penguin), 2007.

18. Compared with Chinese paintings that followed strict rules, Japaneses paintings, according to Dr. Weigl, were more difficult to describe because of the emotion-laden aspect. With her gift with words, she nevertheless was always successful.

19. Yoshida Brewers is featured in Eric Shirai's *Birth of Sake*, a 2012 documentary.

20. Article by Kimiko de Freytas-Tamura, "Sake with Your Burger? Japan Is Looking West to Save a Tradition," *New York Times*, August 5, 2014, p. A4.

Bibliography

Addiss, Stephen. "Singing the Wakan Roei Shu." In J. Thomas Rimer and Jonathan Chaves, trans., *Japanese and Chinese Poems to Sing: The Wakan Roei Shu*, p. 255. New York: Columbia University Press, 1997.

Adriannsz, Willem. *The Kumiuta and Danmono Traditions of Japanese Koto Music*. Berkeley: University of California, 1973.

Benedict, Ruth. *Chrysanthemum and the Sword: Patterns of Japanese Culture*. New York: Houghton Mifflin Harcourt, 1946.

Blasdel, Christopher Y. *The Shakuhachi: A Manual for Learning*. Tokyo: Ongaku no Tomo sha, 1988.

Brooks, David. "The Structure of Gratitude" [op-ed]. *New York Times*, July 28, 2015.

Clarke, Arthur C. *The Nine Billion Names of God*. New York: Harcourt, 1967.

Cooper, Michael, ed. *They Came to Japan: An Anthology of European Reports on Japan, 1543–1640*. Berkeley: University of California Press, 1981.

Dalby, Liza. *Geisha*. Berkeley: University of California Press, 1998.

Dean, Britten. "'Howling' Music: Japanese Hogaku in Contrast to Western Art Music." *Monumenta Nipponica* 40, no. 2 (1985): 147–162.

De Ferranti, Hugh. *Japanese Musical Instruments*. Oxford: Oxford University Press, 2000.

Dissanayake, Ellen. *Art and Intimacy: How the Arts Began*. Seattle: University of Washington Press, 2000.

Freytas-Tamura, Kimiko de. "Sake with Your Burger? Japan Is Looking West to Save a Tradition." *New York Times*, August 5, 2014, A4.

Fujita, Shunichi. *Tomizaki Shunsho Geidan: Ji-uta Sokyoku, Sangen no Hanashi*. Tokyo: Nihon Ongaku-sha, 1968.

Hamaguchi, Esyun. *Nihon Rashisa no Saihakken* [Rediscovery of Japaneseness]. Tokyo: Nihon Keizai Shinbun sha, 1977.

Harich-Schneider, Eta. *A History of Japanese Music*. London: Oxford University Press, 1973.

Harich-Schneider, Eta. *The Music Anthology of the Orient*, Vol. 4: *Buddhist Music*. UNESCO Collection, August 7, 1957.

Harich-Schneider, Eta. *The Music of Japan: Record V, Shinto Music*. London: Oxford University Press, 1973.

Hayashi, Ryoichi. *The Silk Road and the Shoso-in*. New York: Weatherhill, 1975.

Hearn, Lafcadio. "Insect Musicians." *Exotics and Retrospectives*. Boston: Little, Brown, 1916.

Hearn, Lafcadio. "A Street Singer." *Kokoro: Hints and Echoes of Japanese Inner Life*. Rutland, Vermont: Charles E. Tuttle, 1980.

Hoshi, Akira. *Nippon Ongaku no Rekishi to Kansho*. Tokyo: Ongaku no Tomo-sha, 1971.

Humphrey, Doug. *Buddha in the Land of the Kami* [video]. Films on Demand, Digital Educational Video, April 1, 2009.

Inoura, Yoshinobu, and Toshio Kawatake. *The Traditional Theater of Japan*. New York: Weatherhill, 1981.

Johnson, Henry. *The Koto: A Traditional Instrument in Contemporary Japan*. Netherlands: Hotei, 2004.

Kageyama, Yuri. "From Imperial Court to Food Court: An Ancient Japanese Music Finds a Crossover Champion." *Washington Post*, April 24, 1999, C10.

Kawakami, Ai, Kiyoshi Furukawa, Kentaro Katahira, and Kazuo Okanoya. "Sad Music Induces Pleasant Emotion." *Frontiers in Psychology* 4 (2013): 311.

Keller, Helen. *The Story of My Life*. New York: Grosset and Dunlap, 1905.

Kikkawa, Eisi. *A History of Japanese Koto Music and Ziuta with Two CDs*. Trans. Leonard C. Holvik. Tokyo, Japan: Mita, 1997.

Kikkawa, Eishi. *Kono Hito Nari Miyagi Michiyo Den*. Tokyo: Shincho Shappan, 1962.

Kikkawa, Eishi. *Nihon Ongaku no Rekishi*. Osaka: Sogen-sha, 1965.

Kishibe, Shigeo. *The Traditional Music of Japan*. Tokyo: Ongaku no Tomo sha, 1984.

Kishibe, Shigeo, and Kenji Hirano. *Nihon Ongaku no Ayumi* [album notes]. VictorVP3005. Tokyo: Chikuma Shobo. Hogaku Taikei Furoku, 1970–1972.

Kitagawa, Hiroshi, and Bruce T. Tsuchida, trans. *Tale of the Heike*. Tokyo: University of Tokyo Press, 1975.

Kitagawa, Joseph M. "Preface." In Donald L. Philippi, *Norito: A Translation of the Ancient Japanese Ritual Prayers*. Princeton: Princeton University Press, 1990.

Kobayashi, Tatsuo. *Jomon Doki wo Yomu* [Reading the Jomon Pots]. Tokyo: Yokoyama, 2012.

Kobayashi, Tatsuo. *Jomon Reflections: Forager Life and Culture in the Prehistoric Japanese Archipelago*. Oxford: Oxbow, 2004.

Kodani, the Rev. Masao, ed. *Senshin Buddhist Temple*. Los Angeles: Senshin Buddhist Temple, 2001.

Koizumi, Fumio. *Nihon Dento Ongaku no Kenkyu I*. Tokyo: Ongaku no Tomo sha, 1979.

Koizumi, Fumio, Yoshihiko Tokumaru, and Osamu Yamaguchi, eds. "Kokyu." *Asian Musics in an Asian Perspective*. Tokyo: Heibonsha, 1977.

Kominz, Laurence R. *The Stars Who Created Kabuki: Their Lives, Loves and Legacy*. Tokyo: Kodansha, 1997.

Komiya, Toyotaka, ed. *Japanese Music and Drama in the Meiji Era*. Trans. Donald Keene and Edward G. Seidensticker. Tokyo: Obunsha, 1956.

Komodo, Haruko. "The Musical Narrative of the *Tale of the Heike*." Chap. 4: *The Ashgate Research Companion to Japanese Music*. Burlington, VT: Ashgate, 2008.

Komparu, Kunio. *The Noh Theater: Principles and Perspectives*. New York: Weatherhill/Tankosha, 1983.

Koyama, Hiroshi. *Nihon Koten Bungaku Taikei 43: Kyogen Shu*, vol. 2. Tokyo: Iwanami Shoten, 1983.

Kriesberg, Matthias. "Japan's New Generation of Composers." *New York Times*, February 6, 2000.

Kubota, Jun. *Iwanami Nihon Koten Bungaku Jite*. Tokyo: Iwanami Shoten, 2007.

Kubota, the Rev. Akira. *Houki Ini Kashu*. Private publication, 2001.

Kurahashi, Yodo. "Brilliance of Bamboo: The 40th Anniversary of Mujuan" [program notes]. October 25, 2014.

Leidy, Denise Patry. "Buddhist Art in a Secular Space: Case Studies from the Metropolitan Museum of Art." Lecture at American University, March 27, 2015.

Levitin, Daniel J. *This Is Your Brain on Music: The Science of a Human Obsession*. New York: Plume, 2007.

MacGregor, Neil. *A History of the Word in 100 Objects*. New York: Viking Penguin, 2008.

Machlis, Joseph, and Kristine Forney. *The Enjoyment of Music*, 8th ed. New York: W.W. Norton, 1999.

Magnier, Mark. "Hatsuko Kikuhara, 102; Master of Japanese Folk Music." *Los Angeles Times*, September 16, 2001.

Malm, William P. *Japanese Music and Musical Instruments*. Clarendon, Vermont: Tuttle, 1959; rev. ed. Tokyo: Kodansha, 2001.

Manyoshu [(Ten Thousand Leaves); poetry collection, 347–759]. Eighth century.

Matsue, Jennifer Milioto. *Focus: Music in Contemporary Japan*. Abingdon, United Kingdom: Routledge/Taylor, 2016.

Mexia, S. J. Lourenco. "Their Music." In Michael Cooper, ed., *They Came to Japan: An Anthology of European Reports on Japan, 1543–1640*, 256–257. Berkeley: University of California Press, 1981.

Mishima, Yukio. *Kinkakuji* (The Temple of the Golden Pavilion). Trans. Ivan Morris. New York: Alfred A. Knopf, 1959, 1971.

Mitsuoka, Tadanari. *Ceramic Art of Japan*. Tokyo: Japan Travel Bureau, 1956.

Mizumura, Minae. *The Fall of Language in the Age of English*. New York: Columbia University Press, 2008.

Morse, Edward S. *Japan Day by Day, 1877, 1878–79, 1882–83*, vol. 2. Boston: Houghton Mifflin, 1917.

Nelson, John K. *A Year in the Life of a Shinto Shrine*. Seattle: University of Washington Press, 1996.

Nihongi: Chronicles of Japan from Earliest Times to AD 697. Trans. W. G. Aston. Rutland, Vermont: Tuttle, 1972.

Nishiyama, Matsunosuke. *Edo Culture: Daily Life and Diversion in Urban Japan, 1600–1868*. Honolulu: University of Hawaii Press, 1977.

Nishiyama, Matsunosuke, Esyun Hamaguchi, and Noboru Haga. "Iemoto Seido to Nihon no Shakai [Iemoto World and Japanese Society]." *Rekishi Koro* [History Journal] 4, no. 4 (1978): 12.

Nomura, Hideki. *Koto no Shoshiki to Gakuri no Ohanashi*. Nagoya: Shogenshu Hanbu, 1973.

Nuwer, Rachel. "Playing Mozart's Piano Pieces as Mozart Did." *New York Times*, Science section, July 20, 2015.

Ono, Masafumi, and Tsutsumu Takashi, eds. *Jomon Bijitsukan Shashin* [Jomon Museum Photos]. Tokyo: Heibon sha, 2013.

Ortolani, Benito. *Japanese Theater: From Shamanistic Ritual to Contemporary Pluralism*. Princeton: Princeton University Press, 1990.

Philippi, Donald L. *Norito: A Translation of the Ancient Japanese Ritual Prayers*. Princeton: Princeton University Press, 1990.

Philippi, Donald L., trans. *Kojiki*. Tokyo: Tokyo University Press, 1968.

Plutschow, Herbert. *Japan's Name Culture: The Significance of Names in a Religious, Political and Social Context*. Kent: Japan Library, 1995.

Popper, Karl. *Objective Knowledge: An Evolutionary Approach*. Oxford, United Kingdom: Oxford Press, 1972.

Rimer, J. Thomas, and Yamazaki Masakazu, trans. *On the Art of the No Drama: The Major Treatises of Zeami*. Princeton: Princeton University Press, 1984.

Ryotaro, Shiba Ryotaro. *Kukai: The Universal Scenes from His Life*. Trans. Akiko Takemoto. New York: ICG Muse, 2003.

Sansom, G. B. *Japan: A Short Cultural History*. Stanford: Stanford University Press, 1987.

Satow, Sir Ernest M. "Ancient Japanese Ritual." Cited in Joseph M. Kitagawa's "Preface," in Donald L. Philippi, *Norito: A Translation of the Ancient Japanese Ritual Prayers*. Princeton: Princeton University Press, 1990.

Satow, Sir Ernest M. "The Shintau-Temples of Ise." *Transactions of the Asiatic Society of Japan*, III. Yokohama: 1874.

Seikin, Tomiyama, and Imai Kinzaburo, eds. *Seikin Ji-uta Shugyo*. Tokyo: Geino Hakkojyo. 1966.

Shikibu, Murasaki, and Royall Tyler, trans. *Tale of Genji*. New York: Viking/Penguin, 2001.

Shirai, Akehiro, and Kazuhiro Aruga. *Nihon no Nanajuni Ko wo Tanoshimu* [Enjoying the 72 Seasons of Japan]. Tokyo: Toho, 2013.

Shonagon, Sei. *Pillow Book*. Trans. Ivan Morris. New York: Columbia University Press, 1967.

Stein, Jess M. ed. *Random House College Dictionary,* rev. ed. New York: Random House, 1980.
Sugiura, So. "Basic Knowledge about Pure Hogaku, Traditional Japanese Music." Japan Foundation, Performing Arts Network Japan, January 19, 2005.
Takemitsu, Makoto. *Nippon Tanjo* [Japan's Birth]. Tokyo: Bungei Shunju, 1991.
Tamba, Akira. *The Musical Structure of No.* Trans. Patricia Matore. Tokyo: Tokai University Press, 1981.
Tanabe, Hisao. *Japanese Music.* Tokyo: Kokusai Bunka Shinkokai, 1959.
Tanaka, Giichi. *Gendai Sankyoku Tenbo,* vol. 3. Osaka: Shakuhachi Nihon-sha, 1973.
Tetsuji, Teranaka, and Hirose Ryohei. "The Oldest Japanese Flute?" *The East* 12, no. 2 (1976).
Tierney, John. "A Generation's Vanity, Heard Through Lyrics." *New York Times,* April 26, 2011.
Tokita, Alison McQueen. *Kiyomoto-bushi: Narrative Music of the Kabuki Theatre.* Kassel, Germany: Bärenreiter, 1999.
Tokito, Alison, and David W. Hughes, eds. *The Ashgate Companion to Japanese Music.* Farnham, United Kingdom: Ashgate, 2008.
Traditions of Jodoshinshu Hongwanji-ha. Los Angeles: Senshin Buddhist Temple, 1982.
Umehara, Takeshi. "Forest Culture and Japan." Lecture at the International Research Center for Japan Studies, June 27, 1991.
Umehara, Takeshi. *Nihonjin no Syukyo* [lecture]. Shinscho Cassette Kouen, December 1987.
Vitello, Paul. "Peter Marler, Graphic Decoder of Birdsong, Dies at 86." *New York Times,* July 28, 2014.
Wade, Bonnie. *Music in Japan: Experiencing Music, Expressing Culture.* Oxford: Oxford University Press, 2004.
Wade, Bonnie. *Tegotomono: Music for the Japanese Koto.* Westport, Connecticut: Greenwood, 1976.
Welford, John Noble. "Flute Music Wafted in Caves 35,000 Years Ago." *New York Times,* International section, June 25, 2009, A12.
Westphal, David, and Peter Grilli. *Shinto: Nature, Gods and Man in Japan* [video]. New York: Japan Society with Togg Films.
Wulf, Andrea. *The Invention of Nature: Alexander Von Humboldt's New World.* New York: Vintage, 2016.
Yoshikami, Mieko. *Sarasoju* by Minojo. Private publication, 1998.

Index

Note: Translation from Japanese to English comes with spelling, name order, and cultural challenges. Alternative spellings are in parentheses after the entry and names are cross-referenced if deemed helpful. Illustrations and tables are noted by ***bold italics***.

Addiss, Stephen 87, 89, 215*n*20, 215*n*21, 215*n*23
aesthetics 2, 7, 8, 11–22, 29, 30, 32, 40, 42, 43, 47, 49, 67, 68, 96, 101, 159, 176, 179, 187, 189, 208*n*2, 208*n*17, 209*n*35
Agatsuma, Hiromitsu 180, 185, 214*n*6, 224*n*53
age-uta 71, 91, 94
ai-no-te ***15***, 124, 128, 129, 142, ***142***, 157
aidagara 170
Ainu 28, 46, 210*n*31, 214*n*5
Aioi no Kyoku 158, 223*n*25
Akashi Kakuichi ***53***, 91, 165, 221*n*20
Akatsuki no Uta 181, 223*n*29
Aki Kaze no Kyoku 77, 116, ***118***, 158, 209*n*31, 218*n*36
akino choshi 79
ama-no-iwafue 28, 46, 212*n*4
amadera 91
Amaterasu 24, 25, 32, 36, 40, 55, 159, 212*n*22, 220*n*9
American West 5
Ananiyashi 83
Ando, Masakazu 188, 224*n*6
anime 107, 176, 186, 208*n*15, 224*n*58
anoyo 25, 28, 46, 210*n*26
Aomori 44, 184, 209*n*15
applause 13, 92, 96, 208*n*7
aragoto 132
Ariwara no Narihira 18
Asakura 33, 36, 37, ***38***, 39, 68, 83, 111–112, 146, 211*n*69

Ascending-IN (A-IN mode) 69, 77, ***78***, 79, 81, 217*n*10
Ashikaga Yoshimitsu 94
ashirai 148
asobi 5, 6, 7, 111
asobi-o 6
Asuka Era 29
ato osae 154
ato-uta 128, 129, 140
AUN J 62, 180, 184, 225*n*15
Awaji-shima ***102***, 102, ***103***, 209*n*29
awase 158
awasezume 106, ***153***
Azuma asobi (Azuma-asobi) 6, 37, 39, 53, 112

bachi 55, 58, 59, 61, 150, 163, 183
banshiki *see* scale/mode, ritsu
Banshiki-gaku 148
Basho 183, 224*n*46
be 119, 161, 220*n*6
Benten *see* Benzaiten
Benzaiten 55, 157, 167, 209*n*33
Betto 165, ***166–167***, 221*n*20; *see also* Tōdō Shoku Yashiki
bi-musical 1
biwa 2, 5, 7, 8, 12, 51, 52, ***53***, 54, 55, 57, 58, 59, ***60***, 63, 67, 72, ***73***, 74, ***74***, 83, 86, 90, 91, ***92***, ***93***, 94, 96, 98, 105, 108, 110, 111, 113, 119, ***120***, 122, 126, 132, 146, 149, 150, 152, 158, 168, 169, 178, 183, 186, 189, 212*n*25, 213*n*34, 214*n*54, 219*n*6, 221*n*19, 225*n*13; Chikuzen biwa 54, 71, 72, 94; construction of 54;

gagaku 51, 71, 91; -hoshi 53, 54, 57, 63, 90, 119, *120*; Heike 94, 119, 132; moso 71, 90, 215n26; Satsuma 54, 55, 72, 91, *93*, 94, 119
blind musicians 13, 53–54, 58, 59, 89, 91, 94, 101, 118, 124, 127, 129, 131-133, 141, 159–175, 177, 180, 215n29, 218n31, 221n20
Buddhism 11, 21, 29, 46, 47, 48, 53, *53*, 54, 64, *84*, 84, 90, 113, 160, 179, 207n4, 208n2, 209n35, 212n14, 222n12; chants 8, 47, 57, 68–110, 119, 185, 186, 211n55, 214n7, 215n6, 215n9; Sunday school 1, *114*
bugaku 50, 113, 212n24
bunraku 7, 8, 36, *60*, 85, 94, 96, 99–100, 120, 122, 131, 132, *133*, 133, 137, 138, 163, 165, 171, 176, 188, 212n6, 216n43, 216n49, 218n19, 222n2
bushido 6
Butokuraku 113
Butsudan 28
buyo 7, 25, 36, *60*, 134, *135*, 135, 137, 149, 150, 172

ceramics 7, 28, 141, 208n4, 210n36, 211n50
chado *see* Four Principles of the Way of Tea
chidori 20, 104, 176
Chidori no Kyoku 15, 63, 77, 102, *103*, 106, *107*, 176, 186, 208n17, 209n29, 213n47, 214n14, 214n17, 216n51, 217n11, 218n36, 219n12, 221n17
Chigo Zakura 19, 157
Chijo Tachibana 94
Chikamatsu Harima 127
Chikamatsu Monzaemon 100, 132
ch'in 89, 215n24
China 1, 2, 6, 8, 17, *18*, 26, 28, 29, 33, 40, 46–51, 53, 54, 55, 57, 64, 66, 68, *70*, 75, 79, 84–86, *88*, 112–113, 114, *117*, 118, 122, 148, 163, 177, 183, 188, 208n3, 208n23, 209n1, 209n31, 209n33, 211n74, 213n53, 214ch4n2, 214ch5n2, 214n3, 214n7, 215n16, 217n10, 219n22, 220n2, 220n25, 222n2, 222n5, 224n4, 225n18
chinkon-sai 36
chirashi 129
chirizume 153
chu-kin 47
Chudai, Emperor 29
chukyoku 113
classical music (Western) 5, 7, 126; *see also* Western music; yogaku
Classical Performing Arts Friendship Mission of Japan (University of California, Los Angeles) 1, 214n12
coda *117*, 119, *120*, 129, 136, 149
Collection of Ten Thousand Pages see Manyoshu
Confucianism 11, 21, 29, 160
cowboy music 5

Daigo, Emperor 86
daikin (dai-kin) 47, 48
daimyos 169
dan-awase 129
dan-giri 136, 149
dan-mono 82, 116, 118, *118*, 154, 172, 220n24, 220n25
dengaku 94, 211n55, 213n31
Dengyo Daishi *see* Saicho
Department of the Affairs of the Kami 32
Dissanayake, Ellen 83, 214n5
dora 48
Dowager Empress 179

Early Nara Era 29
Ebisu (god) 20, 209n33
Echigojishi 107, 130, 138, *139–140*, 149, 167
Edo Era 5, 7, 12, 14, 28, 58, *60*, 79, *95*, 101, *105*, 111, 122, 126, 128, 131, 134–135, 137, 159, 161, *162*, 165, 169, 173, 176, 214n2, 218n23, 218n25, 218n30, 218n44, 221n24, 222n41, 223n23, 224n46
eisho 119
emperor *see* Chudai; Daigo; Go-Shirakawa; Ingyo; Kimmei; Komyo; Nimmyo; Saga; Shomu; Suzaku
empress *see* Dowager; Jingu; Suiko
enka 138, 216n56
Enoshima no Kyoku 157
Enryakuji 54
era *see* Asuka; Early Nara; Edo; Genroku; Heian; Jomon; Kofun; Meiji; Nara; Tumulus; Yamato; Yayoi
Eto Kimio 1, *71*, 143
Etten-utai-mono 89
Ettenraku 75, 79, 89, *90*, 113, *114*, 114, *115*, *117*, 146, 214n14, 215n25, 224n8
Ettenraku-imayo 89

Fenollosa, Earnest 179
Four Principles of the Way of Tea 7, 11–14, *12*, 21, 169
fu 86
Fujieda, Mamoru 183, 223n45
Fujii Kunie 127
Fujiue Kengyo 62
Fujiwara *see* Urabe
Fujiwara no Kinto *see Wakan Roei-shu*
Fujiwara no Mototoshi *see Shinsen-Roei-shu*
Fujiwara Sadotoshi 54
Fuke sect 63–64
Fuki 89, *90*, 116, *116*, *117*, 207n8, 215n25, 217n7, 217n8
fukiawase 64
fushi 91
fushi mono 94
fushimawashi (fushi-mawashi) *73*, 85, 87, 96, 104, 108–109; *see also* mawashi
Futari Daimyo 98
Futotama (god) 25, 36

gagaku 1, 2, 3, 6, 29, 47, 48, **49**, 49, 50, **50**, 51, 52, 53, 57, 63, 67, 69, 71, **73**, 75, **76**, 77, 86, 89, **90**, 110, 113, **114, 115**, 128, 146, 158, 161, 168, 177, 178–179, 183, 184, 188, 207n4, 212n13, 212n19, 212n21, 212n23, 212n25, 212n26, 214n16, 215n16, 215n22, 217n4, 217n5, 222n5, 223n24
gagaku-ryo 48
gaikyoku (gai-kyoku) 62, 63, 64, 131, 156, 157, 219n52
gaku choshi 79
gaku-no-te 157
gakubiwa *see* biwa
gakusoh (gaku-so, gaku-soh) 51, 75, **152**, 152
Ge datsu no kourin 70, **72**, 85, 122
geido 5, 6, 7
geisha 62, 108, 127, **128**, 180, 218n30, 219n17
Geki-bushi 132
Gempei War 6, 90, 119
Genji Monogatari see *Tale of Genji*
genkan 179
Genroku Era 126, 136
Genso Kotei **118**, 209n31, 217n10
geza 150, 177
gidayu 62, 96, 99–100, 104, 133, 134, 137, 163, 165, 216n43, 216n44, 216n45, 216n49, 218n38, 218n41
gigaku 47, 186, 207n4, 212n13, 224n57
gin no shirabe 128
Ginsekai 20, 77, 209n32
ginsho 119
Go-Shirakawa, Emperor 89
Godan Ginuta 17, 19, 218n36, 224n8
goze 62, 138, 167–168, 215n30
Grant, Ulysses S 179
Great Eye Opening Ceremony 54

ha-uta 123, 124, 125, **125**, 126, **126**, 127, 128, **129**, 169, 220n25
Hachi dan 118
hade-gumi 123
Hagoromo 6, 70, 71, **73**, 96, **97**, 207n3, 221n37
haisho 179
hajiki 150, 151
hakase 94
han-kake 157
han-kumoi 77
Hana no Sode 70, **72**, 85, 122
Hanago 98, **99**
Hanazono 142, 144
Handa Hiromu 143
Handayu-bushi 133
haraita 150
Harich-Schneider, Eta 32, 37, 111, 210n42, 211n64, 211n69, 211n72, 211n73, 212n10, 215n18, 215n26, 217n2, 222n4, 222n5
harmony cultural 11, 12, 14, 21, 26, 111, 208n3; musical 8, **81**, 101, 142, 143, 158, 185, 215n19, 220n36, 222n41

Haru no Enoshima 157, 176, 180, 223n28
Haru no Umi 82, 142, 143, **143**, 181, 189, 223n31, 224n8
Haru no Yo 90, 157
Hase Kengyo 59
Hatano school 94
Hatsune no Kyoku 116
Hauk, Camilia Mignon (Minnie) 179
hayari-uta 126
hayashi 96, 120, 121, **136**, 149, 151, 217n14, 219n9, 219n18, 224n56
Hearn, Lafcadio 14, 108, 208n13, 217n70, 219n2
Heian Era 46, 53, 54, 63, 66, 68, 114, 126, 146, 161, 169, 214n5, 221n16, 223n24; court 89
Heike Monogatari see *Tale of the Heike*
hi-gumi 123
hichiriki 36, 39, 40, **49**, 49, 51, **52**, 63, 75, 86, 113, 146, 178, 212n23, 214n14, 223n12
hiji 94
hiki 71, 154
Hikita Awajinojo 132
hirajyoshi 75, **77**, 77, **78**, **81**, 214n4
Hirano Shrine (Kyoto) 40; Hirano Matsuri (festival) 34, 211n57
Hisamoto Genshi 143, 181
Hitoyasu Shinno, Prince 54, 221n20
Hizen-bushi 133
Hokkaido 28, 44, 182
hokyo 179
hon joshi (hon-joshi) 74
hon-sarugaku 97, **122**
honkyoku (hon-kyoku) 63, 64, 131, 156–157, 181, 185
honte 62, 67
honte-gumi 123
hoshi 53–54, 57, 63, 90, 119, 213n31
Hoshi, Akira 86, 134, 215n12, 215n14, 215n16, 215n17, 218n24, 218n43, 218n44
Hoshi to Hana to 79, 158, 223n26
Hotaru no Hikari 178, 222n7
Hototogisu no Kyoku 79, 103, 158, 223n26
Hundred Waka Poems by a Hundred Poets see karuta
Hyakunin Isshu see karuta
hyo 86
hyoshi-ai 148

Ichiura Kengyo 157, 177
iemoto 95, **95**, **102**, 135, 159, 160, 161, 162, 163, 169, 218n40, 221n23
iemoto system (iemoto seido) 3, 7, 9, 25, 33, 54, 159–175, 176, 188, 207n6, 215n30, 216n56, 221n38, 221n39, 222n40, 224n7; dendritic 161, 169, 172, 175; direct lineal 160, 161, 163, 175; quasi-lineal 163, 175; umbrella **160**, 161, 165, 169, 175
Ihara Saisaku 127
iki 7, 12

Ikuta Kengyo 124, 137, *138*, *142*, 152, 157, 158, 174, 218n26, 218n27
Ikuta-ryu 124, 137, 138, *142*, 152, 157–158
imayo 75, 83, 89, 114, 126
IN mode *see* scale/mode
Inari (god) 20, 219n18
ingaku 7
Ingyo, Emperor 47
inkin 48
Inoue Harimanojo 132
Irare no Kure Koto Hiki 47
Ise Shrine 159, 161, 173, 189
ishibue *see* ama-no-iwafue
Ishikawa Kōtō 129, 217n11
Ishimura Kengyo (Naka Koji) 58, 123, 131, 213n40, 218n22
Itchu-bushi 133, *134*, 134, *135*, 137
Itchu Miyakodayu 134
Iwaki, Hiroyuki 1, 207n1
Izanagi (god) 24, 83
Izanami (god) 24, 83
Izawa, Shuji 178
Izumo Shrine 23, 40, 112, 212n82

ji *38*, 39, 91, 152, 157, 211n70, 220n31
ji-goe 96
ji-uta 8, 58, 59, *61*, 61, 96, 100, 101, 104, 107, 112, 124, 128, *129*, 131, 138, *139–140*, *151*, 157, 167, 171, 172, 180, 188, 207n6, 211n60, 212n1, 216n45, 216n46, 216n50, 218n19, 219n13, 219n14, 225n14; bachi 59; sangen 101, 157; shamisen 8, *61*, 96, 101, 104, 180
jiki-deshi 169–170, *170*, 172, *172*
Jimmu-tenno 25, 32, 36
Jingu, Empress 29, 211n70, 212n23, 225n15
Jisei 68, 87, 113, 176, 214n5, 215n22
Jishin-kyo 90; *see also* biwa, moso
jo-ha-kyu 12, 39, 42, 110–144, 218n18
Jodo Shinshu sect 70, 84, *85*, *151*, 210n20, 212n15, 215n8, 215n10, 215n11
Jomon Era 2, 5, 14, 20, 23, 28, *30*, 32, 46, 111, 112, *162*, 210n36; people 7, 8, 11, 17, *18*, 21, 23–28, *27*, 33, 44, 46, 55, 145, 175, 187, 209n3, 209n14, 209n17, 209n18, 210n23, 210n24, 210n25, 210n32, 212n3; pottery 7, 8, 17, 26, 29, 31–32, 42, 145, 210n33, 210n34, 210n36, 211n50, 211n67, 219n1
joruri (music type) 99–100, 132
Joruri, Princess (*Joruri Hime Monogatari*) 94, 216n42
Joun Satsuma 132, *133*
J.S. Bach Is Alive and Well and Doing His Thing on the Koto 181; *see also* Sawai Kazue

kabuki 8, 25, 36, *60*, 62, 63, 96, 100, 120, 122, 124, 131, 132, *133*, *134*, 134–138, *135*, *139–140*, 149, 150, 163, 171, 176, 180, 188, 207n7, 208n9, 212n6, 218n19, 218n44, 218n46; nagauta 20, 213n32

kaede 107, 129, 130, 140, 157, 177, 220n30
Kagawa Seishi 1, 172
Kagoyahime, the Bamboo Princess 20
kagura 5, 6, 36, 40, 52, 53, 63, 110, 111, 112, 120, 211n75, 215n12
kagura-bue 36, 212n24
Kaji Makura 127, 218n32, 219n18
kakegoe 57, 146, 148, *148*, 151
kakezume 116, *116*, *117*, 153, *153*, 207n8, 217n8
kakko 50, 113, 146
kaku 68, 75, *77*, 77, 152
kami koma 59
Kanami Kiyotsugu 94, 213n31, 220n14
kando 118, 154
kangen 50, 113, 146
karuta 102, 186
kasaiki 157
Kasuga Shrine 23, 40, 214n6
katari mono (katari-mono) 8, 131
Katoh-bushi 133, *134*, 134, 137
Katsusaka 31, *31*
Keller, Helen 22, 209n36
Kengyo *53*, 132, 165, *166–167*, 216n49, 221n20; *see also* Fujiue; Hase; Ichiura; Ikuta; Ishimura; Kikuhara; Kikuzuka; Mitsuzaki; Sawazumi; Sayama; Tateyama; Tōdō Shoku Yashiki; Torazawa; Tsuguyama; Tsuyama; Yaezaki; Yamada; Yanagawa; Yatsuhashi; Yoshizawa II
Kenjun of Kyushu (priest) 89
keshi zume 154
Kikkawa, Eishi 33, 82, 214ch5n3, 214ch5n4, 223n32
Kikkawa, Kazuo 183
Kikuhara Kengyo 77, 180, 209n32, 223n27
Kikuzuka Kengyo 79, 172, 180, 223n25
Kimmei, Emperor 47
Kimpira-bushi 132
Kinko-ryu 64
Kitagawa, Joseph 32, 210n38, 210n39, 210n43, 210n45, 211n58, 211n59
Kiyari no Dan 100, *100*, 133
Kiyomoto 134, *135*, 135, *136*, 137, 172, 218n46
Kiyotsune (warrior) 146, *147*
ko-tsuzumi 1, 55, 56–57, 67, 95, 140, 146, *148*, 149, 167, 213n36
Kobayashi, Tatsuo 26, 27, 28, 209n3, 209n9, 209n10, 209n11, 209n12, 209n14, 209n17, 210n22, 210n24, 212n3, 219n1
Kobo Daishi *see* Kukai
Kodani, Masao 83, 215n7
Kofun Era 29
Koizumi, Fumio 104, 213n45, 216n59
Kojiki 13, 24, 29, 82, 209n1, 210n29, 211n79, 212n8
kojin-kyo *see* biwa, moso
Kokaji 20, 153, 219n18
Kokinshu 142

kokyu 58, 62–63, 156, 213*n*45, 213*n*47
koma 58, 59, **60**
Koma clan 179
Komagaku 50
Komparu, Kunio 96, 121, 148, 212*n*2, 213*n*33, 216*n*37, 217*n*13, 217*n*15, 218*n*18, 219*n*8; school 95
Komyo, Emperor 48, 66
konoyo 25, 27, 28, 46, 175, 210*n*26
Korea 29, 33, 39, 46, 47, 50, **50**, 53, 113, 177, 181, 211*n*74, 212*n*12; komabue (koma-bue) 39, 212*n*24
koto 1, 2, 5, 6, 8, 13, **19**, 20, 29, 36, 40, 44–158, 165, 168, 169, 171, 173, 174, 176, 180–181, 183, 184, 186, 188, 189, 207*n*6, 212*n*7, 212*n*19, 212*n*26, 213*n*34, 213*n*36, 214*n*14, 214*n*54, 214*n*55, 214*n*56, 215*n*15, 215*n*24, 216*n*58, 217*n*6, 218*n*27, 218*n*34, 218*n*35, 218*n*37, 219*n*4, 219*n*6, 219*n*15, 219*n*21, 220*n*24, 220*n*27, 220*n*28, 220*n*37, 221*n*18, 221*n*32, 221*n*39, 222*n*8, 223*n*33, 223*n*34, 223*n*35, 224*n*1, 224*n*2, 224*n*3, 224*n*11, 224*n*52, 225*n*16; gagaku 75, **76**, 77, 79, 89, **90**, 151, **152**, 153, 157, 212*n*26; Tsukushi 13, 57, 75, 79, 89, 114
Kōtō **15**, **53**, 132, 165, **166–167**, 216*n*49, 221*n*20; *see also* Ishikawa; Minezaki; Mitsuzaki; Tōdō Shoku Yashiki; Yamazumi
kotoba 25, 96
Kubi Nobu 127, **128**
kuchi-jamisen 151, 155, 158, 219*n*21
Kudan 118
Kukai 48, **84**, 168, 212*n*16
kume-mai 53
kume-uta 32
kumi-uta 89, 102, 114, 116, **116**, 118, **118**, 122, 123, **123**, 124, **124**, 126, 128, **129**, **152**, 172, 217*n*33, 218*n*25, 220*n*18
kumoi jyoshi 75, **77**, **78**
Kurahashi, Yodo 63, 185, 213*n*49, 213*n*50, 213*n*52, 218*n*24, 222*n*1, 222*n*9, 224*n*9
Kure-mai 112
Kuribayashi, Hideaki 184
Kuroda-bushi 107, 113, **114**, 212*n*7
Kurokami 20, 124, 126, 150, **151**, 216*n*31, 219*n*15, 225*n*14
Kurokawa noh 40, 211*n*55, 214*n*6
Kurosawa Kinko 64
Kusunoto 218*n*31
Kwaidan (film) 189, 216*n*31, 225*n*13
Kyo Sukeroku 134
kyogen 1, 7, 25, 40, 70, **72**, 94, 95–96, **95**, **98**, 98, **99**, 108, 121, 122, **122**, **162**, 214*n*12, 216*n*34, 217*n*12, 221*n*37, 224*n*56
Kyojijyo 89
kyoku setsu 94
kyotaiko 48
Kyui (Kyu-I) see *Nine Steps*
Kyushu 24, 25, 54, 59, 89, 94, **173**, 174, 177, 215*n*26, 215*n*29, 220*n*24

Leidy, Denise Patry 2, 207*n*2
Life of Chikuzan 189
Love Suicides of Amijima 133
Love Suicides of Sonezaki 133

MacGregor, Neil 32, 210*n*35
mae-uta 128, 129, 140, 142, 157
Maeda school 94
maki 168, 169
Makioka Sisters 189, 225*n*14
makura 129
Makura no Soshi see *Pillow Book*
Mama no Kawa 126–127, **127**, 216*n*51, 218*n*32
manga 176
Man'ichi (priest) 54
Mansei-in (priest) 54
Manyoshu [Collection of Ten Thousand Pages (Leaves)] 49, 85, 212*n*18
Manzai Raku 180, 223*n*28
Mason, Luther Whiting 178
Matsu no kokage ni 82, **83**, 216*n*59
Matsu no Uchi 134
Matsumura, Teizo 184, 223*n*36, 224*n*51
mawashi 71, **73**; *see also* fushimawashi
Mayuzumi, Toshiro see *Nirvana Symphony*
meigen 46
Meiji Era 5, 20, 64, 69, 86, 94, 111, 141, 158, 173, 177, 178, 180, 190, 208*n*20, 215*n*19, 218*n*29, 218*n*37, 220*n*36, 222*n*10, 222*n*41, 223*n*16, 223*n*18
Meiji Shochikubai 79, **81**, 223*n*25
Metropolitan Museum of Art's Department of Asian Art 2, 207*n*2
michiyuki 136
Midare 118, 221*n*37
Miko dance music 8, **41**, 112, 146; *Miko Dance Music* 40, 112
Minamoto Hiramasa 63
Minekiya Chizaburo 132
Minezaki Kōtō 131, 218*n*31, 218*n*36
minyo 7, 69
Mitsu Seichi 59
mitsuji 148, **148**
Mitsuzaki Kengyo 220*n*34, 221*n*17
Mitsuzaki Kōtō 116, 209*n*31
Miura, Naoyuki 182, 223*n*36
Miyagi Michio 1, 64, 82, 104, 142, **142**, **143**, 157, 181, 189, 212*n*19, 213*n*46, 221*n*31, 224*n*12
Miyako Wasure 15, **15**, 82, **83**, 104, **142**, 181, 216*n*59, 217*n*11, 223*n*29
Miyakoji Bungonojo 134, **135**, 135, **136**
Miyakoji Mojitayu 62, 134, 135, **135**, 135, **136**, 137, 172
Mizu Jyoshi 134
Mizu no Hentai 77, 142, **142**, 181
mode *see* scale/mode
Monbusho 188, 189, 224*n*8

Morse, Edward S. 13, 108, 179, 208n11, 208n12, 210n37, 217n68, 223n19
Mount Hiei 54
Mumonsai/Miyako-Itchu XII 62
Murasaki Shikibu 49, 208n18; see also Tale of Genji
My Horse see Waga Koma
Myotoku-in (musician) 54

Na no Hana 126
nagauta (naga-uta) 20, *21*, 123, 124, *125*, 126, *126*, 127, 128, *129*, 134, 135–136, *136*, 137, 138, *139–140*, 140, 149, *151*, 157, 169, 213n32, 218n25, 219n17, 220n25
Nagoya Obi 15
Nagoya Shinju 134
Naka Koji see Ishimura Kengyo
Nakano-takane 148
Nakashima, Chihoko 1, 219n15
Nakashima, Utahiko 143, 181
Nakatomi see Urabe
nakazora tuning 77
namu amida butsu 119
Nara Era 29, 66
Nasu no Yoichi 91, *92*, 93, *93*, 119, 219n11
natori 170, *170*, 171, 172, *172*, 221n23
natsuyama tuning 79, 223n26
nature 11, 21, 28, 30, 42, 46, 101, 110, 112, 145, 182, 183, 189, 212n7, 212n82
nayashi 157
Nelson, John 33, 211n53, 211n54
neo 58, 59, *60*
ni-agari 74
Nihon no Geino 184
Nihon Shoki 24, 47, 82, 209n1, 212n11, 220n9
Niimi, Tokuhide 182–184, 223n36, 223n38, 223n39
Nimmyo, Emperor 54
Nine Steps 94, 164, *164*, 208n10
Ninigi-no Mikoto 25
Nippon Hoso Kyokai (NHK) orchestra 1
Nirvana Symphony 215n9
Nishimura, Akira 182, 183, 223n36, 223n38, 224n49
nogi tuning 79
noh 1, 2, 6, 7, 8, 17, 19, 25, 30, 36, 40, 55, 57, 70, 71, *73*, 83, 85, 89, 90, 94–96, *95*, 99, 108, 109, 110, 111, 119–121, *121*, *122*, 126, 128, 130, 132, 136, 137, 138, 141, *141*, 146, *147*, 148, 158, 161, *162*, 164, 168, 171, 174, 176, 179, 186, 188, 208n7, 208n24, 211n55, 211n71, 212n2, 213n28, 213n31, 213n33, 213n34, 214n6, 216n31, 216n34, 216n36, 216n37, 216n39, 217n13, 217n17, 218n18, 219n8, 220n11, 223n20, 223n21
noh bayashi (noh-bayashi) *56*, 137, 149, 213n32
noh-utai 169
nohgaku 94, *95*, 122, *147*, 216n34

nohkan (flute) 46, 55, 57, 95, 148, *149*, 212n6, 217n14, 219n6
Nori no Miyama 113, *114*
norito 2, 5, 7, 8, 32, 33–34, *34*, *35*, 36, 39, 40, 83, 84, 110, 111, 186, 211n55, 211n57, 211n62
November Steps 150, 219n12

o-hichiriki 179
Ogi no Mato 91, *93*, 119, 219n11
Ogura Hyakunin Isshu see karuta
Okamoto, Taro 32, 210n36
okawa see o-tsuzumi
oki 136
Okina 132
Okinawan tuning 79
Okoto to Sasuke 189
Okuninushi (god) 17
Okyagari Kobooshi 98, *98*, 122
Omoide no Uta goe 79, *81*, 214n56
Onagahimi, Princess 29
Onoe Kikuyuki 172
Onono Yoshiki 68
ori 39
oru 157
Osaka 40, 47, 57, 61, 62, 124, 131, 132, *132*, 172, 180, 207n6, 213n28, 213n30, 214n3, 214n4, 214n6, 218n23, 219n47, 221n21
oshiki see scale/mode, ritsu
Otomo no Yakamochi see Manyoshu
otsuzumi (o-tsuzumi) 55–56, 57, *95*, 95, 146, 148, *148*, 149, 217n14
Ozatsuma 136, 218n40
Ozatsuma-bushi 132

Paulownia 19, 37, 44, 55, 64, 66
Philippi, Donald 33, 210n29, 210n38, 210n39, 210n43, 211n56, 211n57, 211n58, 211n59, 211n79, 212n8
Pillow Book (*Makura no Soshi* by Sei Shonagon) 49, *117*, 209n26
Pleasure Quarters *15*, *105*, 127–128, 142, 180, 213n39, 223n22
plectrum 51, 55, *60*, 62, 91, 150, 152, 153, 165, 213n46
Poeme 184

raindrop beat (rhythm) 70, 91
Reigaku 179, 183, 224n48
Renjishi 137, 149
Renshobu (teacher) 54
ritsu see scale/mode
Robertson, Marta 142
roei 50, 86–87, 112
Roei Kyujishusho 86
Rokudan 116, 118, 154, *156*, 158, 173–174, *173*, 184, 185, 214n4, 217n6, 219n12, 220n26, 220n28, 223n25, 224n8
rosho 119
ryo see scale/mode

Ryukyu gumi (*Ryukyu-gumi*) 123, *124*
Ryusen 54
ryuteki 51, 57, 75, 86, *113*, 146, 178, 212n24, 214n14

Sabi 11, 101, 133
Saga, Emperor 49, 67, 210n28
saho 50, 86
saibara 37, 50, 75, 83, 85–86, 89, 112, 126, 215n12, 215n15, 215n16
Saicho 48, 54, 168
Sakagami 213n28
Sakamoto Jinoichi 59, 150, 219n14
Sakamoto Tsutomu 143, 181
Sakura, Sakura 69, 77, 214n4, 214n17
Sambaso 55, 132, 210n21
Sambukyo 70, *70*, 84, *85*
samurai 6, 7, 18, 63, 64, *95*, 100, 122, 128, 178, 221n30
san-sagari 74
sangen *see* shamisen
sankyoku 57, 63, 130, 146, 155, 172
sanpo-kakeai 137
sansen 57, 58, *60*, 122, 213n40
sao 58, 59, *61*, 62, 133, 150
Sarawasti 55
sarugaku 6, 55, 94, *95*, 95, 211n55, 213n31; no noh 94, 96, *122*
sato-kagura 6, 33, 39, 40, 52, 111, 112
Sato no Ko 129, 223n28
Sawai Kazue 126, 173
Sawai Koto Academy 173
Sawai Tadao 77, 143, 173, 181, 184, 216n52
sawari 48, 59, *60*, 149
Sawazumi Kengyo 132
Sayama Kengyo 124, 135, 218n25
scale/mode IN 8, 36, 37, 40, 68–81, 85, 87, *88*, 91, 93, 96, *103*, 98, 102, 104, 119, 154, 174, 214n1, 214n4, 216n40, 217n6; noh 70; ritsu 69, 75, 77, *76*, 214n8; ryo 75, *76*, 165; YO 8, 37, *37*, 68–81, 74, 75, 103, *173*, 174, 217n6, 223n26
Sei Shonagon *see* (*Pillow Book*)
Semimaru 54; *see also Sakagami*
Sen Rikyu 11, 162
Senzai no Ho 37
settaku 48
shakubyoshi 36, *37*, 37, *38*, 39, 52, 86
shakuhachi 2, 5, 6, *49*, 57, 58, 63–64, 66, 67, 69, 74, 75, 111, 129, 131, 146, 150, 155–158, *166–167*, 169, 180, 181, 183, 184, 208n6, 209n28, 213n30, 213n51, 218n35, 220n27, 221n25, 222n9, 223n35, 224n9
shakushi 51, 55
shamisen 2, 6, 14, *19*, 44–67, 69, 71, 74, *74*, 75, 83, 90, 94, 96, 100, *100*, *105*, 105, 107, 108, 111, 118, 122–124, *123*, 126, 129, 130, 131, *132*, 133, 135, 136, *136*, 137, 138, 140, 146, 149–152, *149*, 155, 156, 157, 158, 163, 165, 168, 171, 180, 184, 186, 188, 213n32,

213n34, 213n44, 213n50, 214n54, 215n30, 216n45, 218n19, 218n35, 218n37, 219n13, 219n19, 219n20, 221n22
share-biki *see* kaede
Shiba Sukeyasu 179, 212n19, 219n4
shibai-uta 126
shihan 170, *170*, 172
Shika no Tone 131, 209n28, 224n8
Shin Kokinshu 142
Shin Sugomori 20, 157
Shingon Buddhism 48, 70, *84*, 168, 215n10
shinkyoku 180
shinobue 184
Shinran Shonin *see Shoshinge*
Shinsen-Roei-shu 86
Shinto 2, 3, 5, 7, 11, 13, 20, 21, 23, 24, 25, 28, 29, 32, 33, 36, 42, 46, 47, 52, 53, 64, 67, 68, 69, 83, 84, 96, 98, 107, 108, 110, 111, 112, 123, 159, 160, 161, 174, 175, 186, 208n2, 210n23, 210n42, 211n49, 211n53, 211n55, 211n62, 211n67, 212n13, 212n24, 212n82, 214n6, 222n40, 224n12
shiragi 47
shitsu 66, 219n4
shizugaki 152, 153
sho 40, 49, 50, 51, 52, 75, 86, 113, *113*, 146, 178, 179, 219n4
Shobutsu (priest) 90
Shochikubai 79, *81*, 129, 130, *168*, 169, 223n25
shoga 152, *152*, 153, *153*, 154, *155*, 155, *156*, 158, 219n6, 219n21
shogun 54, 91, 94, *95*, 95, 99, 161, 174, 179, 213n39, 221n19
Shojo 121
shoka 148
Shoka no Ogawa 181, 223n29
shoko 50, 51, 113, 146
shokyoku 113
Shomu, Emperor 48
Shoshinge 70, *71*, 84, *85*, 85, 119, *120*, 129, 214n10
Shotoku Taishi, Prince 47
shugen 96
shugyo 6, 7
Shunkin Monogatari 163, 189, 224n12
Shunoten (*Shuno-ten*) 181, 223n29
Society for the Study of Noh Literature 179
Sofuren 215n16
soh no koto 64
Sokkyoku Taiisho see Yamada Shokoku
sorane 157
Sue no Chigiri 127, 218n32
Suehirogari 137, 149
sugagaki *152*, 152, 219n24
Sugiyama Tangonojo 132, *133*, 133
Suiko, Empress 47
Sukeroku Yakari no Edo Zakura 134
sukui 150, 151, 152, 157
suri-sage 157
Susanowo (god) 25

sutebyoshi 157
Suzaku, Emperor 86
suzu 40

taiko 55, **56**, 57, 95, **95**, 113, 136, 146, 217*n*14
taikyoku 113
Takahashi Chikuzan 63, 189, 213*n*50, 225*n*12; see also shamisen
Takasago 17, 138, 140, **141**, 141, 208*n*24
Takemitsu, Makoto 29, 209*n*8, 210*n*27
Takemitsu, Toru 150, 223*n*36, 224*n*50, 225*n*15
Takemoto Gidayu 99, 132, **77**
Takobuku 54
Tale of Genji 15, 49, 51, 86, **117**, 208*n*18
Tale of the Heike 119, 215*n*27, 215*n*28, 216*n*32
Tancho no Tsuru 20, **21**
tanka see waka
Taoism 11, 21, 160
Tateyama Noboru Kengyo 79, 103, 158, 180, 220*n*33, 223*n*26
teahouses 127, 218*n*30
tegoto 116, 124, 128, **129**, 129, **130**, 130, 140, 142, **142**, 180, 181, 217*n*11, 218*n*34, 220*n*25
Tendai 48, 54, 70, 90
timbre 8, 9, 31, 36, 42–43, 51, 55, 64, 66, 67, **71**, 104, 106, 107, 109, 131, 146, 149–158, **155**, 176, 183, 184, 212*n*7, 214*n*56, 224*n*50
Todaiji 49, 55
Tōdō Kai of Kyoto 67, 169, 172, 218*n*21
Tōdō Ongaku Kai 169, 172, 180, 221*n*21
Tōdō Shoku Yashiki 54, 58, **58**, 91, 116, 131, 137, 141, 165, 168, **166–167**, **168**, 169, 180, 213*n*30, 221*n*18; see also Betto; Kengyo; Kōtō; Zato
Tōdōza see Tōdō Shoku Yashiki
Togan 68, 87, **88**, 113
Togi (family) 161; Hideki 78, 87, 178–179, 184, 214*n*5, 215*n*22, 222*n*11; Suenobu 178
Tohoku region 6, 26
Tokiwazu Mojitayu see Miyakoji Mojitayu
Tomimoto Buzendayu 134, 137; school 135
Tomimoto Itsukidayu 135
Tominari Seijo 116, 172, 216*n*47, 217*n*9, 224*n*52
Tomiyama Seikin 1, 15, **16**, 44, 101, 104, 163, 171, 172, 180, 181, 212*n*1, 216*n*46, 216*n*47, 216*n*48, 216*n*59, 217*n*11, 218*n*20, 221*n*31
Tomiyama Seikin II (Kiyotaka) 171
Tomizaki Shunsho 101, 109, 129, 168, 169, 180, 213*n*41, 216*n*45, 216*n*50, 220*n*32, 221*n*31
tomo see be
tonkori 46
Torazawa Kengyo 123, 132
Torii Kiyomatsu 63
Tozan Nakao 64
Tozan-ryu 64
Tsubouchi Shoyo 179, 223*n*17, 224*n*57
tsubu iri 165
Tsuchitori Toshiyuki 44, 212*n*2

Tsugaru shamisen music 62, 63, 69, 123, 171, 180, 184, 185, 189
Tsuguyama Kengyo 218*n*27
Tsukiyomi (god) 25
tsume 39, 152, 154, **155**
Tsumigusa 77
Tsuyama Kengyo **61**, 61
Tsuyama sao 59, **458**
tsuzumi see ko-tsunami
Tumulus Era 29, 46
tuning 68–81

U 49, 179
uchi-awase 158
uho 50
Uji Kaganojo (Kaga no Jo) 99, 132
uke 25, 29, 46
Umehara, Takeshi 11, 26, 209*n*6, 210*n*21, 210*n*23, 210*n*26, 210*n*44
unkaku **65**
ura-goe 96
ura gumi 123
Urabe (family) 34, 47, 48, 161, 210*n*40
uta 7, 8, 42, 82–109, 110, 112, **118**, 186
utai 14, **73**, 85, 96, 108, 121, 138, 208*n*24, 213*n*39; noh utai 85, 108, 138, **141**, 169, 179, 216*n*36
utai-ji 96, 120
utaimono (utai-mono) 8, 131
utsu 20, 150, 219*n*16
Uzume (goddess) 25, 46, 161

viola 1, 2

wa-gon 29, 36, **37**, 37, **38**, 39, 46, **49**, 64, 112, 183, 189, 211*n*70
wa-san 70, **72**, 122
Waga Koma 85
waka 15, 36, 37, 102, **103**, 112, 119, 142
wakan-roei 52, 68, 83, 85, 86, 87, **88**, 112, **113**, 116, 126
Wakan Roei-shu 86
warizume **116**, **117**, 153, **153**, **156**
Wasure Shoka 104, **105**
Way of Tea see Four Principles of the Way of Tea
Way of the Art see geido
Way of the Kami 23, 24, 24, 28, 42
Western music 1, 2, 5, 7, 9, **81**, 104, 111, 142–144, **143**, 177–178, 180–183, 185–186, 189, 208*n*8, 208*n*14, 210*n*37, 212*n*17, 212*n*19, 215*n*9, 217*n*68, 218*n*29, 220*n*27, 220*n*36, 223*n*33, 224*n*47; see also classical music; yogaku
Woman Killer and the Hell of Oil 133
woodblocks 7, 63, 164, 180

Yachiyo Jishi 63
Yae Goromo 129
Yaezaki Kengyo 129, 188

Index

yamabushi 122
Yamada Kengyo 116, 137, *138*; koto 62, *134*, 134, 137, 157, 174
Yamada Masami *see* Yamada Kengyo
Yamada Shokoku 137
Yamamoto Tosanojo 134
Yamato clan 25
Yamato Era 29
Yamato-mai 53
Yamato-uta 32
Yamazumi Kōtō 171
Yanagawa Kengyo 123, 218n21; -ryu 59, *61*, 61, 218n27
Yang Kei Fei *see* Yohiki
Yasutane (poet) 68
Yatsuhashi Kengyo 62, 75, 79, 89, *117*, 171, 174, 188, 213n46, 217n9, 218n26, 218n33
Yayoi Era (Period) 28–29, 46; people 28–29, 210n25
YO mode *see* scale/mode
yogaku 5; *see also* classical music; Western music

Yohiki *118*, 217n10
Yoru no Amigasa 134
Yoshida Bros 180, 184, 213n44, 214n6
Yoshida Seifu 181
Yoshida Takeko 94, 192
Yoshizawa Kengyo II 63, 77, 131, 209n29, 214n14, 214n16, 217n11, 218n34, 218n36, 221n17
Yuasa, Joji 182–184, 223n36, 223n38, 224n46
Yuki 14, *15*, 20, 127, 128, 218n32
yurushi system 168, 169; mono *168*; seido 168, 169, 224n7

zan *38*, 39, 211n70
zato 101
Zato *166–167*, 221n20; *see also* Tōdō Shoku Yashiki
Zeami Motokiyo 94, 164; *see also Kyui (Nine Steps)*
Zen 63, 64, 70, *99*, 165, 185, 208n2, 209n35, 215n10
zokkyoku 6, 219n24

www.ingramcontent.com/pod-product-compliance
Lightning Source LLC
Chambersburg PA
CBHW071407300426
44114CB00016B/2213